THE HINDU EQUILIBRIUM

VOLUME I

CULTURAL STABILITY
AND
ECONOMIC STAGNATION

India
c1500 BC–AD 1980

DEEPAK LAL

CLARENDON PRESS · OXFORD

1988

Oxford University Press, Walton Street, Oxford OX2 6DP
Oxford New York Toronto
Delhi Bombay Calcutta Madras Karachi
Petaling Jaya Singapore Hong Kong Tokyo
Nairobi Dar es Salaam Cape Town
Melbourne Auckland
and associated companies in
Berlin Ibadan

Oxford is a trade mark of Oxford University Press

Published in the United States
by Oxford University Press, New York

British Library Cataloguing in Publication Data
Deepak, Lal
The Hindu equilibrium.
Vol. 1 : Cultural stability and economic stagnation : India c. 1500 B.C.—A.D. 1980
1. India, history
I. Title
954
ISBN 0-19-828498-5

.Library of Congress Cataloging in Publication Data
Lal, Deepak.
Cultural stability and economic stagnation : India, c. 1500 BC—AD 1980/Deepak Lal.
p. cm.—(The Hindu equilibrium; v. 1)
Bibliography: p. Includes index.
1. India—Economic conditions. 2. India—Social conditions. 3. India—History.
I. Title. II. Series: Lal, Deepak. Hindu equilibrium; v. 1.
HC434.L35 1988 330.954—dc19 88-17916
ISBN 0-19-828498-5

Typeset by Colset Pte. Ltd. Singapore
Printed and bound in
Great Britain by Biddles Ltd,
Guildford and King's Lynn

For Deepika and Akshay

PREFACE

The origins of this book are of some interest, as they might help to explain its scope and nature. It began in 1973–4 when I was a full-time consultant to the Project Appraisal Division of the Indian Planning Commission and had to assemble and analyse the available data on wages and employment in order to estimate shadow wage-rates for the Indian economy. The analysis and derivations were published in Lal (1980a), but there was still a large amount of material concerned with labour market issues which I felt could be worked into a study of Indian labour markets. Moreover, as the existing literature on the workings of these markets was in my view rather thin and unanalytical, this was also a task worth doing. As a preliminary, therefore, some of the material was worked into articles and published as Lal (1976a, b), and has been used in Volume II of this study.

In 1978 I joined the Employment and Rural Development Division of the World Bank for two years, on leave from University College London, to work on a research project on Wage and Employment Trends and Structures in developing countries. It seemed natural to build on my earlier Planning Commission work and to include a study of India as part of this project.[1] The research and writing of Volume II has thus been financed in part by the World Bank's Research Committee, and I am extremely grateful for this support. It should be emphasized, however, even more than usual that the views and analysis in this study are my own and should not in any way be identified with those of the Bank or its affiliates. I owe a particular debt to Mark Leiserson, for getting me to Washington and for his continuing support of this work.

I first thought that the major lacuna to be filled in my Planning Commission work was in the analysis of the urban, particularly industrial, labour market, and in charting the long-term trends (extending back beyond the period following Independence in 1947) in wages and employment. To this end two survey papers were commissioned from three collaborators in Indian universities. The first was a 'Survey of Industrial Wage Structures in India', by Dr Bhaskar Dutta of the Indian Statistical Institute, and part of Chapter 9 in volume II is based on this paper. The second was on 'The Evolution of Labour Markets in India, 1857–1947', by Professor Dharma Kumar and Dr J. Krishnamurthy of the Delhi School of Economics. I have made use of this at the appropriate places, with due acknowledgements, in Volume II of this study.

Another major task was to fill in the gaps in the available data on wages and employment in my earlier compilations for the Indian Planning Commission (Lal (1974b, c, d, e)). I was fortunate in being able to obtain the services of Y. Satyanarayana as a full-time research assistant on this study from August 1979 until September 1980. This compilation and analysis of the often confusing and diverse sources of data on wages and employment in India are available in Satyanarayana (1980 *a, b*), and should be useful to other researchers working on wage–employment issues in India. To all these individuals whose collaboration on this study has been essential for its completion I am most grateful, though they are absolved of any responsibility for the use I have made of this work. As part of the design of the project I prepared two papers, one a survey of the new theories of industrial wage structures (Lal (1979*a*)) and another on the issues and methodology concerning the role of labour in development, (Lal (1980*a*)). These are also contained in Volume II of the present study.

The final and (it is to be hoped) more novel ingredient of this study, however, has had a much longer gestation, and involved, the indirect financial and intellectual contributions of so many individuals and institutions so that a list would read like a personal history! For as I began mulling over on the shape of this study two things became apparent. First, many supposedly narrow labour market issues were at the heart of much more general controversies about the causes of and cures for India's continuing poverty. Moreover, most of these controversies pre-dated India's independence. Secondly, numerous observers[2]—mainly non-Indian—have blamed the social stratification and segmentation of labour markets flowing from that unique Indian institution, the caste system, as a major cause of Indian economic stagnation. This, like most other so-called 'institutionalist' explanations is unsatisfactory because it raises the question: Why did the caste system arise and why has it survived? Surprisingly, despite the prodigious literature on the description and consequences of the caste system, I was unable to find much discussion of its origins.[3] And yet once I began to mull over the labour market issues, it became clear that it was essential to assess the reasons for the rise of the caste system not only because the subsequent evolution (or lack of it) of labour markets has been fashioned by the caste system, but also because it might help to explain the relative imperviousness to change of the long-term parameters governing the Indian economy. These origins were shrouded in the mists of the distant past, and obviously the historical context in which the caste system was forged would be essential in determining both its origins and its continuation. For the latter is equally puzzling, as since about AD 1000 India has been ruled by foreigners whose social predilections were diametrically opposed to those perpetuated by the caste system. My hunch was that there must be certain 'environmental' parameters which have remained unchanged since the days when the caste system first arose, and which would explain its continuation. This meant that, in assessing a major feature of present-day Indian labour markets and their role in aiding or arresting economic development, the social, political and economic history of India since about 1500 BC becomes relevant. This subject has now become the self-contained first volume of this study.

This might be considered a daunting task, except that for a long time I have also been thinking and reading about these aspects of India. Though by no means wishing to claim any great expertise in historical studies, I would like to acknowledge an important debt to Messrs Amin and Kapadia of St Stephen's College, Delhi for whatever I learnt of Indian history, in the course of obtaining my first degree, which has after a long lapse of time borne such surprising fruit! Equally fortunately, in retrospect, I married a sociologist (Barbara Ballis Lal). Unbeknownst to her, I have been raiding my wife's library on sociology, and I have also over the years been receiving informal instruction at home in the mysteries of that subject. All I had been able to absorb in this area of knowledge now also seemed to find a place. Knowing as she does my view of her subject, my wife will be surprised to learn that without her indirect intellectual contribution this book could not have been written.

Finally, a very important ingredient in the story I have to tell is the role of climatic factors and of irrigation. It was fortunate that a large part of my early work was on irrigation (Lal (1972a), Lal and Duane (1972)), and that I could build on what I had then learnt about agronomy and hydrology.

All these ingredients which have thus turned this study from its original narrowly technical economic framework into one more broadly based and interdisciplinary will I hope make the book both more stimulating and entertaining. It is now in two parts. Volume I is a general and wide-ranging interpretation of Indian social and economic history. Volume II is concerned with more technical and narrowly labour market aspects of Indian economic development. This does not mean that Volume I of this study is in any sense what a historian or sociologist would recognize as an economic or social history of India. Far from it. This is what I would term an analytical social and economic history,[4] which uses history and sociology to provide the evidence on the nature of the parameters which have, as I argue, determined 'the Hindu equilibrium', but then uses conventional economic analysis to tell an analytical story, in which issues concerning the supply and demand for labour and its earnings are central in explaining both how the Indian economy came to be where it is, and on how the Hindu equilibrium might be altered. In the process this study also outlines an analytical story at variance with the dominant labour market and growth model which still imprisons the imagination and thinking of so many development economists—the surplus labour model. To that extent, the work might have a wider theoretical relevance than its more obvious and limited application to India. This may seem a bold claim, particularly as I take issue with a large body of conventional knowledge in India on the causes and cures of Indian poverty. I hope that these books will thus also illumine the sources of the current deepseated misperceptions (in my view) of the functioning of the Indian economy, and of its labour markets in particular, which colour most of the panaceas propounded by many of my colleagues in India, and which have so patently failed to date to alter the Hindu equilibrium.

I must add that it would be presumptuous in a work of this nature (particularly in the speculative parts of Volume I) to claim any definitiveness in either treatment or coverage of the various topics dealt with. In the present volume I have merely provided an interpretation, which I hope will be both novel and stimulating, of the historical record, which I believe is of some relevance in understanding how the real income of Indians can be raised.

The initial draft of a single manuscript which covered both the current volumes was finished in late 1981. Numerous friends and colleagues who have over the years read this draft (or parts of the manuscript), gave me some confidence that my interpretations, though unavoidably controversial, were not vacuous. For their help, encouragement, and suggestions I would like to thank the following (without of course implicating them in any way in what is contained in these pages): Pranab Bardhan, Peter Bauer, Sarvepalli Gopal, Dharma Kumar, David Henderson, Ian Little, Angus Maddison, Hla Myint, Amartya Sen, Julian Simon, T. N. Srinivasan, and Romilla Thapar.

Apart from altering the structure of the original manuscript to form two self-contained books, I have taken account of the immensely valuable *Cambridge Economic History of India* which appeared since the draft was written, as well as of various other references suggested to me by various readers. But I have made no attempt (except very superficially) to take account either of events or of analyses of Indian economic development since 1980. If the argument in this book is correct, these are but brief moments in an epic story which has not altered in its essentials.

Finally I should say that, despite the doleful nature of the subject matter, the days spent in thinking and writing this book have been very enjoyable, in no small part because they have coincided with the arrival and early progress of our two children. This book is therefore dedicated to them, in the hope that, by the time they are able to read and understand it, the Hindu equilibrium will at last have begun to be shattered.

D. L.

London and Washington
May–September 1981 and July–August 1985

NOTES

1. The two other studies I have been associated with in the series of studies in the project are with Paul Collier, on Kenya (Collier and Lal (1980, 1986) and a study I did of the Philippines (Lal (1980b)).
2. See for instance, Myrdal (1968), Barrington Moore (1966).
3. Two exceptions are Klass (1980) and McNeill (1976): but see ch. 3 for the reasons why I do not find these explanations persuasive.
4. In the same sense as in Hicks (1969). But this has its perils, as noted by Bauer (1971).

CONTENTS

LIST OF MAPS

LIST OF FIGURES

LIST OF TABLES

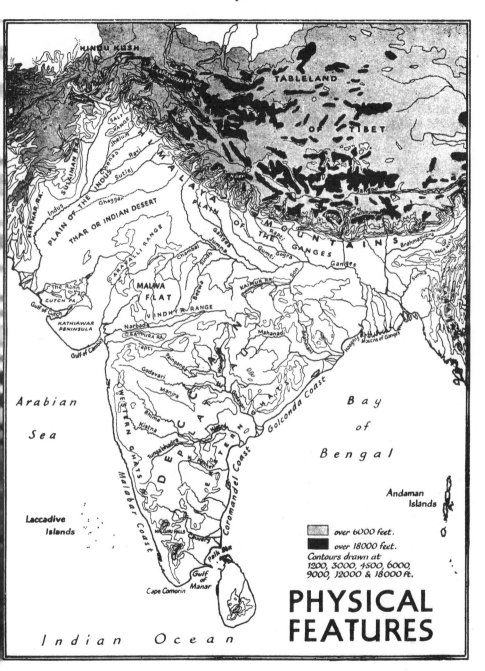

PHYSICAL
FEATURES

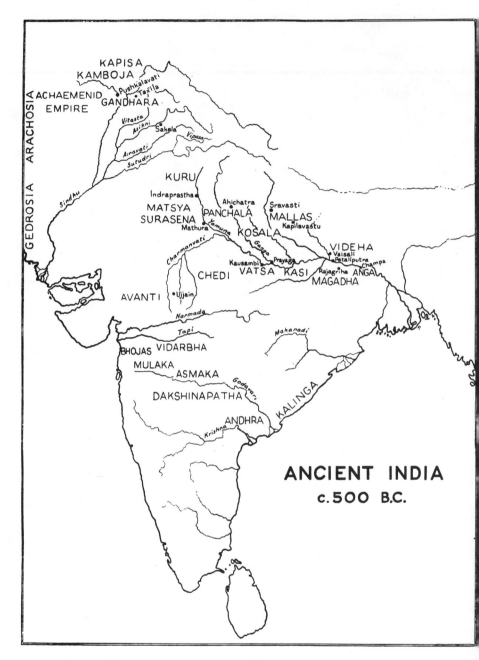

KAPISA
KAMBOJA
ACHAEMENID
GEDROSIA ARACHOSIA
EMPIRE
GANDHARA
Pushkalavati
Taxila
Vitasta
Asikni
Sakala
Vipasa
Airavati
Sutudri
Sindhu
KURU
Indraprastha
MATSYA
SURASENA
Mathura
Yamuna
Charmanvati
PANCHALA
Ahichatra
Sravasti
MALLAS
Kapilavastu
KOSALA
Ganga
VIDEHA
Vaisali
Pataliputra
Prayaga
Champa
Kausambi
CHEDI
VATSA
KASI
Rajagriha
ANGA
MAGADHA
AVANTI
Ujjain
Narmada
Tapi
Mahanadi
BHOJAS
VIDARBHA
MULAKA
ASMAKA
Godavari
DAKSHINAPATHA
KALINGA
Krishna
ANDHRA

ANCIENT INDIA
c.500 B.C.

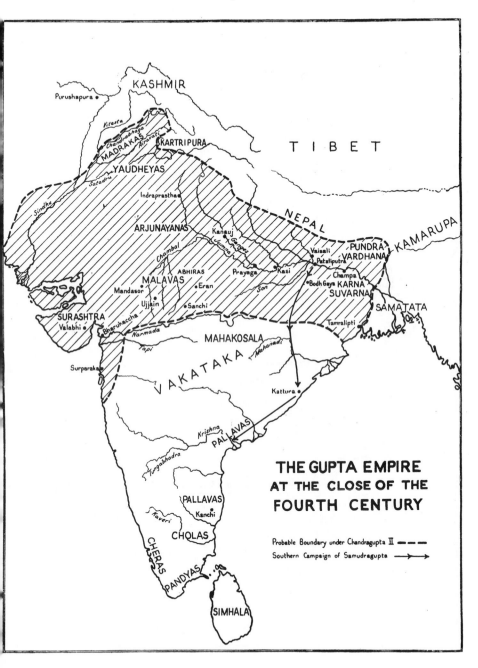

THE GUPTA EMPIRE
AT THE CLOSE OF THE
FOURTH CENTURY

Probable Boundary under Chandragupta II — — —
Southern Campaign of Samudragupta ——————→

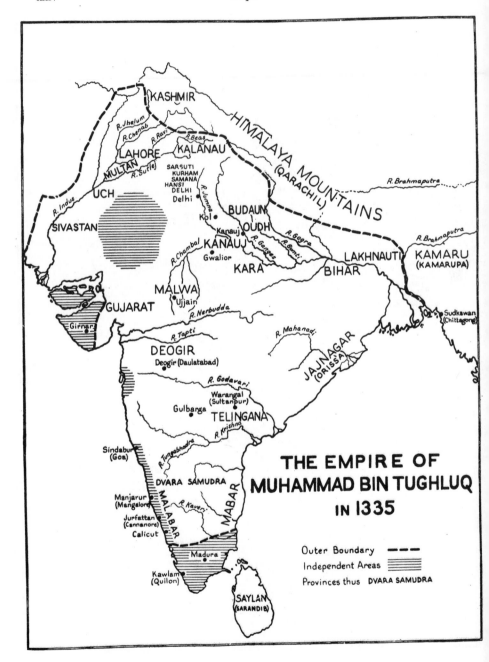

THE EMPIRE OF
MUHAMMAD BIN TUGHLUQ
IN 1335

Outer Boundary ▬ ▬ ▬
Independent Areas ▬▬▬▬
Provinces thus   DVARA SAMUDRA

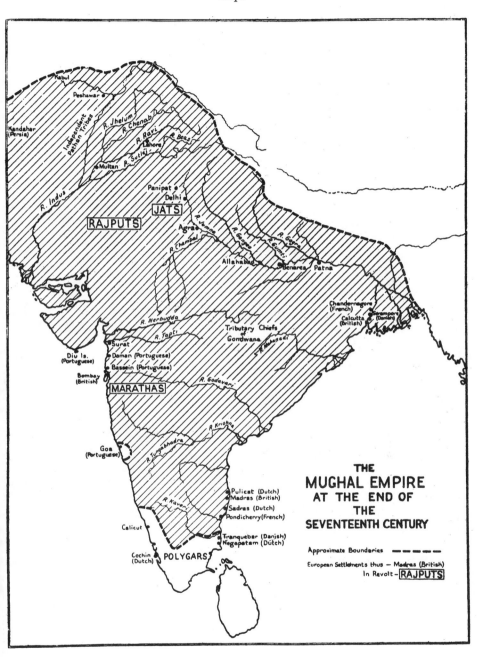

THE
MUGHAL EMPIRE
AT THE END OF
THE
SEVENTEENTH CENTURY

Approximate Boundaries — — — — —

European Settlements thus — Madras (British)

In Revolt — RAJPUTS

INDIA
(1753-1890)

Showing the Sequence of Territorial Acquisition

Indian States

INTRODUCTION

'The fox knows many things, but the hedgehog knows one big thing.'

Archilochus[1]

Most people would like to be foxes, but *faute de mieux* end up as hedgehogs. This is especially true of development economists. For there are a few powerful hedgehog visions which have held them in thrall—visions, moreover, which relate essentially to various aspects of the supply and demand of that most elemental of human resources—raw labour. The three major hedgehog visions are associated with the names of three of the greatest economists, Thomas Malthus, Karl Marx, and Arthur Lewis. A major aim of this book (as well as the companion volume, *Aspects of Indian Labour*) is to provide arguments and evidence to subvert these visions, and to show how their continuing hold is an important element in the continuing misdiagnoses of the causes and cures of India's chronic poverty. This is a bold claim, and to substantiate it this is a long book. For we have had to employ innumerable fox-like stratagems, and make forays into territory not normally entered by economists, to develop our argument.

A common view on the causes and cures for Indian poverty can be briefly stated. Following Malthus, it is contented that the country has been swamped by a massive increase in labour supply, and has been over-populated for over a century, so that for all practical purposes there are large surpluses of grossly under-employed and poor labourers (*à la* Lewis) available at virtually no cost for developmental purposes. However, the mobilization of this surplus labour to yield equitable and rapid growth cannot be left to private capitalists—in part because, on one line of argument, Indian capitalists are still imbued with a trading rather than an entrepreneurial spirit and in part, by another, slightly more sophisticated view, because the private cost of using this labour is likely to exceed its social opportunity cost. Furthermore, it is assumed that capitalist growth, if it does occur, will be inegalitarian, and likely to lead to increased proletarianization and immiserization of the mass of workers (*à la* Marx). The panacea offered is centralized planning of the Soviet or Maoist variety, which attempts to raise the savings rate of the economy and to mobilize the surplus labour for the socially most productive uses. These uses are to be determined by the derivation of material balances which detail the available resources, both financial and physical, and the socially specified requirements in terms of different commodities; and the plan is to be implemented in the industrial sector through detailed industrial, trade, and credit controls, and in agriculture (*a*) through land reform to alter the existing rural asset distribution and (*b*) through the provision of subsidized credit, extension, and infrastructural services to small holder beneficiaries.

The continuing Indian poverty is then blamed on the failure of past governments to acquire the requisite political will faithfully to implement the above measures, in large part because the levers of State in the existing 'bourgeois democratic' system have been systematically hijacked by various vested interests. Next, depending upon the particular political persuasion of the commentator, either an inevitable revolutionary upheaval, which will usher in a socialist utopia, is seen as the outcome of the rising poverty and unemployment (open and disguised), or else, more commonly, exhortations are made to stiffen the will of politicians and bureaucrats to implement the consensual panaceas.

As is the case with most hedgehog visions, its power depends upon its inherent plausibility, in terms of the interpretations it provides not only of the current situation but also of the past. The period of the British Raj in particular is seen as having set back Indian progress through its twin policies of *laissez-faire* and free trade which, whilst promoting industrial capitalism amongst some of the traditional trading groups, led to the immiserization and increased proletarianization of both the rural and the urban masses. The economic policies of the Raj were adduced to have led to the deindustrialization of India, a commercialization of agriculture which, by inducing a substitution of commercial crops for food crops, aggravated the endemic problems of famine, the introduction of land tenure systems which were inimical to rural development, and a heavy tax burden which siphoned off a large part of the meagre savings of the Indian people to finance those notorious 'Home' charges. Free trade and *laissez-faire* are thus still identified as the two villains which halted Indian economic progress during the near-century of fully fledged British rule in India (see pt. II below).

In escaping from this hedgehog vision, I believe it is necessary to reassess the historical record, not only because, as I argue in Part I below, the basic parameters of what I term the 'Hindu' equilibrium[2] were set very early on in Indian history, but because it is the failure to alter these, rather than the more commonly adduced policy failures of the past and the present, which has led to the relative economic stagnation of India in the decades following the Second World War. There are however two aspects of this past which are central to the argument of this book, and which are documented (to the extent available research allows) in Parts I and II. The first is that, despite current appearances to the contrary, India has historically been a labour-scarce economy.[3] That unique feature of its society and economy, the caste system, is—as I argue in Chapter 3—an ingenious second-best method of dealing with the uncertainty of labour supply in the ecological and political environment that faced the ancient Hindu monarchies in the Indo-Gangetic plains. It is these ecological, political, and demographic parameters which we chart in Part I.

The second important feature of the Hindu equilibrium established around the fourth to sixth centuries BC has been its stability over the centuries despite the fact that since about AD 1000 India has been ruled by foreigners out of sympathy with the social philosophy of its central social institution, the caste system. Chapter 4 and Part II of the book are therefore concerned with delineating both the attempts as well as the failures of these foreign rulers to alter the Hindu equilibrium. I argue that the reason for these failures was in part the success of the Hindu equilibrium established in ancient times in maintaining an average standard of living for the populace which, though stagnant and low by current standards, was for millennia not surpassed by most other countries of the world. This has meant that the mass of Hindus (until fairly recently) had little incentive to alter a system which in this historical perspective has more than proved its worth.

But equally importantly, an essential feature of this Hindu equilibrium was its provision of an economic and local administrative structure which could be (and was) readily taken over by any new political overlord for the extraction of that revenue from the land which down to our day has been sought by India's various rulers. Most of these have, therefore, found it easy to succumb to the blandishments of a system which provided the means—with little effort on their part—to fund their courts, armies, and imperial ambitions. As a result, the local administrative structure established in Mauryan times has scarcely altered in its essentials over the millennia. We thus also trace the feeble, and in the end vain, attempts by both India's Muslim and British conquerors to alter the system. For this political and administrative history must form an important part of the explanation for the perpetuation of the Hindu equilibrium.

Whilst the above themes can be considered to be our positive contribution towards providing an alternative to the conventional views on the causes of Indian poverty, there is also the equally important task of questioning the empirical bases of the conventional wisdom. These emphasize the deleterious effects of the British impact on the structure and levels of employment and earnings of Indians. Some of these deleterious effects are supposed to flow from sins of commission—such as the policy of free trade, the introduction of new tenurial systems, and the promotion of the commercialization of agriculture though improvements in communications. Others are sins of omission—such as the failure to protect infant Indian industries, to develop irrigation facilities more fully, and to expand education, research, and rural extension services. We deal with the controversies surrounding these areas in Part II, whose Chapter 10 provides a summary for the busy reader. Volume II and Part III of the present volume attack contemporary conventional widsom directly, by examining the theoretical and empirical underpinnings of its tripartite base—(*a*) the existence of vast rural surplus labour and growing rural and urban unemployment in independent India, (*b*) the non-economic and vague customary or institutionalist determinants of wages and earnings, and (*c*) the purported worsening of the conditions of the poor both absolutely and relatively through the promotion of supposedly capitalist growth in both rural and urban India. The technical and empirical details are in Volume II, whilst Part III of the present more general volume provides a survey.

As this is primarily a work of exorcism, which may have as much therapeutic value in the treatment of some pathologies as more conventional medicines, the so-called 'policy conclusions' which can be derived from the study are only briefly discussed in Chapter 13, which also contains some observations on the relationship of this work to some general theories of economic history and political economy, and in the Summary. There is little novel about the policy conclusions, and I (along with many others) have reiterated them in the past.[4] As it is clearly not ignorance or lack of understanding which stands in the way of their adoption, it is important to assess the reasons why they and the evidence in their support are not found to be persuasive. A subsidiary aim of this book is also, therefore, to provide some reasons for the grip of certain ideas and ideals on the Hindu mind. Writing both as an Indian and as a Hindu, this I have found as much a task of self-analysis as it is of reading other minds! But it is for the reader to judge whether the story I tell in the following pages is not only novel but also credible.

Before we begin, there are however some seemingly tedious questions concerning terminology and methodology to be cleared up: an explanation and justification of the implicit 'ecological' perspective which underlies some of this work; the meaning of the notion of 'equilibrium' that is used; and a discussion of the robustness, from a positivist viewpoint, of the methods of argument employed in this book. These are the subject-matter of the following section of this Introduction. As are other, relatively more technical discussions in the rest of this volume which the general reader may skip without losing the thread of the argument, this section is starred. For the busy or general reader, Chapters 1–3, 10, and 14 would provide a synopsis of my thesis.

* *Ecology, Equilibrium, and Method*

Ecologists tell us[5] that *Homo sapiens*, like all other animals, tends to adapt himself to his physical environment. For a species to survive, that is, to have a long posterity, the animal must be fit to get food and to breed well in its environment. Food and sex are thus the basic goods sought by all animals.

For most animal populations, the particular environment dictates the size. Other species adapt to a change in the physical environment and the continual competitive pressure from rival species for *Lebensraum*, *by forming new species* which can survive in the new environment. The human animal is unique because its intelligence gives it the ability to *change its environment by learning*. It does not have to mutate into a new species to adapt to a change in its environment. *It learns new ways of surviving in the changed environment and then fixes them by social custom*. Colinvaux writes:

it seems certain that the most important dimensions of the ancient human niche were learned. Even the simplest of tribal lives is complicated by the standards of animal lives. Tribal peoples who have survived to our own times exist in a matrix of custom, ritual and taboo. The things all the people do, from gathering food to going to war, are done by the rules of custom; they are learned. Yet to the ecological eye all these learned things fit the people to get their livelihoods and persist as tribes down long spans of generations. The habits serve each individuals of the tribe as the programmed food search of a bird species serves the individual bird. Custom and ritual define the boundaries of these tribal niches. . . . Ancient people learned their professions of life, just as the followers of modern professions learn theirs. It was this fact that made us ready for the dramatic changes of niche that were to come later. But that ability to learn could serve our forefathers only if it was used with caution—learn and stick by what you have learned had to be the rule, because chopping and changing of life styles would have been fatal. . . . So it was essential to the ancient human niche that people not change their habits easily. Learn the niche, yes; but stick to what the elders teach you. The power to change the niche by learning, therefore, was coupled from the earliest days with a necessary conservatism that resists the change. Both power to change and resistance to that change are fundamental properties of the human niche.[6]

The ability to change the environment, to live in a wide variety of environments each with its own set of resources, and to expand particular environments through 'technology' and 'industry' are unique characteristics of the human animal. How and why the environments of the human animals inhabiting the Indian subcontinent have changed and how the new adaptations to them have been fixed by particular social customs or a social order, is an important part of our enterprise in this book. Its major thesis is that the ancient Hindus established a social order particularly suited to the physical environment of the vast Indo-Gangetic plain. The standard of living this provided for a fairly large population was relatively high by contemporary standards for nearly a thousand years. The resulting social and economic order therefore must be viewed as a particularly successful adaptation to the environment facing the anciet Hindus. It is only in more recent times, under external stimulus, that the environment has altered. We will try to identify these changes in the environment and the resulting responses of the intelligent animals inhabiting the subcontinent.

This long cultural stability and seeming economic stagnation I label the 'Hindu equilibrium'. The term 'Hindu' is not to be taken in its religious sense. It signifies the features of a particular *social order* into which many groups other than Hindus have been absorbed over millennia on the subcontinent. It denotes the set of customs and beliefs which on the whole have been shared by and have moulded the habitual behaviour of the inhabitants of the subcontinent.

The term 'equilibrium' requires further comment. The notion of equilibrium in economics has unfortunately in recent years come to be identified with a very special form of equilibrium—that of a perfectly competitive neo-classical economy.[7] But, as Hahn (1973) has argued, this is a very restrictive notion of equilibrium in economics. He therefore proposes a more general notion of economic equilibrium which also fits nicely with the social and ecological equilibrium which is my concern in this book. He describes an equilibrium state as one in which self-seeking agents learn nothing new so that their behaviour is routinized. It represents an adaptation by agents to the economic environment in which the economy 'generates messages which do not cause agents to change the theories which they hold or the policies which they pursue'.[8] Note that this notion of equilibrium is close to that which ecologists describe as the routine or regular behaviour labelled as social custom which fixes a particular human niche. On this view, the equilibrium will be disturbed if the environment changes, and so the human agents have to change and/or learn a new way of living. This equilibrium notion implies that in the subsequent process of adjustment the human agents would have to abandon their past theories as these would now be systematically falsified. To survive they must learn through a process of trial and error—to adapt to their new environment. When this learning ceases, we will again observe a 'new' social equilibrium with routine behaviour by human agents adapted to the new environment.

It is in this (if I may so label it) 'Hahnian' sense that I shall argue that a Hindu equilibrium was established in the subcontinent in about the sixth and fifth centuries BC. It relates to a state of society and 'economy in which agents have adapted themselves to their economic environment and where their expectations in the widest sense are in the proper meaning not falsified' (Hahn (1973, p. 28)).

This notion of equilibrium does not entail that a particular equilibrium is unique given the environmental parameters. Many other conceivable social equilibria could have been accommodated within the niche established and learnt by the ancient Hindus. What it does suggest is that once a particular socio-economic order was established and it proved to be an adequate adaptation to the new environment, it was stable, as there was no reason for the human agents to alter it in any fundamental manner, *unless and until the environmental parameters altered.* Thus, both in assessing the survival of the Hindu social system and in speculating on ways in which it might have changed or is likely to change, we need to delineate the parameters of the changing ecological environment which would have first created this social order and those whose subsequent alteration requires new adaptations by human agents to reformulate new theories and new habits.[9]

Nor, it should be said at the outset, is it any part of my thesis that this social order was the result of a deliberate rationalist plan. It is not that people, understanding the usefulness of some or other institution or social custom, took a common decision to live in one way or another. Economists at least since Adam Smith have been familiar with the notion that an unplanned but coherent and seemingly planned social system can emerge from the independent actions of many individuals pursuing their different ends and in which the final outcomes could be very different from those intended by the individual agents.[10] It is in this spirit that I shall apply the standard tools of neo-classical economics to explain the establishment and persistence of the Hindu equilibrium.

Even at this stage it may be useful to defuse the positivist discontent which the following pages will undoubtedly arouse. It has become uncritically fashionable (particularly but not only in Chicago) to dismiss any 'theory' which does not provide falsifiable predictions. But this is a very narrow view of both the purpose and uses of economics.[11] A much more general and, I would argue, useful purpose of economic theory is to understand or explain events—to tell a plausible story. 'It is plain', writes Hahn,

that we can claim understanding of an event without claiming that we can predict it. Geophysicists for instance believe that they understand earthquakes but cannot predict them; biologists claim to understand the process of speciation but in general cannot predict the next occurrence. . . . In all these cases there are very many elements which enter into the explanation of an event. This in turn hinders prediction and so also falsification. In economics it is certainly hard to think of any thing which has been conclusively falsified.[12]

Another possible source of methodological discontent is the heuristic use of what may appear to be a form of functionalism, in my discussion of the origins of the caste system. Despite their central role in the work of many anthropologists since Malinowski (1927), functionalist explanations of institutions have constantly been under attack. This is on the grounds that 'there is a difference between questions about the function of an institution and about the cause (s) of (the particular once-and-for-all events leading to the origin of, or the recurring events which make up) that institution'.[13] A recent broadside against functionalist explanations in the social sciences is to be found in Elster (1979), which is somewhat qualified in Elster (1983). By contrast, Flew (1985) and Dore (1961) provide more balanced assessments of the uses and abuses of functionalism. As Dore notes, questions about functions are relevant to answers about causation 'only (legitimately) via human motives or evolutionary selection'.[14] Even though the 'ecological' perspective involved in the Hahnian notion of 'equilibrium' I have used may suggest that I am wedded to an evolutionary theory of society (analogously with Elster (1979, 1983)), I should state that this is not so. Thus I do *not* wish to argue (as Hayek does, for instance) that 'social evolution proceeds by the natural selection not of individuals but of social groups or populations via the practical competition of their codes of conduct'.[15] Instead I seek to provide explanations based (*a*) on individual motivation within a historical context (speculative though such explanations may be) and (*b*) on what Dore calls 'the static approach which concentrates on societies which have been stable over long periods of time and seeks for the causal relations between the recurring events which make up their institutions'.[16] I hope that as a result this work will pass Elster's tests[17] and be absolved of any vulgar 'functionalist fallacy'.

There is however one important qualification which must be borne in mind in what follows. The various explanatory economic models we employ must inevitably make contingent assumptions based on the historical record. Unfortunately, unlike China, reliable historical records for India—particularly for antiquity—are scarce.[18] As much of our argument hinges on speculations concerning the establishment of the Hindu equilibrium in ancient India, it is particularly distressing that there are few hard historical facts to be relied on. Recent archaeological advances have helped, but in large part the sources for reconstructing much of ancient Indian history are notoriously unreliable literary records and the subjective accounts of various foreign travellers which have survived the ravages of time. Apart from the undeciphered Indus script, the earliest written records in India are the third century BC inscription of the Mauryan emperor Ashoka. But there is a large and varied body of literature transmitted orally, which goes back to the *Rigveda*, estimated to have been completed about 1500–1300 BC. The later Vedic literature is presumed to pertain to the next seven centuries. So there is a period of over a thousand years for which there is only limited literary evidence on which much of the reconstruction of the early Aryan past in India is based. Thus, in describing the course of events of Indian history statements that '*X* happened' or '*Y* did something' must be taken with more than the usual grain of salt. Nevertheless, as we will not be deviating from the accepted reconstruction of Indian history by its contemporary historians, the suspension of disbelief required in the following narration of historical 'facts' should be no greater than for any other existing work on ancient Indian history.

The only viable method to be pursued in the circumstances is what I call 'analytical economic history'. This involves using theoretical constructs to order whatever evidence is available to tell as plausible a 'story' as the facts will bear. The method is analogous to the deliberations of a jury in a court of law using their general knowledge and implicit theories of human action in sifting through all the available evidence and reaching a verdict on the most plausible of the different interpretations of the facts. In this book I present my interpretation of the broad (though by no means hard) 'facts' of India's social and economic history. It cannot by its very nature claim any definitiveness. But it does provide a different interpretation from the one most commonly accepted in India today. If this book makes the reader question this orthodox interpretation (even partially), or if it stimulates others to provide alternative interpretations, it will have been worth writing. It is in this spirit that we begin our story with an account of the natural environment within which the inhabitants of the subcontinent have pursued their basic individual biological ends of breeding and feeding.

NOTES

1. Quoted in Berlin (1978).
2. The term 'Hindu' is used, not in its religious sense, but to describe the social order within which most inhabitants of Hindustan—the Indian subcontinent—have lived since about the 2nd century BC.

3. Thus even in 1965–70, although by some standards India was amongst the most densely populated countries in the world, its agricultural resources base per capita was better than Japan's. Thus Boserup (1981, p. 171) presents the following figures for area of agricultural land per inhabitant in Japan, China, and India, for about 1965–70.

	Japan	China (ha.)	India
Irrigated and multi-cropped	0.01	0.06	0.04
Irrigated and cropped annually	0.02	0.04	0.01
Rain-fed and cropped annually	0.02	0.05	0.17
Rain-fed and used for short fallow.	0.00	—	0.08
Permanent pastureland	0.01	0.23	0.03
Total agricultural area	0.06	0.38	0.33

4. See Lal (1973, 1980).
5. Ecology in our sense is coterminous with population biology and socio-biology, and is concerned to explain 'the observed inter-relationship among the various forms of life—organisms, species, and broader groupings and communities and between forms of life and their external environment' (Hirshleifer (1977, p. 1)). See Wilson (1975) for the authoritative text on the subject. Colinvaux (1983) and Hirshleifer (1977, 1982) present applications of the ecological or biological perspective to history, law, and economics respectively. Socio-biology, Wilson maintains, encompasses all the social sciences. Hirshleifer (1977) notes that 'the fundamental organising concepts of the dominant analytical structures employed in economics and in socio-biology are strikingly parallel.' Thus the 'optimizing' by individual agents in economics is called 'adapting' by the biologist, whilst both consider the social or aggregate result of the interaction of competing individual agents. Socio-biology is of course a close cousin to that body of thought which has been labelled 'social Darwinism'. The illegitimate moral (ethical) inferences drawn by this body of thought from biological premises has rightly led to its rejection. But, as Hirshleifer maintains, this does not undermine the value of that part of this body of thought which is concerned with 'the entirely scientific contention that man's biological endowment has significant implications for his social behaviour' (ibid., 8).
6. Colinvaux (1983, pp. 34–5).
7. This is the so-called 'Arrow–Debreu equilibrium'. However, general equilibrium theorists have shown that, more generally, equilibrium states defined as 'states of the economy which if they obtained would leave us no plausible reason for supposing that these states would change' (Hahn (1973, p. 10)) are all in the so-called 'core' of the economy. The core is a game-theoretic notion: a feasible state of an economy in which no coalition of self-seeking agents could improve themselves. Though every Arrow–Debreu equilibrium is in the core, the converse is only true under the extremely restrictive assumption that the number of agents in the economy is so large that each agent is without power. The core eqilibrium is thus the more general notion of equilibrium in economics, and, as Hahn notes, 'The core indeed has some claim to be regarded as a concept of social equilibrium in the sense that for a Core-state we can think of no reason why self-seeking agents would wish to combine to upset the status-quo' (Hahn (1973, p. 11)).
8. (Hahn (1973, p. 25)). Hahn considers the economic agent as a Bayesian econometrician constructing a model of the economy in which he is an actor. He processes the exogenous messages (those which are independent of his own actions) from his environment (the economy and nature) and has a theory. The 'agent is *learning* if his theory is not independent of the date. It will be a condition of the agent being in equilibrium that he is not learning' (p. 19). This does not imply that his expectations about the future must remain constant, but if 'the method by which he makes forecasts is the same at all dates he will not be learning' (p. 20). The equilibrium action of an agent could therefore be described by an observing econometrician 'by structurally stable equations' (p. 20). Nor does this notion imply that falsification of the theory in the small (e.g. if there is always some housewife who finds some shop that has run out of what she wants) indicates that the economy is out of equilibrium.
9. Nor does it imply 'that in equilibrium any quantities and prices or rates of change of these are constant. What is required is a frequency distribution of prices conditional on exogenous events

which in some precise sense corresponds closely enough with the prior conditional distribution held by agents' (Hahn (1973, p. 27)).

10. See Hayek (1967), Arrow and Hahn (1971).
11. See Caldwell (1982) for an appraisal and critique of positivist methodology in economics.
12. Hahn (1984, pp. 4–5).
13. Dore (1961, p. 79).
14. Ibid., 79.
15. Gray (1987, p. 42).
16. Dore (1961, p. 80).
17. Elster (1983, ch. 2).
18. As a recent Indian historian notes, 'Expression of grave regret over lack of adequate information on almost all crucial points of the social history of ancient and medieval India is perhaps the inevitable starting point of all historical research on this period. . . . If, therefore, what follows in the pages below appears to be a string of conjectures and speculations, at least part of it could, perhaps, be blamed on the collective misfortune of historians that so little of the evidence from India's ancient and medieval centuries has survived' (Mukhia (1981, p. 284)). This is a suitable epigraph for Part I of this book.

Part I

The Pre-colonial Millennia
1500 BC–AD 1757

1

Pre-Aryan India[1]

1. THE GEOGRAPHICAL ENVRONMENT

Bounded by the Himalayas—the highest mountain range in the world—in the north, and with lower ranges to the east and west running down to the sea which encloses the southern peninsula, the Indian subcontinent forms a natural geographical region. This subcontinent can in turn be divided into three distinct geographical subregions (see Map section).

First of these is the Deccan peninsula, which is separated from the north by low hills and which itself consists of hills, plateau, and scarps interspersed with some substantial alluvial plains. These have formed geographical subregions in the South, and have been the nuclei of subregional population clusters. Second is the vast Indo-Gangetic alluvial plain, spanning virtually the whole of northern India. This has been the theatre for much of Indian history. It is in turn divisible into two major regions dominated by the two great river systems of India—the Indus and its tributaries in the west, and the Ganges and Brahmaputra and their tributaries in the centre and the east.

These two great river valley systems of the northern plain have been separated by a relatively arid region—the western part of modern-day Rajasthan and Sind. Rainfall from the south-east monsoon is heaviest in the eastern part of the plain and diminishes as we move westwards. But over millennia there have been important climatic changes related to the waxing and waning of ice ages which have affected the relative aridity of this north-western dry zone. When climatic changes made it into a virtual desert, the Deccan peninsula was effectively cut off from the northern plain. But during the last ice age (about 9,000 years ago), the dry zone had a more humid phase and the two broad northern and southern regions were more closely integrated.

Ecologists and archaeologists recognize the last ice age as being a great divide in human history. As the oceans shrank to make the giant ice-cap which spread down from the North Pole, many shallow seas became part of the continental plains. The ice age provided an expansion of an environment where the primeval human animal liked to live: 'good land, with warm, dry continental summers, supporting grass rather than forest, a proper place for hunter-gatherer peoples to be' (Colinvaux (1983, p. 43)).

This period when man, in India as elsewhere, was essentially a hunter-gatherer ended at the close of the ice age—about 10,000 years ago. The subsequent climatic changes left the world's—and India's—geography and climate much as it is today. The major change in India as elsewhere must have been a reduction in the 'good land' of savannah and grassland. In India this meant that the western dry zone, which had been moist and had supported savannah, became arid and turned into the Thar desert that we know today.

2. THE EMERGENCE OF PASTORALISM AND AGRICULTURE

The end of the ice age diminished the new environment's capacity for carrying hunter-gatherer populations. The human animal, in India as elsewhere adapted by changing its habitual behaviour. It was aided by the unique human ability to adapt to a new environment, and by a genetically determined digestive system which allows it to feed on a variety of foodstuffs.

The great divide in human history emphasized by ecologists was the new environmental adaptation of herding rather than hunting animals and the cultivation of the first food crops. As hunter-gatherers in the ice age, humans had to compete with other carnivores for their prey. By herding their prey they could keep them for themselves and, more importantly, could now carry over stocks of food calories which would allow a smoothing of food consumption over time. The nomadic pastoralism which developed as a social form would now be a way of living in which inter-temporal acts of savings and investment—the essential elements, for economists, of economic growth—would have become part of the cultural habits of the human animal.

Of even greater importance than herding was the new habit of growing crops. This for animal species was a revolutionary change, as it allowed the human animal to move down the food chain as it took to agriculture. 'It was as if a tiger had taken to growing corn. It was an event completely without precedent in the history of life on earth. And its consequence was a change in the density of human populations.'[2]

When man was a hunter-gatherer, like all carnivores he had to rely on a very inefficient method of obtaining food calories down a long food chain. Plants obtain their energy from the sun, herbivorous animals from plants, and carnivores from eating herbivores. At each stage there is a loss in efficiency in terms of the energy transferred. By switching to eating plants, human beings greatly expanded the potential supply of food calories available and thus 'broke the primeval restraints on number and marched down a food chain to where the energy was'.[3]

As in the Indian subcontinent groups of hunter-gatherers, pastoral nomads, shifting cultivators, and settled agriculturalists have survived to this day, it must be assumed that there were large local variations in the adaptations of man in India to the ending of the ice age. These in turn were due to the large variations in climate and environment which have always prevailed over the subcontinent, which have provided a variety of niches, in some of which more primitive ways of earning a living have survived to our day. But given the broad brush with which we are painting our picture, whilst the importance of local and regional variations must always be borne in mind in what follows, the major subcontinent-wide tendencies are what concern us, and these would suggest nomadic pastoralism and settled agriculture as the major ways of earning a living in India (as elsewhere) after the end of the last ice age.

From the archaeological record it appears that, at least in north-west India, the domestication of animals on which the 'new' nomadic pastoralist way of life was based goes back about 7,000–10,000 years.[4] It is more difficult to date the domestication of plants and the emergence of settled agriculture in the subcontinent. What appears certain from recent archaeological research is that between 8000–5000 BC to the west of the Indus valley (in what is today Baluchistan) there were settlements which cultivated wheat and barley[5] and also saw the first domestication of the Indian cow—*Bos Indicus*. In the succeeding period there is evidence of the cultivation of cotton, and also that the wheat produced was of a local rather than an imported variety.

These agricultural settlements then spread along the Western edges of the Indus. However, as Allchin and Allchin observe, 'until positive evidence is available to disprove it, we must assume that during all this time there was no settled agriculture elsewhere in the subcontinent' (p. 121). By about 3500 BC agricultural settlements began to emerge in other parts of the Indus system and perhaps also on the Indus plain. Allchin and Allchin suggest that it is likely this period also saw the emergence of settlements in eastern, central, and peninsular India.[6]

By the middle of the fourth millennium BC there was a spread of settlements and an accompanying growth of population throughout the Indus system. These settlements practiced agriculture on the flood-plains of the Indus,[7] which has always been a highly unstable river, changing its course as it deposits large quantities of silt during its annual inundation along a wide flood-plain. With the recession of the annual inundation from June to September the alluvial plain is highly fertile. 'Wheat and barley sown at that time ripen by the following spring, *without either ploughing or manuring of the ground*.'[8] The banks of the river had forests with wild game, whilst the plains beyond the alluvial plain would have produced a rich and varied grassland vegetation which provided grazing for wild as well as for domestic animals.[9]. It was on this flood-plain that by the beginning of the third millennium BC a radically new human niche was firmly established in India.

3. THE INDUS VALLEY CIVILIZATION

Once the agricultural opportunities offered by the annual inundation had been grasped, and a means of flood defence in the form of burnt brick walls discovered,[10] the way was set for the development of what goes by the name of the Indus valley civilization.

This was the first urban civilization on the subcontinent, which was based on the agriculture and animal husbandry of the Indus flood-plain which 'appears to have been extraordinarily like that of recent centuries in the Indus valley'. It also appears that by this time the 'wooden plough or 'ard' was employed' and some of the cropping patterns used 'have survived locally till today'.[12]

The archaeological remains at Mohenjodaro (Sind) and Harappa (west Punjab) also bear witness to the existence of a highly civilized urban community in the Indus valley some 4,000–5,000 years ago. Apart from what can be reconstructed from the artefacts found at those sites, little is known about this civilization, as to date no one has broken the secret of the writing on the few seals that have been found. Their existence, however, suggests that it was a civilization which traded with other parts of Asia; and it appears that the Indus valley civilization bears many striking resemblances to the ancient civilizations in Sumeria and Mesopotamia.

The level of living of the urban inhabitants of Mohenjodaro appears to have been high by contemporary standards, judging by the artefacts and archaeological structures that have been discovered.[13] A little more can be said about the sources of earning a living, but not about the social system of this ancient civilization or the reasons for its demise. What is known is that, since its establishment about 5,000 years ago, Mohenjodaro was successively destroyed and rebuilt seven times[14] before being finally abandoned after a number of centuries.

Whilst it lasted, there must also have been a flourishing agriculture in the hinterland—which is known to be exceptionally fertile—with wheat, barley, and cotton being cultivated. The existence of granaries in the cities according to recent excavations at Kot Diji (Sind), suggests that the towns were fed by the surplus produce of the countryside. There must also have been groups of highly skilled artisans who knew 'the potter's wheel, kiln-burnt brick, the boring of hard substances like carnelian, and the casting and alloy of metals'.[15]

NOTES

1. Based on Allchin and Allchin (1968), (1982), Colinvaux (1983), Kosambi (1981), Sankalia (1977), Piggott (1950), Majumdar *et al* (1978), and Basham (1967). See also Smith (1981).
2. Colinvaux (1983, p. 36).
3. Ibid., 41.
4. Allchin and Allchin (1982, p. 97).
5. Ibid., 108.
6. Ibid., 127.
7. Ibid, 141.
8. Ibid., 104 (emphasis added).
9. Ibid., 105
10. Ibid., 117.
11. Ibid., 190.
12. Ibid., 192.
13. ' On the whole, the ruins leave no doubt that there was on this site a large populous and flourishing town whose inhabitants freely enjoyed, to a degree unknown elsewhere in the ancient world, not only the sanitary conveniences but also the luxuries and comforts of a highly

developed municipal life. We must also conclude that the art of building had reached a high degree of perfection' (Majumdar *et al* (1978, 17–18).

14. Ibid., 15.
15. Ibid., 20.

2
Hindu India

By *c.*1500 BC the Indus civilization had disintegrated. Various tribes, less similar in their ethnic origins than in the common origin of their languages in the Aryan (Indo-European) speech group, started migrating from the north-western passes into what is now Punjab. These were the 'Aryan-speaking peoples' whose evolution has determined the social and cultural milieu of the subcontinent to our day. It is not our purpose to trace the progress of these pastoral peoples across the breadth and length of India over the succeeding centuries and their gradual evolution from semi-nomadic cattle-breeding pastoralists into settled agriculturists who also gradually re-established another urban civilization (initially) in the Indo-Gangetic plains.[1] In this process they also evolved a social system—the caste system—which has provided the basic social framework for the daily lives of the majority of the peoples of the subcontinent, who are now called Hindus, and which has survived innumerable foreign invasions, internal turmoil, colonization, and probably economic vicissitudes—so much so that, after over 2,000 years, it is still of vital importance in understanding the society and politics of India.[2] We therefore turn to a brief outline of the historical evolution of this social system, as well as an outline of its major features, in the rest of this chapter, before turning in the next to an examination of its probable rationale, continuing relevance, and possible economic effects.

1. FROM TRIBE TO CASTE

It is now believed[3] on the basis of archaeological evidence that the Indus valley civilization had completely disintegrated by the time the Aryan tribes entered north-west India around 1500 BC 'They were a people of warlike stockbreeders, organised in tribes rather than kingdoms. Their culture bears a generic likeness to that of *Beowulf*, the earlier Icelandic sagas, and the old Irish prose epics, and was somewhat less advanced than that in the Iliad.'[4] The Aryans had harnessed the horse to the chariot and knew the uses of iron. Their success in overcoming the original inhabitants of India was based on 'their unequalled mobility due to the movable supply of cattle, the horse-chariot for war and ox carts for heavy transport'.[5]

They entered the plains of the Punjab in search of pasture for their herds, and only gradually settled in small village communities in forest clearings in the western Gangetic plain, where they combined with the remnants of the pre-Aryan settlements and took up the agriculture which was the chief occupation of the previous Indus valley civilization.[6] But unlike the Harappans (the people of the

Indus valley civilization), they were innocent of any urban or city civilization, which only gradually evolved over the succeeding centuries with the spread of their village communities across the Indo-Gangetic plain. From *c.* 800–600 BC, the so-called 'later Vedic period', the Aryans spread over modern-day Punjab, Haryana, Uttar Pradesh, and the adjoining areas of Rajasthan. This expansion was based on clearing thin vegetation in the region and later through burning the forests they reached in eastern Uttar Pradesh and northern Bihar by about 600 BC. They also began to use the iron axe for clearing the forests at about this time, and gradually introduced the iron ploughshare for the deep ploughing which became an essential feature of their agricultural practices.[7]

There seem to have been two distinct stages in the eastward movement of the Aryans beyond the western Gangetic plain (including Haryana and western Uttar Pradesh). The earlier spread was along two routes encircling the Ganges valley—north along the Himalayan foothills and south along the base of the Vindhyas. The former was more important. This first eastward spread along the foothills of the Gangetic plains was in search of mineral deposits that the Aryans needed for their weapons and the iron tools on which their new-found agricultural settlements were increasingly dependent. They could not at this stage advance through the central Gangetic plain, which was marshy and covered with dense tropical forest. By contrast, the thinner forest of the foothills could be burnt down. There was thus a chain of Aryan settlements established along the Himalayan foothills in southern Nepal which swung southwards (near the Camparan district of Bihar) to reach the ores which 'lay beyond the hills of Rajgir, the one early Aryan settlement south of the great river'.[8] The availability of the ores enabled iron-age implements to be forged and to be used with fire to clear the Gangetic riparian jungle.

Initially wheat and barley were the main crops in the west, but rice was also cultivated.[9]

By about 700 BC the Vedic texts speak of 'ploughs drawn by twelve-ox teams; such ploughs are in use to this day, indispensable for driving deep furrows and turning over heavy soil which otherwise will not yield well or retain its fertility. The strong plough could be made of wood trimmed down by bronze tools, but the ploughshare in east Punjab, particularly on strong soil near the watershed, had to be of iron. . . . The metals began to come in significant quantities from the east from about 800 BC. India's finest deposits of iron and copper ores lie at the eastern end of the Gangetic basin in southeast Bihar.'[10]

With the introduction of iron ploughshares, and the clearing of the jungles of eastern Uttar Pradesh and Bihar (using iron-ore implements), rice and sugar cultivation based on deep ploughing began. 'A significant development in cultivation was the beginning of transplantation of paddy. . . . Paddy now became a winter crop, and wet paddy production enormously added to the yield making it double or more.'[11]

This middle Ganges plain was a new ecological region for the Aryan settlers.

Intensive wet rice cultivation became their major agricultural activity,[12] particularly on the wide flood-plains of northern Bihar and eastern Uttar Pradesh. During this spread of the Aryans across the Gangetic plain there was a gradual increase in social stratification and the emergence of States from tribes—a process which is not central to our purposes.[13]

The tribes, from the outset, were much given to internecine warfare, the chief cause of which was cattle-stealing or land disputes.[14] Faced, however, with the darker, snub-nosed, indigenous non-Aryan peoples of north-western India, whom they referred to as 'Dasas' (a term later to be synonymous with 'slave'), they tended to unite against a common enemy of whom they were both fearful and contemptuous. As the Aryans spread through the western Gangetic plain the indigenous peoples were either absorbed or pushed to the edges of the Aryan settlements that were established.[15] The subsequent treatment of the Dasas as beyond the social pale was, perhaps, the first step towards the establishment of caste, as described by the term 'varna' (which was the division between the fairer, twice-born[16] (dvija) Aryans, and the darker, non-Aryan Dasas).[17]

The Aryans themselves were divided into three broad social classes (not castes) when they first came to India—the three well-known ones, viz. the Brahmanas (priests), Kshatriyas (warriors and aristocracy), and Vaishyas (common people). With the incorporation of the conquered Dasas and the progeny of Aryan–Dasa alliances into Aryan society, these three classes, together with a fourth comprising the Shudras, gave birth to the four class varnas (or, as it is mistakenly called, the caste system).[18] 'The first three castes were probably a theoretical framework evolved by the Brahmanas, into which they systematically arranged various professions. Combinations and permutations within the latter were inevitable and were explained as originating in the intermixing of castes. The fourth caste, however, appears to have been based both on race as well as occupation.'[19]

Over long periods, the caste status of an occupation could change. Thus, with the transition from nomadic pastoralism to an agrarian economy, the extension of Aryan settlements with the clearing of the forests on the Indo-Gangetic plain, and the gradual growth of urban centres, trading, and money-lending came to be the main occupation of the Vaishyas. The Shudras became cultivators but were still separated from the Aryans by being denied 'twice-born' status and participation in Aryan Vedic rituals. 'There was thus a natural separation between the agriculturalists, those who cleared and colonised the land, and the traders, those who established the economic links between the settlements, the latter coming from the class of wealthier landowners who could afford economic speculation.'[20]

Agricultural development came to be largely dependent on the Shudras, most of whom in the earlier phase of Aryan expansion were landless and hence of very low status.[21] However, by about the second half of the sixth century BC a social category even lower than the Sudras appeared—the untouchables—who were considered to be outcasts, and beyond the pale of Aryan society. 'They may well have been an aboriginal tribe, gradually edged away to the frontiers of areas of Aryan control, where they lived by hunting and food-gathering. They are all described as having their own language, distinct from Aryan speech. Their occupations, such as rush-weaving and hunting, came to be looked upon as extremely low.'[22]

Whilst the four varnas provided the broad theoretical framework for the evolving Hindu society, in practice the social system consists of numerous hierarchically ranked occupation- and often region-specific subcastes (jatis).[23] The interweaving of these hierarchically arranged subcastes is the real fabric of the Indian caste system, rather than the varnas.

The gradual evolution of the caste system was accompanied by an important change in the polity of the Aryans. The nomadic Aryan tribes were organized into patriarchal groups. Their chief was a mere tribal leader without any pretensions to kingship. With the gradual establishment of Aryan agrarian settlements, however, the need for common protection became greater and 'the most capable protector was elected chief'.[24] But monarchical tendencies were still kept at bay by the importance of two tribal assemblies (called the 'Sabha' and the 'Samiti').[25] The idea of the divinity of kings emerged gradually. The military leaders—the Aryan chiefs—sought this status with the assistance of special sacrifices performed by the Brahmin priests. The Brahmins came to be looked upon as intermediaries between men and gods. The increasing revenue that could be extracted from the newly prosperous agriculture provided the means to found powerful ruling monarchies in the Indo-Gangetic plain. The result was a series of kingdoms, where kingship increasingly became hereditary.[26] In this process, the republican tribal assemblies, the Sabha and Samiti, became attenuated. But not all Aryan communities in the period of the consolidation of Aryan domination over the plain became monarchical; a large number of republican communities prevailed until about the fourth century AD.

More importantly for our purposes, the geographical distribution of these Aryan monarchies and republics is of some importance, as are the differences in their social structures. The monarchies covered the Indo-Gangetic plain. The republics were to be found in the Himalayan foothills and in Punjab around the northern periphery of the kingdoms. The republics (except for those in the Punjab) occupied less fertile, hilly areas, and are likely to have pre-dated the monarchies, if, as noted above, the wooded low-lying hills were more easily cleared than the marshy jungles of the plain. Later, with the establishment of the Gangetic monarchies, more independently minded Aryan settlers in the plains might have rebelled against the growing centralization of the monarchies, and established communities in the hills more in keeping with their ancient tribal traditions, as in the early settlements in the Punjab.[27]

The exact sequence of the establishment of the republics and monarchies is not important for our purposes. However, their geographical distribution provides an important clue to the likely differences in the agrarian systems in these two different types of Aryan community.

The settled Gangetic agrarian communities, which by and large were monarchies, would have required a more labour-intensive type of economic organization than those of the republican foothills. The reason for this is that both the clearing of the foothills and the subsequent system of agriculture practised thereon was probably based on bush fallow which would require less labour per acre than the form of cultivation on the plains. On the Indo-Gangetic plain, the clearing of the forests and marshes and the introduction of more intensive cultivation (e.g. in wet rice), with shorter periods of fallow in agricultural operations, would have required greater inputs of labour than in the foothills.[28] There is thus likely to have been a markedly different pattern and intensity of agricultural labour demand in the two geographical regions covered by the republics and the monarchies.

Moreover, whereas the older Aryan tribal loyalties and their institutional expression in the republican Sabhas and Samitis withered in the Gangetic monarchies—being replaced by the caste system—they survived in the republican foothills. The natural geographical barriers on the foothills would also have limited the size of the republics, and helped in the survival of their special political form which required frequent meetings of tribal councils.[29] By contrast, there was a natural tendency for kingdoms in the Indo-Gangetic plain to expand over a larger geographical area, as there were few geographical barriers impeding the progress of imperial arms once the forests on the plain had been cleared. This tendency towards the growth of geographically large polities would have made it difficult to maintain republican forms, with their frequent meetings of popular tribal councils, on the Gangetic plain.

The important point for our purpose here is that there was probably a significant correlation between the social, economic (agrarian), and ecological variables of the two types of Aryan polity. On the one hand, there are the republics in the foothills following a less intensive form of agriculture and with an older tribal social structure. On the other, the feuding but powerful monarchies of the Indo-Gangetic plain, with their more intensive agriculture and with a recently evolved caste system providing the framework for maintaining social order.

The leaders of the two most important anti-casteist religious movements in India—Buddhism and Jainism—were from the republics, thus further highlighting the differing extents of the influence of the emerging Vedic orthodoxy—as embodied in the caste system—in the republics and monarchies. These new sects offered the strongest ideological challenge to caste. The resulting conflict between tribe and caste, which was reflected in that between the Aryan republics and monarchies, was not finally settled until the fourth century AD when Samudra Gupta destroyed the Lichchhavi republics in the west. This marked the final triumph of caste over tribe.

But until then the republics provided a haven for anti-casteist thought and spawned numerous anti-caste sects, the most important of which were Buddhism and Jainism. It took a long time for the caste system to win its fight against this spiritual response of the republican tradition to Brahmanism. We need to fill in some details of this story.

2. CASTE VERSUS SECT

With the settling of the Gangetic plain, its rivers became arteries of trade. Towns expanded and provided a congenial environment for a growing number of artisans who came to be organized into guilds. The artisans who were concentrated in particular parts of the town, and whose occupations became hereditary and close-knit, were regarded as subcastes (jatis) by about the sixth century BC.

This growth of trade and commerce in the sixth to fourth centuries BC led to the growing prosperity of the mercantile classes, who were classified as Vaishyas under the varna system. Their economic power was not, however, matched by political power, which was held by the two upper varnas.[30] This led to social tension, as the caste system became a major obstacle in any attempt by the mercantile guilds to translate their growing economic strength into political powers.[31] The rise of the heterodox sects of Jainism and Buddhism provided them, and others oppressed by the caste system, with an avenue of escape.[32] Later, in the medieval period, the Bhakti movement was also a non-casteist movement of mainly lower castes in urban centres. This tendency for oppressed castes to opt out of the existing Hindu social order by joining a non-casteist sect has continued to the present day.

The outcome of the conflict between the mercantile caste and the Brahmins can be traced in the relative growth and decline of Buddhism in India. Over the centuries, the fortunes of Buddhism and the mercantile caste waxed and waned together. Their final decline was partly caused by an increase in internecine warfare in northern India after the Gupta period, as well as by the start of a series of invasions from the north-west. Both must have disrupted inland and overseas trade—the major sources of the economic power of the mercantile caste. By the time of the advent of the crescent in India (c.AD 1000), Brahmanism was victorious and caste had finally triumphed over sect.

3. CASTE TRIUMPHANT

In its practical aspects, the basis of the caste system as it evolved was not so much the four varnas or great classes (or castes) but the interrelationships and adjustments of numerous subcastes (jatis). These subcastes were based on occupational specialization, but mobility was possible, and did occur within the inter- or intra-caste status hierarchy. This vertical mobility was dependent on the whole caste (and not just its individual members) moving up the social hierarchy. This was usually done by adopting a different occupation, possibly migrating to a new region and demanding a higher ritual status.[33] Apart from offsetting some of the more obvious rigidities of an occupational hierarchy, this group (but not individual) mobility also allowed the effective supply of labour in different occupations to change as demand, technology, and resources—including the subcastes' relative population growth-rates—in the economy altered. Thus, it appears from manuscripts[34] that during the Gupta period a guild of silk-weavers in western India, finding they could not earn a decent living in their traditional occupation, moved to another part of western India, where they adopted higher status professions as archers, soldiers, bards, and scholars! Similarly, it is unlikely that over the millennia all Brahmins could have earned a living as priests. The Scriptures (the *Smriti*) laid down what different classes should do in distress. They 'carefully define what a man may legitimately do when he cannot earn a living by the calling normally followed by his class, and by these provisions, Brahmins might pursue all manner of trades and professions'.[35]

The very complicated vertical hierarchy of castes also made it easier to absorb new ethnic groups who arrived in successive waves throughout Indian history. Their place in the social hierarchy was determined partly by their occupation and sometimes by their social origins.[36]

During its evolution, the caste system had also been provided with a ritual and philosophical rationale and justification, which need not concern us, even though we recognize that the resulting ideology must have been important in buttressing the system.[37] The important point is that by the end of the sixth century AD, with the victory of caste over tribe and caste over sect, Indian society developed a social structure whose major features have survived to our day.

4. ADMINISTRATION, LAND TENURE, AND THE VILLAGE COMMUNITIES

The land was communally owned in the first Aryan agrarian settlements. But with the decline of tribal units land came to be divided amongst the families in the village, and private property in land was instituted. Bigger holdings were largely run with hired labour. Slaves were not kept in large numbers and were primarily engaged as domestic servants.[38] As the Aryan settlements expanded along the Ganges, it became a natural trading artery and a number of market towns developed on its banks. Some of the richer landlords then became traders.

Following the accession of Bimbisara in the second half of the sixth century BC and the ascendancy of his kingdom of Magadha, the beginnings of an administrative structure are discernible in the monarchies. This became necessary as these feuding Aryan monarchies became more dependent for their survival upon the revenue they could extract from the agricultural settlements. However, an administrative system was not fully developed in ancient India until the reign of the imperial Mauryas in the third century BC. Its basis (as was that of the empire) was land revenue.

Officials were appointed to measure the land under cultivation and to evaluate the crop. Regular assessments were made to increase the revenues from an expanding economy. Each village was under the jurisdiction of a headman who was responsible for collecting taxes,[39] and these were shipped to the royal treasury by yet other officials.

The villages were stockaded. Beyond their fields and pasture lay waste lands and jungles which were the property of the king. He alone could sanction their clearance and, as the land was thus theoretically owned by the king, he usually extracted about one-sixth of its produce as tax.[40]

To clear the forests of new settlements, the Government deported large bodies of 'Shudras' from over-populated areas. These Shudra settlers, who had to give up the surplus from their crops to the king, worked on clearing the forests or as cultivators. They were not allowed to bear arms. As soon as these new settlements became economically viable, other members of complementary castes and occupations moved in voluntarily. The Government was also responsible for the construction and maintenance of various irrigation facilities, which it financed by a water tax on users.[41]

The Mauryas thus established the first centralized bureaucracy in India. Ashoka's empire was divided into four provinces, under royal princes, who were the emperor's viceroys. Each province was subdivided into districts, which in turn were divided into groups of villages. The village was the lowest unit of administration.[42] This general pattern for administering the Indian empire has remained virtually unchanged, despite local and temporal variations, over the intervening centuries.

For each group of villages, there was an accountant above the village headman, who was responsible for maintaining a land register, boundaries, records of live-stock, and a census of the population. In addition, a tax collector determined and levied land revenue. These lower-level, rural bureaucrats were paid 'either by a remission of tax or by land grants'.[43] Salaries were paid to the higher-level administrators which, together with expenditure on public works, absorbed about a quarter of the total revenue.

With the decline of the Mauryas, northern India once again disintegrated into feuding kingdoms and the centralized administrative apparatus of the Mauryas collapsed. Now, large kingdoms typically 'had a central core of directly adminis-tered territory and a circle of vassal kingdoms subordinate in varying degrees to the emperor. These vassals had vassals of their own in petty local chieftains call-ing themselves *rajas*. The Indian system differed from that of Europe in that the relations of overlord and vassal were not regularly based on contract. . . . When decisively defeated in battle, a king might render homage to his conqueror and retain his throne. Thus, vassals usually became so by conquest rather than by contract'.[44]

By the time of the Guptas (AD 319), it became apparent that the centralized empire of the Mauryas could not be replicated. The local administrators (the rajas) thereby acquired a great deal of autonomy. Moreover, from the sixth cen-tury AD the salaries of officials came to be paid in land grants and not in cash.[45]

These land grants did not absolve the officials from paying land taxes. The Brahmins alone received a type of land grant (agrahara), which was tax-free. The secular officers, by contrast, became tax-farmers. Land grants were made from the fallow or waste land owned by the State. When such a grant was made in lieu of a salary, the donee did not acquire complete rights over the land. He could not evict tenants, and had a right to one-third to one-half of the produce.[46] The other major sources of taxation were the urban guilds of artisans, who had prospered with the establishment of peace and political stability and the ensuing increase in trade and commerce under the Mauryan empire.

But it was the village communities which came to be the primary economic unit of the Indian economy. They and the caste system provided stability to a common society which was torn by internecine warfare amongst feuding Indian monarchies, subjected to numerous foreign invasions, and ravaged periodically by pestilence and famine.

The caste system's vocational segregation meant that war was a game for the professional warrior castes which excluded most of the other castes. This was fortunate for the latter, particularly as, until the Islamic invasions, the Hindu code of chivalry, which maintained the sanctity of non-combatants, was respected.

From the days of Megasthenes (*c*. 315 BC) to those of the Muhammedans (*c*. AD 1000), the immunity of the village communities from pillage and destruction in times of war was an established fact. Except where anarchy reigned, normally, society was protected by its autonomous institutions which were too deep-rooted to be disturbed by even the chronic instability of kingdoms of the Middle Age (600–1200 AD). The secret of the present Hindu civilisation is, therefore, to be found in the enduring social structure.[47]

Though the village communities were not completely autarkic, their trading links were probably fairly localized.[48] Within the village economy, the relationship between the different caste groups took a particular form. This patron–client relationship, called 'jajmani' in the north, continues to this day. In writing about the social structure of modern-day Indian villages, Srinivas states:

The essential artisan and servicing castes are paid annually in grain at harvest. In some parts of India, the artisans and the servicing castes are also provided with free food, clothing, fodder and a residential site. On such occasions as birth, marriage and death, these castes perform extra duties for which they are paid a customary sum of money and some gifts of land . . . although, primarily, an economic or ritual tie, it has a tendency to spread to other fields and become a patron–client relationship. The relationship is generally stable and usually inherited. The right to serve is hereditary, transferable, saleable, mortgageable and partible. The *jajmani* system bound together the different castes living in a village or a group of neighbouring villages. The castewise division of labour and the consequent linking up of different castes in enduring and pervasive relationships provided a pattern which cut across the ties of caste.[49]

5. CULTURAL STABILITY AMIDST POLITICAL INSTABILITY

Numerous authors have attested to the stabilizing effects of the resulting system based on the twin pillars of caste and the village community. As the caste system provided room for group though not for individual social mobility, it had an important stabilizing effect by putting 'a damper, so to speak, on the rise of the parvenu'.[50]

It also helped the survival of Hindu society for millennia, because 'integrated as it was to both politics and professional activity, [it] localised many of the functions which would normally be associated with a truly "oriental despotism".'[51]

More importantly, the survival of Hindu society was probably due, as Dumont has emphasized, to the ideology underlying the system which created a disjunction between status and power.[52] This arose at an early stage of the evolution of the caste system. Dumont[53] hypothesizes that pre-Aryan India had chiefdoms rather like the ones Hocart[54] studied in Fiji and whose social structure Hocart found remarkably similar to that of the Kandyan kingdom in Ceylon that he later studied. In Fiji the chief has both status and power (he is both priest and king), and there is no distinction between the pure and impure. However, there is a religious specialization of labour services by various 'lineages'. These services are those commanded by the taboo person of the chief.

The centre-piece of the Hindu system, however, particularly in its rituals, is the importance attached to notions of pollution, and of purity and impurity. Thus, 'In Fiji, the system is centred on the chief—let us say the king, and the pure and the impure are not distinguished. In India, the king or his equivalent is indeed the main employer, but the Brahmin, the priest, is superior to him, and, correspondingly, the pure and impure are opposed.'[55] This 'disjunction between status and power,' argues Dumont, 'which was after all Indo-European, led to the transformation of the "Hocartian" system into the caste system.'[56]

Moreover, the subordination of the king to the priest (the Kshatriya to the Brahmin) in the status ranking made power inferior to status, and thus enabled Hindu society both to absorb all types of ruler within its fold and to preserve its essential structure. As Dumont aptly remarks:

It is thought that in ancient India the accession to the throne, and to the dignity of Kshatriya, by dynasties of a different origin, was an irregularity. This assumes that heredity is more important than function, which is true of caste (jati) but not the Varnas (the four great classes of Hindu society). So far as the Varnas are concerned, he who rules in a stable way, and places himself under the Brahmin, is a Kshatriya . . . since function is related to force, it was easier to become king than Brahman: Kshatriya and untouchable are the two levels on which it is easy to enter the caste society from outside.[57]

The status rules were ritualized in terms of notions of pollution, which many anthropologists[58] consider to be the central ideological principle underlying the caste system. As these notions of pollution apply to all aspects of what Americans would call an individual or group's 'life-style', parvenus seeking to raise their status to a level commensurate with their power (political or economic) have, throughout Indian history and to our day, sought to emulate the life-styles of the caste to whose status they aspire.[59]

Thus, 'the institution of caste, independent of the government and with social ostracism as its most severe sanction, was a powerful factor in the survival of Hinduism. The Hindu, living under an alien political order imposed from above, retained his cultural individuality largely through his caste, which received most of the loyalty elsewhere felt towards king, nation and city. Caste was so strong that, until recent years, all attempts at breaking it down have ended in failure.'[60] Various religious reformers like Kabir have tried. The Sikhs, despite the specific injunctions of their religion, never overcame caste feelings. The Roman Catholic and other converts to Christianity brought and perpetuated their caste prejudices, and even the Muslims with their egalitarian religion, once settled in India, organized themselves into castes.[61] The notion of caste has thus formed the framework for the material life of all the peoples in the subcontinent.

Without, therefore, attempting to downgrade the ideological and ritualistic underpinnings of caste, it is necessary, in our view, to ascertain whether the material interests of the Indian peoples have been well served by this unique social institution. For even someone who does not adhere to any crude materialist view of history must presume that the caste system was not economically dysfunctional over 2,000 years of Indian history. Otherwise it would be difficult to explain the survival of an institution which, whilst not hampering, certainly did not promote political unity, and against which serious challenges, both ideological and political, were periodically mounted—from the days of Buddhism and Jainism to those of Islam and the utilitarianism of the early British Raj. Hence in the next chapter we seek to provide an economic rationale for the caste system—that set of social customs which has governed the habitual behaviour of Indians for nearly 2,000 years.

NOTES

1. But see Thapar (1966), (1984), Kosambi (1981), Allchin and Allchin (1982) for a reconstruction.
2. Many historians have attested to this continuing cultural stability of India. Thus, e.g., R. S. Sharma (1954) writes: 'Except in India, wherever Muhammedans succeeded in establishing themselves, they transformed society and culture beyond recognition. Islam simply came, saw and conquered. Hindu India (on the eve of the Muslim invasions *c*.1000 AD was weak, divided and decadent. And yet, after centuries of continuous fighting, India could not be equally submerged. Paradoxical as it might seem, therefore, India, on the eve of the Muslim invasions, was both weak and inconquerable. She was politically most vulnerable but, culturally, all but impregnable' (pp. 2–3). This cultural stability has even outlasted the second great cultural onslaught—that of the West. Not surprisingly, as we shall see, it is in the Hindu social structure, established in c.300 BC, that historians have identified the source of this cultural stability. Thus, Sharma writes: 'The secret of the preservation of Hindu civilisation is . . . to be found in the enduring social structure. The rigidity of the caste system is often referred to as one of the causes of our decline. By no means a defensible institution, under modern conditions, it nevertheless

made its own contributions to our cultural survival. Fortresses were taken, capitals changed their masters, kingdoms rose and fell, but Hindu society was hardly affected. This inviolability of its main character has been due to two institutions, viz. caste and the village community' (ibid., 28).

3. See Thapar (1966, p. 29).
4. Basham (1967, p. 34)).
5. Kosambi (1981, p. 76).
6. Thapar (1966, p. 30). She also notes that there were sedentary agriculturalists in this region (Doab) prior to the Vedic period, as is evident from the archaeological record. The Asuras, for example, are said to have had a correct knowledge of the seasons for agricultural activities (Thapar (1984, p. 27)).
7. Sharma (1983, p. 115)).
8. Kosambi (1981, p. 90).
9. 'Remains of rice, ascribable to about the 8th century BC, have been found at Hastinapura [in the Punjab–Harayan area]. At this stage however rice was of the untransplanted variety' (Sharma (1983, p. 115)).
10. Kosambi (1981, p. 89).
11. Sharma (1983, p. 122).
12. See Thapar (1984, p. 72)).
13. Ibid., and Sharma (1980a).
14. Thapar (1984, p. 32). One of the most famous Indian epics, the *Mahabharata*, concerns the tribal war between the Kauravas and Pandavas over land rights. Their descendants in modern Indian villages have not ceased their internecine strife over the same issues.
15. Ibid., 28.
16. The 3 upper castes of Hindus were called 'twice-born' because their males wore the sacred thread on being initiated (born again) into the sacred rites at puberty.
17. Thapar (1966, p. 38). See also Kosambi (1981).
18. See Basham (1967, pp. 148–9), for the origin of the confusion between 'varna' (class) and 'jati' (caste).
19. Thapar (1966, p. 38).
20. Ibid., 39.
21. Ibid., 56. See also Sharma (1980a).
22. Thapar (1966, p. 56). See also Sharma (1980a).
23. Hutton (1963), Dumont (1970), Srinivas (1965).
24. Thapar (1966, p. 36).
25. The former was probably the council of tribal elders, the latter of the entire tribe. For a fuller description of the Aryan polity see Thapar (1984).
26. Thapar (1966, p. 37).
27. Ibid., 50.
28. See Boserup (1965) for the importance of these differing types of fallow as determining the labour intensity and hence productivity of agriculture. See Thapar (1984), Kosambi (1981) on the likely differences in agriculture practices.
29. Although there were confederacies of republics such as the Vriji confederacy, but with the tribes remaining independent and retaining equality of status. See Thapar (1966, p. 51).
30. 'Ashoka's emphatic plea for social harmony would suggest the existence of social tension. Guild leaders in urban centres had the factual control of urban institutions yet the social code denied them the position or prestige to which they felt entitled. A practical expression of their resentment was their support for the heterodox sects, Buddhism in particular' (Ibid., 82).
31. The seizing of political power on the part of a given guild would require that it first ally itself with other guilds in order to obtain their loyalty, without which no political ambitions were likely to be achieved. Such co-operation may have been effectively prevented by caste rules, such as that forbidding eating together, which was an effective barrier between guilds of different caste (ibid., 112).
32. Ibid., 68.
33. Ibid., 40.
34. Ibid., 153.
35. Basham (1967, p. 141).

36. Thapar (1966, p. 39).
37. But see the various important studies of the Indian caste system which emphasize this aspect Dumont (1970), Ketkar (1909), Hocart (1950). See also Hutton (1963), and p. 44 below.
38. See Sharma (1980a), Kosambi (1981), Thapar (1984).
39. Thapar (1966, p. 55).
40. Ibid., 76.
41. This irrigation tax was 'between one-fifth and one-third . . . the total would amount to one-half of the produce for peasants paying one-third as irrigation cess. The laws books had "unalterably" laid down the rate of land revenue demand in the range of one-twelfth to one-sixth depending on the nature of the soil and its yields. Yet the actual collection varied between one-tenth and one-third according to the status of the ruler' (Mukhia (1981, p. 292)).
42. Thapar (1966, p. 84).
43. Ibid., 55.
44. Basham (1967, p. 95).
45. Ibid., 97.
46. Thapar (1966, p. 146).
47. Sharma (1954, p. 28).
48. Thus Srinivas (1965) writes, 'Most Indian villages do not have more than a few of the essential castes and depend upon neighbouring villages for other services, skills and goods.'
49. Ibid., 511. He goes on: 'The modern "caste problem" is to some extent the result of the weakening, in the last 50 years or more, of those vertical and local ties and the consequent strengthening of horizontal ties over wide areas.' See also Dumont (1970, p. 4).
50. Hutton (1963, p. 122).
51. Thapar (1966, p. 19).
52. Dumont (1970, chs. 3, 7, 10).
53. Ibid., 213.
54. Hocart (1950).
55. Dumont (1970, p. 49).
56. Ibid., 213.
57. Ibid., 74.
58. Ibid., Ketkar (1909).
59. See Srinivas (1965) for the relevance of this form of social climbing even today.
60. Basham (1967, p. 152).
61. See Frykenberg (1985) for a review of recent works which show how the British, having failed to alter the caste system, adapted to it.

3

An Economic Rationale for the Hindu Social System

INTRODUCTION

Few attempts have been made, to the best of our knowledge, to provide an *economic* rationale for the emergence and continuance of the Hindu social system and in particular its most important pillar—the caste system.[1] It is however difficult to believe that the caste system could have survived so long if it were economically dysfunctional.[2] Lacking, as it does, any official Church, Hinduism could not enforce its social system through a clergy; and, at least from AD 1000 onwards, the secular force in the land was in foreign hands (first of the Muslims and then the British) whose relatively egalitarian religious and social precepts were at complete variance with the hierarchical structure and world view of the caste system. More importantly, despite their initial prejudice against the system and attempts at reform, both sets of invaders came in time to adapt their secular power to its norms—however half-heartedly and with whatever mixture of motives. The Muslims, in time, even took over its social prejudices.

In this chapter, therefore, we attempt to provide the sketch of an economic theory which might be able to explain both the origins and the resilience of the Hindu social system as expressed in its twin pillars, the caste system and the village 'community'. We will also deal with another novel aspect of Hindu customs—its ban on cow slaughter. In what follows we will concentrate upon the north, and in particular on the Indo-Gangetic plain, which was (as we saw in the last chapter) the crucible of Hinduism, and its social expression in the caste system. However, we also need briefly to outline the variant of the Hindu social system that was established in the southern peninsula by about the sixth to ninth centuries AD, and the reasons for the form it took. This is done in the penultimate section of this chapter.

1. SOME EMPIRICAL HYPOTHESES

There are some crucial empirical assumptions underlying the following theoretical speculations; one of these can be thoroughly documented from India's history, but the evidence on the others is still largely speculative.

(a) Political instability

The first assumption we make, and one which can be fairly well established, is the political instability and the ensuing periodic breakdown of any centrally imposed law and order over large parts of the country. The ancient Hindu texts recognized the continual feuding amongst the Aryan monarchies in terms of the political doctrine of 'matsyanyaya'—unbridled competition in which the powerful preyed upon the weak without restraint, or, to use the language of the texts: 'where the big fish swallowed the little fish in a condition of anarchy'.[3]

The large, rich alluvial, and geographically homogenous Indo-Gangetic plain has formed a natural 'core-area', to use Eric Jones's term, for an Indian State.[4] But given its size, its domination by a single State, with the available military and transport technologies, has been episodic. Nor have there been geographical barriers within the area to provide a 'natural' States system as in Europe. The history of northern India is one of the rise and fall of Indo-Gangetic empires, which from time to time also extended to the south. The resulting endemic political instability and the periodic breakdown of any centrally imposed law and order accompanied by cultural and (more contentiously) economic stability has been remarked upon by historians, one of whom aptly states:

Fortresses were taken, capitals changed their masters, kingdoms rose and fell, but Hindu society was hardly affected. . . . This inviolability of its main character has been due to two institutions, viz the caste system and the village community. India was, as it were, covered by innumerable circles, some of them concentric and some intersecting. The circle of the village community stood within the village but intersected both the circle of the village and the larger circle of the kingdom, being linked up with members of the same caste outside the village and the kingdom. The network of castes and villages sustained its balance and remained intact even when the larger circle of the kingdom was broken into or destroyed. The kingdoms were the variables, and villages and castes the constant factors in the Hindu socio-political equation.[5]

Since the establishment of numerous feuding Aryan monarchies in the Indo-Gangetic plain, the lodestone of every petty Indian chieftain has been the establishment of a pan-north Indian or subcontinental empire, based on the exploitation of the large revenue base provided by the relatively productive agrarian system which was gradually established in the region. This is the first ecological–empirical assumption we make.

The other three empirical assumptions are more speculative. The first concerns the ecology of the early Aryan agrarian settlements, and the likely balance between the demand for agricultural labour and available supply. The second concerns the likely stability in the land to man ratio. The third concerns the 'equilibrium' levels of living during the periods of political stability of the Indian rural masses from about 300 BC till the beginning of the end of the Moghul empire in the late seventeenth century AD. Periods of political instability presumably led to declines in the population and levels of living from these 'equilibrium' levels.

We next summarize the available evidence for these three ecological–economic assumptions, before taking up their implications and those of the more solidly established fact of Indian political instability.

(b) Stability of crop patterns and agrarian technology

The first ecological fact which we wish to emphasize is the difference between the agricultural conditions (noted in chapter 2) faced by the early Aryan settlers in the Indo-Gangetic plain and those of the Himalayan foothills. In the latter, the Aryan settlements established by clearing the relatively thin forests probably followed a less labour-intensive method of cultivation than the settlements on the Indo-Gangetic plain. The latter was marshy, and once cleared was suitable for producing labour-intensive crops. The Gangetic settlements hence probably required a higher labour input per acre both for clearing the land and in the agricultural practices adopted.

There is evidence from the writings of the Chinese traveller Huan Tsiang that at the time of Harsha (AD 606–47) sugar-cane and wheat were the main crops of the north-western Indo-Gangetic plains, and rice in the region of Magadha (modern-day Bihar) and points further east. Given the similarity between these and modern cropping patterns in the region, the pattern of crops cultivated in the Indo-Gangetic plain as well as the technology appears to have remained largely unchanged for nearly twenty centuries.[6] We have no similar information on the crops grown in the republican foothills, but we hypothesize that they are unlikely to have been cultivated with the same degree of labour intensity as the crops of the monarchical plains—sugar-cane, wheat, and rice. This is the second ecological–empirical assumption we make.

(c) Stability of population size

The third assumption concerns the size of the population at the time of the evolution of the caste system in the monarchies of the Indo-Gangetic plain. India today is considered to be a heavily populated country. However, until the early part of the twentieth century, the land–man ratio in the country was very favourable. Certainly the country could not have reached its land frontier in the fifth century BC, as the cultivated area has been increasing in the country until fairly recently (and with it agricultural output—see Table 3.1).

More surprisingly, perhaps, there is some tentative evidence (admittedly little better than guesses for antiquity) which suggests that the size of the population and hence the land–man ratio in times of peace and political stability (which could be termed the 'equilibrium' level) remained relatively constant from the time of the Mauryas (*c*. 320 BC) till the late eighteenth century.[7]

Thus Datta (1962) has estimated that the population of India in about 320 BC was 181 million. But as this was based on Greek estimates of the size of the Indian army facing Alexander, it is likely to have an upward bias—as the Greek writers, by exaggerating the size of the opposition they would have faced, wanted to provide an apologetic for Alexander's failure to move into the Ganges valley.[8] Thapar therefore suggests a figure of about 100 million or less for this period. Another estimate by Pran Nath for the seventh to tenth centuries AD puts the

TABLE 3.1. Agricultural and Population Rates of Growth, India (% p.a.)

	Area cultivated	Yield	Agricultural product	Population
1900–19	0.29	0.24	0.53	0.25
1920–39	0.24	– 0.44	0.20	0.83
1940–9	0.66	– 1.63	– 0.97	1.32
1950–60	1.18	2.34	3.52	1.98

Source: Sen (1965), cited in Clark and Haswell (1967, p. 83).

total population of the subcontinent between 100 and 140 million. A figure which, Basham observes, 'seems reasonable, though based on very slender evidence'.[9]

A hundred million is the estimate made by Moreland (1920) for India's late sixteenth-century population, for the period of Moghul stability during the reign of Akbar. Davis (1951) adjusts Moreland's figures to yield a population for 1600 of 125 million.[10] The best available estimates of the subsequent population of undivided India have been derived by Angus Maddison from various sources and are given in Table 3.2. This likely relative stability, for nearly 2,000 years after the establishment of Hindu civilization on the subcontinent, in the *upper limit* of the size of the population until the beginning of the nineteenth century is the second important non-political stylized assumption we make.[11]

The estimates for 320 BC and AD 1600 (if valid) refer to periods of relative peace, stability, and prosperity in the turbulent history of the subcontinent. They therefore reflect the 'equilibrium' population which the social and economic system could support with available technology. There were likely to have been large deviations around this 'equilibrium' level over the centuries, due to the four horsemen of the Apocalypse—famine, disease, pestilence, and war. But there is virtually no quantitative data available on these aspects till the mid-nineteenth century.

(d) Unchanging levels of living

The final empirical assumption we make concerns levels of living. Ashok Desai (1972), using data contained in Abul Fazl's *Ain-I-Akbari* (a contemporary record) has tried to determine the level of real urban wages and of mean per capita consumption and output of agricultural goods in Akbar's time (1595) as compared with their level in 1961. This methodology has been criticized by Heston (1977) and Moosvi (1973, 1977). The details are beyond our remit. The important point to note is that, although Desai's original hypothesis of seventeenth-century standards of living being about 1.4 to 1.8 times the levels in 1960–1 has not stood up to the criticism, the general thrust of the revisions made by Heston, Moosvi (1978), and Desai himself (1978) suggests no marked

TABLE 3.2. Population of Undivided India (Including Native States), Benchmark
and Census Years 1600–1941 (millions)

	Undivided India	Native States	British India
1600	125.0	—	—
1700	153.0	—	—
1800	186.0	—	—
1856	227.0	—	—
1871	255.2	—	—
1881	257.4	—	—
1891	282.1	—	—
1901	285.3	62.3	222.2
1911	303.0	71.0	232.1
1921	305.7	72.0	233.7
1931	338.2	82.0	256.2
1941	389.0	93.0	296.0

Source: Maddison (1971, p. 164); derived by him from Davis (1951, pp. 26–7). Burma is excluded throughout. The figures for 1931 and 1941 are from the census; 1871–1921 include Davis's adjustment for under-coverage. The figure for 1600 is Davis's adjustment of Moreland's (1929) figure. The figure for 1856 is from Mukherjee (1969). Figures for 1700 and 1800 are Maddison's interpolation of 1600 and 1856. Maddison assumes that before 1800 the British conquest made little significant difference to population trends and that the growth path for 1600 to 1800 was smooth at 0.2% a year, and from 1800 to 1856 at 0.4%. Proportions in British India and Indian States from Sivasubramonian (1965).

improvement in levels of living between 1595 and 1960, though equally there has probably been no marked worsening. Maddison's estimate is that 'India's per capita income in 1750 was probably similar to that in 1960, at about $150 at 1965 US prices'.[12] Similarly Raychaudhuri (1968) has argued that the likely path of per capita output followed that of changes in the level of peace and stability between 1575 and 1900 as charted in Fig. 3.1.

We lack even the meagre and speculative estimates of levels of living during Akbar's reign for the earlier periods. However, as the size of the population was likely to have been stable during periods of peace and prosperity from the Mauryas to the Moghul and British empires (at least till 1900), the likelihood that the cropping pattern was relatively unchanged in the Indo-Gangetic plain over this period, and that from the days of the Aryan settlement Indian agriculture probably stagnated at what, by the standards of the second century BC, was a technologically fairly advanced level (for instance it used animal power, light ploughs as well as water-wheels), it might be not be a wild guess that the standard of living was about the same in 320 BC as they were in AD 1595. In any case, we will hypothesize that this was so, with (obviously) falling population and standard of living in the long periods (sometimes centuries) during which the country

FIG 3.1

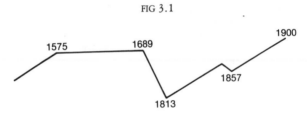

Source: Raychaudhuri (1968), p. 90.

was engulfed by wars against invaders or else between feuding Indian chieftains trying to established a pan-Indian empire.

If this guess is right it would be in accordance with the few descriptions of the life of the Hindus left by pre-Moghul foreign travellers,[13] which suggest that Indians enjoyed a fairly high standard of living by comparison with other contemporary civilizations. For then Indians for 2000 years would have enjoyed a fluctuating per capita income which, at its peak of about US $150 at 1965 prices, was about the same as in Elizabethan England.[14] As the new-found prosperity of Elizabethan England marked a radical change in the standard of living of most European peoples, the same relatively stagnant Indian standard of living since the fourth century BC must have appeared the height of prosperity to foreign observers from other countries and earlier times.

The last three empirical assumptions taken together suggest that by about the fourth to third centuries BC India had evolved an economic system which maintained living standards (at least at times of political stability and normal rainfall) which were roughly comparable to those in about 1960. The caste system and the village economy as it had evolved by the fourth or third century, BC were, we would hypothesize, an essential ingredient in maintaining this 'equilibrium', ableit at a relatively low level by modern standards. What is more, for a long time after this human adaptation to the 'new' environment faced by the Aryans was developed it enabled a standard of living which was probably fairly high compared to other contemporaneous countries and civilizations.

2. THE BOSERUP THEORY AND THE ARYAN ECONOMIC PROBLEM

In explaining the determinants of this Aryan behavioural adaptation to their new environment, we need to ask: what was the economic problem that the Aryan agrarian settlements faced during their period of expansion in the Indo-Gangetic plain? We would hypothesize that it was the danger of a shortage of labour.

As we noted in the last chapter, the clearing of the forests and the establishment of the new settlements was made possible by the existence of the 'shudras', who were probably the peoples vanquished and absorbed by the Aryans in their march across the Indo-Gangetic plains. The importance of the shudras lies in their augmentation of the supply of labour available to the Aryans from within their own tribes. The availability of shudra labourers both enabled and impelled the Aryans to change their way of life from nomadic pastoralism towards a form of settled agriculture.

The role of increasing population pressure on land in both inducing and facilitating the adoption of more intensive forms of agriculture has been persuasively argued by Boserup (1965).[15] She argues that population pressure is a necessary but not sufficient condition for technical change in agriculture (in the form of an intensive use of both labour and capital). She identifies the differing labour input per hectare requirements of different types of agrarian system by the frequency with which a particular piece of land is cropped. Thus nomadic pastoralism, the dominant form of activity amongst the pre-Vedic Aryan tribes, is more labour- and capital-intensive than hunting and gathering, or the slash-and-burn type agriculture practised by many African tribes.

According to Boserup, different agrarian systems can be ordered in terms of their periods of fallow on a spectrum from the most primitive—slash-and-burn—to the most advanced—multiple cropping with modern inputs. What distinguishes these systems is both the relative frequency with which a particular piece of land is cropped and the ensuing increase in direct and indirect labour inputs required to maintain a constant per capita food output. The crucial economic variable in different types of subsistence agriculture is the amount of labour required per unit of food (say grain) produced. Thus in those earlier agrarian systems where land is not scarce relative to labour, it is the yield *per unit of labour* rather than the absolute yield *per hectare* which is important for the farmer. Thus, contrary to the classical Malthusian presumption, Boserup argues that, instead of population growth being induced by technological advances, it is population growth which leads to the adoption of more advanced techniques (that is, techniques which raise yields *per hectare*). The farmer in a land-surplus, labour-scarce economy will be concerned with the labour requirements of the new advanced techniques. These generally require increased labour effort. They will not be adopted until rising population reduces the per capita food output that can be produced with existing techniques and forces a change.

Both Boserup and Clark and Haswell provide a wealth of historical evidence from different regions and periods to support this theory, which explains changes in forms of agricultural production[16] from 'forest fallow'—the most primitive type of shifting agriculture (with low densities of population to land)—to 'bush fallow' to 'short fallow' to settled agriculture based on the plough (with high densities of population to land).[17] We have described in Chapters 1 and 2 the changing ecological circumstances which led to this sequence of agricultural development in India.

3. LABOUR SUPPLY, SLAVERY, AND CASTE

The shift from nomadic pastoralism to settled agriculture of the Aryan tribes, with its higher labour requirements, must have been induced and made possible by the presence of the indigenous shudras who (as we saw in the last chapter) were initially used to clear the forests. But once the forests had been cleared, the labour requirements per unit of food produced would have differed in the two regions—the marshy Indo-Gangetic plain and the more 'fertile' Himalayan foothills. We do not have any data on the likely yields (i) per man-hour or (ii) per hectare, or on the labour input required per unit of grain produced in the two ecological regions of Aryan India. Our hypothesis would be that there were longer systems of fallow (with some variants of slash-and-burn) in the republican foothills and shorter systems of fallow with more labour-intensive cultivation in the monarchical plains.[18]

There is some relatively recent data (for 1949–51) from Sarawak[19] where the land Dayaks produce rice both in the sedentary swamps as well as on the hills. Ecologically, the conditions seem similar to those in Aryan India. Geddes found that, even though output per acre was higher on the sedentary swamp (yield per worker was 1,903 kg of paddy) as compared with the hills (1,578 kg), the Dayaks invariably preferred to produce rice on the hills cleared by 'slash-and-burn' methods. This was because the *yield per man hour* worked, with a total input of 2,165 hours/ha on the swamp and 1,663 hours in the hills, was lower (only 0.87 kg/man hour) in the swamps than in the hills (0.95 kg/man hour).

The monarchies of the plains therefore would have required a larger labour supply to maintain a reasonable output of food per capita than the republics of the foothills. Once the Aryans had left their nomadic ways and established monarchies based on the revenue from agricultural settlements in the Indo-Gangetic plain, any drastic decrease in labour supply was likely to threaten their new-found way of life, with its high demand for labour. Given the relative abundance of land there must always have been the danger that part of the labour supply on the new Aryan settlements might melt into the remaining forests to start their own settlements, or else, and more likely, take to more primitive forms of agriculture.

The control and maintenance of an adequate supply of labour is, therefore, likely to have been an important consideration underlying the viability of the socio-economic system that evolved in the Indo-Gangetic plain. By contrast the republics would not have been under the same pressure to control their labour supply, as the demand for labour to maintain their agrarian system would have been lower. The caste system we hypothesize was the Aryan response in the monarchical plains to the problem of maintaining an adequate labour supply to carry on settled agriculture. As similar pressures were less intense in the republican foothills, we would expect, as was the case (see ch. 2), that the need for and adherence to a caste-based society in these regions would be weaker.

To add plausibility to this view (to be further developed below), we need to show why some of the other responses that other societies have made when faced by a similar danger of a shortage of labour were not viable. The most obvious response is that of enslaving a part of the population.

A surprising feature of ancient Indian society is that 'India unlike some other ancient civilizations was never economically dependent on slavery; the labourer, farm worker and craftsman were normally free men, and the *Latifundia* of the Roman magnate had no counterpart in India.'[20] Though there were some slaves, these were usually domestic servants. Why?

The shudra cultivators in Hindu caste society were the descendants of the earlier Aryan enemies, the Dasas, and of mixed Aryan–Dasan liaisons.[21] The word 'dasa' later came to mean a slave, and it would be surprising if this did not imply that at least some of the Dasas were initially enslaved.

In the absence of a centralized administrative system to register and enforce slave 'contracts', a necessary condition for slavery to persist is the ease with which slaves can be distinguished from free men by some attribute such as pigmentation or language—the former being more inescapable than the latter. The Dasas were distinct in their appearance from the Aryans[22] and spoke a different language. Thus it would have been possible for the Aryans to have enforced their enslavement, even without the centralized political system needed to enforce a more colour-blind type of slave system. It is likely that, in the original development of the caste (varna) system, the Dasas were enslaved in some form and put beyond the Aryan social pale. Gradually, however, though not accorded the twice-born status of the Aryans, they were incorporated as shudras into the Hindu caste system as cultivators of land. Though some slavery continued, it took the form of debt peonage. It was often contractual, with free men selling themselves and their families into slavery in times of distress.[23]

The Dasas, unlike the Aryans (who were pastoralists), probably knew the technology for settled agriculture[24]—a technology which the remains of the Harappan civilization and more recent archaeological evidence testify (see Chapter 1) was known in India before the Aryan invasions. The agriculture of the Aryan settlements in the Indo-Gangetic plain was based on this technology and its various extensions. Three reasons could explain the emancipation of the Dasan slaves and their incorporation into Hindu society, albeit with a lowly status.

First, the skills in cultivation required for a viable settled agriculture, which the Aryans needed to learn from the Dasas, could presumably only be demonstrated by doing—which of course implies the *willingness* of the Dasas to demonstrate these skills. Secondly, having practised these skills in the past, the Dasas were likely to have had an absolute advantage in the exercise of these skills (at least initially) as compared with the Aryans. Thirdly, as is well known from the experience of various forms of collectivized agriculture, agricultural technology (even of the subsistence type) cannot be described in terms of any precise set of input–output coefficients. Hence it is very difficult to monitor the effort of peasants and coerce them to perform according to an efficiency norm, for there are no unambiguous indicators of this norm. Thus it would have been more efficient for the above incentive and informational reasons[25] to have emancipated the

Dasan slaves, and to have given them autonomy in decision-making and control over agricultural operations.

Besides slavery, various other means for maintaining the rural labour supply in the Indo-Gangetic plains, such as poll taxation,[26] limitations on migration, and various forms of indenture, would also have been impossible at the time the Aryan social system evolved, as they all require the power of a centralized State and its attendant bureaucracy for their enforcement. However, because of our first stylized fact—the endemic political instability during this period—any such alternative would have been built on sand. With plentiful land and the waxing and waning of political authority over a particular region, there would always have been the danger that more directly coerced peasants would have fled the settlements (as they nevertheless did, off and on, for instance, in later Moghul times) whenever political authority was weakened by internecine conflict amongst the monarchies.

The caste system provided a more subtle and enduring answer to the Aryan's problem of maintaining their rural labour supply. It established a decentralized system of control which did not require any overall (and larger) political community to exist for its survival, and it ensured that any attempt to start new settlements outside its framework would be difficult if not impossible. The division of labour by caste and its enforcement by local social ostracism were central to the schema. There were two aspects of the caste system as described in the previous chapter which are relevant.

The first is the endogamous specialization of the complementary services required as inputs in the functioning of a viable settlement. Any oppressed group planning to leave a particular village to set up on its own would find that, if it were confined to a single caste group, it would not have the necessary complementary skills specific to other castes to start a new settlement. They would therefore have to recruit members of other complementary castes to join them in fleeing the Aryan settlement. The likelihood of that would be remote. For some of these other complementary castes would already have a high ritual and economic status, with little incentive to move to the more uncertain environment of a new settlement.

The caste-wise division of labour could also be maintained purely through the instrument of social ostracism without a central Church or political coercion. For if the oppressed lower castes (or individuals in them) could have acquired the necessary complementary skills they could have overcome the difficulty of putting together the required coalition to form a new settlement from within a single oppressed caste. This, however, was unlikely to happen, as it would not be profitable for other caste groups to impart the knowledge of these complementary skills. For the ostracism involved in breaking the caste code, either as a consumer or producer (at each level of the caste hierarchy), would entail higher costs than any gains from performing any profitable arbitrage in the labour market (including imparting knowledge of complementary skills) that the casteist segmentation of labour might entail.[27] This can be shown more rigorously, in terms of a model developed by Akerloff (1976, 1980).

*4. A SIMPLE ECONOMIC MODEL OF A CASTE ECONOMY

Consider a simple economy in which there are only two castes, Vaishyas and Shudras (V and S) who are specialized according to the caste code in the provision of labour for two types of task which are labelled skilled and unskilled. All workers are homogeneous except for the accident of their birth as a Vaishya or Shudra. Labourers can produce only one product, firms can produce only one product, and everyone wishes to purchase more than one product. Goods are produced by profit-maximizing firms who follow the caste code by only employing Vaishyas in the skilled tasks and Shudras in the unskilled tasks. According to the caste code, anyone consuming the products of a firm which produces goods without following the caste code would be made an outcaste. Assume that the wages paid are competitively determined for each of the two types of labour and are:

w_s for the skilled Vaishya tasks
w_u for the unskilled Shudra tasks
with $w_s > w_u$

also let the output per unit of labour in each of the different types of task be the same in every industry, of which there are n, producing the 1 . . . n goods in the economy.

Thus, a_s is the output per unit of labour in skilled tasks and a_u is the output per unit of labour in unskilled tasks

If the amount of Vaishya labour allocated to the skilled tasks in industry i is L_{si} and of Shudra labour to unskilled tasks L_{ui}, then the output of industry i, x_i is

$$x_i = a_s L_{si} + a_u L_{ui} \qquad (i = 1 \ldots n)$$

If the price of the output of industry i is p_i (taking industry 1's price as the numeraire), then the profit-maximizing condition entails that for each industry i

$$p_i [a_s L_{si} + a_u L_{ui}] - [w_s L_{si} + w_u L_{ui}] = 0 \qquad (4.1)$$

One possible equilibrium which would satisfy (4.1) is if:

$$w_s = a_s \qquad (4.2)$$
$$w_u = a_u$$

and hence $$p_i = 1$$

We also assume that if there is any outcaste labour it receives a wage of $w_o = a_o$.

As labour is homogeneous, in the absence of the caste code, it would pay producers to hire cheaper Shudra labour at the lower wage rate w_u to perform the skilled tasks (note $w_s > w_u$, so that if a Shudra worker is hired to perform a skilled task where his productivity, *ex hypothesi*, will be $a_s = w_s$, and only paid w_u, the producer will make an additional profit of $a_s - w_u = w_s - w_u$). In fact, it would pay him to do so, as long as the price at which he could sell his output p_i^* was such that

$$p_i^* a_s - w_u = p_i^* a_s - a_u > 0$$

or if
$$p_i^* \geq a_u / a_s \qquad (4.3)$$

But under many circumstances (to be specified below) it will not be worthwhile for *consumers* to buy goods from such a producer who has broken the caste code, because to do so would put them outside the pale, and lower *their own earning opportunities* to those of outcastes, namely w_o ($< w_u < w_s$). Suppose these potential consumers were found amongst the Shudra caste. Their earnings would decline from w_u to w_o. What would be the change in their utility. Assume that, having been outcaste, the Shudra buys α units of the non-caste good i[29] at the price p_i^*. He will then have

$$w_o - \alpha p_i^* \qquad (4.4)$$

of his lower income to purchase the other goods being produced by caste firms, whose price (see (4.2)) is unity, so expression (4.4) will give the units of the other goods he can purchase. Assuming utility depends only on the consumption of the n goods, the consumer who has been made an outcaste will now have a utility level:

$$\alpha + (w_o - \alpha p_i^*)$$

or
$$\alpha (1 - p_i^*) + w_o$$

If he had not been outcaste, he would have had an income of w_u, which would also yield the same units of consumption of goods (as prices from 4.2 are all unity), and thence his utility level. Hence it would only be worth his while patronizing a non-caste firm, and thereby being outcaste if his utility level after being outcaste was at least as great as that from his retaining his caste status by not buying from the non-casteist firm, that is if

$$\alpha(1 - p_i^*) + w_o \geq w_u \qquad (4.5)$$

or only if
$$\alpha > [w_u - w_o]/(1 - p_i^*)$$

or substituting for p_i^* from 4.2 and 4.3 if

$$\alpha > [a_u - w_o]/[1 - a_u/a_s] \qquad (4.6)$$

or
$$\alpha > [w_u - w_o]/[1 - w_u/w_s]$$

As the value of α is a parameter of the utility function, it cannot be inherently implausible that α will be *less* than the expression on the right-hand side of (4.6). Suppose that

$$\alpha < \left[\frac{w_u - w_0}{1 - \dfrac{w_o}{w_s}} \right] \qquad (4.7)$$

Then as $(w_s - w_o) > (w_s - w_u)$, (4.6) cannot hold.

It would not be in the interest of producers or of Shudras or any other caste to break the code against producing and buying goods which have been produced by firms which circumvent the caste differentiation of labour. But why shouldn't the producer, knowing that some customers will become outcastes for buying their non-caste goods, also offer to hire them at a marginally higher wage than the outcaste wage of w_o and put them to work in skilled tasks (occupation)? He will not do so, for if he can then sell this product (i^{**}) at the price p_i^{**}, his maximum profits will be given by

$$p_i^{**} a_s - w_o \geq 0$$
or
$$p_i^{**} \geq w_o / a_s \qquad (4.8)$$

But at this price, no consumer will be willing to buy the non-caste good and to be ostracized. As before, suppose the new outcaste buys α units of the non-caste good at the price p_i^{**}, then by an argument similar to the one given above, he will be able to obtain $w_o - \alpha p_i^{**}$ of the other caste goods, yielding a utility level:

$$w_o - \alpha p_i^{**} + \alpha$$

and this utility level will only be greater than w_u if he had not been outcaste if

$$w_o - \alpha p_i^{**} + \alpha > w_u$$
or if
$$\alpha > [w_u - w_o] / [1 - p_i^{**}]$$

by substitution this leads to

$$\alpha > [w_u - w_o] / \left[1 - \frac{w_o}{w_s} \right] \qquad (4.9)$$

But in (4.7) we have already assumed that α is less than the right-hand side of (4.9), so it is clear that (4.9) cannot hold, and hence no consumer will be willing to break the caste code.

Thus it would appear that it would not be in the self-interest of any single producer to break the caste code, essentially because the price at which he could then sell the 'polluted' good and earn a profit would be too high for any consumer, who would then suffer ostracism (and an ensuing cut in income) if he purchased it.

But suppose that, instead of just one producer, a coalition of producers (each, *ex hypothesi*, supplying a separate good along the goods spectrum (1 . . . *n*)) decides to break the caste rules on employment. It is obvious that, if all producers did so in collusion, then the system would collapse and all labour would be paid a homogenous wage, and this would obviously represent a Pareto improvement.

So the interesting question is: what is the minimum size of the coalition of producers required to break the caste system?

Let the required number be k and let the price they sell their products produced by outcaste labour used in skilled occupations be given by

$$p_i^{***} a_s - w_o \geq o$$

or
$$p_i^{***} \geq w_o/a_s \qquad\qquad (4.10)$$

As before, outcaste consumers' utility taking account of their ostracism will be the amount of non-caste goods they can purchase αk, and caste goods, $w_o - \alpha k$ p_i^{***}, or, that is,

$$w_o - \alpha k p_i^{***} + \alpha k$$
,
and for this move to be in their interests, the utility level will have to be greater than that from their caste-level earnings, namely $w_u = a_u$,

or
$$w_o + \alpha k (1 - p_i^{***}) > w_u \qquad\qquad (4.11)$$

which yields the value of k (after substituting for p_i^{***} from (4.10) and (4.2)). Thus the size of the caste-breaking coalition of producers k is given by:

$$k > [w_u - w_o]/\alpha \left[1 - \frac{w_o}{w_s}\right] \qquad\qquad (4.12)$$

so for suitable parameter values, it is possible that (4.12) will not be satisfied, and no caste-breaking coalition of producers will form.

The above model, however, does allow the formation of a caste-breaking coalition if the 'free-rider' problem can be solved. To explain the perpetuation of the system Kuran (1987) has provided a model which supplements Akerloff's by showing how 'bandwagon effects' can create a climate of opinion in which it is virtually impossible for dissenters to reveal themselves and thereby organize caste-breaking coalitions. The caste system discourages open protests and disagreements; it uses open voting, rather than the secret ballot, at meetings of caste councils to resolve disputes; and it also provides sanctions against disagreements with the judgements of these councils. These three features of the system, taken together, mean that 'its potential opponents do not air their opposition and doubters of its wisdom do not publicise their doubts. To the extent these factors do come into play, the existence of economically viable anti-caste coalitions will remain a secret.' Moreover, the sanctions against even questioning the validity of the system mean that over time most opponents of the system will keep their preferences and beliefs private. 'As a result new generations grow up hearing much in favour of the system and almost nothing against it. Their thought processes vitiated by the climate of opinion, they come to see the desirability of the inherited order as self evident.'[30] Kuran provides a formal model of this form of collective conservatism. Taken together with Akerloff's model, it provides an economic explanation for the perpetuation of the beliefs which make the internal undermining of the caste system difficult, if not impossible—once, for the reasons we have given, it comes to be established.

5. LABOUR SEGMENTATION, LOCALIZATION, AND VILLAGE AUTARKY

We have thus, we hope, provided an economic rationale for the origins of the caste system. In summary, in an environment of endemic political instability, the caste system provided, first, an 'incentive-compatible' system for co-opting vanquished peoples with the agricultural skills required to establish Aryan settlements on the Indo-Gangetic plain. Secondly, through its occupational segmentation enforced by social ostracism, the caste system provided a subtle and enduring decentralized social system, requiring neither a centralized State nor Church, to tie down an adequate labour supply in the labour-intensive tasks required to settle the new Aryan niche in the plains.

But the system was not completely rigid. Designed to maintain the labour supply in a land surplus economy, the casteist segmentation of labour inhibited but did not completely prevent labour mobility between occupations. Both in theory and practise (see Chapter 2) over-populated castes, who would suffer a cut in earnings if all their members crowded the occupation, could and did take up other occupations. There has thus always been both occupational and status (social) *group* mobility within the caste system. However, unlike more individualist and impersonal economic systems, these processes of mobility were slower to work over time. Thus the economic efficiency of the system must have been lower than that posited in the textbook models of perfectly competitive labour markets. However, given the need to ensure an adequate labour supply under unaltering *average* economic conditions, and with the assumed lack of any centralized political authority for considerable periods of time, the system may have been the most efficient available—that is, in economists' jargon it may have been second-best Pareto efficient.

The other two aspects of the Aryan settlements on the plain—the autarkic nature of the village community and the patron–client (jajmani) relationships between the castes—are more easily explicable. As noted at the beginning of this chapter, the Hindu social system evolved at a time of continually feuding monarchies and republics in northern India. The endemic political instability would explain the autarky of the villages. A viable socio-economic system would have to overcome the periodic interruption of interregional trade and commerce. Even taking account of the primitive systems of transport and communications in ancient India, which would have converted many goods in the regional or subregional economies into non-traded goods, the uncertainty induced by the continual political instability must have made a further move towards subregional or village autarky economically rational.

A simple model

Some rough idea of this can be presented in terms of a very simple model.

Consider a closed economy, which under autarky can achieve a per capita income of Y^{AUT}.[31] If the subregional economy had become specialized by engaging in interregional trade, and if this trade were not disrupted, it could earn a per capita income of Y^F_{MAX}. However, once specialized, suppose that trade was disrupted for some reason, so that its commodity terms of trade deteriorated drastically, as the effective price of its imports rose and exports fell. For these traded goods would now have to incur the costs of brigandage, pillage, and other symptoms of the breakdown of interregional law and order. Then its per capita income would only be Y^F_{MIN}. We also assume, not unrealistically, that

$$Y^F_{MAX} > Y^{AUT} > Y^F_{MIN} \tag{5.1}$$

Thus we assume that, as compared with the autarkic alternative, the 'free-trade' one is subject to considerable income uncertainty. Without any method of spreading this risk, the subregional economy, say the village, could not be risk-neutral in assessing the fluctuating income associated with the trading alternative. The villagers should then act as expected *utility-* rather than expected *profit-*maximizers.

Suppose that the utility function is of the constant-elasticity type, namely

$$U(Y) = \left(\frac{b^e}{1-e}\right) Y^{1-e} \tag{5.2}$$

where e is the elasticity of marginal utility and also the Arrow–Pratt measure of relative risk aversion (see e.g. Hey (1979 p. 49)). Furthermore, suppose the probability that trade will not be disrupted over the relevant period of choice is p, and of being disrupted is $1-p$. Then the expected utility from the trading alternative (U^F) is simply

$$U^F = p.U(Y^F_{MAX}) + (1-p)U(Y^F_{MIN}) \tag{5.3}$$

Whilst *ex hypothesi* the autarkic income accrues with certainty, the utility level associated with it is

$$U^A = U(Y^{AUT}) \tag{5.4}$$

Next suppose that the value of the parameter elasticity of marginal utility e is 2.[32] Then it will be desirable to choose the trading alternative if

$$U^F > U^A$$

which from (5.2), (5.3), (5.4) yields

$$\frac{1}{Y_{AUT}} < p\,\frac{1}{Y^F_{MAX}} + (1-p)\,\frac{1}{Y^F_{MIN}} \tag{5.5}$$

Further denote

$$Y^F_{MAX} = nY^{AUT} \text{ (with } n > 1 \text{ from (5.1))}$$

then (5.5) yields the condition for the trading equilibrium to yield greater utility as:

$$Y^F_{MIN} > \left(\frac{1 - p}{1 - \dfrac{p}{n}}\right) Y^{AUT} \qquad (5.6)$$

In Table 3.3 we give, for different values of p and n, the values for

$$k = \left(\frac{1 - p}{1 - \dfrac{p}{n}}\right) \qquad (5.6)$$

that is, the percentage of the autarkic income level Y^{AUT}, below which the minimum income under trading at times of political instability Y^F_{MIN} cannot fall.

What is likely to have been the probability of political instability?[33] With the advantage of hindsight, we can provide some rough estimates from the course of Indian history from the fourth century BC to the nineteenth century AD. Assume that each generation's time horizon is roughly a century. Then we can examine the historical record for the number of years in each century since 300 BC, when there was a period of relative political stability and, at least for North India, law and order. The data is given in Table 3.4. From this we can construct two probabilities. One is that any given century will have some years of stability, and people being optimistic assume that the whole century will follow the same pattern. On this assumption the probability of centuries in which there was political stability and pan-north Indian law and order are eight out of the twenty-two centuries between 300 BC and 1900 AD, yielding a probability of 0.36. If, on the other hand, we are more pessimistic and realistic, and actually weigh the centuries in which there was political stability by the ratio of the number of years to the total in the century in which there was political stability, we get a probability estimate of 0.19.

From Table 3.3, for these two values of p = 0.35 and 0.20, it is apparent that even if the gains from trade doubled per capita incomes over their autarkic level (an extremely optimistic assumption) during periods of political stability, the

TABLE 3.3. The Value of k for Different Values of p and n

p =	.10	.15	.20	.25	.30	.35	.40	.50	.75
n = 1.25	.98	.97	.95	.94	.92	.90	.88	.83	.63
1.50	.96	.94	.92	.90	.88	.85	.82	.75	.50
1.75	.95	.93	.90	.88	.84	.81	.78	.70	.44
2.00	.95	.92	.89	.86	.82	.79	.75	.67	.40
3.00	.93	.89	.86	.82	.78	.74	.69	.60	.33

Source: Derived from equation (5.6).

TABLE 3.4.   Periods of Stability in North Indian History

300–200 BC	Ashoka: 268–31 BC Mauryan (50 years)
200–100 BC	
100–AD 0	
AD 0–100	
AD 100–200	
AD 200–300	
AD 300–400	Accession of Samudra Gupta AD 335 Gupta (80 years)
	Chandragupta II AD 375–415
AD 400–500	
AD 500–600	
AD 600–700	Harshavardhana AD 606–47 (40 years)
AD 700–800	
AD 800–900	
AD 900–1000	
AD 1000–1100	
AD 1100–1200	
AD 1200–1300	Alauddin Khiljii AD 1296–1316
AD 1300–1400	Mohammed Tughlaq AD 1325–51
	Firoz Shah Tughlaq AD 1357–88
AD 1400–1500	
AD 1500–1600	Akbar AD 1556–1605
AD 1600–1700	Aurangzeb AD 1658–1707
AD 1800–1900	British Raj. *c.* AD 1847–1947

trading alternative would only be superior if at times of trade disruption, incomes did not fall to less than 80–90 per cent of the autarkic levels. For more realistic gains from trade, the levels of income at times of disruption under trade should not fall below 95 per cent of the autarkic levels if the trading alternative were to be utility-maximizing.

It is not surprising therefore that, given the political instability during the time the Indian village communities were forged, they should have been relatively autarkic. This, given the endemic instability of subsequent Indian political history, was a happy choice, which must have contributed to the continuance of these communities for 2,000 years.

6. THE JAJMANI SYSTEM AND IMPLICIT CONTRACTS

The customary Jajmani relationships, and their relatively unchanging character, can also be provided with an economic rationale. The relevant economic model is that of implicit contracts.[34] In a fairly autarkic village community, relative prices of inputs and outputs would be determined primarily by local demand and supply. We have argued above that cropping patterns, agricultural techniques, population, and standards of living were probably stable on average over the fairly long run. Hence there was probably not much variation in the long-run equilibrium configuration of village-level relative prices. This does not imply that there were no variations in the shorter run. The variability of Indian climatic conditions would in themselves have led to annual variations in agricultural output as well as in the demand for different types of labour. The resulting variability in short-run equilibrium relative prices would entail considerable variability over time in the incomes of different types of labour. The ability to bear the risks of this income variability would depend partly on relative wealth, and its most important determinant in an autarkic village environment—the relative size of food stocks held by the different occupational groups. Both overall wealth and food stocks are likely to be highly correlated with the size of landholdings. Thus the bigger landlords (who were and are the dominant castes in Indian villages[35]) would most easily be able to bear the income variability of tropical agriculture, which most likely would make them slightly less risk-averse than the members of poorer castes in the village.

Now consider the possible systems of payment for the labour services provided by various service castes, such as barbers, washermen, potters, or carpenters in a village. For simplicity, assume just one such service caste, also that the derived demand and hence equilibrium earnings (in the short run, given a fixed labour supply) vary with the variations in the climatically determined level of agricultural income. Furthermore, for simplicity, assume that the landowning employer caste is risk-neutral but their employees are not.[36]

Suppose that the fluctuating value-marginal product of the service workers who are risk averse is either w_o or w_1, in Fig. 3.2, where OU is their utility function. Then, if they are paid a wage equal to their variable marginal product, their utility level will be $\overline{U}$ corresponding to the expected wage w. They would however be equally well off with the certainty-equivalent fixed wage $\overline{w}$. Moreover, the latter type of labour contract would also be preferred by the risk-neutral

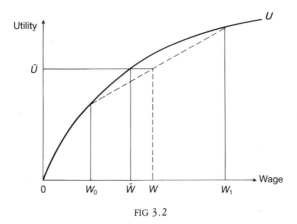

FIG 3.2

employers, for whom the average wage payment would decline from the mean of the fluctuating wage, namely from w to the lower $\bar{w}$. We would thus expect that the dominant castes would offer a fixed wage contract of $\bar{w}$. Moreover, given that the underlying conditions of demand and supply (including their stochastic components) stay constant for long periods of time, this fixed wage will not alter. To the observer, the fixed wage payment of $\bar{w}$ will appear as a customary payment. In years when the value-marginal product of labour is low, the relevant labour will be underemployed but its 'customary' wage payment will remain unchanged.[37]

Moreover, with the constancy of relative prices in the village on average (for the reasons given earlier) and the limited monetization of the village economy, this 'customary' wage would be paid in kind, usually in grain. Thus, the jajmani system with its apparently custom-based payments from patrons to clients can be explained as a 'second-best optimal' economic response to an environment in which there is income uncertainty, and in the absence of an insurance market the patron in effect provides a form of insurance policy to his client.

7. SACRED COWS

We need now to examine the economic rationale of a feature of Hindu caste society which, at least in its contemporary variants, does seem prima facie uneconomic. This is the veneration of the cow, and the restrictions on cow slaughter. It is particularly strange that a nomadic pastoralist people should have imposed a ban on cow slaughter. Our preliminary hypothesis must be that, if they did so, it was something the Aryans had to learn in adapting to the new environment of settled agriculture. India is a country which is identified with both 'surplus' labour and 'surplus' cattle, and it is usually argued that if the Hindu's objection to cow slaughter could be overcome, at least part of the above problem could be overcome by killing off the 'surplus' cattle.

First, it should be recognized that the bovine population still serves (and presumably did for the ancient Indian Aryans) the three economic functions of providing milk, traction in agricultural operations, and a source of fertilizer and fuel in the form of dung. There is one set of issues concerning India's sacred cows which can be easily settled with contemporary data. This concerns the determinants of an economic livestock population in terms of size and its age and sex distribution. Though we do not have any data on the size and sex distribution of the bovine population in ancient India, we can nevertheless examine to what extent Hindu attitudes to cows are uneconomic by examining whether, in contemporary India, the stock and sex distribution of livestock can be shown to depart from these 'rational considerations'. As this discussion is relatively technical and may not interest the general reader, it is banished to a starred section below. All the general reader need note is that the evidence suggests that Hindus have been culling their bovine population to maintain an 'optimum' stock for millennia. This culling, however, is not done by slaughtering cattle in deference to the long-standing Hindu ban on cow slaughter. The rationality of this form of culling is considered in the second section.

(a) Sex distribution

Consider the following simple model[38] of a relatively autarkic peasant community, which has a fixed land area and population, which we normalize at unity by suitable choice of units. The only two goods consumed and produced are grain (G) and milk (M), and we denote the ratio of the marginal utilities in consumption of milk in terms of grain as p_m.

For simplicity, we assume a fixed coefficients technology in both grain and milk production. Thus the requirements of animal power per acre are g 'bull units' per acre. Hence for N acres gN bulls are required. The resulting *gross* output of grain in pN, where p is the grain output/acre.

Furthermore, we assume that both bulls and cows require k units of grain per unit period as feedstock, so that the feedstock requirements of grain for the bulls is $kg.N$, leaving a *net output* of grain (Y) for human consumption or as feedstock for cows as

$$Y = pN - kgN \tag{7.1}$$

The transformation frontier between the grain available for human consumption (G) and milk (M) can then be readily derived as follows. The output of milk, will depend upon the number of cows kept (C), and their milk productivity (m that is, output of milk per cow), so that

$$M = mC \tag{7.2}$$

But as each cow, *ex hypothesi*, requires k units of grain as feedstock the grain available for human consumption (G) will then be

$$G = Y - kC = (p - kg)N - kC \tag{7.3}$$

From (2) and (3), by total differentiation, and noting that p, k, g, and m are assumed to be constant, and for a given N, we have

$$dG/dM = -k/m \tag{7.4}$$

This must obviously be equal to the ratio of marginal utilities (marginal rate of substitution in consumption $1/p_m$). However, as is apparent from (7.4), the transformation frontier in this simple economy is a straight line (see Fig. 3.3), and hence if the same production conditions face two communities, with the same population and land acreage (N) but with different tastes (represented in Fig. 3.3 by indifference curves, $IoIo$ and $I'oI'o$), the 'relative price' of milk to grain will be the same in both communities, but the one with a greater preference for milk relative to grain (i.e. with $I'oI'o$ indifference curves) will have a higher C, that is, a larger number of cows, but (as N is the same) the same number of bulls, so that the cows per 100 bulls will be higher at $P'o$ than at Po.

Various comparative static propositions can be inferred from this simple model.

First, an increase in cropped area (*dN*) *ceteris paribus* will mean a parallel shift in the transformation frontier outwards to $T'T'$. Given the fixed coefficient of bull input per acre of *g*, this will increase the number of bulls required by *gdN*. This will also (from (7.1)) increase net output of grain by *dN*, and hence real income in terms of grain by *dN*. The change in the number of cows will depend upon where the income–consumption curve intersects the $T'T'$ line. If tastes are homothetic, then the income–consumption curve will be the straight line *OC* and the demand for milk and hence for cows will rise proportionately to output, and the ratio of cows to bulls will remain unchanged. However, if the demand for milk is relatively more (less) income-elastic than for grain, the income–consumption curve will intersect the $T'T'$ line between $P_2P_3(P_1P_2)$ and the demand for milk and for cows will then increase proportionately more (less) than that for net output and for bulls, leading to a higher (lower) ratio of cows to bulls.[39]

Secondly, suppose real income in terms of net per capita grain output rises, either because of a rise in the productivity of land (*p*) or because of a decrease in population (note that all the equations (7.1)–(7.3) are in per capita terms, as we had normalized the population at unity). As, *ex hypothesi*, with no change in acreage the number of bulls required remain unchanged (at *gN*), the sex ratio will depend only upon whether or not with the increase in income the demand for milk remains constant, rises, or falls. From Fig. 3.3, it is clear that as long as milk is a normal good, the real income rise will lead to a rise in the number of cows, and hence in the ratio of cows to bulls.

Finally, we can consider various changes in the technological parameters, concerning the above economy, namely the milk productivity of cows, (*m*), the traction requirements in terms of bulls per acre (*g*), and the feedstock requirements (*k*) of cattle. It is apparent that changes in *k* and *m* will from (7.4) alter the

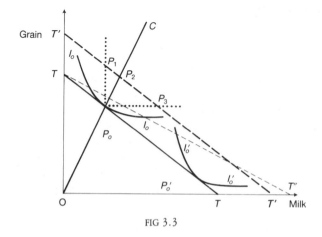

FIG 3.3

slope of the transformation frontier *TT*, with either a lowering of *k* or raising of *m*, reducing the slope of the frontier to *TT''*. As long as milk is not an inferior good in consumption, the resulting implicit lowering of the relative price of milk (in terms of grain) will increase milk consumption, and hence the number of cows; with an unchanged number of bulls (as land acreage has not changed), the ratio of cows to bulls will rise. Similarly, the effects of a reduction in the traction requirements of bulls in agriculture, due for instance to a substitution of mechanical for bull power, will mean a fall in *g* and hence the number of bulls required for a given acreage *N* will fall; but because of the resulting rise in real income (as *Y* – net grain output will now be higher), the demand for milk, if it is a normal good, will rise along with the number of cows and hence the ratio of cows to bulls will improve.

We can now apply some tests to the data on the sex ratio of adult livestock holdings in India, in different regions, as given by the livestock survey of 1972, to see whether the interregional variations in this sex ratio can be explained in terms of the above economic model. For if this were the case, then that should at least provide some prima-facie evidence to suggest that the caste system even now (and hence probably more so in the past) does not run counter to economic considerations.

Table 3.5 (col. 1) provides data from the 1972 livestock census on the sex ratio (*s*) of adult female to male bovines (cattle plus buffaloes).[40] From our model, it is apparent that the three variables which we might expect to affect *s* are the population density per hectare of cropped land (*P*), the level of real per capita rural income (*Y*), and the extent of mechanization measured by the number of tractors per hectare of cropped area (*T*).

The available data on these variables is summarized in col. 2–4 of Table 3.5. It should be noted that we have taken the money earnings/wage per man day for males aged 15–44 amongst non-cultivating wage-earners' households from the National Sample Survey (NSS) 25th Round (1970–1) (NSS Report 233) as the index of per capita money income in the different states. To convert these into real (interregionally comparable) income levels, they have been deflated by the index numbers for interregional rural price differentials computed by Rath (1973) for 1961 for the different States (see Lal (1974b) for a survey of the available index numbers).

We then ran an ordinary least squares (OLS) cross-section regression of the form

$$S = a_o - a_1 P + a_2 Y + a_3 T$$

where the expected signs of the coefficients on the basis of our model are as shown.

The estimated regression equations are

(1) $S = 65 - 7.77 P^{**} + 31.57 Y^{***} - 1.93 T$
$$R^2 = 0.43; F = 3.27^{**}$$

TABLE 3.5. Data on Livestock Regressions for India

	Sex ratio S (1)	Population density P (2)	Real income Y (3)	Mechanization T (4)
Andhra Pradesh	113	2.9	1.61	0.44
Assam	80	4.5	3.07	2.55
Bihar	76	4.6	1.63	0.69
Gujarat	125	1.9	2.50	0.79
Haryana	198	1.7	3.67	5.37
Himachal Pradesh	118	3.5	4.12	0.00
Jammu and Kashmir	142	4.3	3.99	0.00
Karnataka	135	2.2	1.55	0.54
Kerala	236	5.9	4.29	0.90
Madhya Pradesh	95	1.7	1.46	0.26
Maharashtra	99	2.0	2.22	0.34
Orissa	85	2.5	2.03	0.30
Punjab	157	1.9	4.57	11.19
Rajasthan	174	1.2	2.69	0.70
Tamil Nadu	102	3.8	1.82	1.52
UP	87	3.3	2.73	1.65
W. Bengal	76	4.7	2.13	0.18

Sources: S: From Vaidyanathan (1978) — sex ratio is defined as females per 100 males. P: As for S, except 1969–70 from *Statistical Abstract of India* 1972, pp. 3, 43. Y: From NSS Report 223, Tables 2.1–2.9. T: National Commission for Agriculture, pt. 2, table 3.27, p. 282.

(2) $S = 65 - 6.28P + 28.56Y^{***}$

$$R^2 = 0.42; F = 5.02^{**}$$

** Significant at 5%
*** Significant at 1%

The mechanization variable is of the wrong sign, but the others are of the right sign, and the overall regression as well as the coefficient on the income variable are statistically significant.

Though the above regression does not support our model's effects on the sex ratio of the increase of mechanical power, some further evidence, on the effects of mechanization on the number of adult male bovines used per cropped hectare in India, to some extent does. At the all-India level the stock of adult male bovines between 1951 and 1972 has grown more slowly than the increase in cropped area, so that over time the number of adult male bovines/hectare has consistently fallen as the mechanical horsepower/hectare has risen (see Table 3.6).[41]

TABLE 3.6.   Trends in Animal and Mechanical Power used in Agriculture: All India, 1951–1972

	1951	1956	1961	1966	1972
No. of working animals[a] (m.)	67.3	70.7	80.4	81.4	82
Gross sown area[b] (10^6 ha)	127.9	145.7	155.2	158	164
No. of tractors (000)	8.64	17.73	27.3	54	148
No. of pumpsets (000)	108.6	169.2	390.1	886	3,176
No. of cane crushers (000)	21.3	23.3	33.3	45	87
Total horsepower[c] (000)	782	1,227	2,527	5,465	18,535
Working animals/ha	.526	.485	.518	.515	.500
Mechanical power (hp/ha)	.006	.008	.016	.035	.113

a. Including working adult females, and, hence not strictly equal to adult males.
b. Three-year average centred around each year at the head of the column.
c. Assuming that a tractor has an average power of 15 hp and all other items of equipment 5 hp each.
Source: Derived from livestock censuses in Vaidyanathan (1978, p. 19, table 15).

This would tend to provide some support for our case that the sex composition of India's bovine stock is likely to be adjusted in line with economic considerations.

Nor is this economic sex ratio likely to have been the result of divine design. From Table 3.7 it would appear that there have been persistent differences in the sex ratios of the bovine population when examined at different ages. As natural mortality is unlikely to exhibit the particular age- or sex-specific pattern required to yield the observed age-specific sex ratios of Table 3.7, it is a fair surmise that India's sacred cows are not as sacred in practice as in theory. Various methods of disposing of surplus cattle—such as starving them, or passing them on to untouchable scavenging castes who are not required to adhere to Hindu caste restrictions on cow slaughter—are obviously being employed.[42] Lest it be thought that the variations in aggregrate sex ratios conceal interregional differences in stockholding amongst Hindus and non-Hindus which would be compatible with non-economic religious considerations being the major determinants for the Hindus, Table 3.8 provides data on the sex ratio of cattle (from the 1956 livestock survey) for various districts of Uttar Pradesh along with their proportions of Muslim and Hindu population. As is apparent, the sex ratio does not seem to be religiously determined. In fact, as Raj (1969) notes, 'it is precisely in some districts in which the Hindu population is dominant, and very orthodox (e.g. Banaras) that the percentage of cows maintained is low' (p. 81, n. 31).

Two questions remain. The first is whether the overall size of the stock is optimal in each region. This should take account of the fact that the productivity of any existing stock (which hitherto we had assumed to be constant) can be increased (for both traction and milk) by better feeding of a smaller stock, given

TABLE 3.7(A). Trends in Sex ratio of Cattle and Buffaloes by Age Group: All India, 1951–1972

	1951	1956	1961	1966	1972
Cattle					
Sex ratio:[a]					
0–1	104.8	103.2	101.2	100.7	—
1–3	97.8	95.9	90.3	89.6	—
3 +	124.0	131.8	135.6	136.2	132.1
Mortality rate:					
1–3 male	—	.547	.441	.443	—
female	—	.423	.381	.378	—
Buffaloes					
Sex ratio:					
0–1	68.6	68.6	69.7	67.5	—
1–3	45.2	37.9	41.1	38.7	—
3 +	31.0	29.9	31.5	32.3	27.6
Mortality rate:					
1–3 male	—	.820	.790	.802	—
female	—	.524	.489	.488	—

a. Sex ratio is defined as the no. of males per 100 females.

Source: Derived from livestock censuses in Vaidyanathan (1978, p. 13, table 11).

the same available land area and hence feedstock for supporting cattle.

The second is a puzzle thrown up by the data in Táble 3.7, namely, why the sex ratios for cattle follow the odd pattern they do (falling dramatically and consistently over the years for cattle aged 1–3 years), unlike those for buffaloes.[43]

We will deal with the second question first, as it is more easily disposed of. Consider a very simple intertemporal steady state stocking model. In the steady state, the desired (equilibrium) ratio of adult female bovines (L^f) to male bovines (L^m) is L^f/L^m. Say the natural mortality rate for adult cattle is the same for males and females, d.[44] Noting that cows are also producer goods, their desired stock will also depend upon their function of breeding other cows and bulls for the future. However, the breeding habits of any population of cows is likely to have some random (stochastic) element in it. Thus suppose that of any 100 new cows born, the *ex ante* probability that any one of them will turn out to be an 'efficient breeder' is p. This means that, of the 100 new cows, only p100 will, when adult, turn out to be breeding cows. All we require is to determine the optimal sex ratios, in the steady state, for different-aged bovines, given L^f/L^m, and d.

Assume for simplicity, that there are only three relevant age-groups for bovines. The new-born (0–1 years), an intermediate age-group (say 1–3 years), and adults (3 + years). The relevant steady-state sex ratios (females per 100 males) for the three age-groups S_1, S_2, S_3 can then be determined as follows. S_1,

TABLE 3.7(B).   Annual Death-rate of Cattle and Buffaloes at Different Age-groups: All India, 1950–1951 (average death-rate per thousand animals)

Age-group	Cattle			Buffaloes		
	Bullocks	Cows	Calves	Males	Females	Calves
Below 1	—	—	263.2	—	—	386.5
1–2	—	—	84.5	—	—	194.7
2–3	—	—	55.2	—	—	154.8
3–4	60.9	85.9	—	149.3	83.2	—
4–5	60.9	85.9	—	149.3	83.2	—
5–6	60.9	85.9	—	198.7	74.9	—
6–7	41.0 .	94.1	—	151.8	88.6	—
7–8	26.6	94.1	—	151.8	88.6	—
8–9	26.6	126.0	—	151.8	88.6	—
Over 9	128.6	174.0	—	164.4	136.4	—

Notes:
1. The basis for these estimates are explained thus: 'Data on distribution by age of different animals as well as on deaths and slaughter in four weeks prior to the interview were collected. The latter related to the former gives four weekly death rates in different age groups. In order to derive annual death rates from the above data, the following procedure was adopted for the age groups 0–1 and 1–2: For the age group 0–1, the weekly death rates for successive 13 periods were obtained from the four weekly death rates for 0–1 and 1–2 (namely, 35.7 and 8.6 for cattle) by taking weighted averages, the weights being 13, 0; 1, 72; 2, 11; . . . 12, 1. These death rates were then successively applied to survivals at the end of each to get annual death rates of the 0–1. This measures the proportion of calves below 1 year age which will die in the course of the year. (This is rather different from infant mortality rate as usually measured, namely, the number of live-born calves which live to year 1.) The death rate for 1–2 is derived on the basis of four weekly death rates from this age group successively 13 times to the survivals at the end of each four weekly period' (Dandekar (1954, p. 67)).
2. The above estimates of mortality are based on sample data on age distribution which seem defective, especially in the young age-groups; the ratio of young stock aged less than one year to those of 1–3 years age derived from the Gokhale Institute data is much less than obtained from the livestock census and subsequent National Sample Survey Reports. Also on the basis of data on birth-rates given on pp. 75–6 of the livestock census report, and the data on the population in the 0–1 age-group, the infant mortality rates would seem to be very much higher than shown in the above table.

Source: Derived from Dandekar (1954, p. 67) in Vaidyanathan (1978, p. 15, table 13).

that is, the ratio of female to adult new-born bovines, is determined by nature, and this (from Table 3.7) appears to be close to unity. The farmers, however, have to make decisions about disposing of the unrequired bovines as this cohort becomes 1–3 years old.

Given that they will need d breeding females and d males to replenish the steady-state adult stocks of male and female bovines each year, they will obviously only wish to carry the required numbers of each sex that will yield this addition of adult (3 +) stock. As far as the males of the intermediate age are concerned, the decision is relatively simple. Of every 100 infant males born, only d

TABLE 3.8.　Human and Animal Population in Uttar Pradesh

District	Percentage of total population, 1961		No. of female cattle per 100 male cattle, 1956
	Muslims	Hindus, Jains, etc.	
Saharanpur	31.8	69.2	49.0
Muzaffarnagar	28.0	72.0	37.0
Bahraich	25.5	74.5	73.1
Aligarch	19.0	81.0	33.2
Azamgarh	12.6	87.4	37.0
Allahabad	22.9	88.1	48.3
Deoria	11.5	88.5	43.2
Banaras	10.3	89.7	48.4

Source:　Raj (1969, p. 81).

will be required as adults (to replenish the d per 100 of the adult male livestock dying from natural causes each year). Hence in the intermediate age-group there will only be d males for 100 units of stock.

For the female stock in the intermediate age-group, the problem is more difficult. The farmers do not know which of the 100 female infants born each year is likely to turn out to be an efficient breeder. Given that p per cent of infants are likely to turn out to be efficient breeders, and that they will need d 'efficient breeders' to replace the d adult cows dying each year, they will have to carry d/p females per 100 in the intermediate age-group. So the sex ratio (females per 100 adults) in the intermediate age-group will be $S_2 = d/p/d = 1/p$. As the value of p is likely to be less than unity, S_2 will be greater than one.

When the intermediate-age stock becomes adult, the breeding characteristics of the teenage females which were hitherto uncertain will become known, and the non-breeders will be reduced so that the net addition to the adult female stock is the required replacement of d per 100 adult females, to yield the steady-state adult sex ratio $S_3 = L^f/L^m$ it being noted that in our simple model the male stock had already been adjusted to the desired level at the intermediate stage. The sex ratios of the three age-groups in a steady state process will thus be:

$$S_o = 1$$
$$S_1 = 1/p > 1 \qquad \text{(as } p < 1)$$
$$S_3 = L^f/L^m$$

For cattle, for the reasons we have noted earlier, and as is verified by the empirical evidence presented for India, $S_3 < 1$, and hence we get the pattern of observed sex ratios by age for cattle as shown in Table 3.7 which are exactly those our model would predict. Similarly for buffaloes, the desired S_3 is greater than unity, as buffaloes in India are used rarely (except in some paddy-growing areas) as draught animals but mainly to produce milk, and this means that more adult females than males are desired in the adult buffalo population. We would therefore expect, as we do, that the sex ratio rises between 1–3 + years (see Table 3.7).

(b) Size of the stock

Even if the sex ratio of the Indian stock of bovines is altered in line with economic considerations, there is still the unanswered question: is the overall size of the stock not uneconomic (and has it not been so for centuries)? Linked to this is the further question of whether, as emphasized by Dandekar (1969, 1970) the religious ban on cow slaughter has led to economic methods of adjusting the size and composition of the stock, such as slow starvation?

The answer to the first question depends on the relative costs and benefits of cattle stocks of different sizes, taking account of the varied uses of the bovine population in traction, milk, and dung production for use both as fuel and as fertilizer. No serious study is available as the basis for any judgement whether the overall size of the current stock is optimal in this sense; whether by using the feedstock released by reducing the number of cows it would be more economic to raise the nutritional status, and hence the productivity, of the bovine population as a whole in all its different uses. However, as our earlier evidence from contemporary India shows, and as is further corroborated by Mishra (1970), the Indian stock of cattle has been constantly adjusted over the 1920–66 period, to 'admit (1) a higher degree of specialization in the production of milk and draught power, (2) a higher degree of breeding performance via reduction in bull–cow ratio and increase in the ratio of breeding females to non-breeding females and finally (3) a higher degree of rationalization through reduction in the proportion of useless animals and culling of the unnecessary youngstock'. Clearly, therefore, Hindu religious predilections have not prevented necessary adjustments in the cattle stock in the light of changing demographic and economic considerations. For our purpose, therefore, the question whether, given current economic and technological conditions, the existing cattle stock represents a large or small surplus element (in a technological sense) is redundant. However, Raj (1971) is surely right in emphasizing that, given that Indian peasants do adjust their stocks to changing environmental circumstances, 'no dramatic changes can be expected in regard to the holdings of cattle in India unless effective substitutes can be offered for the various goods and services which the cattle now provide directly and indirectly' (Raj (1971, p. 721).

(c) Ban on cow slaughter

The only remaining basis for indicting the caste system of economic irrationality is the uneconomic method of cattle stock adjustment that is used—slow starvation. The likely inefficiency of starving rather than slaughtering redundant cattle is argued by Dandekar: 'The carcass of a healthy and wellfed animal has many uses and is thus of much economic value. The same animal put through a long process of starvation eats up most of its economic value and finally leaves behind a carcass with nothing but bones and much inferior hide. But the process is uneconomic for other reasons as well. Slaughter, while it kills some, enables the rest to be fed better. The process of starvation on the other hand requires a much larger number to be underfed and starved than need be eliminated.'[45]

This is a powerful argument in support of the economic irrationality of the Hindu ban on cow slaughter. We are less concerned with the current validity of this argument; what concerns us is whether such a ban would have been irrational for the ancient Hindus.

First it should be noted that this ban evolved gradually during Vedic times. It is apparent from the Hindu sacred texts that it was not until the later *Puranas* were written (which were probably reflecting conditions about the fifth and sixth centuries AD) that bans on cow slaughter became firmly established as part of the Hindu moral code. Thus the Vedic literature of the early nomadic Aryan invaders does not have any absolute prohibition on cow slaughter, nor does the *Manu Smriti*, which provides the codification of the caste system,[46] nor does the *Arthashastra*. All these sources stress the usefulness of bovines in providing food and traction, and seem to suggest that in normal times cattle, particularly cows, were not to be slaughtered because they were productive and of economic value: 'it [*sic*] has or could have a calf, or it gives or could give milk, and is not barren, economically without value.'[47] But the *Arthashastra* refers to 'cattle which are fit only for the supply of flesh', thus indicating that not all cattle were inviolable.[48]

The doctrine banning cow slaughter probably originated with the republican sects of Buddhism and Jainism but, even in the reign of Harsha (AD 606–64), 'the doctrine of *Ahima* and the sanctity of the cow are still fighting their way against popular resistance or apathy'.[49] It was not until the Muslim invasions and conquests (about AD 1000), 'when the Hindus were shocked by the constantly recurring examples of cow slaughter',[50] that the doctrine comes into its own.

Kosambi argues that, when the Gangetic settlements were established, 'both agriculturalists and traders suffered from the constant warfare which was regularly preceded by Vedic *Yajna* fire sacrifice'.[51] Naturally, in a predominantly pastoral society the main sacrifice was of cattle. 'Cattle and other animals were requisitioned in increasing numbers' by the feuding warriors for 'the *yajna* without payment'.[52] Once private property in land and in farm animals had been established in the monarchies, this confiscation and sacrifice of village cattle became uneconomic for the cultivators, and the later Hindu ban on cow slaughter and beef-eating, argues Kosambi, drove this out of fashion. This view, which emphasizes the role of a ban on cow slaughter as a way primarily of influencing the otherwise uneconomic and predatory behaviour of the upper castes (Brahmins and Kshatriyas) during the period of feuding Gangetic monarchies, is also supported by the evidence of Sanskritization in modern India, whereby lower castes seek to rise in the hierarchy by emulating the social habits of the upper castes. A major aspect of this Sanskritization is eschewing, certainly beef, often all meat, and liquor. This suggests that these are upper-caste manners.

But, as Kosambi emphasizes, this was not always so: 'a modern orthodox Hindu would place beef-eating on the same level as cannibalism, whereas Vedic brahmins had fattened upon a steady diet of sacrificed beef'.[53]

Moreover, the lower castes, even though they did not own cattle, could (as they still do) eat dead cattle. Indeed, this was their charge for the 'free disposal' of dead cattle. So what we need to explain is the emergence of the ban on cow slaughter and the eating of beef amongst the cattle-owning upper castes in the late Vedic period.

Marvin Harris (1975) has argued that the taboo on cow slaughter is a rational response in the face of the periodic droughts and famine to which Indian agriculture has historically been prone. The monsoon rains fail on average in one year out of four. He argues that the Indian 'Zebu cattle have small bodies, energy storing humps on their backs, and great powers of recuperation. The native breeds are capable of surviving for long periods with little food or water and are highly resistant to diseases that afflict other breeds in tropical climates.'[54] They are more likely to survive a drought or famine than their human owners. He then asserts:

During droughts and famines, farmers are severely tempted to kill or sell their livestock. Those who succumb to this temptation seal their doom, even if they survive the drought, for when the rains come, they will be unable to plough their fields. I want to be even more emphatic: Massive slaughter of cattle under the duress of famine constitutes a much greater threat to aggregate welfare than any likely miscalculation by particular farmers concerning the usefulness of their animals during normal times. It seems probable that the sense of unutterable profanity elicited by cow slaughter has its roots in the excruciating contradictions between immediate needs and long run conditions of survival. . . . To western experts it looks as if 'The Indian farmer would rather starve to death than eat his cow'. . . . They don't realise that the farmer would rather eat his cow than starve but that he will starve if he does eat it![55]

There is a germ of a good and probably valid idea in this passage, but it is confused by Harris's implicit assertion that it is solely *myopic* individual actions which make it rational to ban cow slaughter, in effect, to save the individual from himself! An economist finds this is unconvincing. For consider Harris's postulated starving farmer—if he knows he *is* going to die if he doesn't eat his cow, it is surely rational to do so, for even if it is asserted that as a result he will starve *tomorrow*, at least he would have prolonged his life by one period, with the obvious positive addition of *some* utility today. If the choice is between starving and dying today or tomorrow, most rational individuals would prefer to put off the evil day. To make Harris's explanation plausible, what is required is some reason why, even though it may be rational for the individual farmer to eat his cow, this leads to external diseconomies which made it socially harmful (for the Aryan society) to do so.

A reason can be provided if we consider the relative autarky of the Aryans' village communities. The supply of cattle, particularly draught animals, would be dependent on local supply. In particular, it would depend upon the numbers of 'mother machines' to produce cattle, namely cows. Given the positive association between the optimal level and sex composition of the bovine stock and the levels of living of the inhabitants of the village community, any depletion of the stock *at the village level* would obviously hamper the levels of living of the community. Much worse, if this depletion from the steady-state levels were due to a reduction in the number of cows, it would be more difficult in the future to build up the optimal level. A reduction in the number of cows from the steady-state level could be equivalent to a destruction of part of the steady-state capital stock.

Assume that fluctuations in the population of humans and bovines around their mean steady-state levels (which are optimal given the existing technology and ecology) are due entirely to droughts and famines caused by climatic variations. However, given the differing resistance of humans and bovines (in particular India's Zebu cattle) to drought, the mortality rate amongst the human population is higher than amongst the bovines. From the viewpoint of the community this implies that to maintain a particular (mean) steady-state population of humans and bovines, the ratio of the population of humans in a good year (without famine) to the mean steady-state population would have to be higher than the same ratio for bovines.[56]

Suppose that we have an economy which by some fluke has achieved this steady state. Now let a famine or drought occur, and also assume that, within the village, there is implicit or explicit exchange of bovine services or output. With the onset of the famine, each human knows that he has a finite probability of starving to death which he can stave off by killing his cattle. With non-cooperation amongst the individuals, they are all now faced by the classic Prisoner's Dilemma (Luce and Raiffa (1966, pp. 94 ff.)). For suppose that there are only two people in the village community, A and B. Each has the choice of killing or not killing his cow to prevent starvation. If neither kills his cow, then their expected utilities will be those attaching to the steady-state levels of per capita income, say U^s. If either A or B kills his cattle whilst the other does not, then the expected utility level of the person who has killed his cattle will be higher (say U^{kn} than that of the person who hasn't killed his cattle, say U^{nk}), but below the level U^s. This is because, for the person who has killed his cattle and survives the drought, there is no certainty that the post-drought number of cattle and of humans will be at the steady-state level required to maintain per capita income intact. Whilst clearly, for the person who did not kill his cattle, there is still the added uncertainty that he might not survive the drought (so $U^s > U^{kn} > U^{nk}$). The final choice is that both kill their cattle. In this case both will have an expected utility level U^{kk}, which will obviously be less than U^s and U^{kn} but greater than U^{nk}, because in this case they will both at least stave off the uncertainty of starvation in the current period. This last consideration is likely to weigh quite heavily in the expected utility sum for most individuals who value current life very highly, however uncertain the future. Thus the pay-off matrix of the utilities of A and B is likely to look as follows:

		B	
		not kill his cow	*kill his cow*
A	*now kill his cow*	(U_a^s, U_b^s)	(U_a^{nk}, U_b^{kn})
	kill his cow	(U_a^{kn}, U_b^{nk})	(U_a^{kk}, U_b^{kk})
	(with $U^s > U^{kn} > U^{kk} > U^{nk}$)		

From this it is apparent that in the non-cooperative game both will end up killing their cows, with disastrous effects on the post-drought cattle stock and hence on their future levels of living. A co-operative solution, whereby both eschew killing their cows, would be Pareto optimal.[57] However, given the political anarchy of ancient India, this co-operative solution could not be enforced by a central government. However, it could be attained by an internalized social or moral code (see Arrow), which banned the killing of cows during a drought.

This still does not, however, yield a justification for banning cow slaughter, come rain or shine! It could be argued that a moral code which only banned cow slaughter during droughts would be subject to problems of cheating (moral hazard) which would not arise if there were a total ban covering both good and bad years—the ban being even more effective if at the same time there were also a ban on the eating of beef which led to an in-built abhorrence of the flesh of bovines. This would provide the form of precommitment required to avoid the problems of *akrasia* which would arise during a drought if there were only a partial ban on cow slaughter. Faced with the pangs of hunger during a drought, only a Ulysses tied to the mast by his natural abhorrence of beef could survive the song of the Sirens to kill his cows![58] Moreover, if on account of long climatic cycles the frequency of drought had increased between the Vedic and the post-Vedic period, it would explain the gradual emergence of the ban in the later period.

But we must not carry too far these purely economic arguments to explain the total Hindu ban on cow slaughter. For, as our discussion of the likely historical evolution of the doctrine suggests, in the early period of the development of Hindu civilization, though the cow was venerated for its economic functions, cow slaughter was discouraged (presumably because of its deleterious effects during periods of drought and famine and to regulate the predatory behaviour of the upper castes) but not banned. Hence the more efficient killing of livestock during 'normal' times was probably allowed. All this changed with the Muslim invasion. As our thesis is that the elements of the Hindu social system were really set by the political and economic conditions during the time of the village settlements, this later extension of the veneration of the cow (which could be economically rational) to a total ban on cow slaughter (which might not have been), must have been part of the general Hindu response to foreign domination, by drawing in its horns. The growing abhorrence of the killing of cows and eating their flesh, even as it tended to reduce the problem of moral hazard during times of famine and drought, could now also be used as the distinguishing feature and rallying cry of Hindu culture against an alien culture which gloried in cow slaughter.

8. THE 'HINDU' REVENUE STATE

Suppose then that the social structure of the village communities was economically rational (being a second-best Pareto efficient adaptation to the environmental and political constraints faced by the earlier Aryans). Nevertheless, over time, why did the changing political masters of India not seek to alter this society, particularly when, as with the Muslims, it conflicted so sharply with their ideology and views of the ideal society? The major part of the explanation would lie in the system's ability to allow a decentralized rural economy to function without the need for any large centralized resources, whilst providing an easy administrative unit to be milked for the revenue from the rural surplus which all rulers of India or its regions have coveted to finance their armies, and which has thus formed the economic basis for the maintenance and extension of their territorial power.

The system of land taxation had developed well before Mauryan times. It was a fixed proportion of the crop paid in kind, which according to the texts should be one-sixth, but Megasthenes cites a figure of one-quarter; whilst in the *Arthashastra* the suggested rate is as high as one-third, and it appears that even in the relatively benevolent Asokas reign it was as high as one-quarter.[59] As we have seen, in order to determine the tax base land was regularly surveyed and land titles were registered. But the bureaucracy performing this function was local, and probably hereditary.[60] It is likely that this lowest tier of the bureaucracy was not altered when, with a change in political overlordship, the other intersecting chains in the bureaucracy were replaced.

The centripetal tendencies towards an Indian empire have been counterbalanced by the endemic centrifugal forces due to geography, and the associated difficulties of communications in holding the subcontinent together. Though the most prosperous and glorious periods of Indian history have been the periods of stability under dynastic imperial rule, the difficulty of maintaining the imperial unity of India has in its long history made such periods relatively infrequent. The great strength of the social and economic system set up by the ancient Hindus, therefore, was its highly decentralized nature, which provided specific incentives to warring chieftains to disturb as little as possible the ongoing life of the relatively autarkic village communities. This was done in part by making war the trade of professionals and thus saving the mass of the populace from being inducted into the deadly disputes of India's changing rulers. Equally important, however, was the creation of a local administration and revenue structure, and a tradition of paying a certain customary share of the village output as revenue to the current overlord, which meant that any new political victor had a ready and willing source of tribute in place. It would be a foolhardy monarch who would seek to change these local arrangements, which greatly reduced the effort required on his part to finance his armies and court. The village communities in turn bought relative peace and quiet and could carry on their daily business relatively undisturbed beneath the hurly-burly of continuing aristocratic conflict over the tax base. This explains both the continuity of the village communities, and the (prima-facie) surprising supineness Indians have shown faced with a new ruler.

Apart from financing the court and the army, the tribute obtained from rural India was generally 'stored, and the wealth of even small kingdoms is attested by foreign travellers and by the records of the booty obtained by Muslim invaders'.[61] This unproductive use of the rural economic surplus could not have aided economic development.

However, there were pressures on the Aryan kings to undertake various public works—such as building roads, irrigation systems, and planting trees (no doubt to arrest the deforestation and attendant soil erosion which might have become a problem in some parts of the Indo-Gangetic plain even in ancient India). The good kings were distinguished from the bad ones in ancient India by the number of public works they undertook. The sacred texts provided a spur to a ruler's beneficence by urging him to be concerned with his subjects' welfare. But it is also likely that, as land revenue varied positively with rural output, it would have been in the interest of the monarchs to invest part of their tribute in various public works which raised agricultural output. The Magadhan kingdom in fact used its revenue to pursue an aggressive policy of opening up and settling new lands.[62] But we have no estimates of the proportion this productive public expenditure composed of the annual tribute received by ancient Indian monarchs.

9. SOUTH INDIA

The early history of South India is even more speculative than that of the North. It is based partly on archaeological finds dating back to neolithic times, and on early Tamil literature going back probably to the first few centuries AD.[63] Harder evidence based on Chola inscriptions is available from about the ninth century AD.

Stein, following Day (1949), argues that the southern peninsula contained another 'core' of Hindu India (the Hindu–Dravidian mode) on another alluvial plain, that of the Coromandel with its extension to the tablelands of the interior peninsula.[64] But, unlike the large extensive and unified Gangetic plain (the core of the north Indian Hindu–Aryan civilization), the Coromandel plain and its extensions have consisted of separate river basins which can support and have supported relatively dense and prosperous agrarian populations. These have been the 'scattered and isolated nodes of prosperity and civilization surrounded by forest-clad uplands capable of supporting only small and often predatory populations'.[65]

The Aryans of the Indo-Gangetic plain began moving into the peninsula from about the sixth century BC,[66] primarily as traders. The earlier route was probably from the west. Kosambi argues that the major motivation for the later Aryan cultural thrust to the south was their insatiable demand for metals. By the time of Ashoka the Gangetic supply of iron ore (in Bihar) began to lag behind demand for its use, particularly for making the steel required to forge the instruments for colonization on the Gangetic plain—swords and ploughshares. The early Aryan traders in the south had located new sources of iron in the Deccan. But it was probably not until the Magadhan invasion of the south which reached the edge of the Mysore plateau that the long symbiosis between the north Aryan and local Dravidian peoples began.[67]

The iron ores in the south were to be found in scattered pockets in the jungles of Andhra and Mysore. But the peninsula could not be settled by the Aryans as in the north, 'for the best soil was concentrated in scattered pockets, and of a totally different kind of that in Magadha. The future development of this third part of the Magadhan empire would mean a new growth of local population, local languages and local kingdoms'.[68]

There seems to be no evidence of any massive migration of Aryans from the north. What appears to have happened over the centuries (until the rise of the Pallavas in the sixth century AD) is a gradual process of Sanskritization[69] of the local population, so that by about the ninth century a distinct Hindu–Dravidian society and polity are discernible in the southern macro-region. This had certain unique features which distinguished it from the northern Hindu polity and society.[70]

The caste system in the south was based on a tripartite division of society. At the top were the Brahmins, in a secular alliance with respectable ('sat') agricultural Sudra castes and the rest of the lower castes—also designated as Sudras in terms of varna—who in turn were divided into left-hand and right-hand castes. Usually 'right hand castes were associated primarily with agricultural production and local trade in agricultural commodities with left hand castes associated with mobile artisan production and relatively extensive trade in non-agricultural commodities.'[71] The Kshatriya (or warrior) caste is notable for its absence[72] and the merchant (Vaishya) castes of the north seem to be merged into the two bifurcated lower castes of Sudras.

There was also a distinctive polity in the south, which Stein calls a 'segmentary' State. By this he implies a State which consists of virtually independent local units which at times recognize the moral (but not real) overlordship of a sacred ruler.[73] There was no south Indian equivalent of the constantly feuding Kshatriya kingdoms of the north. These local units, which were composed of a number of large and densely populated villages—the segments of the segmentary State—were governed by assemblies ('sabhas') of the local Brahmin and

·dominant landed Shudra castes. The constituents governed by these assemblies inhabited a single territorial unit.

Unlike the situation in the north, the Brahmins had secular authority in the south. This was based both on their sacerdotal functions but more importantly on 'the power which they possessed by virtue of their direct control over land and those dependent on the land. . . . In no other portion of the sub-continent did elaborate and powerful Brahmin villages (brahmadeyas) exist as they did in the Coromandel and in many parts of the contiguous tableland during the period.'[74]

Most of these centres of peasant civilization in the scattered pockets of alluvium along the extended Coromandel plain did, however, need to mount defences against the raids by the less sedentary peasants, the hill tribes and forest peoples of the non-coastal western Deccan plateau. But this warfare (as well as the predatory raids periodically mounted by the agriculturists themselves) were conducted by armies consisting of the local corporate groups, 'soldiers of the left and right division of castes, certain artisan groups, guilds'.[75]

The conflict which we noted in the north, between settled agriculturalists, mainly Hindu, pursuing a relatively labour-intensive form of agriculture in the plains and the 'hill people', mainly Buddhist and Jain, following less labour-intensive forms of agriculture, also occurred in the south.

For a period some time before the seventh century AD[76] the people of the Coromandel plain seem to have been conquered by hill people called the Kalabhara. These 'interlopers', as Sastry (p. 121) calls them,[77] were Jains. Jain and Buddhist ideas had spread to the south with the monks who established cave monasteries in the north western Deccan from about the time of Ashoka. The 'hill people' were attracted to these anti-casteist sects which provided them with 'Aryan' respectability without committing them to according Brahminism and the sedentary peasant agriculture the primacy it held in the Hindu–Dravidian milieu.[78] Also, as in the north, 'the towns of the Coromandel region were bastions of Jain and Buddhist influence'.[79]

As in the north, there was a spirited ideological and presumably military response against these sects from the Hindus of the Deccan coastal plain. By the time of the great South India–Hindu Saint Sankara (ninth century AD), 'the victory of [a] new devotional [Hindu] orthodoxy over Jainism and Buddhism had been assured as a consequence of the assimilation of the folk religion and by [a] crucial shift of popular support to the puranic cults of Siva and Vishnu'.[80]

In explaining these similarities and contrasts between the southern Hindu–Dravidian society and its northern Hindu–Aryan cousin, we would expect ecological factors to have played a part. Also, there are some speculations by Kosambi about the process of Sanskritization in the south which are relevant. Taking these together, it would appear that the alluvial river valleys and plains of the Deccan provided the physical environment for the type of sedentary agriculture and its complementary social system that the Aryans had firmly established in the north by about the fourth to third centuries BC.

By the time of Ashoka, Kosambi tells us the Brahmins had become the spear-heads for the spread of Aryan caste society in undeveloped areas all over India.

They first brought plough agriculture to replace slash and burn cultivation, or food-gathering. New crops, knowledge of distant markets, organization of village settlements, and trade also came with them. As a result kings or kings-to-be invited Brahmins, generally from the distant, Gangetic basin, to settle in unopened localities. Almost all extant copper plates are charters which—from the twelfth century onwards—record land grants to Brahmins unconnected with any temple.[81]

Here then seems to be the origin of the distinctive Brahmin villages of the south. We may see the Brahmins moving into the south some time in the early years of the Christian era as akin to modern technical assistance experts! Given a high status as well as substantial economic rewards, they would be the advisers to the locally dominant groups who wanted to establish and/or extend peasant agri-culture. As with modern-day technical experts, worried about their bodies facing different germs in encounters with a different people, they established their separate 'cantonments'—the 'brahmadeyas'.[82]

By the time of the Aryan penetration of the south the technology—plough agriculture—for settlements on alluvial plains must have been fairly well diffused through all the social strata in the Indo-Gangetic plain. This tech-nology—particularly for wet rice cultivation—is as we have noted fairly labour-intensive. The Brahmins moving to the south probably provided not only the technical expertise for transferring this Gangetic technology but also the form of social organization and an ideology (the caste system) to tie down the large agri-cultural supply to the land which was essential for the technology's adoption. This social system being peddled by the Brahmins would also have met the needs of the cultivators on the Coromandel plain 'to assimilate new people to the pea-sant order and to preserve their own place of ascending in that order'.[83]

As the Brahmins had not come in the wake of a martial conquest, they would not have required any warrior class to maintain their position in the secular order (as they did in the north). 'Collaboration with would-be Kshatriya warriors could not strengthen, but only weaken, Brahmin secular authority.'[84] They only needed to maintain their alliance with the dominant landed castes in their local-ity—groups which were probably responsible for inviting them as technical and ideological experts in the first place.[85]

Furthermore, unlike the large and unified Northern plain, 'the most distinc-tive characteristic of the Coromandel plain north of the Kaveri basin, the oldest and most dense region of peasant agriculture and settlement in the region, was that of numerous and scattered peasant localities separated by large and small tracts of inhospitable land'.[86] These natural barriers between the localities would have made the unification of the region under one ruler problematic. The sabhas and the corporatist nature of the institutions for defence and governance of the localities could have been an adaptation by the Brahmins of the 'caste system' to the older tribal forms of government—with the difference that these were now controlled by the local dominant groups—the Brahmins and the upper-caste landlords.

Finally, the success and need for an albeit modified version of the Aryan caste system on the southern alluvial plains, as opposed to the more inhospitable plateau and hills of the Deccan, is consistent with our theory about the origins of the caste system in India—as a subtle method of labour control. But the differences in the two systems of caste, with a virtual two-tier class system and with much less differentiation between the upper and lower Shudra orders in the south, would have been due to two vital differences. First, as we have argued, in the north the indigenous people absorbed by the Aryans provided not merely labour but also the human repository of the technology they required for establishing their agrarian settlements in the Gangetic plain. A social system which, we have argued, was impelled by the Aryan need both to tie down an adequate labour supply to the land and to provide an 'incentive-compatible' system for the northern Shudras to transmit their technical knowledge by doing could, once it was established in the north, be transferred to other ecological areas where the problem (once the Aryans had learned the technology) was purely one of tying down the local labour supply. The same degree of caste differentiation would no longer have been necessary.

Secondly, for the dominant peasant cultivators in the south the Brahminical ideology was probably most useful in maintaining their ascendancy.[87] This was particularly important after the Kalabhra interregnum had posed a serious threat to their security.

Peasant groups may have felt considerable need for greater ideological coherence as a means of unifying the diverse segments of peasant society against similar threats in the future. . . . Beyond this threat of conquest, the leading cultivating groups were also faced with the need to assimilate new people to the peasant order and to preserve their own place of ascendancy in that order. The means for accomplishing these objectives could be found in the system of stratification according to ascribed ritual purity in which the respectable and powerful cultivators were acknowledged to be next only to Brahmins in moral standing.[88]

The caste system, therefore, which with its ideological trappings was created to deal with the particular economic problems of settled agriculture in north India, was adopted primarily for its ideological usefulness in establishing and maintaining a peasant society and polity in South India. This could account for the variations of the caste theme between the north and south noted above.

Once established, by about the ninth century AD, 'this peasant "ecosystem" ' remained virtually unaltered up to the nineteenth century.[89] A constant factor apart from the natural environment, to which it was an adaptation, was technology. Stein tells us that there is considerable direct evidence that 'techniques and devices with which South Indian peasants manipulated their environment in order to produce food and other valuable products appeared to have remained unchanged over the several centuries covered'.[90]

Thus by the time of the Islamic invasions of north India, the whole of the subcontinent was in the grip of that equilibrium marked by cultural stability (albeit with variations between the north and the south) and economic stagnation which I have labelled 'the Hindu equilibrium'.

10. INDIAN FEUDALISM?

Finally, there is one largely scholastic matter which must be briefly discussed. This is the question: was the ancient Hindu social order just a variant of European feudalism? R.S. Sharma in his *Indian Feudalism* (1980b) gives an affirmative answer, and there is a large neo-Marxist historical literature which has propounded various theories of 'feudalism' and 'semi-feudalism' to explain ancient as well as contemporary Indian society. Ashok Rudra (1981) has recently provided a critique of the thesis that the Indian social system can be put in the straitjacket of European feudalism.[91] He contrasts a dubious universalist definition of feudalism due to Coulborn (1956) with the more authoritative particularistic view of Bloch (1961). On the universalist definition, feudalism is essentially a form of government 'in which the essential relation is not between ruler and subject, nor State and citizen, but between lord and vassal'.[92] As Rudra rightly remarks, 'the definition is virtually useless in categorizing alternative social structures as these features may be expected to occur in all pre-capitalist and preindustrial societies subject to conditions which make decentralized government more suitable than an obsolutist state apparatus for the extraction and distribution of social surplus.'[93] Nor is the Soviet Marxist universalist view much use. For them feudalism 'is a residual category: whatever is pre-capitalist and whatever is not slavery is feudal!'[94]

Bloch (1961) by contrast has a succinct description of the particulars of European feudalism:

a subject peasantry; widespread use of the service tenement (i.e., the fief) instead of a salary, which was out of the question; the supremacy of a class of specialized warriors; ties of obedience and protection which bind man to man and, within the warrior class, assume the distinctive form called vassalage; fragmentation of authority—leading inevitably to disorder; and, in the midst of all this, the survival of other forms of association, family and state.[95]

There are obvious parallels between some of these features of European feudalism and Indian caste society. But the underlying social ethic was nevertheless very different. Bloch tells us that feudalism 'was an unequal society, rather than a hierarchical one', and that 'in an age of disorder, the place of the adventurer was too important, the memory of men too short, the regularity of social classification too uncertain, to admit of the strict formation of regular castes'.[96] By contrast a hierarchical caste society was the essence of the Hindu social order.

But more importantly, the central economic institutions of European feudalism are not to be found in India. Thus there is no record of serfdom associated with the feudal institution of a manor in India.[97] Nor was forced labour a part of the agricultural production process. As Mukhia (1981) notes in demolishing the arguments of various proponents of Indian feudalism, 'The primarily free peasant form of agricultural production, being formed from the post-Mauryan times, thus continued to characterize the agrarian economy of ancient and medieval India.' Nor are the feudal notions of vassalage, fiefdoms, and homage to be found in India—though of course there are some similarities in that bureaucratic functionaries rarely received salaries but were provided remuneration through some form of tax-farming.

But the crux of the difference between the Hindu social system and European feudalism lies in their very different conceptions of the mutual ties between one man and another. Rudra sums this up rather well: ' "Imagine two men face to face" says Marc Bloch while describing the ritual of homage; well, we simply cannot imagine two men face to face in the context of Indian social history.'[98] Thus whereas under European feudalism social ties including those of dominance were between *individuals*, in Hindu society the relationships were always in terms of *groups*—castes. We must agree with Rudra: 'The caste system is a characteristic product of the Indian genius, just as feudalism was a typical product of the European genius. If it should be considered laughable to write European history in caste terms by the same token applying feudalism in India history should be treated as maladroit.'[99]

11. CONCLUSIONS

This has been a long, probably discursive, and certainly speculative chapter. It is, however, central to the major thesis of this book. A summary of the argument of this chapter and its relevance to what follows may hence be in order.

Throughout his history man has lived in a highly uncertain environment, where he did not know if he would be able to feed and breed tomorrow, and never more so than in the thousands of years before the emergence of modern industrial economies. The latter have provided, for at best a minority of the world's present-day population, both the institutional structures and the material means for alleviating this uncertainty and hence reducing the prospects of a continuing Hobbesian state of nature, in which life was 'nasty, brutish, and short'. For the rest, from their primeval origins in the savannahs of Africa, disaster has lurked around every corner for millennia. It would be surprising, therefore, if over the years one of the primary concerns of human social and economic systems were not with economic security. As the way in which men and women earn their living and the ways in which their economy can adapt to change and exogenous fluctuations in environmental variables is an important determinant of the stability of their future income streams, the institutional structures that they erect to provide this stability will naturally have a profound effect on the abstract labour market which mediates the demand and supply of their most fundamental services.

Amongst human institutions, the caste system has been both unique and one of the most enduring. Apart from its direct effects on the labour market, in terms of its segmentation by occupationally segregated and imperfectly (though *not* completely) immobile endogamous groups, it also provides a *Weltanschauung* which can be expected to colour its adherents' attitudes to economic change. It is therefore important to form a judgement (*a*) whether or not it was an economically rational form of institution in the past and (*b*) whether or not its persistence into the contemporary era is a hindrance to economic progress,[100] and thereby to the greater degree of economic security at higher levels of living which is feasible by a transition to a modern developed economy.

This chapter has essentially been concerned with the first of these questions, and provided some hints towards answering the second. Economists (and social scientists in general) have with a few notable exceptions found little economic rationality in the caste system. This was because they have assessed it within a framework which assumes away problems of uncertainty and analyses the efficiency of an economic or social system in terms of its deviation from a theoretical perfectly competitive economy. Within such a framework it is easy to show that the caste system could not conceivably have been Pareto efficient.[101] However, once the peculiar environmental constraints facing the ancient Hindus are recognized and the irreducible uncertainty which has haunted mankind is allowed to play its part, then the relevant question becomes not one of first-best Pareto efficiency, but whether, given the relevant constraints, a second-best Pareto efficient outcome was achieved by the institution of the caste system. The major thesis of this chapter is that in theory such a case can be made, whilst in practice the persistence of the system for 2,000 years should be a powerful *prima-facie* argument in support of this case.

We have argued that the caste system was probably a second-best optimal response to the problems faced by the ancient Indians concerning (i) endemic political instability, (ii) obtaining a secure labour supply for labour-intensive settled agriculture in the Indo-Gangetic plains, and (iii) the uncertainty concerning the outputs and inputs of their major form of economic activity—tropical agriculture—arising from the vagaries of the monsoon. We have shown how some simple economic models, based on 'game theory' and of rational decision-making under uncertainty, can provide a rationale for many of the surprisingly irrational features of the caste system. We have also provided speculative, but we hope not implausible, evidence in support of the assumptions of these models. If these arguments are correct, they also provide powerful reasons for the survival of the caste system as a second-best optimal response to various environmental constraints. In subsequent chapters, we also hope to show why subsequent attempts to effect change without affecting these environmental parameters have failed.

We have also argued that the socio-economic system established by the ancient Hindus provided them with a standard of living which, though low by modern standards, remained relatively high by the standards of bygone years, for many centuries. Most economists, whilst speculating on the effects of the caste system, have rarely tended to go back in time beyond the Moghul period in the sixteenth century. They have found this system correlated with technological and economic stagnation at levels of living which, by the standards of European countries of the time, were slipping. This however is to take an extremely myopic view of the system, which by then had already existed for nearly 2,000 years, and moreover (on the admittedly speculative and tentative evidence cited in this chapter) had provided a standard of living on average which was probably unparalleled in most other regions and countries over such a long period. It is this *relative economic success of the caste system for 2,000 years of Indian history which is extraordinary and requires explanation*, rather than its possible contribution to the relative decline in the subcontinent's standard of living because of the possible impediments it may have put in the way of the adoption of modern technology and ideas in the last 400 years. But, as we shall see, even the latter inference is probably unfounded.[102]

Finally, it is necessary to make a number of disclaimers to avoid any misunderstanding of the nature and import of the arguments in this chapter. As an economist I have naturally tried to find an economic rationale for the caste system. This does not mean that I subscribe to the vulgar materialist fallacy of believing that man lives by bread alone! Obviously the religious, philosophical, and ritual elements in Hinduism are equally (if not more) important in perpetuating the system. The relative primacy of one or the other factor in originating or perpetuating the system is not of importance for my purpose. What is important is that the economic and non-economic aspects of the system mutually reinforced each other.

Thus I would accept that, as Dumont emphasizes, the unique feature distinguishing the caste system from other modes of social stratification is the disjunction of power and status in the caste hierarchy. But I would argue that it is the peculiar environmental circumstances of endemic political instability in the ancient Hindu monarchies for which the system was forged which makes this disjunction economically rational and ritually enforceable!

The second disclaimer I wish to make is more important. Much of the modern abhorrence of the caste system is due to the legitimate dislike, in my view, of the system of economic and social inequality it perpetuates. The argument in this chapter might be construed as an apologetic for these inequalities. But, as Dumont has stressed, this is to judge this system by an ethic which is completely alien to its spirit. This does not mean that those of us who subscribe to a different ethic should not seek to change the deep-seated Hindu belief in a system predicated on the continuation of '*Homo hierarchicus*'. As a Hindu member of a

Westernized 'caste,' I write this book as one infected by the agnostic, liberal, and egalitarian ethic of the European Enlightenment. But I am deeply conscious of the fact that I am only a member of what is at best a small 'caste' in this Hindu system, and that, whilst tolerating my ethical prejudices, the system as a whole may be unresponsive to my prescriptions. Are the panaceas offered based on this Western ethic which advise a frontal assault on *'Homo hierarchicus'* likely to succeed in undermining an ancient and functional social system, particularly if the ethics on which they are based goes against its grain? Or are there other methods (more subtle and hence not so easily resisted) which, whilst serving our Westernized subversive ends, are likely to be more successful? What are the parameters of the ancient system that need to be changed in this more covert assault, and what environmental conditions need to be fostered for the assault to succeed? These are the major policy questions which we will ultimately address. But meanwhile it will be instructive to see how two other attempts (by the Muslims and the British) fared in their attempts at changing what we can now term the 'Hindu equilibrium'. It is to these that we turn in the following chapters.

NOTES

1. But see Weber and Marx. The numerous Marxian writings which attempt explanations in terms of various Marxist categories such as varieties of feudalism are, in our view, an extreme form of scholasticism. On this see Thorner (1980). There is a medical rationale provided by McNeill (1976), which we discuss in n. 81 below.
2. Even though many observers have laid the blame for Indian economic backwardness at its door. See Maddison (1971), Moore (1967).
3. Thapar (1966, p. 46).
4. Jones (1981, ch. 6) argues that the uniqueness of Europe was that because of its geography it allowed a 'State system' to develop. This was a unique system which 'necessitated the maintenance of a balance of power for its very survival. . . . It seems to have been based on a characteristic of the environment. This, *fons et origo*, was the scatter of regions of high arable potential set in a continent of wastes and forests. . . . Major natural barriers protect several parcels of territory the size of modern nation-states and the more durable polities expanded to fit the framework and then stop. . . . Enough states were constructed each about its core and all of a similar enough strength to resist the logical conclusion of conquest and amalgamation: a single unified European state. . . . A long lasting states system is a miracle' (pp. 105–8); and Jones claims it gave rise to the market economy which led to Europe's miraculous economic growth in the 18th and 19th centuries.
5. Sharma (1954, p. 28).
6. Thapar (1966, p. 146). Also, we know that cropping patterns and technology at the time of Akbar were similar to those today (see ch. 4 below and references cited therein). Our presumption therefore is that the agrarian economy maintained the same technology and cropping patterns for over 2,000 years, with agricultural output keeping up with population through the expansion of the cultivated area.
7. Thus as Raychaudhuri (1968) notes, 'virgin land was available in plenty until population increased substantially after 1921 generating the problem of unfavourable land–man ratio and that the pre-1921 situation could be adequately explained simply in terms of a very favourable land–man ratio. Even in 1872 India's population was only 255 million' (p. 82). See also Durand (1977).
8. See Thapar (1966, p. 27).
9. Basham (1967, p. 91).

10. See also Desai (1972) and Moosvi (1973) for alternative estimates. Desai's estimate of 70 m. is close to Moreland's (1920) estimate for Akbar's empire (a subset of undivided India). Moosvi's estimate is 150 m. for undivided India.

11. This is the common assumption made about Indian population growth. Thus Simon notes: 'India's population was "virtually stationary" during the 2000 years prior to 1600 at perhaps 100 million people, about the same as Europe's population at that time. If anything it "declined rather than increased" over that period. Sustained population growth began in India about 1600, but growth was slow until perhaps the middle of the 19th century, when much more rapid population growth began. After 1600 and well into the 20th century, Europe's population, however, grew much more rapidly after 1600 than did India's' (Simon (1977, p. 208)).

12. Maddison (1971, p. 18).

13. Amongst these early travellers' accounts are those by Megasthenes (*c.* 315 BC), Huan-Tsiang (AD 630–44), Fa Hsien (AD 405–411), and Alberuni (AD 1030).

14. See Maddison (1971, p. 18) for this estimate.

15. See also Clark and Haswell (1967, ch. 3). Dairty (1980) provides a formalization of the Boserup 'growth model'.

16. For those unfamiliar with the increasing labour requirements as the period of fallow is shortened, the following succinct account by Clark and Haswell may prove useful. 'The repetition of the process of "cut and burn", with gradually increasing frequency, affects not only the fertility of the soil, as measured by its chemical components, but also its physical condition. In the first phase, described as "forest fallow", burning a mature forest growth, it leaves a soil which is loose and friable and also weed-free, which can be planted and cultivated with little effort. Repeated burning of less mature growth brings us to the stage described as "bush fallow", where the soil has become less friable and more compact, requiring much greater effort to cultivate it with hoes; while at the same time weed infestation has become more serious. In the final stage, described as 'short fallow' the soil has become infested with perennial rooted weeds, which cannot be controlled by hoeing without exceptional effort. At this stage the cultivator may advance to plough agriculture, if he can keep draught animals; or, as may have happened in some cases, relapse into nomadism, using extensive areas of low-rainfall land for grazing and living predominantly or solely in livestock products' (Clark and Haswell (1967, pp. 51–2).

17. Thus Clark and Haswell (1967, pp. 26–7) cite various sources which suggest that, in the hunting and gathering phase, 30 km^2–140 km^2 per head may be required depending upon the climate and natural resources of the region. 'Primitive agriculture reduces space requirements to something between 1 and 5 sq. km. per head according to Ratzel. With the domesticity of animals this falls to 1/2. However, by the time people are living in settled villages and really taking agriculture seriously, the figure may go on falling down on 0.15' (p. 27).

18. Kosambi (1981) notes: 'Indian tribal lands, always ample in extent and generally under shifting cultivation, remained territory rather than property. A holding was formally subject to reassignment by tribal assembly. . . . In contrast, the very existence of the absolute monarchies depended upon regular taxes from permanently fixed primitive holdings in steadily cultivated plots' (p. 122).

19. Geddes (1954) cited in Clark and Haswell (1967, pp. 35–6).

20. Basham (1967, p. 154). Also see Kumar and Krishnamurthy (1981) for the estimates made by various economic historians of the numbers of slaves in British times.

21. Thapar (1966, pp. 34, 38). See also Sharma (1980a).

22. The texts describe them as being dark and flat-featured compared with the fair and clear-cut features of the Aryans.

23. Basham (1967, p. 153).

24. Thus Thapar (1966) tells us that the Aryan's 'fight with the Dasas was more protracted as they *were well settled on the land*' (p. 34).

25. The caste system thus arose because in the technical jargon it was an 'incentive-compatible' system.

26. As in Kenya, to provide a cheap labour supply to the white settler farms. See Collier and Lal (1986).

27. Some readers of the draft version of this book have asked: why didn't the Shudras leave the

Aryan society whilst the caste system was being set up over the centuries, as they would have had the complementary agricultural skills required amongst themselves at that stage? My answer would be that they didn't because (*a*) the Shudra status in Aryan society was an improvement over their earlier one as slaves; (*b*) if they did run away, because of their distinctive physical features they would have been easily identified, caught, and enslaved. They would therefore have preferred the lowly but 'free' status of Shudras. (*c*) With time and the gradual endogamous specialization of work amongst Shudra subcastes, some of these subcastes would be doing better than others, and they again would not find it in their interests to break the caste code.

28. The following model of sanctions, as Akerlof notes, leads to the probability of small coalitions being able to break the sanctions equilibrium. However, a more complicated model, which incorporates the value of reputation as well as those of belief and the costs of disobeying the social code in the utility function, yields more 'stable' sanctions equilibria. See Akerlof (1980).

29. α is thus a parameter of the consumer's utility function.

30. Kuran (1987, p. 663).

31. Leaving aside all problems about real income comparisons.

32. This is the value which seems consistent with modern consumer expenditure survey data in India. See Lal (1972a, appendix).

33. The following exercise is purely illustrative and is based on a number of simplifying and unrealistic assumptions. First, we are implicitly assuming that the future course of Indian history was known in ancient India, so that p can be based on *ex post* frequencies of instability. Secondly, we are assuming that there were no regional variations in p, nor in the relative regional dislocation caused by internecine warfare.

34. Azariadis (1975), Gordon (1974), Akerlof and Miyazaki (1980) for the formal theory and Lal (1980a) for a partial survey!

35. See Srinivas (1965).

36. Though the argument only requires them to be less risk-averse in the Arrow–Pratt relative risk-aversion sense.

37. The workers will however not be unemployed, for a fixed-wage-cum-employment contract will dominate a fixed-wage and variable employment contract for risk-averse workers. The wage they will accept as part of the former contract will obviously be lower than that with variable employment. This feature will make the fixed-wage-cum-employment contract also attractive for cost-minimizing but less risk-averse employers (see Lal (1980c) for the details).

38. The economic rationality of the composition and size of India's bovine population is discussed in Raj (1969, 1971), Dandekar (1964, 1969, 1970), Mishra (1970), Harris (1975), Vaidyanathan (1978).

39. This can be readily shown algebraically—suppose $(M_0 G_0)$ and $(M_1 G_1)$ are the consumption of milk and grain when the transformation curve is TT and $T_1 T_1$ respectively. Let the change in the number of cows to produce M_1 rather than M_0 of milk be $\triangle C$, and the change in net grain output be $\triangle Y = \triangle N$ (from (7.1)). Where if N_1 is the new land acreage $\triangle N = N_1 - N_0$. Then if

$$\frac{M_0}{G_0} \gtreqless \frac{M_1}{G_1} \qquad \text{(i)}$$

we have by substitution from (7.2) and (7.1) that

$$\frac{C_0}{[(p - kg)N_0 - . kC_0]} \gtreqless \frac{C_0 + \triangle C}{(p - kg)[N_0 + \triangle N] - k[C_0 + \triangle C]} \qquad \text{(ii)}$$

which after simplification yields that

$$\frac{C_0}{N_0} \gtreqless \frac{(C_0 + \triangle C)}{(N_0 + \triangle N)} \qquad \text{(iii)}$$

But as *ex hypothesi* the number of bulls is given by gN, we have the sex ratio of cows (C) to bulls ($B = gN$), given by (multiplying both denominators in (iii) by g), $C_{0/B_0} \gtreqless (C_0 + \triangle C)/(B0 + \triangle B)$.

40. Buffaloes in India are primarily used for milk (see below), and hence are predominantly female. They should be taken as close substitutes for cows for our purposes.

41. More firm conclusions, at the State level or by landholding classes in each State, on the relationship between mechanical and animal power/ha are not easily derived. Thus Vaidyanathan (1978) found that in regressions of draught animals/average size holding and mechanized power per ha, for a cross section of States (from the 1961 and 1971 livestock census), and for landholding by size class in 5 States (from the National Sample Survey), the results were as shown below. There is some support (although not overwhelming) for the postulated substitution of animal by mechanical power, on the basis of our model.

1. *Relation between draught animal/ha (Y): average holding size (X_1); mechanical power per ha (X_2) (All India – State cross-section):*

$$Y = 139.07 - 26.8\,X_1^{**} - 0.066\,X_2\,(R^2 = 0.78)$$
$$(4.64)\qquad\quad (0.321)$$

2. *Landholding classes: States:*

Punjab $\text{Log } Y = 4.95 - 0.089X_1^{**} - .883X_2^{**}\,(R^2 = 0.90)$
                     $(0.013)\quad\ (0.405)$

Kerala $y = 42.357 - 1.288X_1 + 3.971X_2\,(R^2 = 0.26)$

Karnataka $Y = 111.569 - 4.299X_1^{**} - 297.302X_2^{*}\,(R^2 = 0.56)$

Andhra $\text{Log } Y = 4.434 - 0.056X_1^{**} + 0.832X_2\,(R^2 = 0.55)$
Pradesh $(.016)\qquad\quad (3.904)$

Tamil Nadu $Y = 231.26 - 2.527X_1 - 334.26X_2^{**}\,(R^2 = 0.62)$
                   $(2.486)\quad (115.691)$

     *   significant at 5%
     **   significant at 10%

42. See Raj (1969), Harris (1975).

43. Vaidyanathan (1978, pp. 13–14) seems to suggest that the observed pattern reflects irrational behaviour.

44. From data collected by Dandekar (1954) cited in Vaidyanathan (1978), it appears that by the age of 9 years the mortality ratios for bullocks and cows converge. The differing ratios in the earlier age groups for the two sexes reflect human decisions to alter the sex composition of the stock towards its desired equilibrium value. See Table 3.7(*b*).

45. Dandekar (1964, p. 355). Dandekar also states that 'elimination by starvation is indiscriminate whereas weeding through slaughter can be selective' (ibid., 355); but this is a *non sequitur*. For there is no reason (and no evidence presented) why a peasant should not starve the *particular* cattle he wants to get rid of, rather than the whole herd, in order to obtain the level and sex composition of the bovine stock he desires.

46. See Brown (1964).

47. Ibid., 246, quoting the *Arthashastra*.

48. Ibid., 247.

49. Ibid., 249.

50. Ibid., 254.

51. Kosambi (1981, p. 101).

52. Ibid., 102.

53. Ibid.

54. Harris (1975, p. 21).

55. Ibid., 54.

56. Thus suppose that the probability of famine in any year is p. If a famine occurs, the mortality rate among humans is m, and among bovines is m^1 (with $m > m^1$). If the 'steady-state' population of humans and bovines are H^* and B^* respectively, the desired stock of humans (H) and bovines (B) to be carried in each year is given by:

$$p\,(1 - m)H + (1-p)H = H^* \qquad\qquad \text{(i)}$$

and

$$p\,(1 - m^1)\,B + (1 \quad p)\,B = B^* \qquad\qquad \text{(ii)}$$

which, given that, $m > m^1$ yields $H/H^* > B/B^*$ as asserted above.

57. Pareto optimality implies that it is not possible to make one person better off without making another one worse off.
58. See Elster (1979) for a splendid discussion of the variety of problems surrounding rationality in the face of akrasia.
59. Basham (1967, p. 108).
60. Ibid., 106.
61. Ibid., 112.
62. See Kosambi (1981, pp. 150 ff.).
63. See Stein (1980, 1982), Sastri (1976).
64. Stein (1980, p. 32).
65. Stein (1982, p. 17).
66. See Kosambi (1981, p. 126).
67. Ibid., 163.
68. Ibid., 164.
69. Stein (1980, p. 66).
70. Stein (1980, p. 52) summarizes the distinctive features of the social structure as 'the great secular authority and significant secular functions of South Indian Brahmms; the dual division of lower social groups (into left hand and right hand castes); and the territorial segmentation of all social hierarchies'.
71. Ibid., 52.
72. In Kerala however these warrior lineages did emerge, but as far as the Brahmins were concerned they always regarded them as Sudras: 'Nayar "Kshatriyahood" has thus been a case of enriched Sudra status' (Stein (1980, p. 48)).
73. Stein (1980, p. 23). In Stein (1982) he writes: 'whereas in northern India localized political units were rarely capable of being linked to kings whose sovereignty might for a time be recognized by local chiefly figures, such linkage was the normative condition in South India. South Indian kings were in all cases effectively in control of only a small portion of the macro-region, but the legitimacy of their hegemonic claims—which were ceremonial rather than real in any case—could be recognized by local rulers far removed from this core of real power. What was insisted upon by those who extended recognition to an overlord was a style of "dharmic" kingship as that which was expressed in the Sanskrit tradition of the age' (p. 33).
74. Stein (1980, p. 53).
75. Ibid., 49.
76. Ibid., 76 ff.
77. Sastri (1976, p. 121).
78. Stein (1980, p. 79).
79. Ibid., 73.
80. Ibid., 81.
81. Kosambi (1981, p. 172).
82. This may be the place briefly to discuss McNeill's (1976, pp. 65 ff., 81 ff.) epidemiological theory of the origins of the caste system. He argues that 'the caste organization of Indian society may have partly been a response to the kind of epidemiological standoff that arose when intrusive Aryans, who had probably learned to live with some acute "civilized" diseases—e.g. perhaps smallpox—encountered various "forest folk" who had acquired tolerances for formidable local infections that flourished in the warmth and moisture of southern and eastern India' (pp. 83–4). And 'the taboos on personal contact across caste lines, and the elaborate rules for bodily purification in case of inadvertent infringement of such taboos, suggest the importance fear of disease probably had in defining a safe distance between the various social groups that became the castes of historic Indian society. Only after a prolonged process of epidemiological encounter, during which antibody immunity and tolerances of parasitic infestation were gradually equalized (or initial differences sharply reduced) did it become safe for Aryan-speaking intruders to live side by side with speakers of Tamil and other ancient tongues' (p. 66). The trouble with this theory in explaining the origins of the caste system is that its implicit dates seem to be wrong. Whilst it might be plausible in explaining the separation of the Aryans from the Dravidian population in their early encounters in the south, and hence in the establishment of distinct and separate Brahmin villages in the Deccan, it cannot explain the taboos and casteist segmentation *amongst* the Aryan 'twice-born' castes them-

selves in the north, which antedates the Aryan penetration of the south.

83. Stein (1980, p. 84).
84. Ibid., 71.
85. The relative physical separation of the Brahmin villages being explained by the factors emphasized by McNeill.
86. Stein (1980, p. 73).
87. Ibid., 84 ff.
88. Ibid., 84.
89. Stein (p. 25) describes 'an ecotype as a socio-cultural sub-system to be understood within a larger socio-cultural context'.
90. Ibid., 24.
91. Mukhia (1981) provides a demolition of the feudalism thesis from the viewpoint of a historian. Alice Thorner (1982) surveys the large contemporary literature on semi-feudalism. Her concluding comments are worth quoting: 'Although the arguments have sometimes been couched in highly abstract language, the mode of production debate cannot be dismissed as a scholastic quarrel over definitions. The participants are, without exception, engaged or concerned scholars, who hope through their research and writing to contribute to leftwing political action. . . . If someone with no personal experience of mass leadership maybe permitted to pass comment on her fellow academics, I would say that most of the political prescriptions smack of the armchair and the scholar's candle' (p. 2064). And Rudra rightly notes that the proponents of the 'semi-feudal' thesis 'must presumably think that the mode of production in India was feudal at some time in the past of which some remnants are surviving in present-day Indian agriculture. If that be so they must be blissfully ignorant of the fact that the premise cannot be taken for granted; that the majority of Indian historians who have taken up the question have rejected the idea of feudalism in the context of Indian history' (Rudra (1981, p. 2133)).
92. Coulborn (1956).
93. Rudra (1981, p. 2135).
94. Ibid.
95. Bloch (1961, p. 446).
96. Ibid., 443.
97. See Rudra (1981), Mukhia (1981).
98. Ibid., 2144.
99. Ibid., 2146.
100. Numerous authors, amongst whom we may cite Maddison (1971) and Moore (1967), have held the caste system in part responsible for Indian economic stagnation. As we have hoped to show in this chapter, though caste and stagnation are correlated, the direction of causation usually asserted is at best a half-truth!
101. Pareto efficiency implies that the economy is operating on the technically efficient production possibility frontier.
102. Also see Rudolph and Rudolph (1967) for a critique of the facile view that the traditional Hindu social structure is an impediment to social and economic development.

4

Muslim India

INTRODUCTION

Muslim India dates from the establishment of the first Turkish sultanate in AD 1206 in northern India, ending with the decline of the Moghul empire after the death of Aurangzeb in 1707. Broadly speaking, this period covered the relatively unstable Turkish and Afghan sultanates (AD 1206–1526) and nearly 200 years of more stable rule under the Moghuls in the sixteenth and seventeenth centuries.

Despite the emergence of two near-pan-Indian empires—during the sultanates of the Khiljis (1296–1316) and the Tughlaqs (1325–88)—this earlier period of Muslim rule was still characterized by the endemic political instability of ancient India. In the 320 years AD 1206–1526 there were about thirty-two sultans who ruled at Delhi, from Aibaq to Babur, making an average of ten years for every sultan. Firuz Tughlaq reigned the longest (AD 1351–88) whilst the widest dominions were those of Alauddin Khilji and his successors down to Muhammed Tughlaq (AD 1311–35). By contrast, there were six Moghul emperors between AD 1526 and AD 1707 and two of them, Akbar and Aurangzeb, dominated India for the major part of the sixteenth and seventeenth centuries. It was during their reigns (in particular that of Akbar, and in the early part of Aurangzeb's) that Muslim India probably reached its economic zenith. Thus, it is by the economic conditions during the reign of Akbar and his immediate successors that we shall judge the difference made by Muslim rule in India to the levels and ways of earning a living of the Indian populace. In forming this judgement, we shall also briefly refer to the conditions and the contributions of the various sultanates in the early years of Muslim rule in India.

The continuing paucity of any quantitative data on which to base these assessments, particularly for the earlier period, should be emphasized. Nevertheless, certain broad features are discernible from the sources studied by historians so far.

The important point (which will we hope emerge from this chapter) is that, despite its very different ideology, Islam failed to alter the underlying parameters of the economy, society, and polity established in ancient India. Although there were some changes in institutions (to be discussed below), these for the most part reinforced the conditions yielding what we have termed the 'Hindu equilibrium' on the subcontinent. The chapter is in three parts, covering the polity, society, and economy under Muslim India, with a brief concluding section.

1. POLITY

The first amazing feature of the Muslim conquest was the apparent ease with which it was effected. Within about a century after Mohammed Ghori's defeat of Prithviraj Chauhan in AD 1192, the major part of the subcontinent was being ruled by dynasties of Turkish and Afghan descent. But this represented little other than a transfer of suzerainty.[1]

The characteristic feature of Hindu India that, with the transfer of power from one king to another, the lower levels of the state and village level administration remained unaltered, also suited the new rulers. Nor was the constant feuding amongst ambitious Muslim nobles, seeking to acquire independent kingdoms, novel by ancient Indian standards. As in the past, a central authority was rarely established, except for brief periods, and thus the long-standing Indian problem of political instability remained.

Early in their sojourn in India, the Muslim rulers adopted ancient Indian notions of kingship and the conjoint dream of establishing a pan-Indian empire based on the surplus of the agrarian economy. The predatory attitudes of the State to the predominantly agrarian society remained unchanged from those in ancient India. The adoption of the Hindu notion of kingship also entailed the right of the king to tribute, which continued to take the ancient Indian form of a share in the gross agricultural output.[2] The availability of this land revenue, moreover, provided both the incentive and the means to extend a particular kingdom's frontiers by force of arms. It thus kept the idea of a pan-Indian empire, first implanted by the Mauryas, alive and well in the Indian polity.

The Koran does not contain the notion of divine kingship. However, India's new Turkish rulers were familiar with the notion, 'having known of it through the Sassanian kings of Persia. On arriving in India, they discovered that this was already an accepted notion. It merely required the sanction of the theologians to incorporate it into the political framework of the sultanate.'[3]

The Muslim theologians—the Ulema—like the Brahmins before them in ancient India, were willing to oblige by 'interpreting passages from the Koran which would authorize these innovations on condition that the sultan would allow the Ulema to be the religious and legal arbiters in State matter'.[4] Not all sultans were willing to make these concessions. Nevertheless, there is a similarity between this process and the similar compact between priests and monarchs through which the more democratic and republican traditions of the early Aryans were transformed into those of divine kingship.[5]

It is unlikely that it is merely the Indian air which makes invaders with different political institutions adopt the typically Indian form of divine kingship, in which theologians legitimized the extant secular power. It is more likely, as we have argued in the previous chapter, that this notion of kingship and accompanying administrative structure was an indigenous form evolved in the fifth and sixth century BC which has well suited both the rulers and the ruled.

It suited the rulers as it sanctioned their right to a part of the national income in the form of land revenue. Moreover, given their need for this revenue to maintain their courts and armies, any new ruler would be loath to disturb an existing system which provided him both with a ready-made instrument for obtaining this revenue at little cost to himself (on which more below) and with an easy means for acquiring the necessary rights to it.

Given the difficulty that most Indian kings have had in establishing (although even more in maintaining) a pan-Indian empire, it was equally in the interests of the ruled to accept a system in which their daily lives were not being constantly upset by the continual internecine warfare amongst various self-aggrandizing kingdoms.

Once the essentially predatory nature of secular power for most of Indian history is accepted,[6] the fundamental continuity of the polity established in ancient India is more easily understood—the limits to the predatory exactions being set by the easy availability of land, and hence the potential flight of peasants baulking at unreasonable revenue demands (see below). If all rulers are predatory, it makes no sense to prefer one over another. What the people need is a system which minimizes their exactions. Thus it is not surprising that, in line with ancient Indian practice, the impact of the continual dynastic changes under the Muslims had little impact on the lives of the mass of the people but was confined to the highest circles of the administration.[7]

Nevertheless, there were attempts to impose greater centralization in the king's dealings with his major source of financial succour—the peasants. The first such attempt was by Alauddin Khilji. He was worried by the political danger posed by the independence which local chieftains and headmen were acquiring by keeping back a share of the income due to the State. 'Consequently, Alauddin set chiefs and headmen aside, and entered into direct relations with the peasants of a large portion of the kingdom, selecting for general adoption one of the various methods of detailed assessment which prevailed at the time.'[8] But the system did not last for long. Although temporarily revived during the reign of Sher Shah (1539–45) and briefly during the reign of Abbar, the ancient Indian practice of dealing directly between the monarch and the village as a whole for land revenue continued until the end of Muslim rule. This was largely due to the administrative costs of establishing a more centralized system of revenue administration. 'The village was there, and the line of least resistance was to bargain for its revenue, either with its headmen or with a [tax-] farmer, as circumstances might permit.'[9] Finally, the system begun in Hindu India of allowing government officials a share in land revenue in lieu of salaries was extended, and eventually became the dominant method of payment for administrative service in Muslim India.

There were three different types of intermediary between the peasants and the king created by this process, according to Moreland.[10] The first were the assignees, to whom, 'instead of paying cash, the State provided for future pecuniary claims by assigning to the claimant the king's share of the produce of a specified area, the assignment carrying with it the grant of executive authority sufficient, at any rate, to enable the assignee to assess and collect the amount due. . . . The area might be an entire province or a single village: the claim to be satisfied might represent the cost of maintaining troops, or salaries for civil or military service.'[11] Whilst *assignments* were conditional on future service, *grants* with similar conditions were given for past services. Both were held strictly during the king's pleasures. Finally, there were *tax-farmers*, given the right to farm the king's share of revenue over a province or smaller area, in return for an under-taking to pay a fixed annual sum (usually assessed and paid in cash) to the exchequer. Along with this complex welter of land rights there was a slow but clear tendency for the growth of marketable property rights in land.[12]

The imperial bureaucracy built by Akbar and maintained by his successors consisted of mansabdars, who were paid by assignments of land revenue.[13] Two methods were employed to prevent their acquiring a territorial base for revolt. First, every three to four years, they were rotated from one office to another, as were the jagirs from which they farmed the revenue. Habib[14] has suggested that, except for a brief period under Akbar, at least 80 per cent of the empire's terri-tories were assigned to mansabdars as jagirs. Secondly, the emperor resumed their property at death.[15]

Raychaudhiri has characterized the resulting system as a 'conquest state'. The State 'was created by, and largely existed for, acts of conquest. . . .' The Empire, held together by force, needed a vast machinery of co-ercion and, hence, adequate resources to sustain it. And as it expanded to ensure adequate supply of resources, its needs increased more than in proportion.'[16]

2. SOCIETY

The idolatrous, caste-ridden society the Muslim invaders found in India was dia-metrically opposed in many ways to their social predilections. But, after many centuries of conflict, it was Hinduism which wrought a greater change in Islam rather than vice versa.

The earlier Muslim conquerors of India, apart from plundering the temples and royal treasuries, also followed the injunctions in the Koran on the forced or voluntary conversion of infidels. In addition, under the sultanate (and epi-sodically later), a major discriminatory feature of Muslim rule (particularly in the second half of Aurangzeb's reign) was the levy of 'jizya', the poll-tax on non-Muslims. It was levied according to the whim of the sultan, and was never counted a major source of revenue.[17] The jizya imposed by Aurangzeb in 1679 did impose an additional burden, particularly on the poor. It has been estimated that it was equal to about a month's wages of an unskilled urban labourer.[18]

Gradually the persecution of Hinduism gave way to the assimilation by Islam of the Hindu social mores. This was facilitated by the severance of the channels

for large-scale Muslim immigration from western Asia after the Mongol invasions.[19] 'Each year the sea brought a mere handful of traders who settled in the
west-coast ports. Islam therefore had to rely increasingly on Hindu converts.'[20]
But the Hindus seemed reluctant to be converted, despite the seeming attraction
of Islam's social democracy to those suffering from the social and economic
inequities of the Hindu caste society. This may have been because 'at the lower
levels of society, the advantages to be gained by conversion were not spectacular.
The Muslim community consisted mainly of converted Hindus, and, obviously,
their pattern of living would not differ radically from that of the larger community in the midst of which they lived.'[21]

The Muslims soon developed the caste consciousness of the Hindus. It began
with an ethnic distinction between the families of foreign extraction, the
descendants of the Arab, Turkish, Afghan, and Persian invaders who formed the
highest caste ('Ashraf') and the indigenous converts from Hinduism ('Ajlaf').
Amongst the latter, the upper-caste Hindu converts, for example Muslim
Rajputs, formed the next highest caste. Finally, there were two occupational
castes, one 'clean' and the other 'unclean'.[22] The former included the artisans
and other professional people, and the latter were the scavengers and those associated with unclean work. As in the case of Hindu subcastes, an individual could
only improve his status if the entire 'zat' (jati, or subcaste) moved up the social
scale. Muslim restrictions on inter-dining were less severe than amongst Hindus
but they did extend to unclean castes. Caste endogamy was the basis of mar-
riages. 'The grafting of caste onto profession was so firm and strong by now that
no minority community could hope to dislodge it, and this was at the very root of
social relationships.'[23]

As in ancient India, various heterodox anti-casteist sects arose, the most
important of which became part of the Bhakti movement (AD 1440–1534).
Akbar sought to create a new official Indian religion, incorporating (as he
thought) the good elements of existing religions. Although the latter never got
off the ground, the followers of the two major Bhakti saints, Kabir and Nanak,
founded independent religious groups—the Kabir 'panthis' and the Sikhs, of
whom only the latter have survived to our day. But even the Sikhs, despite the
message of social equality preached by their saints, have not remained immune
to caste.

The relatively elastic nature of the caste system enabled the Hindus at least to
tolerate if not to formally absorb all these emerging groups—including Islam.
The earlier foreign invaders (the Greeks, the Scythians, the Parthians, and the
Huns) were absorbed as Kshatriyas into the Hindu social system. Formally, the
Muslims were not similarly absorbed. But

in spite of its egalitarian philosophy, the influence of Islam did not lead to the disappearance of caste. The fact that Islam in India succumbed to and accepted caste society
reduced the social dynamism of Islam. Where the *Shaikhs* and the *Sayyids* (members of
the high Ashraf caste) had a caste status analogous to that of the *dvijas* (the twice-born

Hindus), the threat to the caste system was slight. Authority and social prestige remained with the castes traditionally associated with power.[24]

3. ECONOMY

In Chapter 3 we have already surveyed some of the available evidence on the economic condition of Muslim India, particularly during the reign of Akbar in the sixteenth century. This showed that during times of peace and law and order the population was probably stagnant at about 100 million, and that levels of living during Akbar's time were probably not much lower than those of India at the time of Independence in 1947. But over this long time-span there were obviously periods of famine, war, and disease, with large falls from this 'equilibrium' income level. The two most prosperous periods were the centuries of stability, the fourteenth and sixteenth,[25] and, if our arguments in Chapter 3 are acceptable, the sixteenth century probably returned India to the same levels of living that existed in the fourteenth, and which were destroyed in the fifteenth century by internal chaos and invasions by foreign marauders.

The standard of living of the masses of the Indian people at the height of the Moghul empire was probably comparable with that in Elizabethan England.[26] 'The average peasant had more to eat than his European counterpart, and suffered no more oppression from the lords. It is possible that the strength of custom and the intricacies of the caste system gave him greater protection. On the other hand, he was more liable to the disaster of flood and famine, when his rulers could not help him much even if they would.'[27] He was also probably more prone to disease and thus, all in all, his expectation of life was probably lower than in contemporary Europe.

We next look at agricultural conditions, industry, trade, technology, and productivity in turn.

(i) Agricultural conditions

The early Muslim sultans took over the existing system of revenue administration and land tenure. The land revenue was about one-fifth of gross agricultural output during the sultanate. But, under some sultans such as Alauddin Khilji and, later, Mohammed Tughlaq, it rose to nearly one-half, as these monarchs came to be pressed for revenue to finance military campaigns to fulfil their imperial ambitions. But Mohammed Tughlaq found his attempt foiled—as with most of his other schemes—by bad luck.[28] His introduction of the land-tax coincided with a famine in the Doab (the inter-riverine tract between the Ganges and Jumna); the peasants, instead of acquiescing in the increased imposts as during Alauddin's reign, rebelled and the taxation policy was revised.[29] This was probably not the first peasant rebellion against exorbitant taxation but is one of the earliest recorded after the ancient Indian system of land revenue had been established.

The destruction wrought on cultivation in the Doab—the Hindu heart-land—by the subsequent suppression of the rebels, as well as the consequences of the ill-advised shift of the capital from Delhi to Daulatabad in central India, took a long time to repair. The movement of the capital from Delhi removed 'the one large market for the surplus produce of the country'; hence 'there would be no object in raising produce which could not be sold; in other words, cultivation must have been curtailed, and the revenue correspondingly reduced.'[30]

Seeing the havoc his policies had wrought on the agricultural prosperity in the Doab, Mohammed Tughlaq (after the return of the capital to Delhi in 1337) attempted to make amends by constituting a special ministry, and posting officials in the region

with instructions to extend cultivation and improve the standard of cropping. . . . The officials, nearly one hundred in number . . . were an incompetent and esurient lot. They undertook to complete the task in three years, and started out with ample funds for the grant of advances; but much of the money was embezzled, much of the waste land proved to be unfit for cultivation; of 70 odd lakhs issued by the Treasury in the course of two years, 'not one-hundredth or one-thousandth part' produced any effect, and the officials were—naturally—in fear of drastic punishment. Before, however, the fiasco became manifest, the king was called away to the Deccan [in 1355] . . . but he was not destined to return and, under his mild successor, the advances were written off as irrecoverable.[31]

Moreland comments on this sad episode that the ensuing dispersal of peasants in the regions 'must be attributed solely to a series of administrative blunders'. More importantly, however, as he notes, it is the first recorded instance of the idea that 'improvements in cropping should be one of the objects of administrative action'. Henceforth, agricultural improvements by the State[32] were to take two forms: first, as in the past, an extension of the area under cultivation, and secondly, the replacement of inferior by superior crops: 'wheat was to replace barley, sugar-cane to replace wheat, vines and dates to replace sugar-cane.'[33] This episode has been described at some length because it obviously echoes various aspects of Indian agrarian policy and its execution in the modern period. *Plus ça change . . .*!

Thus, during the sultanate, not much changed in the way most Indians, namely those living in the countryside, earned their living. As in the past, 'given reasonably good weather and a reasonable administration, a village would continue to function; failure of crops, or oppressive administration, might send the inhabitants elsewhere; later on, the village might be repopulated, either by its former inhabitants or by new settlers, as the case might be; and another cycle in its history would then begin.'[34]

Table 4.1(*a*) shows an index of yields (normalized on wheat) for various crops around Delhi, put together by Habib for the period 1290–1870. This shows that, yields of gram (chick-peas) and cotton have remained stable since 1290, but with some decline in yields of barley and jowar (sorghum). As the latter are inferior

TABLE 4.1(A). Estimated Agricultural yields, 1290, 1640–1649, 1870

	1290	1640–5	1870
Wheat	100.00	100.00	100.00
Barley	124.44	95.85	86.50
Gram	71.11	71.98	71.43
Juar	88.89	56.12	59.52
Cotton	35.56	42.62	46.43

Source: Habib (*CEHI*, vol. i, p. 50).

grains, the decline in their yields could have been because they were driven off the more fertile lands.[35]

As in the past, the sultans were keen to extend the cultivated region, whenever sufficient numbers of humans were available, with the objective of increasing their tax-base and thence their revenues. The two methods of promoting rural development, in addition to administrative pressure, were the provision of State irrigation works (on which more below) and the granting of cash advances to overcome any shortage of capital. Moreland comments: 'it is safe to infer that capital was the principal requirement for the accepted policy of development; but the records show that, in this period, as in later times, State advances were apt to be embezzled by the officials employed in their distribution and, consequently, the value of the expedient was, in practice, limited.'[36]

The above features of the agrarian economy were not substantially altered under the Moghuls. Slightly firmer evidence on agricultural yields in western Uttar Pradesh and eastern Rajasthan is available for this period. Table 4.1(*b*)

TABLE 4.1(B). Average Crop Yields, Mughal Period

	Man-i-Akbari per *bigha-i-Ilahi*		
	1540–5	Agra, 1870	Delhi, 1870
Wheat	12.96	13.13	12.6
Barley	12.93	12.34	10.9
Gram	10.93	7.12	9.9
Jowar	10.35	7.67	7.5
Bajra	7.62	4.23	7.2
Moth	5.16	3.56	—
Mash	7.77	3.34	—

a. *Man-i-Akbari* is a measure of weight used in Akbar's time and equalled 56 lb. (See Habib (1963, p. 368)‡). *Bigha-i-Ilahi* is a measure of area used in Akbar's time and equalled 0.24 ha. (See Habib (1963, p. 362)‡).

Source: Habib (*CEHI*, vol. i, p. 219).

TABLE 4.2(A).   The Mean of AIN's Highest and Middling Yield and Modern (1892)
Yield from Irrigated Land

Crop	*Man-i-Akbari* per *bigha-i-Ilahi*[a]						
	Ain	Saharanpur	Meerut	Buland Shahr	Aligarh	Agra	Delhi
Wheat	10.0	13.34	14.21	14.21	16.01	10.67	12.13
Barley	15.25	14.23	14.23	14.23	14.23	14.32	10.41
Jawar	11.75	—	—	—	—	—	—
Bajra	9.0	—	—	—	—	—	—
Gram	11.75	10.67	10.67	10.67	10.67	10.67	—
Sugar-cane	11.75	17.78	16.68	22.23	—	—	15.62

shows that between 1540 and 1870 there was little change in the average
productivity of land. This evidence suggests that Desai (1978)[37] is *not* right in
arguing that the data from the Ain-i-Akbari suggest that agricultural yields per
acre were higher in Akbar's days than at the time of Indian Independence in
1947. Moosvi's and Heston's arguments are more persuasive in suggesting that
these yields were probably comparable with those in British India in about 1892
(see Table 4.2). This conclusion can also be supported by some theoretical
arguments.

First, on the Boserup hypothesis—which, as we have argued, seems a plausible
explanation for the relatively unchanging land–man ratio, levels of technology,
and cropping patterns in India for nearly 2,000 years—average yields/acre would
have remained roughly constant. But this constant level would have to include a
substantial surplus that accrued in both Hindu and Muslim India to the State
and its functionaries. With the gradual erosion over the nineteenth and twentieth centuries of this share of gross output paid to the State (as the share of land
revenue in gross (and net) agricultural output has declined precipitately—see
Part III), the same *man-hours*/acre, with unchanging technology and the same
overall land to labour (man) ratio, would now yield a higher income per man-
hour worked to the peasant farmers. As long as income and leisure were normal
goods for them (as is likely—see Volume II of this work), they would substitute
some of their increased income for leisure, thereby (given the same overall levels
of population and land) reducing the man-hours/acre input and hence the out-
put/acre of the land.

The Boserupian process would, however, begin to take over with the expansion of the population, (which only becomes marked in the nineteenth century)
when, to maintain foodgrain output per capita, greater man hours/acre and
thence greater output/acre would be required. Thus, since 1860, when the
land–labour ratio started declining, we would expect the yields to start increasing
from their post-land revenue augmented levels. As the decline in the tax burden

TABLE 4.2(B).   AIN's lowest Yield and Modern Yield from Unirrigated Land

| Crop | *Man-i-Akbari* per *bigha-i-Ilahi*[a] | | | | | | |
	Ain	Saharanpur	Meerut	Buland Shahr	Aligarh	Agra	Delhi
Wheat	8.87	8.89	9.76	9.76	10.67	5.34	5.29
Barley	8.12	9.78	9.78	9.78	9.78	7.11	—
Jawar	7.50	—	7.11	7.11	8.89	6.2	—
Bajra	5.02	4.89	5.34	6.23	7.11	—	—
Gram	7.75	7.11	7.11	7.11	7.11	5.33	—
Sugar-cane	7.50	—	—	—	—	—	—

a. *Man-i-Akbari* = 56 lb; *bigha-i-Ilahi* = 0.24 ha.
b. *Ain-i-Akbari* is a late 16th-century (1595) statistical compilation of official data compiled and edited by Abul Fazl. For a detailed study of this data see Moosvi (1987).
Source: Moosvi (1977).

on agriculture probably went hand in hand with the increase in population in the nineteenth century, any tendency for yields to decline because of the first factor would be counterbalanced by tendencies for them to rise because of the second factor. Taken together, we would find that yields per acre did not alter much between 1595 and 1892 as shown by Moosvi (1977).

A major impetus to agricultural progress probably required both increased capital and the introduction of new technology. The last was available at least in principle in the form of new cropping patterns—as the above discussion of the Doab in the reign of Mohammed Tughlaq demonstrates. However, the spread of tax-farming and the growing practice of assigning land revenue in lieu of salaries to the Moghul nobility and bureaucracy did not provide the necessary levers of change.[38]

The centrifugal political tendencies that might have resulted from creating permanent jagirs were dampened by the mansabdar–jagirdar system, with its temporary assignments. But this reduced the jagirdars' interest in developing their land. As the jagirdars rarely held their jagirs in any one area for more than two or three years, they had no long-term interest in their temporarily assigned territory. Their primary interest was in milking their lands.[39] Moreover, the largest part of the mansabdar's income—about 77 per cent—went to maintain the armed forces, particularly the horsemen they had to retain.[40]

Secondly, to avoid any political threat from the rise of over-mighty subjects, the Moghuls resumed the mansabdars' property at their death, which further sapped their incentives for capital accumulation. Instead, the sums they extracted from the peasants were spent on ostentatious display.[41]

The unwillingness of the jagirdars to inject capital was *not* offset by any massive productive capital expenditure by the State to promote rural development.

Most of the agricultural surplus that accrued to the Moghul ruling class was used to hoard precious metals and jewels, and in the construction of tombs and palaces. Maddison states: 'India's imports of precious metals were equal to practically the whole of its exports and there was also some domestic production of these items.'[42] This hoarding was equivalent to the removal and burial of part of the economy's productive resources.

The importance of irrigation in promoting agricultural growth had been recognized by India's Muslim rulers at least since the time of Firuz Tughlaq, and the building and maintenance of irrigation systems was considered to be a mark of royal beneficence even in ancient India. But even at the height of the Moghul empire in the seventeenth century, the actual extent of public irrigation works was probably fairly limited. Maddison states that 'these were unimportant and probably did not cover more than 5 % of the cultivated land of India'.[43]

Thus, without the assured water supply that could only be provided by irrigation because of the erratic nature of the monsoons, the cultivation of high-value but risky crops was eschewed in favour of coarse grains like millet. The new cropping pattern Mohammed Tughlaq sought to introduce in the Doab (see above) would not have been adopted by farmers in the absence of an assured water supply, as each of these new crops was more risky than the existing crop (in terms of the variance in its output, with the possibility of a disastrous fall in output when the monsoon failed).

Revenue concessions and *taqavi* loans were the major instruments used by the Moghuls to stimulate rural development. These loans came from the State as well as local rulers. But, as Morris (1968b) notes: 'apart from the question of how extensive was the use of taqavi loans, they could not have served as great incentives to actual cultivators because they inevitably resulted in higher tax burdens. Raychaudhri (1965) thinks more of its general significance than I do, but still he does not make the case that it served as a direct incentive to the actual cultivator. The benefits seem to have flowed to the zamindars and local moneylenders.'[44]

Apart from the State, the jagirdars and the peasants, the only other source of capital were 'autonomous chieftains' and local merchant–money-lenders. They might have been able to provide finance for rural investment for which their hereditary territorial links could have provided an incentive. However, it has been argued that they commanded a relatively limited share of the rural surplus as compared with the jagirdars and the State.[45] Nor could the local merchants and money-lenders be expected to contribute substantial capital sums for long-term investment. Their business was mainly short-term arbitrage—buying crops in the villages and selling them outside.[46] Whilst the urban merchants, who by all accounts were very wealthy, seemed to lack both the interest and ability to penetrate and establish control over the rural sector.[47]

The tax burden entailed by the land revenue arrangements was very large by contemporary standards. Maddison estimates that 'the total revenue (of which land revenue was the major part) of the Moghul State and autonomous princelings and chiefs was probably about 15–18% of national income',[48] which can be compared with the estimate of Deane and Cole that, in 1688, tax revenue amounted to 6.3 per cent of national income in England.[49]

Finally, the rural economy always faced the danger of peasants absconding because of heavy taxation, as happened in the seventeenth century during the later part of Aurangzeb's reign.[50] This denudation of villages would have meant the loss, however temporary, of the fixed capital embodied in the peasant's house, animal shelters, cleared land, and irrigation facilities, and would have acted as a further brake on productive agricultural investment.[51]

It might be thought that uneconomic peasant attitudes, possibly engendered by the caste system, were also to blame for the continuing stagnation of India's agricultural economy. However, during the Moghul period, there was some growth of cash crop cultivation where the growth of the market and the State policy of encouraging the cultivation of high revenue-yielding crops provided the right incentives.[52] The spread of tobacco cultivation all over the empire in a period of some fifty years is the most dramatic testimony to this development.[53] Thus it would seem that, wherever there were appropriate incentives and the means to switch to more profitable (expected utility increasing) crops, seventeenth-century peasants were willing to make the necessary substitutions. The caste system in itself is unlikely to have inhibited agricultural progress.

Whilst the cultivator, therefore, did not have the means or the incentive to invest, neither did the State, and the various intermediaries would not invest as they were part of a system which sapped investment incentives, particularly in rural development. But the State and its intermediaries *were* interested in expanding their revenues. There thus arose a tussle between them and the peasants over the sharing out of a stagnant surplus.[54] But, more importantly, the stagnation of revenue provided an impetus to territorial expansion as a source of new revenue-earning areas. 'If military power defined the size of the revenues that a chieftain had at his disposal, then the resources he squeezed out of the rural sector were ploughed back into increasing the supply of armed retainers, the most profitable of all aristocratic investments.'[55]

The total numbers of public servants and their dependents that the system supported were immense. Thus, it has been estimated that nearly 26 million of the estimated population of 100 million in Moghul India were dependent for their livelihoods on 'public service'[56]—a state of affairs that (as we shall see) even the modern Indian revenue state has not succeeded in establishing!

(ii) Trade and industry

Even though agriculture did not benefit from the surplus that was extracted from it, the spending by the Muslim nobility on various luxury goods which it financed did lead to the growth of crafts and small-scale handicraft industries in urban areas. The resultant growth of urban industry was similar to that fostered through the spending of their land revenues by the chiefs and kings of Hindu India.

The Muslim rulers, in particular the Moghuls, continued the ancient Indian practice of employing artisans directly in State factories[57] to produce both the munitions and coins required to maintain and facilitate State power, as well as various manufactures for the consumption of the court and its dependents. In these imperial factories the raw materials were supplied to artisans working to royal instructions and paid on a wage basis. The richer nobles in turn employed skilled artisans at their homes for manufacturing 'fine textiles and various luxury goods for personal use as well as for the purpose of exchanging presents among the nobility or for ceremonial presentations to the king'.[58]

As in ancient India, most of the artisans not directly employed by the court and nobility were organized in guilds. The merchant class grew and prospered (as it did in ancient India) with the expansion of internal and foreign trade in these manufactures of textiles, gold and silver thread and embroidery, various metals (particularly brass and copper), paper, leather, and wood. The merchants provided working capital to the artisans by making advances for raw-material purchasing, and bought up the final output for sale to foreign traders. The artisans were often paid wages for their services. 'Besides the merchants, there were bankers, bullion merchants, moneylenders, brokers and shopkeepers who were all contributing towards a change in industrial organisation of the country.'[59]

The foreign traders (who had emerged on the coasts of India by about the fifteenth century) soon sought to oust these middlemen, by setting up their own handicraft factories employing artisans on a wage basis. These European factories marked the beginning of an industrial system in India. Thus, in Baroda in the seventeenth century, 'the English factors employed 800 workmen for manufacturing textile goods'.[60]

A contemporary Dutch account by De Laet estimated the daily artisan wage of 5 or 6 taccas as equivalent to 4 or 5 Dutch stivers. Prakash[61] translated this (at a rate of exchange of 24 Dutch stivers = Re 1) into three or four annas a day. But it is not clear at which year's price level the last conversion has been made. If at that prevailing in the seventeenth century, then, as from Deane and Cole, it appears that the European price level in the seventeenth century was about the same as in 1913, and we would have a daily artisan wage of about Rs 0.25 in 1913 rupees, which would be equivalent to Rs 1.05 per day in 1950–1 rupees.[62]

It is not possible to estimate either the size or growth of this artisan handicraft industry. But some indication is provided by Maddison's estimate that, before 1780 when they were hit by competition from Europe, the exports from Bengal of textiles were less than £2 million compared with a figure of £12 million for the UK, which had less than a tenth of Bengal's population.[63]

There were various taxes and imposts on the output of these handicrafts, particularly on their export. As with agriculture, a large part of the surplus of industry went to the State through inland tolls and port, provincial, and town duties. The forms of extortions used by the State's functionaries 'ranged from straight-forward plunder to ostensibly legitimate taxation'.[64] But unlike the peasants, the traders could evade these impositions through 'contacts, bribes, organized action and perhaps above all, the spendthrift amir's [official's] dependence on credit. Hence, despite the ambivalences in official attitudes the merchants flour-ished, while the peasant was reduced to bare subsistence.'[65] Something was kept back by the merchants which formed a reserve of capital upon which princes drew at times of war or stress. The major item of the merchant's wealth which escaped official depredation was a proportion of 'the silver bullion, imported annually into the country, which vanished underground. Some of this became rustic work-ing capital, in the form of bangles and jewelry, for wedding expenses, temple offerings and security for advances to purchase seed, etc., while the rest went to small or large hoards in the absence of banks.'[66]

Overseas trade also grew during the period, and was centred on the coastal regions. Besides the colonies of foreign merchants, these coastal cities also had large Indian 'business houses with branches overseas. Wealthy bankers gave loans and took promissory notes, and many lived entirely on lending money to traders. Conditions having been somewhat unsettled (at least during the period of the sultanates), one would have expected cheating and fraud to be common, yet traders and travellers alike testify to the high level of integrity in India.'[67]

Cotton was the major item of export, but the spice trade was important for the Malabar coast, and indigo and saltpetre were the other major items of export, the major imports being luxuries like wine and metals, especially silver.[68]

The effects of this trade were localized in the coastal areas, however, and did not constitute a significant enough force to transform economic conditions in the country as a whole. This was in part due to the one-way flow of internal trade from the rural to urban areas,[69] which nevertheless was substantial, as was the resulting wealth of the merchant classes. The extent of monetization and the penetration of a market economy into the rural hinterland are still controversial. Raychaudhuri (1968) argues that, during the Moghul period, the dependence of the towns on supplies from the rural hinterland, as well as the 'fact of something between a third and a half of the agricultural produce being marketed to meet the revenue demand in cash', suggests 'the emergence of an intricate organiza-tion for commerce and money supply as also vast accumulations of liquid capi-tal'.[70] However, Morris argues against this that 'except within the urban sector itself, this traffic possessed the character of tribute rather than commerce'.[71] He quotes Raychaudhri (1965) against Raychaudhuri (1968): 'The relationship of mutual exchange between towns and country, which developed in Europe in the later Middle Ages, and its consequences in terms of specialization and division of labour are absent from the Indian scene.'[72]

Given the paucity of quantitative evidence, the most one can conclude is that:[73] (i) the partial monetization of the village economy, arising from the growing need to obtain cash to pay the revenue demand, led to the growth at the village level of grain-dealers cum money-lenders; (ii) in the coastal regions various traders and bankers arose, some of whom were extremely wealthy and able to issue bills of exchange ('hundis') for enormous sums which were honoured throughout India as well as large parts of Asia.

Raychaudhuri (1968) feels this emerging urban mercantile class could, as in Europe, have led to the industrial capitalism which many consider to be the hallmark of development![74] Morris, however, rightly in our view, emphasizes the limited extent of their influence and power in transforming the economy. Most towns were appendages of a court and its bureaucracy, and few 'developed an independent viability that was based on intimate commercial interdependence with a large rural hinterland'.[75] Even in Gujarat, he argues, where the rising mercantile classes may not have been entirely dependent upon the court and bureaucracy for their prosperity, the rising bourgeoisie were incapable of establishing and sustaining an independent power base.

The great merchants of Gujarat, being unable to provide themselves with an independent military power, were very vulnerable to bureaucratic pressures. Thus, they could not defend themselves as a collectivity either against imperial demands or the pressure of regional rural-based chieftains. Their inability to establish direct control over their rural hinterland explains, at one and the same time, both their political weakness and their ultimate economic insignificance.[76]

(iii) The continuance of the revenue economy

Thus we see the beginnings of a form of mercantile capitalism in urban India; but its flowering was prevented by various constraints imposed by officialdom and the social restrictions of the caste system.[77] As in the sixth century BC, the economic power of this class was not matched by equivalent political power (see ch. 2 above). The merchants 'did not dare to display their wealth like the merchants of London or Amsterdam; they appeared at court more often as victims of a "squeeze" than as respected financial advisers'.[78]

This point is of some importance, both in explaining the continuance of the system which perpetuated the 'Hindu equilibrium' and in underlining the aspects of the Moghul economy which make it unlikely that it could have transformed itself on its own into a fully-fledged capitalist market economy.[79] For the Hindu equilibrium was the result of the institution of an extremely sophisticated version of what Hicks has termed a 'Revenue Economy', 'in which a "surplus" of food and other necessities is extracted from cultivators and used to provide sustenance for public servants'.[80] The beginning of a market economy is evident in India from the rise of merchants and traders in the urban centres of ancient India in the fifth and sixth centuries BC. In the Moghul period there was a further expansion in the necessary preconditions for the evolution of a market economy—in instituting and enforcing contracts through self-policing amongst the merchants themselves, and by arbitration of conflicts, probably through other merchants.

This form of mercantile development, as Hicks emphasizes, is possible without the need for any direct political initiative or legal developments in the State. But, in this extra-legal and extra-political form, the penetration of the mercantile economy is likely to be fairly limited. Although the rulers may not look upon commerce with indifference, something more is required for the mercantile economy to establish itself as the dominant economic form. 'What is also necessary is that they, together with their judges and administrators, should have a "feel" for trade, so that they can give it the kind of help or, rather, recognition that it needs. This is a difficult requirement to meet, but there is one condition on which it will be met. It will be met if the rulers are themselves merchants or are deeply involved in trade themselves.'[81]

But there was no equivalent in India, even in the coastal commercial areas, of the European city States, which played such an important role in the rise of the market economy and mercantile capitalism in the economic history of Europe.[82] The continuing disjunction between the economic and political power of the merchant class in Muslim India (as had obtained in Hindu India) must be an important part of the reason why, despite the growth of a mercantile urban economy, its values and methods did not penetrate too far into the hinterland.

CONCLUSIONS

Our conclusions can be brief. The Muslim period, although it made some minor changes in the relationships between the rulers and the ruled (in particular, the more extensive use of tax-farmers and assignees of land revenue), did not make any fundamental changes in the polity, society, or economy of India. The Hindu equilibrium was scarcely disturbed. Although this enabled Indians to enjoy a per capita income level even in the sixteenth and seventeenth centuries which was probably as high as that in contemporary Europe, India was slipping in relative terms. It would soon be left far behind as the Industrial Revolution took root in England and spread to other parts of the Western world.

Continuing agricultural stagnation was not altered by any attempt to reinvest the considerable rural surplus extracted by the changing rulers and their functionaries, in productive public works such as widespread irrigation which, by reducing the uncertainty of water supply, would have enabled a shift to more valuable, higher-yielding, but more risky cropping patterns. The surplus was not used for productive investment in industry either, although its expenditure on various luxury goods did lead to the promotion of a wide range of handicrafts and the development of a rudimentary 'putting out' system. The general insecurity of any agglomeration of wealth which could be confiscated at the king's pleasure provided strong disincentives for capital accumulation, whilst the continuing disjunction between the economic and political power of the growing mercantile communities meant that the growth of a vigorous mercantile capitalism, which might have altered the parameters of the Hindu equilibrium, did not occur. Indians therefore continued to earn a standard of living by means which had remained relatively unaltered for nearly 2,000 years.

The collapse of the Moghul empire in the eighteenth century led to another century of political instability in India, during which levels of living must have suffered, but not by much.[83] But, by the end of the century, a new foreign power was to establish its hegemony over the subcontinent. We turn to an examination of the difference India's new imperial rulers—the British—made to its polity, society and economy.

NOTES

1. Thapar (1966, p. 287).
2. This system was similar to the one the Muslims brought with them from Afghanistan. 'They came prepared to claim a share of the produce of the soil, and they found the peasants accustomed to paying a share to whoever might be in a position to take it' (Moreland (1929, p. 16)).
3. Thapar (1966, p. 290).
4. Thapar (1966, p. 290).
5. 'It came to be believed that the sultan was necessary for the very existence and security of the State for, without him, there would be anarchy: a belief not dissimilar to earlier Hindu ideas on the relationship between the king and the State' (ibid.)
6. There were obviously brief interregnums over the millennia, when the rulers sought to promote the public's welfare rather than their own.
7. Moreland states: 'The establishment of Moslem rule could take one of two forms. If the Hindu king or chief submitted, and agreed to pay tribute, things would go on as before, except the chief, no longer a king, would probably try to recover the amount of the tribute from his villages by increasing the demand on them, a process which would be possible in some conditions, if not in all. If the king or chief did not submit, and lost his position by conquest, the conquerors would step into his place and would probably continue the existing relations with the villages as the line of least resistance, until circumstances arose which called for a change' (1929, p. 202).
8. Ibid., 202.
9. Ibid., 203.
10. See also the detailed accounts by Habib in *CEHI*, vol. i, p. 235.
11. Moreland (1929, p. 10)).
12. Raychaudhuri (*CEHI*, vol. i, p. 176).
13. Akbar paid them salaries in cash, but his successors found this too onerous and paid them by revenue assignments instead.
14. Habib (1963, pp. 271–2).
15. 'The assignments of land were for life only; the next generation had to start from the bottom with an official appointment. During life, payments were always in arrears so that they were only able to make ends meet by means of advances from the Treasury. At death, the great man's property was sealed and nothing was released until the advances had been recovered. . . . The Moghul nobility was thus an official aristocracy which was hereditary as a class but not as individuals, which was landholding but not feudal' (ibid.).
16. Raychaudhuri (*CEHI*, vol. i, p. 172).
17. 'Often the tax was used as a legitimate means of increasing the revenue and not necessarily with the intention of persecuting the non-Muslim population. A *jizya* paying citizen would cease to pay the tax on conversion to Islam; thus, increasing conversions could lead to a loss of revenue! The sultans therefore may not have been too eager to encourage large-scale conversions' (Thapar (1966, pp. 271–2)).
18. Habib (*CEHI*, vol. i, p. 238).
19. Ibid.
20. Ibid., 289.

21. Thapar (1966, p. 290).
22. See Ahmad (1966) for a discussion of how the Ashraf–Ajlaf dichotomy is a theoretical one which masked the fully developed caste consciousness amongst Muslims.
23. Thapar (1966, p. 301).
24. Ibid., 320.
25. Spear (1965a, p. 24), Habib and Raychaudhuri, (*CEHI*, vol. i).
26. See Maddison (1971, p. 8; Spear (1965a, p. 47).
27. Spear (1965a, p. 47).
28. Mohammed Tughlaq also introduced the first token in India of brass and copper to replace the silver coinage. The disruption of commerce caused by the token currency led to its withdrawal after 2 years. See S. Digby in *CEHI*, vol. i, p. 97. He also decided to shift his capital to the centre of India at Daulatabad, as Delhi, he rightly argued, was too close to the northern passes which let in numerous marauding invaders, giving little time and warning for the sultan to mobilize his forces before they appeared at the gates of the capital. Having moved every man, woman, and dog from Delhi to Daulatabad, it was soon discovered that the new capital did not have a stable and sufficient water supply for its population, so the capital was shifted back to Delhi with the remnants of those who had survived the first forced long march to Daulatabad. 'When Ibn Batuta visited the capital in 1333 AD, Delhi was being strenuously rehabilitated but it was a long time before the imperial city recovered from the effects of its historic evacuation' (Sharma (1954, p. 141)).
29. See Thapar (1966), Moreland (1929).
30. Moreland (1929, p. 48). See also Habib (*CEHI*, vol. i, p. 63).
31. Moreland (1929, p. 50).
32. Habib (*CEHI*, vol. i, p. 66).
33. Moreland (1929, pp. 50, 51).
34. Ibid., 65.
35. Habib (*CEHI*, vol. i, p. 50).
36. Moreland (1929, p. 65).
37. See the debate between A. Desai, Heston, and Moosvi in the *Indian Economic and Social History Review IESHR*, cited in ch. 3.
38. See Habib (1980) for a detailed review of the evidence on the level of technology in Mughal India. He describes the introduction of the Persian wheel, grafting in horticulture, the crank handle to the spinning wheel, Persian weaving techniques and direct block printing in textiles, the screw in metal work, and the belt drive in the drill as the major technological advances in India during this period. But he emphasizes the surprisingly static nature of Indian technology—most surprising being the failure to introduce book-printing. He concludes: 'while the Indian economy was not closed to innovation and invention, there was no overwhelming enthusiasm for technological change, which in retrospect appears so strikingly to mark 16th- and 17th-century Europe' (p. 33).
39. See Habib (*CEHI*, vol. i, pp. 260, 317) and Raychaudhuri (*CEHI*, vol. i); also Morris (1968b, p. 357).
40. Raychaudhuri (*CEHI*, vol. i, p. 179).
41. Thus Spear (1965a) states: 'The process amounted to death duties of about 100 %. Aware of the fate which hung over them, the Moghul lords accentuated the situation by heavy spending. Why not get the glory to be derived from ostentation and public works when you could pass nothing on to your family? Thus, the Moghul nobles were notable for their ostentation, their crowds of retainers with even more than the average insolence of office, their works of piety in the shape of mosques, wells and resthouses, of ease like their gardens and summerhouses, and of remembrance like their great domed tombs' (p. 41).
42. Maddison (1971, p. 23); whilst Raychaudhuri notes: 'De Laet estimates Akbar's treasures at his death at about 522.4 million florins. The treasure hoarded by nobles was almost equally staggering. In thirteen years as governor of Bengal, Shaista Khan was believed to have accumulated Rs. 380 million. At a more modest level, treasures worth Rs. 3 and 10 million are known to have been left by a number of nobles at their death' (*CEHI*, vol. i, p. 183).
43. Maddison (1971). Also Habib (*CEHI*, vol. i, pp. 255–60) denies that the Moghul State provided any major irrigation facilities. Thus Maddison is right in stating: 'it is misleading in the Indian context to suggest, as Marx did, that the "oriental despotism" of the State apparatus had

a functional justification in the development and protection of irrigation. As far as the economy was concerned, the Moghul State apparatus was parasitic. It therefore seems inappropriate to call the system an agrarian bureaucracy. It was a regime of warlord predators which was less efficient than European feudalism' (ibid., 23–4). Also, as Thapar writes about ancient India: 'The importance of irrigation to Indian agricultural conditions was fully recognised. In certain areas, water for irrigation was distributed and measured. The *Arthashastra* refers to a water tax which was regularly collected wherever the State assisted in providing irrigation. Although the construction and maintenance of reservoirs, tanks, canals, and wells were regarded as part of the functions of the government, there is no ground for holding that the control of irrigation was the key to the political control of the country' (Thapar (1966, pp. 77–8)).

44. Morris (1968b, p. 358).
45. Ibid., 359; Habib (*CEHI*, vol. i, p. 167).
46. Ibid., 359.
47. Ibid., 363–4.
48. Maddison (1971, p. 22).
49. Whilst Habib writes: 'One major aim of Moghul administration stands out, in bold relief: The attempt at securing the bulk of the peasant's surplus. The shares of the crop taken under the *bhaoli* or *kankut* varied with crops and localities but one-half in the less fertile regions, and substantially more in the more fertile seem to have represented the norm' (*CEHI*, vol. i, p. 238).
50. Moreland (1929, p. 14).
51. Morris (1968b, p. 357).
52. Habib (*CEHI*, vol. i, ch. 2).
53. Raychaudhuri (1968).
54. Moreland (1929, pp. 207–8).
55. Morris (1968b, p. 360).
56. Raychaudhuri (*CEHI*, vol. i, p. 179).
57. See Thapar (1966, p. 78) for ancient India, and Prakash (1964) for Moghul India.
58. Prakash (1964, pp. 47–8).
59. Ibid., 49.
60. Ibid.
61. Ibid., 50.
62. Using the price index number in table A2.11 in Mukherjee (1969, p. 94), namely, 26 for 1913 and 109.4 for 1950.
63. Maddison (1971, p. 19). Raychaudhuri summarizes the scanty evidence: 'Even any remotely dependable estimate of output and trends in India's most important manufacture [textiles] is not possible. Stray items of information . . . hint at the vast absolute magnitudes involved . . . it seems reasonably certain, however, that the total output of textiles increased under the Moghuls' (*CEHI*, vol. i, p. 272).
64. Ibid., 185.
65. Ibid., 191.
66. Spear (1965a, p. 46).
67. Thapar (1966, p. 296).
68. Spear (1965a, p. 46).
69. Raychaudhuri (1968, p. 86).
70. Raychaudhuri (1968, p. 86).
71. Morris (1968b, p. 362).
72. Raychaudhuri (1965, p. 119).
73. See Chandra (1966, pp. 327–8).
74. Though more recently (1983) Raychaudhuri seem to be less sanguine: 'If there was a cluster of factors contributing to rapid change in pre-industrial Europe, an oppressive and spendthrift ruling class, a heavily exploited artisanate restricted in its occupational mobility, and a culture without mechanical curiosity represented a different sort of cluster in Moghul India. An expanding market, organizational changes and imitative innovation in technology did constitute a powerful combination of features which could have induced a break with the established traditions in manufacture. But these features evidently did not acquire the magnitude necessary to disrupt an immemorial system functioning at the level of a high equilibrium. Industrial involution is perhaps not an inappropriate label for the history of manufacture in our period' (*CEHI*, vol. i, p. 307).

75. Morris (1968b, p. 363).

76. Ibid., 364.

77. Raychaudhuri notes: 'The unbroken self-sufficiency of the subcontinent's economy implied a failure to profit from possibilities of international specialization. The mini-revolution in commerce, making limited demands on the organization and technology of manufacture, contributed to little more than a near-involution in industry; the imbalance between the major sectors of production was not disturbed, the increased demand could be comfortably absorbed by a system of production ultimately rooted in the reciprocal arrangements of a caste system rather than market and exchange' (*CEHI*, vol. i., p. 305).

78. Spear (1965a, p. 47).

79. An arid and inconclusive debate on the question of whether the Moghul economy could have evolved into a progressive market economy has been perpetuated by various nationalist and, more recently, Marxist writings. The nationalist writings are best represented by R. C. Dutt (1901), The Marxist by R. Palme Dutt (1940) and Bipin Chandra (1968). The counter-attack is led by Morris (1968a), with a reply to his critics in Morris (1968b), whilst Raychaudhuri (1968) attempts to provide some balance to the warring factions.

80. Hicks (1969, pp. 23–4).

81. Ibid., 38.

82. Hicks (Ibid., 38–9) sees their evolution as largely due to geography and finds in this factor the divergence in the economic history of Europe and Asia. It is interesting to note in this context that of the four countries of south-east Asia (South Korea, Taiwan, Hong Kong, and Singapore), collectively known as the Gang of Four, which have had such a spectacular growth performance in the period after the Second World War, two are clearly city States, whilst in all four the political power wielded at least indirectly by merchants is considerable.

83. See Bayly (1983).

Part II

The Colonial Centuries, AD 1757–1947

5

Polity and Society in British India

INTRODUCTION

In 1757, Clive's victory at Plassey (in Bengal) began the process of British conquest of India, which was virtually completed by 1818. Acquired by a band of foreign merchants, Britain's Indian empire at that date ran along the coast from Bengal to Gujarat except for the territorial pockets of Portuguese Goa and French Pondicherry, which were in the hands of the other two European powers who had established footholds in India's coastal economies. Of these the French had for a brief period vied with the British for control of the south. By 1852, the British had absorbed the remaining independent principalities in the north-west—Punjab and Sind.

The causes of the collapse of the Moghul empire and the rapid success of British arms and diplomacy in conquering India are beyond the scope of this study. Nor shall we trace the evolution of British colonial administration, first under the East India Company and then under the Crown, nor the growth and final victory of the nationalist struggle in any detail. For our purposes, it is only important to determine if and to what extent the British succeeded in altering the living conditions of the mass of the Indian people, and whether this latest foreign assault on the Hindu equilibrium established at the beginning of the Christian era was any more successful in altering the basic parameters of India's polity, society, and economy than its predecessor.

The Mutiny of 1857 provides a convenient dividing line for two distinct phases in the colonial impact on Indian polity and society. These phases in turn can be identified with two distinct lines of thought which emerged at the turn of the nineteenth century. These concerned the means for promoting the welfare of the Indian people which had explicitly been made the Company's charge by the English Parliament in the late eighteenth century.

The Mutiny also roughly marks the transition of the British in India from 'nabobs' to 'sahibs'.[1] The nabobs sought to assimilate and to become a traditional Indian power; the sahibs set themselves apart and above their subjects, and sought to promote their good as platonic guardians. The notions of racial exclusiveness and the 'white man's burden', so characteristic of the late imperial phase, were alien to India's early British rulers, who exhibited a more robust delight in both the country's mores and its women.[2]

In the first phase the British who conquered Bengal behaved like a traditional Indian power. There was a strong current of opinion amongst these early colonial rulers, represented for instance by Warren Hastings, that they should govern

India in the traditional way. Like the Moghuls and other past imperial rulers of India, they would have been satisfied to maintain law and order in the countryside in return for the land revenue which had for so long been the loadstone of imperial ambitions. They would have preferred to leave Indian society unaltered, a view which was naturally congenial to English Tories.

The suppression of Christian missionary activity and the toleration of various Indian customs such as infanticide and 'sutee' (widow burning) which such abnegation entailed naturally found disfavour amongst the Evangelicals, Utilitarians, and Radicals who were becoming a growing force in British politics at the time.[3] Both the Evangelicals, with their adherence to the Gospels, and the Radicals and Utilitarians, trusting in the power of reason, believed in the superiority of Western ways—religious and secular. These groups found traditional Indian society deeply offensive, with its idolatry, superstitions, and cruel practices. In the first half of the nineteenth century, they were to be a powerful influence shaping British policy in India.

Wilberforce, the scourge of the slave-traders, along with his fellow Evangelicals, longed for the opportunity to save the millions of heathen Indian souls for Christianity. By the beginning of the nineteenth century they had succeeded in obtaining freedom of entry for missionaries in India. The Radicals, confident that reason could transform a sick and static Indian society, achieved their first victory in 1813 with the triumph of free-trade ideas. This led to the entry of private merchants into India and the end of the East India Company's trading monopoly.

A third intermediate group was also influential in determining colonial policy. It can be labelled Anglo-Indian, in that it consisted of the younger generation of the Company's servants who had taken part in establishing its supremacy, and subsequently held key posts in its administration. Men like Elphinstone in Bombay, Metcalfe in Delhi, and Munro in Madras, while aware like the Liberals of the need to alter Indian society on utilitarian lines, were nevertheless conscious of and to some extent sympathetic to the susceptibilities of traditional Indian society. They argued for a policy of gradual change, and it was their quasi-conservatism which ultimately triumphed in the late nineteenth century.

1. RESTORATION OF LAW AND ORDER

The first task the British faced was to restore law and order. The Moghul empire after Aurangzeb's death (AD 1707) had succumbed to the traditional fissiparous tendencies of India. Feuding kingdoms and Persian invasions, the continual wars of succession amongst Aurangzeb's successors in 1707, 1712, 1713, 1719–20, and 1752–53,[4] made the eighteenth century one of chaos, continual internecine warfare, and plunder.

Unlike some of India's earlier wars for imperial succession, the common populace and the economy were not spared by the recurring political instability of the eighteenth century. Local chiefs, using local revenues, recruited mercenary armies which plundered the countryside. Contemporary Maratha nationalism notwithstanding, the large Maratha armies were looked upon by the rest of the country with terror as they plundered and raided the countryside to collect their 'chauth' (a levy of one-fourth of t⟩ ⟨ revenue). Their practice of using local resources to subjugate different areas was followed by numerous other, less grandiose upstarts.

This process had gone so far by the last years of the century that, in Punjab, any adventurer who could collect some followers might seize a mud fort, terrorize the countryside and, in a few years, build himself up as a recognized raja. . . . Revenue came from the countryside and, in these conditions, could only by collected by moving through it. So it came about that the movements of Indian armies were often determined by the need to collect revenue. Mercenaries demand pay; campaigns would be broken in order to collect revenue to stave off a mutiny for arrears. In these circumstances, Indian generals often feared their own troops more than the enemies.[5]

It was not surprising that when the British first had time to examine their newfound dominion, they found it in ruins. The broken-down fortresses, deserted palaces, neglected canals, banks and roads, decaying towns and depopulated villages testified both to the past glory and prosperity and to the current wretchedness of their new fief—wretchedness to which their own predatoriness had contributed.

But the chaos and economic dislocation of the eighteenth century, which had previously been considered to be widespread over the whole of the subcontinent, appears from recent research to have been localized. This is not surprising given our argument that the socio-economic system which generated the Hindu equilibrium was adapted to withstand the endemic political instability of ancient India.

Recently, Bayly has provided a rich reconstruction of the social and economic history of the eighteenth century. He shows how the political changes during that period led to the strengthening of local ruling groups and the Mughal aristocracy which had been at odds with the empire. This enabled the consolidation and emergence of more compact regional states around core areas of agricultural prosperity. In this process there was a considerable reshuffling of agrarian resources—of capital, labour, and skills—across the country, Bayly shows 'how the withdrawal of resources from some areas was matched by their reinvestment elsewhere'.[6] Thus the decline of some areas (in particular in eastern India) was matched by growth elsewhere (particularly in the west).

Bayly also shows that this decentralization of political power 'encouraged the further growth of a rooted service gentry and a homogenous merchant class operating around small town centres'.[7] The combination of these merchants in various associations was important for the emergence of Indian nationalism in the late nineteenth century.

2. REVENUE ADMINSTRATION AND LAND TENURE

The first task of the British administration, when it was set up in the late eighteenth century, was to restore law and order in British India which, until 1818, consisted of the coastal belt of the Carnatic in the south, and Bengal, Bihar, Orissa, and a tract running to Delhi north of the Ganges. Robbers and dacoits, who had grown like maggots in the disturbed countryside, were put down, although it was not until the 1830s, under Bentinck, that that most notorious gang of religious dacoits, the Thuggees, was finally suppressed.

The second major task which the Company faced under Cornwallis in Bengal was the assessment and collection of the land revenue—the perennial problem of Indian rulers. As the resulting permanent settlement in Bengal and different 'ryotwari' settlements (see p. 108 below) in Madras and Bombay were to have important social and economic effects, we discuss these in some detail below.

When the East India Company took over the Diwani of Bengal (which was the imperial grant from the Moghul Emperor Shah Alam of the revenue authority in Bengal and Bihar), its servants soon became rapacious middlemen. Despite valiant efforts by Clive to discipline them, they siphoned off a large part of the revenue surplus into their own pockets. Warren Hastings, when he took over as Governor, replaced the Indian deputies, who, in traditional Indian fashion, had hitherto acted as the Company's tax collectors, by a board of revenue in Calcutta and English collectors in the districts.[8] Following the Regulating Act of 1773,[9] whereby the British Parliament sought to regulate the dealings of the Company with its new-found subjects, Cornwallis was appointed Governor-General in 1786.

Cornwallis changed the nature of the Company's rule in India by reorganizing its administration. Hitherto, the Company's factors combined commercial, political, and administrative roles:

The Company was essentially still a commercial body administering a state as a sideline. It was only natural that many Company servants should consider that their main business was still to make a fortune with public spirit as a desirable extra. Cornwallis altered all this. The service was divided into commercial and political branches, into one or the other you had to opt. Henceforth, you were either a merchant or an administrator, but not both. As a merchant, you could still trade on your own but as an official you had to be content with a large salary. This was the beginning of the Civil Service as known in the nineteenth century and the beginning of the end of the Company's commercial activities. Government in its world was now more important than trade.[10]

Thus the traditional Indian pattern of a disjunction between trade and public functions, which was briefly blurred by the ascendancy of a bunch of foreign merchants over Indian society, was restored. In time, the 'official' British would treat their mercantile compatriots—labelled the 'boxwallahs'—with that degree of aloofness and contempt which Indian rulers had always adopted towards the indigenous mercantile classes. Political power was once again to be strictly separated from economic power.

Cornwallis, furthermore, completed the policy begun by Hastings of Europeanizing the judicial and revenue services. But, more momentously, he arranged a permanent settlement of the revenue and land rights of Bengal. Like most Indian rulers in the past, the British found it difficult to discover the taxable capacity of the countryside. The traditional tax-farmers of Bengal, the zamindars, annually agreed with the Government the dues that they would have to pay in. What they cound obtain as land revenue from the villages was a closely guarded secret, as 'the difference between what they could squeeze from the village and what the Government could squeeze from them was their living'.[11]

Hastings, in an attempt to get at the 'true' tax base of Bengal, had begun a practice of auctioning the right to collect land revenue to the highest bidder. This brought in various newly prosperous members of the Indian mercantile classes who had benefited from acting as middlemen to many of the Company's factors. After the Bengal famine of 1770, there was perpetual danger of a shortage of rural labour (relative to available land). Many of the old zamindars found they did not have enough tillers for their land and could not meet the Government's revenue demands. They were forced to sell their 'zamindaris', often to non-resident, urban 'banias' (merchants). The principle that zamindars had proprietary, saleable right in land was thus established.

Cornwallis, however, seeking to create a landed aristocracy on the English pattern, frowned on the practice of settling the Government's land revenue demand by auction. He sought to turn the zamindars into a landed Indian aristocracy which, besides promoting rural development, would act as British collaborators in pacifying the countryside. The annual settlement of the revenue demand was first replaced by a settlement for ten years in 1789, but the annual settlement was finally made permanent. A fixed annual payment was now due from the zamindars and, as the cultivators could be evicted for not paying *their* dues (which, at the best of times, were unknown and uncertain) to the zamindars, they became, in effect, tenants-at-will of the zamindars.

However, not all the zamindars profited greatly from this permanent settlement, as the initial assessments were set at a high level at a time when agricultural output prices were not rising. Unable to squeeze the peasants enough to pay their dues, many of them were forced to sell their newly granted zamindaris' to various financial speculators from the cities. Moreover, as zamindari rights were now saleable, and the resulting contracts were enforceable in the newly founded system of British justice, these rights could also be used as a collateral for loans to finance the continued extravagant living of the traditional zamindars. The rising indigenous urban mercantile and money-lending classes found investment in land fairly profitable, and were keen to foreclose on the mortgages of the zamindars. Thus 'zamindaris with more than a fifth of the total revenues of Bengal were put up for sale during 1796–7, and within 20 years after the

Permanent Settlement, more than one-third of the landed property of Bengal was sold for arrears of rent'.[12]

This creation of a legally enforceable and transferable right to the collection of land revenue naturally led to the growth of sub-infeudation, which, although initially against the terms of the Permanent Settlement, was legalized by a regulation of 1819. Under this system, the main zamindar would lease out the management of the whole or part oi his estate to middlemen, who would pay him a fixed sum and who, in turn, settled the revenue of the lands either with the actual cultivators or with other middlemen able to pay a higher rental. Thereby grew the layer of intermediary tenures (called 'patni' in Bengal and 'mukarrari' in Bihar) between the Government and the cultivators.

The system of land settlement in other parts of India was, by contrast, influenced not by Cornwallis's ideas but by those of the Anglo-Indian school distinguished above. The progenitor of this alternative system, known as the 'ryotwari' system, was Thomas Munro in Madras. 'He did not differ from Cornwallis over the institution of private-property rights in lands, but only over the hands in which they were to be lodged.'[13] Unlike the Bengal system, he settled the State's revenue demand directly with the cultivator (the 'ryot'), and did not cede the State's right to waste land, as Cornwallis had done in Bengal, to the zamindars. The major administrative difference made by the ryotwari as opposed to the zamindari system was the need for the administration to be continually involved in 'the vast undertaking of assessing and collecting the demand for each cultivated field'.[14] By contrast, in the zamindari system, the State had freed itself from any detailed assessment and collection, merely taking receipt, from a relatively small number of zamindars, a sum fixed permanently at the level at which it stood in 1793. The ryotwari system also meant that, unlike the arrangement in Bengal, the assessment could not in practice be permanently fixed, and it came to represent 'in its actual working all the features of an annual assessment and of a fluctuating, uncertain demand'.[15]

In Bombay, Elphinstone also strove to recognize every species of hereditary tenurial right. These were the result of various tenures granted by the Marathas to their nobles and public servants. Many of these were similar to the Mughal jagirs, but there were also personal 'inams'—or gifts of land—which were proprietary tenures granted usually to Brahmins who held their lands 'in fee simple'.[16] But the Bombay system, in practice, came to resemble the Madras one, and for all practical purposes we can subsume it as part of the ryotwari system. The major difference between the ryotwari systems established in Madras and Bombay was that, whereas in Madras the revenue was based on a fraction, usually one-half, of the net produce of the farm, in Bombay the assessment was based on the relative notional yield of the soil, without any consideration of the actual yield.[17]

The third major revenue system instituted by the British was the so-called 'Mahalawari' settlement, which was established in the so-called 'north-western provinces', which covered modern Uttar Pradesh and parts of Madhya Pradesh.

This arose after an initial period of confusion, in which it was thought that the dominant customary proprietary interest in the land was, as in Bengal, vested in zamindars. The details of the resulting twists and turns in official policy need not concern us, except to note that, in the process, 'the hereditary proprietors and resident cultivators were (initially) deprived, hastily and absolutely, of their rights, and compelled to sue for leases under some fortunate, perhaps fraudulent, purchaser, whom they hated and despised'.[18] But by 1840 some of the initial errors were redressed and it was recognized that, in this region, there existed a large body of co-sharing village brotherhoods.[19] The mahalawari settlement 'recognized all possessory and proprietary under-tenures. It provided for the registration of each separate share, so that the *malguzar* (payer of the revenue), or the principal person who previously engaged on behalf of inferior sharers, might not have their shares fraudulently auctioned for arrears of revenue.'[20]

When the Punjab was conquered in 1849, John and Henry Lawrence settled the land in favour of the cultivator rather than the chiefs, and something closer to the ryotwari rather than the zamindari system was established.

The net result of all these settlements of land revenue was that, by the mid-nineteenth century, the British had succeeded in replacing the customary systems of land tenure by a more legally based one, in which land rights were defined and recorded and, most important, were enforceable through the courts. All the settlements created private saleable property rights 'through the permanent limitation of the State demand and the relinquishment of a private rent to the proprietor. Their differences merely concerned the class of person to be given the proprietary right, and the timing and method of framing a permanent money tax.'[21]

By defining, guaranteeing, and legally enforcing the interests even of individual sharers of joint property, these new revenue settlements further weakened the hold of the ancient village communities on individuals, for they

tended to free the sharers from the bondage of village communities to which they previously remained attached, because of the fact that their shares were, for all practical purposes, inalienable, forming part, as they did, of the total joint property registered exclusively in the name of one of their number, namely, their chief proprietor who had a major share. He possessed a corporate character especially because it was through him that the State disbursed and realized the public dues. No alienation of any share was possible except through him. With the registration of separate shares, his hold on the community thus began to wane. . . . The revenue laws of the British, in fact, set in motion a process of social mobility. Land became a commodity, and the ease with which it could be transferred afforded opportunity to moneyed people to buy social prestige by purchasing landed estates.[22]

3. THE RULE OF LAW

As important as the land settlement for the further development of the Indian polity, society, and economy was the introduction of the British concept of the rule of law. Cornwallis was determined to root out the authoritarian, arbitrary, discretionary, and personal power of the executive which he saw as the heart of Asian despotism, and to base himself explicitly on the great English Whig tradition.[23] The Government's chief function was to be 'the impartial administrator of fixed and equal laws for the maintenance of property rights. Once these latter were secured, all else followed. Political authority, in the form of the subjection of one man to the will of another, was reduced to its lowest point; and the happy marriage of liberty and security provided the most favourable conditions for the production of wealth.'[24] By separating the judiciary from the executive, anglicizing the British administration, and separating the commercial from the political interests of the British in India, he sought to erect an impersonal government of law, a system upheld by its inherent principles and not by the men who were to have the occasional conduct of it. He also pruned and amended the existing Muslim code of law and produced 'a code much more humane than that of contemporary England and one of the most enlightened in the world.'[25] His greatest achievement was the institution of the rule of law as the keystone of the Indian legal system, through his regulation that

The collectors of revenue and their officers, and, indeed, all officers of the Government, shall be amenable to the courts for acts done in their official capacities, and Government itself, in cases in which it may be a party in matters of property shall submit its rights to be tired in these courts under the existing laws and regulations.[26]

The task of enshrining this rule of law in a fully fledged codification of Indian public law was not completed until 1861, with important contributions by Macaulay, which need not concern us here. When it was completed, 'it introduced English procedures and the assumptions behind them into all the Indian courts. This was the department of public life in which Indians first attained high position and where their subtle minds had fullest play. Here, the interaction of western and eastern ideas and minds was widespread, penetrating and sustained.'[27]

As British law came to cover the most important areas of Indian lives, it was inevitable that there was a vast growth of indigenous lawyers, trained and skilled in operating in the new-style Western courts. They were to provide the backbone of the middle classes, which were to emerge as a significant factor in India's nationalist movement and post-Independence politics.

4. SOCIAL REFORMS

By the time William Bentinck became Governor-General of India in 1826, the English liberal tradition had coalesced into a consensus on the means and aims of the transformation of Indian society which was required for the welfare of its constituents. 'Free trade was its solid foundation. Evangelicalism provided its programme of social reform, its force of character, and its missionary zeal.

Philosophic radicalism gave it an intellectual basis and supplied it with the sciences of political economy, law and government.'[28] The liberal school was keen to assimilate, to anglicize Indian society.

The achievements of the institution of property rights in the major asset of Indians—land—and the rule of law to enforce these rights, were to be buttressed by a series of social reforms instituted by Bentinck, and by the introduction of Western education in India (on which more below).

Bentinck attacked and attempted to reform various Indian social customs in the name of what he considered a universal moral code—Western moral law[29] The most important was the suppression of suttee or the burning of widows on their husband's funeral pyre. This was made illegal in 1828. In the previous fifteen years, recorded suttees alone had varied annually from 500 to 820.[30] There was surprisingly little resistance from the Hindus, and even some support by some newly anglicised Indian groups led by Raja Ram Mohun Roy.[31]

The second major measure was the suppression of infanticide, particularly of female children, whilst the most dramatic was the suppression of 'thuggee', which had involved ritual murder and robbery in the name of the goddess Kali.[32] Other measures were the Caste Disability Removal Act of 1850, which would have made it illegal to forfeit the property or inheritance of someone put outside the pale of caste. Given its potentially subversive nature, caste Hindus petitioned against it and it never came into force. The Widow Remarriage Act of 1856 was initiated by a Hindu Principal of the Sanskrit College at Calcutta. But positive interference stopped here, leaving various other Hindu practices, considered more neutral from a Western ethical viewpoint, untouched. But the most important of Bentinck's reforms, for our purposes, was the reform of education, which we examine in the following section.

5. EDUCATION

The provision of formal education to at least certain groups of the population had a long history in India, going back to the days of the imperial Mauryas. Under the ancient Indian Hindu kingdoms, formal education was provided in both Brahmanical institutions and Buddhist monasteries.[33] Nalanda, near Patna, came to be the leading Buddhist monastery and educational centre in the north, attracting students from South-east Asia and China. These essentially theological institutions were supported by land grants whose revenue covered their expenses and enabled them to provide free education for their students.[34] Buddhist education virtually ceased with the destruction of Nalanda by the Turks, while Brahmanical education, which in the earlier phase of Hindu domination covered such subjects as grammar, rhetoric, prosody, logic, metaphysics, and medicine, had by the sixth century AD become much more narrowly theological. Its medium of instruction—Sanskrit—also increasingly became an artificial language, spoken only by the Brahmins and the privileged few who received a formal education. The urban guilds provided their members with training in the required craft skills. But a contempt for technical knowledge developed in this later Brahmanical tradition, which was to make Indian education moribund for centuries.

With the coming of the Muslims, schools were also attached to mosques, and were financed by the State. But their curricula as well as those of the Hindu schools attached to temples were, aˉ in higher education, exclusively concentrated on theology and linguistics.[35] Furthermore, the two communities' educational facilities tended to exclude each other, and there was little educational or intellectual interchange, except in medicine. Technical knowledge did not form part of formal education, whilst vocational training was provided by artisans or the State workshops.[36]

The Moghuls extended the system of Muslim education, and under Akbar's policy of religious toleration Hindus too were allowed to be trained in the Muslim Madarsas. In any case, many Hindus must have had to learn Persian, the new court language, as—at least during the period when the Moghul Empire was at its height—a large number of Hindus served in the imperial service, particularly in its revenue branch.

The early British under Warren Hastings gave some financial support to this traditional education. They did not look with disfavour upon oriental studies, in which many of them had become proficient and even scholars.[37] This tolerant attitude to native education was to change with the emergence of the liberal consensus on the importance of education in changing the mind of India.[38] The chief architect of British Indian educational policy, Macaulay, shared James Mill's profound contempt for oriental culture, and in his famous Minute of Education summed up the aim of English education as being the raising of an English educated middle class 'who may be interpreters between us and the millions whom we govern; a class of persons, Indian in blood and colour, but English in taste, in opinions, in morals, and in intellect. To that class we may leave it to refine the vernacular dialects of the country, to enrich those dialects with terms of science borrowed from the western nomenclature, and to render them by degrees fit vehicles for conveying knowledge to the great mass of the population.'

Following this, the Government began to set up English-language schools and colleges to train these brown sahibs and clerks. As English had now replaced Persian as the State language, there was a natural incentive for all those having to do business with the English courts or administration on their own or their clients' account to acquire a knowledge of English. Public provision was thus buttressed with the private establishment of colleges and schools to impart the new Western education.

Thus, from 1835, an élitist system of providing secondary and higher education in English to the Indian upper classes was implemented. Three non-teaching universities (which were primarily examining bodies for the affiliated colleges) were established in 1857 at Bombay, Calcutta, and Madras. Given their need for Indians to man the intermediate and lower levels of the bureaucracy, the British encouraged literary and philosophical studies in the new schools and colleges. This literary tradition also fitted in well with the traditional predilections of upper-caste Hindus, who were the first to take to English education.

By contrast, both primary and technical education languished. In 1900, there were 140 English arts colleges with over 17,000 pupils, but only four engineering colleges and four medical colleges. There were 3,097 English secondary schools with 422,187 pupils in them, as against only 84 industrial and technical· schools with 4,977 students.[39] The state of primary education, despite some pious hopes, did not improve in the nineteenth century. 'Between 1896–7 and 1901–02, while the number of pupils in colleges and secondary schools increased by 49,000, the increase in primary school pupils was only 1,000. The number of primary schools declined between 1897 and 1902 from 97,881 to 92,226.'[40] Despite some encouragement by Lord Curzon in the early twentieth century, according to the census in 1911, the literacy rate in India was only fifty-nine per thousand (106 in the case of men and ten in the case of women).[41]

Progress in both technical and primary education accelerated in the later years of the Raj, in part under the prodding of the growing nationalist movement; but, even at Independence, only one-fifth of the children of the requisite age were receiving any primary education.[42] Thus English education was confined to the urban (largely Hindu)[43] elite and, while it enabled them to participate increasingly in the ruling of British India, the ameliorative effects from the introduction of Western education on Hindu society, given the narrow spread of Western education amongst the population, would necessarily have been fairly limited. It did, however, have important long-term effects, not least in engendering the notion of nationalism in India for the first time.

6. THE EMERGENCE OF THE NATIONALIST MOVEMENT

One of the enduring features of the Indian political scene until the late nineteenth century was the absence of any national feeling, such as had provided the cement for the European nation-States at the time of the Renaissance. The caste system doubtless made it more difficult to develop an abstract loyalty to a State over and above that to the vertically and horizontally arranged caste and subcaste groups in the country.

In the old tribal polities of the ancient Indian republics, however, there was an incipient notion of loyalty to a State which went beyond that to the king and government of the day.[44] This was lost with the rise and dominance of the ancient Hindu agrarian monarchies in the Indo-Gangetic plain. 'The monarchical system, which leant heavily on religious orthodoxy, tended slowly to blur the concept of the State and, instead, loyalty was directed to the social order. The interdependence of caste and politics had gradually led to caste being accorded higher status than any political institution.'[45]

Nor did the resulting feuding kingdoms, at the time either of the Muslim or of the later British conquests, think of organizing themselves into a concert of Indian powers to resist the foreign invaders. This absence of the development of any stable balance of power amongst the various warring kingdoms of India was, in large part, due to the imperial tradition established in ancient India by the Mauryas, which in turn was due to the lack of natural geographical barriers to imperial ambition on the vast Indo-Gangetic plain.[46] The ready availability of the revenue from the on-going agrarian settlements, as well as their ready acquiescence in paying their dues to any established power, required little effort on the part of a ruler who had established his supremacy. This revenue provided both the means and incentive for recurrent attempts by the various feuding kingdoms to achieve their imperial ambitions. Thus 'there was never an Indian concept of the balance of power of stable states within the orbit of Indian culture. Instead, there was a continuing tradition of empire and lordship from the *Chakravarti* raja with his horse sacrifice as token of supremacy in ancient times to the great Moghuls of the seventeenth century.'[47] The feuding leaders at the start of both the Muslim and Britist conquests sought either to establish an empire for themselves (like the Marathas in the eighteenth century) or else sought to gain as much territory (with its attendant land revenue) at their rivals' expense. The vanquished continued to rule over their own territory through the ancient Indian practice of accepting the suzerainty of any new imperial power which achieved supremacy on the subcontinent. 'The Indian tradition of imperial unification and the absence of national feeling explain the lack of any sense of shame on the part of Indian rulers either to seek foreign help in defeating a local rival or to accept foreign overlordship when it was seen capable of enforcing it.'[48]

The Marathas under Shivaji saw the first stirrings of a genuine national feeling during the closing years of Aurangzeb's reign. It was fanned by a hatred of Islam, aroused by Aurangzeb's reversal of Akbar's policy of religious tolerance. It was aided by the geographical distinctiveness of the Maratha homeland, and by Shivaji's deft clothing of the rising resentment against India's Muslim rulers into a call for the defence of the homeland and the cow (religion) and in federating various Maratha communities on a functional basis. But Shivaji's successors could not resist the temptations of imperial conquest on the ancient Indian pattern. Besides a continual jockeying for imperial power amongst themselves, they also exploited and ruled non-Maratha areas with a ruthlessness not seen before in India. By the time of Warren Hastings, 'their own nationalism had become a sentiment and memory to themselves and their imperialism a nightmare to others'.[49]

Thus it was not until the infection of Western liberal ideas had been planted in a number of Indian minds as a result of Macaulay's and his successors' educational reforms that ideas of nationalism, civil liberties, and constitutional self-government were adopted by the newly Westernised Indian middle classes. What is more, they were to succeed within a short spell of about eighty years in using these Western ideas and ideals against the British in wresting Indian independence from foreign rulers after nearly 600 years. To Macaulay's credit, he had foreseen, and applauded, this possible consequence of his educational policies for the continuance of British rule. Thus, in 1833, in the Charter Debate in the British Parliament, he stated:

It may be that the public mind of India may expand under our system till it has outgrown that system; that by good government we may educate our subjects into a capacity for better government; that, having become instructed in European knowledge, they may, in some future age, demand European institutions. Whether such a day will ever come I know not. But never will I attempt to avert or retard it. Whenever it comes, it will be the proudest day in English history.[50]

This provision of spiritual weapons to the incipient Indian nationalists in their struggle for self-government was buttressed by the Raj's move towards a more aloof, authoritarian, and paternalist State following the 1857 mutiny. This new face of the Raj provided both the emotional charge and many of the actual issues on which various nationalist struggles were subsequently to be waged.

Even though the Mutiny of 1857 was easily suppressed, it gave a grave shock to British self-confidence in their civilizing mission. The liberal policy of seeking to anglicize India through various social reforms was now directly challenged by a paternalist conservative philosophy whose patron saint was Edmund Burke. This alternative view had been earlier espoused by the youthful Anglo-Indian school of administrators (Munro *et al.*) in the late eighteenth and early nineteenth centuries. The Burkeian conservatives looked with horror on the full-frontal onslaught on a traditional society by liberal reformers moved by at best a highly speculative utilitarian philosophy. For them, change was to be managed and to take account of local susceptibilities. But they were clever enough to take over certain parts of that utilitarian creed for their own purposes. There was always an authoritarian streak in the utilitarian tradition, and this was harnessed by the paternalist school in the post-Mutiny period to create that stereotypical image of the British Raj with its aloof sahibs and memsahibs, who also introduced an element of racial exclusiveness in their dealings with their subjects.

The paternalist system of government had been initiated by the Lawrence brothers in the Punjab after its annexation in 1849.

The essence of the Punjab tradition lay in a masterful attempt to prolong the atmosphere of military conquest, and to force, as it were, at one bound, the elements of an advanced civilized government on the stupified and bewildered people. But the imperiousness of the tradition was mitigated by its respect for indigenous custom and by its type of personal and paternal rule, which brought the district officer into intimate contact and understanding with the people.[51]

This substitution of the 'Mai–Baap' State (the State as the father and mother of the people) for the more co-operative State sought in the earlier period under Bentinck, through the open collaboration of the British and the newly

Westernized middle classes, was to lead to the alienation of Macaulay's 'interpreters between us and the millions whom we govern'.

For one of the major achievements of the administrative, legal, and revenue reforms of the previous period was to create an administrative machinery which, in its efficiency and relative incorruptibility (and unaccountability!) would have warmed the heart of any incipient platonic guardian. But 'paternalism grown bureaucratic tended to lose personal touch with the peasant; liberalism grown efficient tended to lose trust in the Indian middle class.'[52]

By the late nineteenth century, the combined introduction of Western education and bureaucratic paternalism might have produced some potential nationalists in the Indian middle classes, and perhaps some potential grievances amongst the peasant populace. But the transformation of essentially local grievances against the rulers into a truly national movement still remained a problem. Nationalist historians, attempting to glorify the movement, have given it a coherence and all-India character which it lacked. Their view that, with charismatic leadership, the nationalist wave overcame the awesome power of the British empire in a few decades has been questioned by more recent historical research. Finding the nationalist account implausible, these revisionists have sought to construct a more realistic story about the composition of the nationalist movement and the reasons for its success.

There are two important points emphasized by these revisionist historians of the nationalist movement.[53] The first is that a common assumption made by nationalist historians is false: namely, that the imperial power was strong—especially at its height when it had perfected its bureaucratic steel frame. By contrast, the revisionists emphasise that the Raj 'was hobbled at every turn. It depended on local allies. Local conditions might buckle its policies. Often it did not know what it was doing.'[54]

Similarly, a second assumption of nationalist hagiography that, the national movement was an all-Indian movement, is also false. As Seal notes:

It is no longer credible to write about a movement grounded in common aims, led by men with similar backgrounds and recruited from widening groups with compatible interests. That movement looks like a ramshackle coalition throughout its long career. Its unity seems a figment. Its power appears as hollow as that of the imperial authority it was supposedly challenging. Its history was the rivalry between Indian and Indian, its relationship with imperialism that of the mutual clinging of two unsteady men of straw.[55]

Whether or not its initial motivation was profit, by the mid-nineteenth century the British conquest of India could hardly be justified as a commercial success. True, it did provide a system of rather lavish outdoor relief for the members of the British upper classes, but the major reason why Britain clung to its Indian empire was its central role, by the middle of the nineteenth century, in the survival of the overall Empire. Seal notes that

Imperialism is a system of formal or informal expansion, driven by impulses of profit and of power, each of which feeds on the other. India's growing foreign trade helped to push the influence of the British deeper into west and east Asia alike. The growing military power underwrote the informal influence they were developing in those regions, as well as the formal Empire they built in Burma, Malaya and East Africa. India became the second centre for the extension of British power and influence in the world; and when she dropped this role after 1947, the British Empire did not take long to disappear.[56]

But, in order to maintain this imperial system, the British did not want to burden the British tax-payer. Through the 'home charges', the costs of holding India and using its armies were to be paid for by Indian revenues. To collect this revenue at least cost, the traditional Indian system of land revenue was available, and the British gladly took it over—with some reforms, aimed as much at gaining loyal collaborators as improving the lot of the peasant cultivator. But in creating these local collaborators the Raj did not merely ratify the customary rights of existing local magnates (as we have seen); the most important social effect of the legal and administrative reforms which created these collaborators was to stir the social pot by rupturing the relative and ancient autonomy of regions and localities.

However, the land revenue the Raj obtained was relatively inelastic. When the Crown succeeded the East India Company in 1858 it inherited a virtually bankrupt fiscal regime. Until the end of the nineteenth century, this financial weakness could not be overcome.[57] In its consequent search for larger revenues, the Raj had to bear harder on Indians at the local level whom until then it had prudently left alone in the hands of local collaborators. The granting of systems of representation, nomination, and election through various channels (whose creation is all part of the long and arduous constitutional history of India) thus became an integral part of the imperial schema for co-opting Indian collaborators to serve British ends.

The creation of these progressively more representative institutions at local and, later, at provincial levels[58] could not be ignored even by those Indians who were merely concerned with local affairs. For the matters which concerned most Indians *were* local, at which level politics continued to be organized on the traditional basis of caste and its attendant patron–client relationships. But once local autonomies were shattered and local and provincial élites shuffled as a result of the new land revenue settlements and the conversion of land into a saleable asset by the new legal system, the economic power and status of many indians came to depend upon their ways of dealing with their new masters.

Nor could the local bosses who emerged confine their activities merely to their local levels. As provincial officials and legislatures

took more of the decisions and made more of the rules, butting into local sanctuaries, shuffling the standing of men and their share of the booty, they gave district bosses reasons for negotiating with the administration at heights to which they had not previou ly climbed. . . . The Raj itself had cut the steps which these petitioners had to mount; it had also defined the tests they had to pass. The administration had carved its peoples into large administrative blocks; and it had set up a system of representing them. In effect, Indians were now being invited to voice the interests of others, if they could show credentials as the spokesmen of a block. This amounted to a licence, almost a command, to form associations intelligible to Government. For the ambitious politician, the entrance fee was to assert or pretend affinities with those who had been bundled into the same category. . . . Associations, like cricket, were British innovations and, like cricket, became an Indian craze.[59]

With the further expansion in representation after the 1919 Act, with its extension of spending power to Indian provincial politicians,[60] it became necessary for the Indians to organize all-India associations, no matter how diverse and conflicting the interests of the members of the coalitions thereby created. At each stage in the progress of the constitutional juggernaut, one way in which particular associations (provincial or national) could vie with each other in demonstrating their support was by combining various local and hence diverse grievances into a national agitation—a technique perfected by Gandhi.[61] Thus Indian politicans, who soon emerged as a special class of intermediaries and spokesmen, shuttling forth between the various layers of the administrative and legislative structure, operated at various official levels and entered and broke out of fragile political associations at their convenience. 'They stepped nimbly in and out of the All-India organizations, like so many cabs for hire.'[62]

The constitutional stakes were raised with Linlithgow's (1940) and Cripps's (1942) offers to Indians of an immediate share in the central Government. The resulting possibility of the post-war mastery of the subcontinent turned the two major national associations, the Congress and the Muslim League, into the self-proclaimed custodians of a subcontinental Pandora's Box of interests. 'Just as the agitations of the 1920's and 1930's had swung the localities behind the provincial leaderships, so the crisis of the last days of the Raj swung the provinces behind the national leaderships.'[63] They were to be the inheritors of the British Raj.

NOTES

1. For a description of the British as nabobs in the early part of their rule, see Spear (1963).
2. Spear argues that the switch from nabobs to sahibs, in the early part of the nineteenth century, was triggered in part by the arrival of English women in India.
3. See Stokes (1959), Spear (1965).
4. See Spear (1965, p. 112).
5. Ibid., 112.
6. Bayly (1983, p. 37).
7. Ibid., 8.
8. Spear (1965, p. 88).
9. This act was prompted by the impending bankruptcy of the Company, which found that its new conquests, far from yielding a net profit to the Company, was a net liability, largely because of the siphoning off of the land revenues by the Company agents for private purposes.
10. Spear (1965, p. 95).
11. Ibid., 96.

12. Mishra (1961, p. 132); whilst Chandhuri (*CEHI*, vol. ii, p. 96) notes: 'In Orissa 51.6% of the 3,000 "proprietors" of the first settlement of 1804 were wiped out between 1804 and 1818.'
13. Stokes (1959, p. 83).
14. Ibid.
15. Ibid. Munro took over the traditional Indian practice of a one-third share of the produce as the State's share. But he could not make the settlement permanent. For 'the Madras *ryot* lived too near the margin of subsistence to commit himself in perpetuity to the revenue demand on his holding. Accordingly, he was given the right to make annual engagements and to vary the number of fields he cultivated from year ˙ year. But even the sum fixed on each field could not be maintained unaltered. Not merely did allowance have to be made for crop failure, but the demand proved generally too high to be met, except in years of bumper harvest' (ibid., 84).
16. Mishra (1961, p. 142).
17. See Bhattacharya (1979, p. 33).
18. Mishra (1961, p. 137).
19. Stokes (1959, p. 85).
20. Mishra (1961, p. 140).
21. Stokes (1959, p. 86).
22. Mishra (1961, p. 146).
23. Stokes (1959, p. 4).
24. Ibid., 6.
25. Spear (1965, p. 98).
26. *Cornwallis Correspondence*, vol. ii, p. 558, cited in Spear (1965, p. 98).
27. Spear (1965, p. 127).
28. Stokes (1959, p. xiv).
29. Spear (1965, p. 125).
30. Ibid.
31. Although, even today, the practice has surfaced at least once according to press reports (in 1980) in Rajasthan.
32. See John Masters's novel, *The Deceivers*, for an exciting fictional account of Colonel Sleeman's victory over the thugs.
33. See Thapar (1966, pp. 154 ff., 302 ff.) and Basham (1967, pp. 164–6).
34. Although the Chinese traveller, Huan Tsang, who visited Nalanda at the time of Harsha, claimed it provided for no less than 10,000 students, Basham concludes that, from the archaeological remains, it appears that 'it could hardly have accommodated 1,000 monks' (Basham 1967, p. 166).
35. Thapar (1966, p. 303).
36. Ibid.
37. Thus Hastings himself knew Sanskrit and Persian, and one Company official, Sir William Jones, translated a great mass of Sanskrit literature, and founded the Asiatic Society of Bengal in 1785.
38. But see Stokes (1959, pp. 57 ff.). Note also Macaulay's famous and arrogant statement: 'I have no knowledge of either Sanskrit or Arabic. . . . But I have done what I could to form a correct estimate of their value. . . . Who could deny that a single shelf of a good European library was worth the whole native literature of India and Arabia. . . . all the historical information which has been collected from all the books written in the Sanskrit language is less valuable than what may be found in the most paltry abridgments used at preparatory schools in England' (from the text of the minute in Edwardes (1967)). This pales by comparison with the massive and sustained indictment of Hindu and Muslim civilization (this 'hideous state of society') in James Mill's *History of British India*.
39. Basu (1967, p. 361).
40. Basu (1971, p. 284).
41. Ibid., 295.
42. Maddison (1971, p. 43).
43. See Mishra (1961).
44. See Thapar (1966, p. 90).
45. Ibid.
46. See Jones (1981), and ch. 13 below.

47. Spear (1965, p. 110).
48 Ibid., 111.
49. Ibid.
50. Macaulay's speech of 10 July 1833, in Macaulay, *Complete Works*, vol. xi, pp. 585–6.
51. Stokes (1959, p. 268).
52. Ibid., 301.
53. They are members of the South Asian history project at Cambridge directed by Anil Seal and the late John Gallagher. See Gallagher *et al.* (1973) and Seal (1968).
54. Seal (1973, p. 1).
55. Ibid., 2.
56. Ibid., 7.
57. Ibid., 9. Also see Bhattacharya (1971) for a detailed account of the difficulties the British faced in maintaining a sound financial basis for their rule during the post-Mutiny period.
58. The history of the various constitutional changes can be summarized as follows: in 1882, representative municipal and local (district) boards were established in most provinces. The India Council Act of 1861 had already set up provincial legislative councils (with nominated native members) in Madras, Bombay, and Bengal; in 1886 they were extended to the north-western provinces, and to Punjab in 1897. The Act of 1892 introduced a back-door electoral principle for nomination to these councils, as it allowed that recommendations might be made by specific Indian organizations. In 1909, by the Morley–Minto reforms, 12 of the 27 members of the Legislative Council of the Governor-General were to be chosen by the non-official members of the provincial councils, and similarly in the lower level provincial councils, some members were to be elected by the municipal and district boards. Also, special interests, e.g. landlords, Muslims, businessmen, had elected members in both the provincial and Governor-General's councils. The Act of 1935 granted the provinces the substance of self-government and enlarged the electorate. The proposals of Linlithgow and Cripps during the war were the prelude to the full-scale transfer of power in 1947.
59. Seal (1973, pp. 17–19).
60. Motivated again in part by the State's need to increase revenue to finance its increasing administrative and military burdens; thus Seal (1973, p. 21) notes that, between 1880 and 1920, the Madras Government, for example, raised its revenues from Rs 8 to Rs 24 crores (1 crore 1 = 10 m.).
61. See Brown (1972, 1977).
62. Seal (1973, p. 23)—practice which one must ruefully note continues to this day!
63. Ibid., 24.

6
The Economy under the Raj, I:
Overall Trends

INTRODUCTION

In forming a judgement on the economic impact of British rule, there are two hurdles to be overcome. One is at present insurmountable, namely the paucity of a meaningful run of statistical data on the structure and levels of output, employment, and earnings for much of the nineteenth century. The second is the nationalist and (more recently) quasi-Marxist fog in which most interpretations of the effects of British rule have been shrouded.

Preying on the liberal ideals of their rulers, Indian nationalists erected a mythology of the devastating effect of British rule on the traditional, static, subsistence economy of pre-British India.[1] The introduction of Western commercial and industrial competition, founded on the twin economic ideologies of *laissez-faire* and free trade, it is argued, shattered this traditional economy—it destroyed the indigenous handicraft industries and led to a deindustrialization of India which was not matched by any significant development of modern industry; it enfeebled agriculture, created a new class of landless agricultural labourers who were often unemployed or underemployed, and led to the siphoning off of a substantial part of India's investible surplus in the form of 'home charges' to the imperial metropolis.

Indian writers typically stress the exploitative features of British rule as the cause of 19th century decay. Western scholars, to the extent that they do not accept the exploitation thesis, attribute the failure of the Indian economy to respond to the warming influences of the Industrial Revolution, to the society's 'other worldliness', to its lack of enterprise, and to the caste-exclusiveness of groups within the society. But whether one stresses the imperialist or the social-structural features as decisive the classical view sees the 19th century as an era of stagnation and, possibly even of steady deterioration.[2]

We begin this first of three chapters dealing with the economy under the Raj (which the general reader may choose to skip) with a brief survey of the available evidence on the changes in population, income, output, and employment that occured during the near century from 1857 to 1947 of fully-fledged British rule. We then turn to an examination in the next two chapters of the factors which were likely to have been responsible for the modest changes that did occur, and the reasons why, despite the high ideals of the early British liberal reformers, India gained independence with one of the lowest levels of living in the world.

This relatively detailed examination of the effects of British rule is relevant for our purposes for two reasons: first, because there is an influential nationalist view that British policy frustrated Indian economic development, which if true would seem to cast doubt on our major thesis that the Hindu equilibrium established in ancient India would not have been substantially altered by endogenous forces; and secondly, because there are certain elements of British policy—particularly in its earlier phases with its commitm nt to free trade—which we will argue later could (and did to some extent) help India in breaking out of the Hindu equilibrium. However, it is these very aspects of British rule which have been particularly castigated by the nationalists. In assessing the causes of India's continuing economic stagnation, and charting ways to break out of the Hindu equilibrium, we need to form a more balanced assessment of the Raj. The purpose of the following chapters is therefore by no means to provide an apology for British imperialism, but to ascertain the underlying and deep-seated forces which undermined those policies which, if they had been consistently pursued in the past, might have held out some hope of ending India's ancient economic stagnation, and which might do so if followed in the future.

TABLE 6.1. Selected Features of the Indian Population, 1800–1971

Year	Population (m.)		Birth-rate %		Death-rate %	
	Undivided India (UI)	Indian Union (IU)	UI	IU	UI	IU
(1)	(2)	(3)	(4)	(5)	(6)	(7)
1800	179	154	—	—	—	—
1850	223	189	—	—	—	—
1871	255.2	209.1	—	—	—	—
1881	257.4	210.9	—	—	—	—
1891	282.4	231.4	49	—	41	—
1901	285.3	238.4	46	—	44	—
1911	303.0	252.2	49	51	43	43
1921	305.7	251.3	48	49	47	49
1931	338.2	278.9	46	46	36	36
1941	389.0	318.7	45	45	31	31
1951	—	361.1	—	40	—	27
1961	—	439.1	—	42	—	23
1971	—	547.9	—	42	—	23
			—	37	—	16

Sources: Columns 2 and 3: figures for 1800 and 1850 are from Sen Gupta *et al.* (1969, 1970). Columns 4, 6, and the rest of 2 are from Davis, 1951. The figures in columns 5, 7, and most of 3 are from Nanavati and Anjaria (1965). For 1961 and 1971, data are from *Pocket Book of Population Statistics*, Registrar General, Census Commission, New Delhi, 1972, Tables 1, pp. 8 and V5 2, p. 96. Birth-rate and death-rate figures for 1971 are for 1970.

1. POPULATION

Up to 1881, population estimates reveal mere orders of magnitude. Table 6.1 summarizes the best available estimates. It shows a population of about 180 million for undivided India and 154 million for the current Indian Union in 1800. It grew to about 257 million (for undivided India) in 1881, i.e. by about 0.46 per cent per annum (compound). Between 1881 and 1921 it increased to 305 million with a similar compound annual rate growth of about 0.44 per cent. But during these 121 years, there were periods—1871–81, 1891–1901 and 1911–21—when it was largely stagnant, chiefly because of famines (see Table 6.2) and a virulent influenza epidemic in 1916 which took 9–18 million lives.[3]

From 1921, however, there has been a steady increase in population, and an acceleration in its rate of growth, due to a dramatic reduction in mortality (see Table 6.1). This is due to improvements in water supply, inoculation, and vector control in reducing mortality from plague, cholera, malaria, typhoid, kala-azar, and other epidemic diseases.[4] As a result the death rate fell from about 49 per 1,000 in 1921 to 27 per 1,000 in 1951. Though there was some decline in birth rates, it was not as marked as those in death rates.

2. PER CAPITA INCOME

Various economists have attempted to estimate long-term trends in national income.[5] Despite various areas of continuing uncertainty, the best available estimates are those of Heston (1983), summarized in Tables 6.3 and 6.4[6] (which also shows by comparison the previously most plausible estimates namely those of Sivasubramonian). Table 6.4 shows that per capita income steadily rose from about Rs 120 (at 1946–7 prices) in 1868–9 to Rs 171 in 1930, and then declined to Rs 166 in 1945. Thus there was an increase of 40 per cent in per capita income, at

TABLE 6.2(A).   Famine and Mortality in India, 1800–1950

Period	No. of famines	Estimated mortality (m.)
1800–25	5	1.0
1825–50	2	0.4
1850–75	6	5.0
1875–1900	18	26.0
1900–25	17	4.08[a]
1925–50	13	1.5[b]
TOTAL	61	38.7

a. Data do not include the high mortality rates reported in the 1901 Census Report for the Central Indian States of Malwa Agency, Bhopal, Indore Agency, Bhopawar, and Indore Residency.
b. Relates to the Bengal famine of 1943.

Source: Nanavati and Anjaria (1965, p. 31, table 1).

TABLE 6.2(B). Regional Distribution of Famines in India, 1729–1909

Provinces	1729	1770	1781	1783	1790	1791	1799	1802	1803	1805	1812	1823	1832	1837	1854	1860	1865	1868	1873	1877	1885	1888	1890	1891	1897	1909
Bengal	F	F	—	—	—	—	—	—	—	—	—	—	—	—	—	—	F	—	F	—	—	F	—	F	F	—
Bihar	—	F	—	F	—	—	—	—	—	—	—	—	—	—	—	—	F	—	F	—	—	—	—	F	F	—
Orissa	—	—	—	—	—	—	—	—	—	—	—	—	—	—	—	—	F	—	—	—	—	F	—	—	F	F
Oudh	—	—	F	—	—	—	—	—	—	—	—	—	—	—	—	—	—	—	—	—	—	—	—	—	—	—
North-west Provinces	—	—	—	F	—	—	—	—	—	F	—	—	—	F	—	F	—	F	F	—	—	—	—	—	F	—
Punjab	—	—	—	F	—	—	—	—	—	—	—	—	—	—	—	—	—	F	—	—	—	—	—	F	F	—
Central Provinces	—	—	—	—	—	—	—	—	—	—	—	—	—	—	—	—	—	F	—	F	—	—	—	—	F	F
Central India	—	—	—	—	—	—	—	—	—	—	—	—	—	—	—	—	—	F	—	—	—	—	—	F	F	F
Rajputana	—	—	—	—	—	—	—	—	—	—	—	—	—	—	—	—	—	F	—	—	—	—	—	F	F	F
Sind	—	—	—	—	—	—	—	—	—	—	F	—	—	—	—	—	—	—	—	—	—	—	—	—	—	—
Gujarat	—	—	—	—	—	F	F	—	F	—	F	—	—	—	—	—	—	—	—	F	—	—	—	—	F	F
Bombay	—	—	—	—	—	F	F	—	F	—	F	F	—	—	—	—	—	F	—	F	F	—	F	F	F	F
Berar	—	—	—	—	—	—	—	—	—	—	—	—	F	—	F	—	—	—	—	—	—	—	—	—	F	F
Hyderabad	—	—	—	—	—	F	F	F	—	—	—	—	F	—	F	—	—	—	—	F	—	—	F	—	F	F
Madras	—	—	—	F	F	—	—	—	—	—	—	—	—	—	—	—	F	—	—	F	F	F	F	F	F	F
Mysore	—	—	—	—	—	—	—	—	—	—	—	—	—	—	—	—	—	—	—	F	—	—	—	F	—	—
Burmah	—	—	—	—	—	—	—	—	—	—	—	—	—	—	—	—	—	—	—	—	—	—	—	—	—	—
PROVINCES AFFECTED TOTAL	1	2	1	4	1	3	3	1	2	1	3	1	2	1	2	1	4	6	3	6	2	3	3	8	13	9

Source: Sharma (1972).

TABLE 6.3(A). Net Domestic Product, in 1946–1947 Prices, of India by Sector (Selected Years, 1868–1900) (Rs million)

Year	Animal husbandry	Forestry	Fishing	Mining	Manufac- turing	Small-scale and services	House rent	Foreign earnings	Agri- culture	Govern- ment	Net product
1868–9	4,263	100	196	12	41	8,162	717	– 392	15,486	1,708	30,293
1872–3	4,466	111	203	10	61	8,362	729	– 416	16,513	1,743	31,782
1882–3	5,008	128	216	34	282	8,196	738	– 484	17,632	1,833	33,583
1884–5	5,210	132	219	42	332	8,884	752	– 499	17,371	1,851	34,294
1885–6	5,309	134	220	39	353	8,943	759	– 506	18,488	1,861	35,600
1886–7	5,410	136	222	42	362	8,972	766	– 514	17,432	1,870	34,698
1887–8	5,513	138	224	47	404	9,032	773	– 522	19,028	1,880	36,517
1888–9	5,617	140	225	51	446	9,060	780	– 530	19,415	1,889	37,093
1889–90	5,724	142	227	59	481	9,121	787	– 533	18,420	1,898	36,321
1890–1	5,833	145	228	65	518	9,181	794	– 546	20,134	1,908	38,260
1891–2	5,944	148	230	70	545	9,242	801	– 554	16,398	1,917	34,741
1892–3	6,057	151	232	76	557	9,271	802	– 563	19,020	1,927	37,530
1893–4	6,172	153	233	77	589	9,332	803	– 571	19,755	1,937	38,480
1894–5	6,289	155	235	85	661	9,393	804	– 580	20,081	1,947	39,070
1895–6	6,429	158	236	106	685	9,455	805	– 589	18,867	1,957	38,109
1896–7	6,361	161	238	116	747	9,484	806	– 598	16,017	1,967	35,299
1897–8	6,496	163	240	122	774	9,546	806	– 607	22,222	1,977	41,749
1898–9	6,699	166	241	139	792	9,575	807	– 616	22,044	1,987	41,834
1899–1900	6,767	169	243	153	870	9,604	808	– 625	18,590	1,997	38,576

Source: Heston (1983).

TABLE 6.3(B). Net domestic product, in 1946–7 Prices, of India by Sector, 1900–1947

Year	Agriculture (S)	Animal husbandry	Forestry	Fishing	Mining	Manufacturing	Small-scale industry	Government (S)(a)	Professions	Other services	Other commerce	House rent	Foreign trade (H)a	Agriculture	Government (H)	Net product (S)	Net product (H)
1900-1	21,872	6,767	172	244	199	664	3,852	1,032	1,348	530	3,938	809	-635	19,660	2,381	40,792	39,929
1901-2	20,419	6,974	172	255	208	1,023	3,984	1,053	1,431	552	4,680	886	-693	16,000	2,161	40,944	39,633
1902-3	23,058	7,177	189	261	211	1,080	4,153	1,110	1,502	564	4,902	895	-738	21,130	2,104	44,364	43,430
1903-4	23,078	7,237	175	272	231	1,116	4,344	1,179	1,579	610	5,026	982	-802	21,259	2,048	45,027	44,075
1904-5	22,525	7,312	192	284	244	1,161	4,667	1,252	1,669	638	5,099	1,018	-791	20,655	2,004	45,270	44,152
1905-6	21,672	7,439	192	289	258	1,372	4,292	1,277	1,573	592	5,278	1,017	-796	19,719	1,955	44,455	43,180
1906-7	22,791	7,558	172	301	273	1,410	4,397	1,327	1,616	604	4,940	1,003	-688	20,834	1,934	45,704	44,354
1907-8	19,973	7,691	183	315	291	1,236	4,320	1,352	1,632	595	4,741	1,213	-685	18,086	1,891	42,657	41,309
1908-9	20,486	7,693	180	327	293	1,241	4,005	1,301	1,508	539	4,834	1,049	-713	18,905	1,811	42,743	41,672
1909-10	25,483	7,468	192	338	289	1,341	4,554	1,388	1,690	598	5,349	1,147	-857	24,166	1,827	48,980	48,102
1910-11	25,389	7,678	223	347	305	1,270	4,818	1,465	1,798	632	5,437	1,198	-891	24,542	1,897	49,669	49,254
1911-12	24,213	7,831	220	350	307	1,277	5,308	1,559	1,973	690	5,437	1,215	-827	23,514	1,882	49,553	49,177
1912-13	23,521	8,114	243	347	327	1,510	5,009	1,691	1,899	659	5,505	1,253	-788	22,577	1,996	49,290	48,651
1913-14	21,455	8,625	243	341	347	1,415	4,901	1,717	1,835	653	5,465	1,273	-757	20,641	1,999	47,513	46,981
1914-15	23,317	8,254	235	332	340	1,450	4,757	1,720	1,903	681	5,463	1,321	-755	22,881	1,967	49,018	48,829
1915-16	24,370	8,140	237	330	338	1,571	4,883	1,767	1,826	638	5,392	1,325	-685	23,974	1,987	50,132	49,956
1916-17	26,112	7,982	246	321	363	1,537	5,215	1,921	1,995	690	5,182	1,307	-605	25,833	2,102	52,266	52,168
1917-18	25,906	7,844	257	316	370	1,504	5,246	2,084	1,986	706	4,761	1,295	-613	25,340	2,241	51,667	51,258
1918-19	18,481	8,106	249	312	381	1,428	4,957	2,318	1,878	669	4,551	1,330	-443	17,760	2,507	44,217	43,685
1919-20	25,343	8,329	283	310	376	1,517	3,892	2,325	1,518	539	4,811	1,319	-449	25,165	2,644	50,113	50,254
1920-1	21,209	8,615	243	301	347	1,624	4,116	2,369	1,610	570	4,935	1,325	-510	19,068	2,681	46,754	44,925

1921–2	23,784	8,729	272	301	320	1,664	4,218	2,207	1,669	592	5,265	1,517	−663	23,759	2,457	49,855	50,080
1922–?	24,850	8,703	303	304	311	1,649	4,858	2,472	1,943	715	5,490	1,652	−774	24,895	2,616	52,476	52,665
1923–4	22,878	9,033	286	304	338	1,395	5,536	2,713	2,250	872	5,367	1,727	−871	22,885	2,818	51,826	51,940
1924–5	23,357	9,144	280	315	356	1,831	5,736	2,781	2,337	940	6,056	2,064	−882	23,296	2,836	54,310	54,304
1925–6	22,798	8,890	292	312	361	1,882	5,856	2,700	2,423	998	6,609	2,203	−932	22,961	2,755	54,392	54,610
1926–7	22,894	9,355	286	315	372	2,139	5,597	2,699	2,349	995	7,000	2,291	−968	22,857	2,730	55,324	55,318
1927–8	22,345	9,176	292	318	390	2,413	5,819	2,815	2,438	1,072	7,187	2,372	−1,063	22,496	2,800	55,574	55,710
1928–9	23,217	9,298	272	318	390	1,927	5,973	2,859	2,497	1,140	6,848	2,407	−968	23,646	2,805	56,178	56,553
1929–30	23,770	9,568	283	321	410	2,406	6,130	2,956	2,577	1,242	7,285	2,499	−982	24,654	2,850	58,465	59,243
1930–1	24,124	9,204	266	327	387	2,181	6,875	2,959	2,743	1,362	6,308	2,565	−1,010	24,453	2,727	58,291	58,388
1931–2	24,064	9,126	266	330	356	2,286	6,367	2,945	2,743	1,359	6,354	2,690	−1,168	24,746	2,636	57,718	58,091
1932–3	24,140	9,116	266	330	327	2,477	6,342	2,888	2,851	1,392	6,399	2,753	−1,232	24,690	2,539	58,053	58,254
1933–4	23,917	9,152	272	332	331	2,353	6,536	2,972	2,974	1,436	6,280	2,896	−1,391	24,427	2,573	58,060	58,171
1934–5	23,774	9,349	289	338	374	2,653	6,721	3,033	2,866	1,365	6,379	3,081	−1,332	24,444	2,614	58,890	59,141
1935–6	23,597	9,295	312	341	408	2,869	6,176	3,101	2,817	1,343	6,624	3,104	−1,391	24,370	2,742	58,596	59,010
1936–7	26,016	9,617	306	344	414	3,143	5,779	3,149	2,663	1,279	6,510	3,125	−1,471	26,861	2,694	60,874	61,264
1937–8	25,016	9,593	329	344	475	3,351	5,825	3,221	2,574	1,211	7,235	3,086	−1,310	25,874	2,744	60,950	61,331
1938–9	22,298	9,817	355	347	459	3,789	6,324	3,262	2,654	1,254	7,851	3,350	−1,330	23,523	2,746	60,430	61,141
1939–40	24,177	9,910	343	350	475	3,901	6,102	3,468	2,534	1,214	7,596	3,323	−1,068	25,234	2,915	62,325	62,829
1940–1	24,710	9,721	352	355	578	3,963	6,044	3,888	2,432	1,158	7,515	3,200	−938	25,357	3,271	62,978	63,008
1941–2	23,690	9,988	352	355	647	4,765	5,271	4,272	2,244	1,075	7,588	3,131	−557	24,801	3,638	62,821	63,298
1942–3	24,926	9,962	375	358	683	5,191	4,316	5,042	1,807	940	7,318	2,932	−280	26,051	4,469	63,570	64,122
1943–4	26,572	9,970	409	358	616	5,790	3,162	5,121	1,321	622	7,212	2,566	−82	27,515	5,133	63,637	64,592
1944–5	25,459	9,882	438	361	466	5,676	4,791	6,046	2,013	952	8,093	2,503	−63	26,636	5,979	66,617	67,727
1945–6	23,984	10,055	312	361	475	6,124	5,665	6,144	2,386	1,078	9,047	2,557	−57	25,230	6,039	68,131	69,272
1946–7	23,907	10,110	432	364	430	4,841	5,979	5,253	2,432	1,026	8,681	2,501	−49	24,899	5,253	65,907	66,899

a. S = Sivasubramonian's (1965) estimates; H = Heston (1983).

Source: Heston (1983).

TABLE 6.4(A).   Trends in Per Capita Income in India (1946–1947 Prices)

Year	S[a]	H
1868–9	—	120 (73)
1870	—	—
1872–3	—	125 (76)
1890	—	134 (82)
1900	—	145 (88)
1902[b]	147 (90)[c]	147 (90)
1910	157 (96)	154 (90)
1920	164 (100)	164 (100)
1930	171 (104)	171 (104)
1935	166 (101)	166 (101)
1940	169 (100)	169 (100)
1945	163 (99)	166 (101)
1950	—	—

a. Based on (S) Sivasubramonian (1965) and (H) Heston (1983).
b. The 1902 estimates are 3-yr. averages; for all other years after 1900 they are 9-yr. averages.
c. Figures in brackets are index nos. of per capita real income (1920 = 100).
Source: Kumar and Krishnamurty (1981).

TABLE 6.4(B).   Growth of Net Domestic Product, at 1946–1947 Prices, for Selected Sectors

Sector	Average 1900/1–1904/5 (Rs m.)	Average 1940/1–1946/7 (Rs m.)	Increase (%)
1868–1900:			
Agriculture	15,486	20,952[a]	35.3
Manufacturing	41	870	2,022.0
Small-scale manufacturing and services	8,162	9,604	17.67
Government	1,708	1,997	16.92
NDP	30,293	38,576	27.34
1900–1945:			
Agriculture (S)[b]	22,190	24,970	12.6
Agriculture (H)[b]	19,737	25,966	31.6
Manufacturing (S)	1,009	5,524	447.5
Small-scale industry (S)	4,200	4,783	13.9
Government (S)	1,125	5,521	390.8
Government (H)	2,139	5,375	151.3
NDP (S)	43,277	64,572	49.2
NDP (H)	42,244	66,422	57.2
Population (m.) (S)	288.0	405.6	40.8

a. Average of 1897–1900.
b. S = Sivasubramonian (1965); H = Heston (1983).
Source: Heston (1983).

an annual compound rate of growth of 0.60 per cent, in the sixty years between 1868-9 and 1930. This was an extremely modest rate in comparison with Japan, the US, and Germany, but also in comparison with many tropical producers, such as Burma, Thailand, Ceylon, and Malaya.[7] It was also much lower than the annual rate of 1.5 per cent compound achieved to date in post-Independence India (1950-1 to 1977-8).

However, as can be seen from Table 6.4, there is likely to have been a progressive deceleration in the per capita incomes rate of growth between 1902 and 1930, and a decline in the last fifteen years of British rule.

In Tables 6.1, 6.3, and 6.4 show that, since 1920, it has been growth in population (1.22 per cent p.a.) relative to output which explains the downward trend in per capita income. For net domestic product increased rapidly at an overall annual compound rate of growth of 1.55 per cent between 1920 and 1946, with an annual compound rate of growth of 2.6 per cent compound between 1920 and 1930. From the more speculative nineteenth century data it would appear that the rise in per capita income was due to modest increases in output between 1870 and 1890 which were, however, greater than the increases in population during this period. Between 1890 and 1920, there are marked fluctuations in output, but with a steady increase in population. Not too much should of course be read into these figures. What they do show, however, is that it is erroneous to believe that per capita incomes stagnated or even declined, as has been asserted by nationalist historians, economists, and politicians.

3. SECTORAL OUTPUT GROWTH

Heston has estimated the net national product by sector for 1868-1900 (Table 6.3). These figures also show the sectoral growth of output for the nineteenth century. There was a very large increase in manufacturing output, starting from a low base. The growth in government, by contrast, was fairly modest. Table 6.4 (*b*) summarizes Heston and Sivasubramonians estimates of the growth of net domestic product between 1900 and 1946 for selected sectors (at constant 1946-7 prices). Basing ourselves on Heston, it appears that, between 1900 and 1947, in the last half-century of British rule, the fastest-growing sectors were the Government sector (which consists of commercial public undertakings such as railways, irrigation, and electricity, and also the bureaucracy) and modern industry. But even in 1945, having started from a low base, *modern* industry accounted for only 9 per cent of national income. Industry as a whole accounted for 17 per cent of national income in 1945, and its small-scale industrial component grew by about only 14 per cent between 1900-45, according to Sivasubramonian (1977).[8]

4. EMPLOYMENT GROWTH AND OCCUPATIONAL STRUCTURE

Tables 6.5, 6.6, and 6.7 summarize the best available evidence on the structure of employment from 1881 to 1951. The only acceptable assertion that can be made on the basis of these tables is that there was not much change in the

TABLE 6.5. The Industrial Distribution of the Working-force in Undivided India, 1901–1951

Activity	Average	1901 (%)	1911 (%)	1921 (%)	1931 (%)	1951 (%)
Cultivators	M	53.2	53.5	55.9	49.8	54.4
	F	43.6	41.0	48.1	30.4	45.7
	P	50.3	49.6	53.5	44.3	52.2
Agricultural labourers	M	14.3	15.4	14.4	19.5	16.4
	F	30.2	32.5	28.0	43.8	34.5
	P	19.1	20.8	18.6	26.3	21.1
Livestock, forestry, fishing,	M	4.2	4.9	4.3	4.9	2.9
hunting; and plantations,	F	2.9	3.2	3.2	3.8	2.3
orchards and applied	P	3.8	4.4	4.0	4.6	2.4
activities						
Mining and quarrying	M	0.1	0.1	0.2	0.2	0.4
	F	0.1	0.2	0.3	0.2	0.3
	P	0.1	0.2	0.2	0.2	0.4
Manufacturing	M	9.5	9.1	9.0	8.4	9.1
	F	11.4	10.9	8.4	8.8	7.7
	P	10.1	9.6	8.8	8.5	8.7
Construction	M	1.1	1.3	1.1	1.2	1.4
	F	0.8	0.8	0.8	0.9	0.9
	P	1.0	1.2	1.0	1.1	1.3
Trade and commerce	M	5.8	5.5	5.9	5.9	6.1
	F	3.5	5.3	5.2	4.8	2.8
	P	5.1	5.4	5.7	5.6	5.2
Transport, storage and	M	1.5	1.5	1.3	1.4	1.9
communications	F	0.2	0.2	0.2	0.1	0.2
	P	1.1	1.2	1.0	1.1	1.5
Other services	M	10.2	8.3	7.8	8.6	7.8
	F	7.2	5.9	5.7	7.1	5.6
	P	9.3	7.6	7.2	8.2	7.2
TOTAL WORKERS	M	100	100	100	100	100
	F	100	100	100	100	100
	P	100	100	100	100	100

Source: Krishnamurty (*CEHI*, vol. ii, p. 535, table 6.2).

industrial and occupational structure of the work-force over this fairly long period. These all-India trends mask some differing regional trends. 'In Kerala, Maharashtra, Madras and West Bengal there was a relative shift in the work force away from agriculture, while in Orissa and Rajasthan there was a shift towards agriculture. Also within the manufacturing sector, employment in factories grew while employment in the non-factory sector declined between 1901 and 1951.'[9]

TABLE 6.6.   Structure of the Male Work-force 1881–1911

Sector	1881 (%)	1911 (%)
Cultivators	51.7	53.5
Agricultural labourers	10.7	13.4
General labour	8.3	2.7
Plantations, forestry, fishing, etc.	1.7	4.9
Mining and quarrying	0.1	0.1
Manufacturing	10.6	9.1
Construction	0.5	1.1
Trade and commerce	4.9	5.5
Transport, storage, and communication	1.8	1.7
Other services	9.8	7.7
TOTAL WORKERS	100	100

Source: Krishnamurty (*CEHI*, vol. ii, p. 534, table 6.1).

The growth in employment in the three sectors—primary (agriculture), secondary (manufacturing and mining), and tertiary (others)—from 1901 to 1971 is shown in Table 6.7, which also shows (in (*b*)) the average annual compound rates of growth of employment for three periods, 1901–31, 1931–51, and 1951–71, as well as the percentage share of the three sectors in generating employment. The right most column of this table gives the overall all-India participation rate, while Table 6.8 shows the trends in participation rates of males and females, by State, for 1911, 1951 and 1961. The major features these tables highlight are:

(*a*) the possibly small decline in secondary employment in manufacturing and mining between 1900 and 1931;

(*b*) the continuing importance of agriculture in the seventy years 1901–1971 in absorbing 75–80 per cent of the increased employment in the labour force;

(*c*) some fall in the overall participation rate since 1921 when the Indian demographic explosion began (see Table 6.1).

This last factor is explicable in terms of the changes in the age-structure of the population, an increase in schooling, and a relative shift from rural to urban areas, all of which would tend to lower the participation rate.[10]

5. URBANIZATION, LITERACY, AND INFANT MORTALITY

Table 6.9 provides the data on urbanization between 1901 and 71. It shows that, while in 1901 only 11 per cent of the population lived in urban areas, by 1951 this proportion had reached 17 per cent.

TABLE 6.7(A).   Employment by Sector in Indian Union, 1901–1971: Census Data (millions)

Census years	Agriculture: livestock, fishery, and forestry		Mining and manufacturing		Others		Total	Participation rate
	No.	%	No.	%	No.	%		
1901	79.3	—	13.1	—	18.3	—	110.7	46.4
1911	88.2(1)[a]	72.3	12.0(−10)	9.8	21.8(19)	17.9	122.0(11)	48.4
1921	87.7(−1)	73.1	10.8(−11)	9.0	21.5(−1)	17.9	120.0(−2)	48.0
1931	89.2(2)	72.0	10.8(0)	8.7	23.9(11)	19.3	124.0(3)	44.5
1941	89.3(0)	74.0	11.1(3)	9.2	20.3(−18)	16.8	121.0(−3)	38.0
1951	101.9(14)	72.8	13.0(17)	9.3	25.1(24)	17.9	140.0(16)	38.8
1961	137.8(35)	73.0	19.6(51)	10.4	31.3(25)	16.6	188.7(35)	43.0
1971	167.3(21)	73.8	22.4(14)	9.8	37.2(19)	16.4	226.9(20)	41.0

a. Figures in brackets give % change over preceding year.

Sources: (1) Government of India (1980), Annexure l which cites (*a*) Census of India, 1961 Monograph 4, p. 25 for 1911 and 1951; (*b*) Census of India, 1961 general economic tables, pt. II–B(i) for 1961; (*c*) adjusted census data for 1971, estimated by Manpower Planning Division, Planning Commission. (2) 1901 figures are from Satyanarayana (1981, table 4) (based on census data).

TABLE 6.7(B). Changes in Employment, 1900–1971

Period	Agriculture	Mining and manufacturing	Other	Total
1901–31:				
Average annual compound rate of growth (%)	0.39	− 0.64	0.89	0.38
Increase in employment (m.)	9.90	− 2.30	5.60	13.3
Share in employment generated (%)	74	− 17	2	100
1931–51:				
Average annual compound rate of growth (%)	0.67	− 0.93	0.25	0.61
Increase in employment (m.)	12.70	2.20	1.20	16.00
Share in employment generated (%)	79	14	8	100
1951–71:				
Average annual compound rate of growth (%)	2.51	2.76	1.99	2.44
Increase in employment (m.)	65.40	9.40	12.10	86.90
Share in employment generated (%)	75	11	14	100

Sources: as for Table 6.7(*a*).

TABLE 6.8. Trends in Work-force Participation Rates in India and the States, 1911, 1951, and 1961 (Percentages)

	1911		1951		1961	
	Males (%)	Females (%)	Males (%)	Females (%)	Males (%)	Females (%)
Andhra Pradesh	62.5	41.6	52.6	21.2	62.2	41.3
Assam	62.1	39.0	54.4	30.7	54.3	31.8
Bihar	62.5	34.7	49.1	20.7	55.6	27.1
Gujarat	58.6	30.0	51.7	28.0	53.5	27.9
Jammu and Kashmir	59.5	33.7	—	—	57.8	25.6
Kerala	53.6	28.0	46.7	18.1	47.2	19.7
Madhya Pradesh	64.7	47.9	60.4	37.9	60.2	44.0
Madras (Tamil Nadu)	60.6	36.5	45.7	12.7	59.7	31.3
Maharashtra	62.5	39.8	56.8	33.3	57.1	38.1
Mysore (Karnataka)	54.9	25.3	49.6	18.1	58.4	32.0
Orissa	60.6	30.4	56.3	18.8	60.8	26.6
Punjab	60.1	11.9	54.9	17.2	52.9	14.2
Rajasthan	63.5	45.4	59.4	38.3	58.1	35.9

TABLE 6.8. *contd*

	1911		1951		1961	
	Males (%)	Females (%)	Males (%)	Females (%)	Males (%)	Females (%)
Uttar Pradesh	65.1	33.3	59.7	23.6	58.1	18.1
West Bengal	62.9	18.8	54.2	11.6	54.0	9.4
INDIA	62.0	33.9	54.3	23.3	57.1	28.0

Source: Census data, taken from Government of India (1970, p. 1977, tables 2 and 3). This report is hereafter referred to as the Dantwala Committee.

TABLE 6.9. Trends in Literacy, Urbanization, and Infant Mortality, 1901–1971

Year	% literate in total population			% urban population to total	Infant mortality 100% live births
	Average	Male	Female		
1901	5.4	9.8	10.7	10.8	295
1911	5.9	10.6	1.1	10.3	282
1921	7.2	12.2	1.8	11.2	247
1931	9.5	15.6	2.9	12.0	227
1941	16.1	—	—	13.9	199
1951	16.7	25.6	7.9	17.6	146 +
1961	24.0	34.4	13.0	16.0	140 +
1971	29.5	39.5	18.7	19.9	

Sources: Literacy rates from Government of India (1971), series 1, India paper 1 of 1971 supplement, provisional population totals, p. 37. Urbanization figures are from Bose (1965). Estimates of infant mortality and expectation of life are from Das Gupta (1971). 1961 and 1971 infant mortality rates are from Government of India (1971, table VS3).

TABLE 6.10. Expectations of Life at Birth, 1881–1971

Census year	Male	Female
1881	23.67	25.58
1891	24.59	25.54
1901	23.63	23.96
1911	22.59	23.31
1921	19.42	20.91
1931	26.91	26.56
1941	32.09	31.37
1951	32.45	31.66
1961	41.89	40.55
1971[a]	46.40	44.70

a. Based on 10% and 20% urban sample.

Source: Government of India (1980, table 9).

The literacy rate rose from 5 per cent in 1901 to 17 per cent in 1951 and nearly 30 per cent in 1971, but the marked differences in the levels and spread of education between males and females persisted over the period.

Table 6.9 gives the figures for infant mortality and Table 6.10 for life expectancy, derivable from the census for 1901–1971. These show a 33 per cent decline in infant mortality and 39 per cent increase in life expectancy over the period 1901–51. But much of the improvement in life expectancy came in the 1930s.

NOTES

1. The most notable amongst these nationalist analyses is that of R. C. Dutt, while its persistence even in our day is attested to by e.g. Thorner and Thorner (1962) Patel (1965), Chandra (1968), and Bagchi (1976). The major questioning of this 'canonical tradition' is contained in the writings of Morris D. Morris, D. Kumar, A. Maddison, and A. Heston, to cite the major protagonists. The recent *Cambridge Economic History of India*, vol. ii, presents the most balanced scholarly assessment available to date. See also Charlesworth (1982).
2. Morris (1968, p. 3).
3. Davis (1955, p. 280).
4. Ibid., 280.
5. See M. Mukherjee, K. Mukherjee, Blyn, Sivasubramonian, and Maddison.
6. Much of the uncertainty relates to measures of agricultural output, which in turn depends upon estimated agricultural yields. Heston (1973) has criticized Blyn's estimated agricultural yields and, in Heston (1983), also Sivasubramonian on the grounds that the official estimates on which these other authors rely, and which show declining agricultural yields between 1920 and 1947, are implausible (see Kumar and Krishnamurty (1981)). But the controversy continues. See e.g. Maddison (1985), who argues that Heston's post-1900 national income trends are too high. See also the symposium (1985) on the *CEHI*.
7. See Lewis (1970, 1978).
8. However, as Kumar and Krishnamurty (1981) note: 'Output in this sector is very difficult to estimate—Sivasubramonian takes census figures of employment (themselves unreliable), and multiplies by real wages which he estimates to have increased by 69% between 1900 and 1946–47. Heston argues that this increase is too high, although he too feels some increase in labour productivity probably took place' (p. 6).
9. Ibid., 11.
10. Krishnamurty (n.d.), states: 'it is difficult to quantify the contribution of each of these factors as we do not have age-specific WFR's (work force participation rates) for any year prior to 1961. It is, however, clear that the population aged 15–59 declined from 56.4% in 1911 to 54.1% in 1961; the decline was sharper for females, from 56.4% and 54.7% (Sinha 1972).' During the same period the share of urban areas in the total population increased from 10.29% to 19.05% (Bose (1965)).

7

The Economy under the Raj, II: Rural Development

INTRODUCTION

From the compendium of trends presented in Chapter 6, it would be fair to say that there was some modest agricultural growth during the near-century of direct British rule. This is largely dependent on our acceptance of Heston's (1973, 1978) reworking of Blyn's (1966) estimates of agricultural yield per acre.

Blyn's estimates show that, whilst foodgrain output per head, and gross availability of foodgrains per head (which includes domestic production and net supply from foreign trade) rose from 1891 until 1911, it declined thereafter (see Table 7.1). Heston (1973) argues that Blyn's estimates, are flawed as they depend upon an estimated trend decline in yield/acre for foodgrain crops of – 0.18 per cent p.a. during the 1891–1964 period. Using official revenue statistics, Blyn had found that the above overall trend was composed of a small rise in yields of 0.29 per cent p.a. into the first four decades (1891–1921) and then a more marked decline of – 0.44 per cent in the last four decades (1922–47) (see Table 7.2). The revenue yield estimates which Blyn used were designed to determine the revenue demand, and were based on a standard yield and a so-called 'annual condition factor' (for the relevant plots of land). Both these were subjective estimates, and Heston (1973), using comparisons between these revenue yields and more scientific crop-cutting experiments in the post-Independence period, argues that 'there were biases in the official yields per acre—particularly an upward bias from 1886 to 1897 and downward bias from about 1936 to 1946—in several areas of India'.[1] His agricultural growth and national income

TABLE 7.1. Food Output Availability, British India, 1891–1941

	Output food grain		Gross availability	
	lb. per head	Index	lb. per head	Index
1891–2	405	90.4	—	—
1892–3	477	106.4	466	102.4
1900–1	470	104.9	470	103.3
1910–1	565	126.1	497	109.2
1920–1	535	119.4	544	119.5
1930–1	448	100	455	100
1940–1	363	81	365	80.2

Source: Derived by Kumar (1967) from Blyn (1966).

TABLE 7.2. British India Yield per Acre of Crop Aggregates and Individual Crops: Average Trend Rates of Change, 1891–1942

Crop	1891–1942	1891–1911	1926–42
All crops	0.01	0.47	− 0.02
Foodgrains:	− 0.18	0.29	− 0.44
Rice	− 0.24	0.39	− 0.57
Wheat	0.38	1.25	0.02
Non-foodgrains:	0.86	0.81	1.15
Sugar-cane	0.73	1.03	1.20
Cotton	0.95	0.98	1.27

Source: Blyn (1966, p. 151, table 7.1).

TABLE 7.3(A). Average Annual Acreage in Various Categories British India, 1907/8–1916/17 and 1936/7–1945/6

	1907/8–1916/17 (million acres)	1936/7–1945/6 (million acres)	% change
All crop acreage	186.5	196.0	9.5
Total area sown	231.2	241.8	10.6
Area sown more than once	30.0	35.0	5.0
Net area sown	201.2	206.8	5.6
Not available for cultivation	95.6	85.4	− 10.2
Cultivable waste	74.4	73.9	− 0.5
Fallow	42.1	43.6	1.5
Forest	60.2	63.4	3.2
Above four categories	272.3	266.3	− 6.0
Total reported area	473.9	473.3	− 0.6

Source: Blyn (1966, p. 129, table 6.1).

TABLE 7.3(B). Average Trend Rates of Change in Crop Acreage British India, 1891–1941 (% p.a.)

	1891–1941	1891–1911	1926–42
All crops	0.40	0.67	0.35
Foodgrains	0.31	0.35	0.39
Non-foodgrains	0.42	0.86	0.03

Source: Blyn (1966, p. 131, table 6.2).

estimates, cited in Tables 6.4 and 6.5, are based on corrections for these biases. This modest agricultural growth at a compound rate of 0.6 per cent p.a. between 1900 and 1946 was the product of the likely increase (albeit modest) in yields and Blyn's estimates of the increase in cropped area (see Table 7.3).

As a result, food output kept pace with population. But does this mean that the mould in which traditional Indian agriculture had been set in ancient India was broken?

1. THE BOSERUP PROCESS

Following Boserup (see ch. 3), we would expect that, following the population explosion which can be dated from 1921, the Hindu equilibrium in agriculture would have been maintained with some expansion in acreage to meet the increased (near-subsistence) food needs of the mass of the population, but with little incentive for any marked intensification in agricultural technology. After 1921, however, with the rapid growth in population, a further intensification in agriculture would be required to maintain per capita food supplies. Moreover, this intensification would involve the adoption of various land-saving but labour-intensive methods in agricultural production. In Indian climatic conditions, multiple cropping requires the provision of an assured water supply usually through the artificial means of irrigation, which is in effect a method of using capital to substitute for land. From 1921, with the increase in population relative to the (initial) cropped area, we would expect that the Boserup response would be an increase in the ratio both of capital to labour and of capital to land as the ratio of land to labour declined.

Thus, if Boserup's thesis about the stages of agricultural development is correct we would expect that, during the first half-century of British rule, the slow growth of population would have been accommodated by an expansion of the net sown area, with little change in technology. After 1921, we would expect some technological change with an increase in the ratio of the capital input (which, in peasant agriculture, is itself primarily in the form of 'congealed', indirect labour inputs) to labour and to land.

Unfortunately, the available data do not enable us to test this hypothesis with any degree of rigour. Nevertheless, the data assembled in Table 7.4 are suggestive and broadly in support of Boserup's hypothesis. In this table, we present data on rural output and capital stock at constant 1970–1 prices, on agricultural labour force, and on net sown area and total sown area (which includes the area sown more than once) and the percentage of the net sown area irrigated for 1901, 1940–1, and the three end-years of the post-Independence decades, 1950–1, 1960–1, and 1970–1. It should be noted that the acreage figures are not strictly comparable for the pre- and post-Independence period, as the former cover British India and the latter the Indian Union, between which there is not a one-to-one correspondence. For British India includes areas of post-Independence Pakistan and excludes various native Indian States, whereas the figures for the Indian Union exclude the former but include the latter. Also, there are no reli-

TABLE 7.4. Some Macro-aggregates for Indian Agriculture, 1901–1971

	1901	1940–1	1950–1	1960–1	1970–1	% change 1901–40/1	% change 1950/-1970/1
Aggregates:							
NDP in agriculture at constant 1970/1 prices (Rs 10 m.)[a]	5,291	6,961	10,168	13,575	16,989	31.6	67.1
Labour force in agriculture (m.)[b]	79.3	89.3	103.6	119.1	129.9	12.6	25.4
Capital stock (Rs 10 m. constant 1970/1 prices)	—	—	5,848	9,729	13,204	—	125.8
Net sown area (m. ha.)[c]	81.42	83.69	118.75	133.20	140.80	2.8	18.6
Total area sown (m. ha.)[c]	93.56	97.85	131.89	152.77	165.79	4.5	25.7
% of net sown area irrigated[d]	16.9	17.6	17.6	18.5	22.10	4.1	25.6
Ratios:							
Output/labour (Rs/man)	667.2	779.5	981.5	1,139.8	1,206.5	16.8	22.9
Land/labour (ha./man) (i)	1.03	0.94	1.15	1.12	1.38	-8.7	-6.1
(ii)	1.18	1.10	1.27	1.28	1.28	-6.7	0.8
Capital/labour (Rs/man/index nos.)	(110)	(110)	564.5 (100)	816.9	1,016.5	0.0	80.0
Output/land (Rs/ha.) (i)	649.8	831.8	865.25	1,019.14	1,206.61	28.0	40.9
(ii)	565.5	711.4	770.95	888.59	1,024.73	25.8	32.9
Output/capital	—	—	1.74	1.40	1.29	—	-25.0
Capital/land (Rs/ha.) (i)	—	—	492.46	730.40	937.28	—	90.4
(ii)	—	—	443.40	636.84	796.13	—	79.6

	1900–40	1950–70
Elasticities:		
% change in output / % change in labour	2.5	2.5

TABLE 7.4. *contd*

	1900–40	1950–70
% change in land (i)	0.22	0.73
% change in labour (ii)	0.36	1.00
% change in capital		
% change in labour	(1.00)	4.95
% change in output (i)	11.29	3.51
% change in land (ii)	7.02	2.51
% change in output	(2.5)	0.53
% change in capital		
% change in capital (i)	—	6.8
% change in land (ii)	—	4.9

Notes: Brackets indicate approximation; (i) refers to net sown area for land and (ii) to total area sown.

Sources:

1. 1901–40:

   a. Output—Heston's estimates in table 6.4. His 1946–7 constant price estimates have been converted into constant 1970–1 prices by using the following series. From *Gazetteer of India*, vol. iii, p. 920, we have the following index numbers for wholesale prices, Base for 1939 = 100, 1951 = 434.8; the Base for 1952–3 = 100, for 1951 = 120.2, and for 1961 = 127.5. Linking these series together yields a value for the Base 1946–7 = 100 series of 268.08 for 1970–1.

   b. From table 6.7

   c. Net sown area and total sown area from Blyn (1966, p. 129, table 6.1).

   d. From table 7.5 and Government of India 1980. The figure for 1901 is for undivided India, the figure for 1940–1 is for the Indian Union for 1934–5.

2. 1950–70:

   Choudhury (1983) for all the data except for acreage figures from Government of India (1974, p. 45).

3. Capital/labour ratio index numbers are approximations from Shukla (1965) as cited in Shah (1974, p. 463).

able capital stock estimates for Indian agriculture before 1950–1.[2] However, from Shukla's (1965) work, however flawed, it would appear that there was probably little change in the capital/labour ratio in agriculture between 1900 and 1950. This is represented by the index numbers in brackets in row 3 of Table 7.4 (*b*).

Table 7.4 reveals some rather interesting stylized facts about the Indian agricultural economy in the periods 1901–1940/1 and 1950–1970/1. In both periods, there was a rise in the output to labour ratio, which accelerated in the second (post-Independence) period. This was due to a more rapid extension of both the net sown area and the double-cropped area, so that the total cropped area increased between 1950 and 1971 in percentage terms by as much as the rural work-force. More dramatic, however, was the change in the rate of capital formation in agriculture between the two periods, such that the capital/labour ratio, after being stagnant between 1900 and 1941, rose by about 80 per cent between 1950 and 1970. Part of this increased capital formation was of the land-saving variety (mainly in the form of irrigation, which makes multiple cropping possible),[3] but diminishing returns had already set in, with the output/capital ratio declining markedly as more capital was applied to a given land area and labour force. Clearly, in this second period, as compared with the first, capital was being used to substitute for land which was becoming scarce, as is evident from the steady decline in the land/labour ratio over the seventy year period (but note that the land/labour ratios in the two periods are not strictly comparable, for the reasons given above).

The hypothesis that it was the population growth caused by the exogeneous decline in mortality after 1921 (see Table 6.1) which was driving these changes is supported by the various crude elasticity estimates we can derive for our aggregates (Table 7.4). The elasticity of output with respect to labour supply remained relatively constant over the two periods, a corner-stone of Boserup's hypothesis. But the responses to the differing rates of labour supply increase differed markedly in the two periods. It should be noted that, even though the population explosion dates from the great divide of the 1921 census (see Table 6.1), given the lag involved in the maturing of humans (from the time they are born until they enter the labour force), the effects of the increasing population growth-rate on the rural labour supply were not felt until 1951 (see Table 6.7). Thus, whereas the rural work-force increased by 12.6 per cent between 1900 and 1940, it rose by twice that percentage in the twenty years between 1950 and 1971. We would therefore expect, on Boserup's hypothesis, that rising population pressures would be most potent in inducing a switch to more intensive methods of agricultural production in the post-Independence period (1950 onwards).

This is borne out by the elasticity estimates in Table 7.4. Thus, as noted above, whilst the elasticity of output with respect to labour supply remained unaltered, that of land and capital with respect to labour supply increased markedly from the pre-Independence period of low labour supply growth to the post-Independence period of more rapid labour supply growth. The elasticity of land double-cropped with respect to labour supply has risen to unity, both through the increase in new land and in multiple cropping (which, of course, is indirectly the result of the increased capital formation in land-saving techniques such as irrigation). But the most important factor in keeping constant the elasticity of output with respect to labour has been the marked rise in the capital–labour supply elasticity. As much of this capital formation is labour intensive, we can assume, following Boserup, that it is more likely that the increased labour supply has induced this increased capital formation rather than the other way round, a view implicit in much of the conventional wisdom, haunted as it is by the shade of Malthus.

If this argument is correct, it suggests that British agricultural policy in itself did not have a marked deleterious or favourable effect in changing the technological parameters of the Hindu equilibrium in rural India. We need to look instead at the factors which led to the post-1921 population explosion. These factors were: the public health measures which reduced mortality directly; the various indirect effects flowing from the stability engendered by the establishment of law and order; and the integration of the fragmented rural economy into the international economy, which raised per capita income levels (however modestly). They can be adduced as the underlying reasons for creating the incentives for adopting more intensive agricultural techniques—which, if widespread, could constitute an agricultural revolution in India. But before this inference can be accepted it is necessary to examine various obvious objections, and to look at a slightly more disaggregated story.

2. THE ROLE OF LEADING INPUTS: OVERALL TRENDS

In tropical Asian agriculture, the 'leading inputs' required to transform traditional agriculture are irrigation and the complex of complementary inputs represented by fertilizers, new seeds, and pesticides.[4] Two questions, therefore, are of importance in assessing agricultural progress or the lack of it during the British Raj. The first is: to what extent was this intensification of agriculture dependent upon the pursuit of particular public policies, in particular public investment in irrigation, agronomic research, and extension? The second: were public policies pursued with the optimal degree of vigour, given the available resources and technological knowledge? Our purpose in answering this question is not to defend or castigate the British Raj, but rather to show that, despite all efforts (or lack thereof), there was no structural transformation of India's agriculture.

In keeping with the dominant *laissez-faire* economic doctrines of the time, during the early part of British rule in India the Government did little by way of directly promoting agricultural progress. Rural development was sought through the creation of a new system of legally enforceable land rights and tenurial systems, and the development of productive irrigation schemes in the deltas of the major rivers, with the specific aim of raising additional revenues.[5] As for private investment, these irrigation schemes were to pay for themselves through water charges. They were financed by borrowing in London, and the justification for their being in public rather than private hands were the large indivisibilities in the capital expenditure involved, as well as obvious externalities in determining, enforcing, and monitoring water rights in the command areas.

After the 1870s, however, partly because of the series of famines in the country and the steady erosion of faith in the *laissez-faire* doctrines of the earlier era, the paternalist attitude outlined in Chapter 5 became predominant. In 1871, a separate Department of Agriculture was created in the Government of India. In 1880, a famine commission was appointed after the great famine of 1876–8.[6] In 1889, the first serious attempt to frame a policy of agronomic research tailored to Indian needs was made by commissioning a report from Dr J. A. Voelcker, consultant chemist to the Royal Agricultural Society.

Dr Voelcker's 'report has left its impress on all subsequent investigations dealing with agriculture in India and the Royal Commission of 1928 also drew largely on it'.[7] His remedies for the improvement of Indian agriculture were 'irrigation by canals, tanks and wells and the use of manures', better seeds and 'improvements in the system of land tenure'.[8] This advice was sound and has been the conventional wisdom on raising Indian agricultural productivity ever since.

The progress made in the provision of the leading inputs can be gleaned from the following tables. Quinquennial averages of net area irrigated from government and other sources between 1900 and 1930 in British provinces, for which comparable data were available, have been estimated by the National Commission on Agriculture (1976) and are given in Table 7.5 below. This shows the irrigated proportion of net sown area rising from 16.9 per cent in 1904–5 to 22.3 per cent in 1929–30. Until 1919–20, although both the area irrigated by public and private irrigation was expanded, the rate of expansion was greater in private irrigation. In the 1920s the expansion of irrigation slowed, but thereafter, until Independence in 1947, there was a modest expansion of irrigated area, primarily through government irrigation works. From Table 7.6 it is apparent that the greatest progress in irrigation was in Greater Punjab.

During the British period, 'farmyard manure and dung were used to bring about improvements in crop yields, but no statistics are available about the quantities used from year to year. Chemical fertilizers were available in small quantities and used only in coffee and tea plantations and for certain commercial cops. Production of ammonium sulphate in India was about 4.5 thousand tonnes in 1919 and all but 480 tonnes were exported and there were no imports. In 1925, of the estimated production of about 15 thousand tonnes, only about 7 thousand tonnes were retained in India. During the quinquennium ending 1929–30, average imports of chemical fertilizers were of the order of about 48.5 thousand tonnes.'[9] Blyn argues that some upward influence on yields was exerted by use of these inputs, 'but in the aggregate its effect was of virtually negligible significance'.[10]

Table 7.7 shows the progress made in the latter part of British rule in the provision of better seeds for rice, wheat, sugar-cane, cotton, and jute (crops which

TABLE 7.5. Net Area Sown and Area Irrigated, Undivided India, 1900–1930, and Indian Union, 1934–1950

Quinquennium ending	Net area sown (million ha.)	Area irrigated by government works (million ha.)	Area irrigated by wells (million ha.)	Net area irrigated (million ha.)	Percentage of col. 3 to col. 2	Percentage of col. 5 to col. 2
(1)	(2)	(3)	(4)	(5)	(6)	(7)
Undivided India:						
1900–5	78.1	7.5	—	13.2	9.6	16.9
1909–10	82.8	8.6	—	15.9	10.4	19.2
1914–15	84.1	9.5	—	18.0	11.3	21.4
1919–20	82.5	10.5	—	18.8	12.7	22.8
1924–5	84.3	10.4	—	18.6	12.3	22.1
1929–30	84.7	11.0	—	18.9	13.0	22.3
Indian Union:						
1934–5		5.0	4.8	17.1	—	17.6
1949–50		6.4	5.3	19.4	—	19.1

Source: Government of India (1976, p. 209, table 3.9, and p. 201).

TABLE 7.6.   Averages of Irrigated Land / Cultivated Land for Selected Periods, by Region

Region	First period (%)	Second period (%)	Years in each period
British India	21.6	23.6	1908/9–1921/2, 1922/3–1945/6
Greater Bengal	13.3	.15.0	as above
Madras	28.7	27.9	1907/8–1921/2, 1922/3–1945/6
United Provinces	28.7	29.4	1891/2–1917/18, 1918/19–1945/6
Greater Punjab	43.5	55.5	as above
Bombay–Sind	15.5	16.4	1891/2–1918/19, 1919/20–1945/6
Central Provinces	2.9	4.8	1891/2–1917/18, 1918/19–1945/6

Source: Blyn (1966, p. 187, table 8.3). Calculated from annual percentages in Appendix 8A, which are based on net area irrigated and net area sown data in *Agricultural Statistics*. Data for 1946–7 were not available.

TABLE 7.7.   Improved Seed Acreage as % of All-crop Acreage for 1922–1923 and 1938–1939, by Region

Region	1922–3	1938–9
Greater Bengal	0.8	6.2
Madras	1.2	8.5
United Provinces	1.0	5.0
Greater Punjab	5.5	32.9
Bombay–Sind	2.8	15.8
Central Provinces	2.0	8.1
British India	1.9	11.1

Sources: Derived from Blyn (1966, p. 200, table 8.6).

accounted for 90 per cent of the improved seed area). The most outstanding advance was made in wheat and cotton, in Greater Punjab, and to some extent, in Greater Sind.[11] Blyn (1966) estimates that 'if better seed improved yield per acre by as much as 50% on the average for all crops, then the 1938/39 yield per acre in Greater Punjab would have been about 13% higher than in 1922/23; this would represent a constant growth rate of about 0.75% p.a., which is close to the average increase of 0.90% per year in crop yield per acre in the last four reference decades'.[12]

There was also a marked expension in irrigation under the Raj (see Table 7.8). In 1894 about 12 per cent of the cultivated areas was irrigated, by 1938–9 this had doubled to 26 per cent. Over half this expansion in irrigated area was accounted for by public works.

There was some growth in agricultural education, with the number of agricultural colleges increasing from five to nine and their students from 445 to

TABLE 7.8(A). Development of Irrigation[a] in British India

Year	Total cropped area (million acres)	Total irrigated area (million acres)	Area irrigated by government works (million acres)	Percentage of cultivated area irrigated by	
				Government works	Private and public works
1894–5	197	24	—	—	12
1901–2	197	30	18.5	9	15
1913–14	219	46.8	25.0	11	21
1920–1	212	48.9	26.5	13	23
1925–6	226	47.5	27.3	12	21
1930–1	229	49.6	30.9	13	22
1935–6	227	51.0	30.0	13	22
1936–7[b]	231 (213)	51.6 (50.1)	30.4 (30.0)	13 (14)	22 (23)
1937–8[c]	213	52.8	32.5	15	25
1938–9	209	53.6	32.3	15	26

TABLE 7.8(B). Distribution of Irrigation by Province

Province	Area irrigated by government works (%)		% cultivated area, 1938–9[c]	Return on capital (productive works) (%)
	1935–6	1938–9		
Punjab	11.1	12.3	42.8	13.63
Madras	7.5	7.2	20.2	5.97
United Provinces	4.3	5.3	14.9	6.38
Sind	4.3	4.7	86.4	2.73
Bihar	0.6	0.7	3.5	5.71
Orissa	0.3	0.4	12.2	Unproductive
North-west frontier	0.4	0.5	19.4	9.72
Bombay	0.3	0.4	1.5	8.07
Burma	2.1	—	—	—

a. Compiled from *Statistical Abstract for British India*, and *Triennial Review of Irrigation in India*.
b. The figures in brackets exclude Burma.
c. Excluding Burma. In 1938–9 the capital outlay amounted to Rs 152.8 crores; net return on capital 5.89%; of production works only, 7.61%.

Source: Anstey (1952, p. 616, table x).

3,110. But as this growth was minute compared with the potential need for agricultural research and extension workers, it could not have had any marked effect on raising agricultural productivity. Nor was there much change in the type of agricultural equipment used during the first half of this century.[13]

Thus it is primarily through the expansion of irrigation (and the cropped area)

TABLE 7.8(C).　Distribution of Irrigation by Type of Works

Type of irrigation works	Area irrigated	
	1935–6 (%)	1938–9[a] (%)
Government canals	23.6	25.1
Private canals	3.8	3.8
Tanks	5.9	5.8
Wells	12.7	13.49
Other	5.0	6.5
TOTAL	51.3	54.5

a. Excluding Burma.
Source: as for Table 7.8(*b*).

that agricultural growth took place during the Raj. The question which remains is whether public investment in irrigation facilities was adequate—it being noted from Table 7.4 that the growth of the area sown which is irrigated has been much higher in the post-Independence period.

3. IRRIGATION

There are two distinct questions of interest in determining whether or not the mix and level of irrigation provision under the Raj was optimal. First, was it socially profitable? Secondly, given the available public resources, would it have been desirable to expand public irrigation works by even more than was done during the period?

In answering these questions it is necessary to consider the likely effects of irrigation in raising agricultural productivity in the agro-climatic conditions of the subcontinent. Map 7.1 provides a rough average rainfall map of India. It is apparent that, in general, water supply from natural rainfall increases markedly as one travels eastwards. Moreover, as rainfall increases the climatic conditions become favourable for cultivating paddy. Wherever paddy can be grown it is the favoured crop, as 'the per-hectare yield of paddy is the largest of any of the food-grain crops. This is so even in terms of the weight of the edible part or caloric value.'[14] Although rice is grown in India even in regions with less than 25 in. of rainfall in the sowing season, it is grown as an irrigated and not as a rainfed crop and, depending on their relative profitabilities, competes with other irrigated crops for acreage.[15] However, 'in regions of more than 200 inches of rainfall as in the districts adjoining the Western Ghats it is almost the only food crop grown. This crop is largely concentrated in Bengal, Bihar, Orissa, and Madras, and these provinces accounted for ⅔ of the total area under rice in British India.'[16]

Thus the role of irrigation in rice production depends crucially upon the

MAP 7.1   Mean Annual Rainfall and Regions of British India

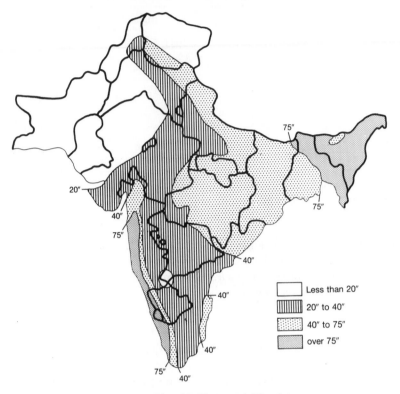

Source: Blyn (1966, p. 136, Fig. 6.2.

climatic conditions under which rice is grown. Ishikawa classifies the rice culture in Asia into four patterns.[17] The first is based on the pattern of floods in some of the principal riverine alluvial plains and deltas in Asia. This is the pattern in the Ganges delta. The paddy is sown with the first monsoon rains, it ripens when the floods that follow are at their height, and is mown after the water has receded.

In the second pattern, followed in the middle reaches of the Ganges, the crop is grown outside the flood season but relies on the utilization of the silt carried by floods.

In the third pattern, the crop is grown under rain-fed conditions or under the system of water fallow.

The fourth pattern is based on both irrigation and flood control or drainage to achieve a controlled water supply throughout the life cycle of the crop. This last system requires greater social-overhead investments in irrigation, flood control, and drainage. But it is the only system under which, with proper manuring and other cultural practices, rice yields can rise above the level of 2.3 tonnes (in terms of paddy) per hectare[18] produced by the other systems. In the other systems, however, irrigation and/or flood control are not essential in yielding the common subsistence yield of 1.3 tonnes per hectare.[19]

Thus paradoxically the marginal (social) returns on irrigation and flood control are likely to be higher in the regions of relatively low rainfall than in the higher rainfall regions. This is because, even without irrigation and flood control, in the flood- or silt-based systems of rice culture, respectable subsistence yields can be obtained. The shift to a more controlled water supply in these regions requires massive investments in multi-purpose irrigation systems incorporating both irrigation and flood control. By contrast, as floods rarely occur in the relatively drier regions, conventional irrigation systems will yield a controlled water supply. There is no need in these regions for the irrigation systems to incorporate expensive flood-control mechanisms.

The second difference is that a controlled water supply requires public investment in the region with flood- and silt-type patterns of rice culture but not in the drier regions. This is because investment in irrigation-cum-flood control systems (which have to cover the whole river basin) is lumpy and there are obvious external effects to be taken into account in flood control. However, as there are no floods to be tamed in the relatively drier regions, more decentralized and hence privately financed and managed irrigation and drainage systems will, depending upon their hydrology, by feasible.

Thus we would expect that in the course of the evolution of the Hindu equilibrium on the subcontinent, the different rice-growing areas would have acquired different degrees of irrigation intensities and thence yields per hectare for essentially climatic reasons. This is borne out by a comparison of West Bengal and Madras.[20] The former State has high rainfall and humidity, and its rice culture is based on annual flooding in the monsoon season. As a result, yields are low (1.6 tonnes/ha. in 1956). On the other hand, in Madras the available water supply from natural rainfall is insufficient for cultivating rain-fed rice. Hence for millennia this region has grown irrigated rice by using the water from wells and tanks. The greater control over the water supply which results gives 'paddy yields in some districts (including Salem and Coimbatore) of around 2.7 tons per hectare, the level of Japan's yield in the early Meiji era'.[21] Where lack of irrigation does not permit rice cultivation, low-value, drought-resistant cereals are grown. Thus, for the above reasons, given the ecological climatic conditions in the two regions, the marginal social returns to irrigation-cum-drainage will be higher in the low-rainfall as compared to the high-rainfall region, primarily because the investments in the irrigation-cum-flood control systems will be very much larger, and the incremental benefits (in terms of the increased value of rice output) lower than in the rain-fed areas.[22]

This also helps to explain the apparent paradox that the Hindu heartland of eastern India (Bihar, Bengal, and West Uttar Pradesh), in which the Aryans first established their highly productive agricultural settlements, has in more recent times become relatively the most backward part of the subcontinent. The prosperity of eastern India was based on the highly productive (in terms of labour and capital input per acre) flood plain method of paddy cultivation. The standard irrigation facilities could not have raised the productivity of this form of agriculture without massive investments in flood control. By contrast, the expansion of irrigation in the previously low-productivity dry regions of the west has led to their rapid agricultural development. The eastern Hindu heartland has thus declined in its relative rather than in its absolute income levels; the latter were set in ancient India and, as I have argued, have remained unsurpassed for millennia.

It has however been argued that there was an absolute decline in incomes in the eastern region during British rule. This is based in large part on the declining agriculture output trends for Bengal shown in Blyn's work. Given Heston's critique of Blyn's yield estimates, these trends are no longer plausible. However, one interpretative problem remains. Despite the growth of population in the region, the acreage cultivated declined by about 0.06 per cent per year between 1898 and 1946.[23] How can this be explained? The answer seems to lie in the natural shifting of river courses and areas of inundation in north-eastern India.[24] The major change was the shift in the flow of the Ganges system from the Bhagirathi–Hoogly River to the more eastern-coursing Padma River. 'This is the change which created the "moribund delta" between the Bhagirathi–Hoogly, Ganges and Padma Rivers.'[25] However, West Bengal's loss in this respect was East Bengal's gain. Thus, Narain notes that between 1900 and 1939, 'in striking contrast to the conditions obtaining in West Bengal, agriculture was undergoing an expansion in the eastern part of the province. . . . The region of expansion belonged to what has been described as the active delta. Here new soils richly endowed by rivers with silt were in a continuing process of formation. Clearance of forest areas and colonization of new "alluvial formations" jointly led to an expansion of agriculture.'[26]

Thus it would appear that eastern India's present agricultural plight is due not so much to public neglect, but to the fact that the Hindu equilibrium which had been established here in the sixth and fifth centuries BC represented a near perfect socio-economic adaptation to the natural environment. This does not mean that the social rate of return on a properly conceived and executed irrigation-cum-flood-control system in parts of eastern India would not be greater than the relevant social rate of discount. What it does suggest is that, *ceteris paribus*, for purely ecological reasons the social return on irrigation projects producing rice in drier regions is likely to be relatively higher. Thus, from a national planning viewpoint, only after these other intra-marginal projects are completed does it make sense to undertake the lower social rate of return investments in irrigation-cum-flood control in eastern India.

'The drier the region, the greater the marginal social returns from irrigation' is the (perhaps obvious) principle we have arrived at from this excursion into the ecology of rice cultivation. In fact there are certain parts of western India where there would scarcely have been any agriculture without irrigation. The agricultural growth in Punjab and Sind was a direct result of the expansion of the irrigated area.[27]

The regional trends in the expansion of the irrigated area under the British Raj (see Table 7.8) thus suggests that the expansion occurred in regions where the social rates of return on irrigation works was high. But there still remains the question whether, even in these regions, the expansion in the public provision of irrigation was desirable and the best use of available public investment resources. For the canal colonies established by the British in Punjab and Sind, there would seems to be little doubt that this was the case—a conclusion which is supported by one of the few cost–benefit studies available of irrigation in India by Raj (1960) of the post-Independence Bhakra dam. The Bhakra scheme, Raj found, would have been a marginal one by comparison with the building of a system of canals in the inter-riverine plains of the Indus. Its own estimated profitability thus confirms the higher social profitability of the earlier and clearly intra-marginal projects undertaken by the British.

The same sanguine view cannot, however, be taken about the need or the outcome of other public irrigation investments, either in British or in post-Independence India. Assessing the need and social profitability of public investment in irrigation essentially involves a comparison of the substitutability and relative profitability of what in Indian parlance are distinguished as major and minor irrigation works—the criterion for distinguishing between them being the relative capital costs of the irrigation structures set up. There is a monotonic relationship between the capital cost and acreage covered by most irrigation schemes. Thus, the major schemes provide water to a larger number of beneficiaries through irrigation structures which are common to the command area and hence implicitly shared by them. This creates obvious externalities which rule out the private, individualistic development of these schemes. By contrast the minor schemes, involving less lumpiness in investment and covering a smaller acreage, also limit their benefits to fewer beneficiaries, and hence can more easily be executed in a decentralized manner.

Secondly, as the minor schemes predominantly tap ground water whilst the major ones (by and large) utilize surface water, the question of public versus private provision of irrigation water is to a large extent a choice between the use of ground or surface water for irrigation.[28] In judging the adequacy of public investment in irrigation we thus first need to assess the potential and need for public investments in the optimal provision of ground water in the country.

(i) Ground water

Broadly speaking, India can be divided into the region of peninsular India covered by the Deccan trap of volcanic rock formation and the alluvial plains of the great northern river systems, the coastal plains, and the river valleys and deltas of the Godavary and Krishna in central and southern India. The 'Deccan trap' refers to the embedded aquiferous beds, trapped within distinct horizontal layers of volcanic rock.[29] These beds are fed by water through percolation from the overlying rocks. A successful well is one which has been bored to tap one of these aquifers. However, the depth at which these beds will be found, their size and likely yield will vary over the relevant region, depending as it does on the pattern of rock formation.

The drilling of a successful well, as well as its costs (which depend both upon the nature of the rock and upon the depth of the aquifer—see Lal (1972)) and its water yield will thus be highly uncertain in the absence of a hydro-geological survey of the region. Thus in the 'rain shadow' district of Ahmednagar in Maharashtra it was found that the probability of striking water in the absence of a hydro-geological survey was about 30 per cent.[30] With this likelihood of striking water, it was found that, even in the 1970s, in Ahmednagar, at positive shadow wage-rates, the social returns to digging wells for irrigating either a cereal or sugar-cane crop were at best marginal,[31] and depended crucially on the assumed output prices of the two crops. By contrast, with an improvement in the siting of wells following a hydro-geological survey, the social and private rates of return would be considerable. However, the relevant hydro-geological survey of the Deccan plateau had only just begun in the 1970s, private financing of such a survey being ruled out by the obvious externalities involved in the enterprise.

As such we would not have expected any dramatic increase in the number of wells in the Deccan plateau during the British Raj. But we would have expected some expansion, as indeed there was. For at certain times, even with the low probability of striking water, the private rates of return from wells would have increased for two reasons. First, as the costs of digging wells is in large part a function of the opportunity cost of labour, an expansion in labour supply would, *ceteris paribus*, have lowered these costs, and hence raised the private rate of return to the digging wells. Secondly, the returns would also vary with variations in the price of the outputs that could be produced with an improved water supply. With the increased market integration of India's village economies as a result of improvements in communications and the expansion of foreign trade, many village communities took up the production of commercial crops whenever their price relative to the more traditional foodgrain crops was favourable.[32] The variations in farm output prices of those villages integrated into a larger market would have followed a different pattern from that generated mainly by climatic variations within autarkic village communities.

Assuming, as is plausible, that the existing water supply had adjusted over the Hindu and Muslim millennia to the expected profitability of digging wells—based on fluctuations in prices which were largely weather-determined—the commercialization of agriculture during the Raj would have raised this expected profitability for two reasons. First was the new opportunity for producing cash crops whose mean value was higher than the traditional subsistence crops. Secondly, to the extent that the variations in the prices of commercial crops (which were linked to world prices) were not perfectly correlated with the weather-determined prices of the traditional subsistence crops (as they were unlikely to be, given India's small share in the export markets for most of these cash crops during the Raj), the variance in the value of the new crop mix would most likely have decreased. Because of the resulting increase in their expected profitability we would expect an increase in wells during the Raj in the Deccan trap regions, even in the absence of public investment in a hydro-geological survey.

Farmers of the alluvial plains—the second broad type of area—are more fortunate in that, once the depth of the water table is known (say by striking a few exploratory wells), it can be assumed that bores made to that approximate depth will strike water.[33] The uncertainty attached to digging a successful well in these regions is therefore considerably reduced. The spread of well irrigation in these regions would depend first upon the costs of digging the well, which would in turn depend upon the depth of the water table, and at least for much of Indian agrarian history (until the more recent development of tube wells) on the opportunity cost of labour—the major input in digging the well. Secondly, the spread of well irrigation would depend upon the returns from the well, which would in turn depend upon the marginal returns to irrigation. The latter depend on agro-climatic conditions as well as on the prices of the inputs and output of crops produced by utilizing the new water supply. As there was not much change in the agro-climatic conditions (except in eastern India, discussed above) nor in the expected prices (which were mainly weather-determined), the Hindu equilibrium of the past millennia would presumably have already taken these into account in determining the optimal supply of irrigation from wells. The new integration into the world market and commercialization of agriculture during the Raj would, however, have altered the expected price pattern from that of the Hindu equilibrium. This would mean that, even in this region, we would expect the relative profitability of wells to have changed and induced some changes in the acreage irrigated by them during the Raj. Our presumption being that, for the reasons given above, the mean and variance of the distribution of expected profitability of the crop mix chosen would have increased and decreased respectively.

(ii) Surface Water

The other major source of irrigation in India has been through surface water provided by tanks and canals. The latter source needs to be distinguished from both wells and tanks, as it requires large indivisible capital investments with the attendant problem of extracting their maintenance and running costs from the beneficiaries of the system. They normally, therefore, require some form of public investment and management (for keeping the canals in good repair), unlike the other two sources which, being small-scale, can be more easily financed by the savings of peasant families or village communities. The question then arises whether the public provision of irrigation was adequate under the British, noting (see Chapter 4) that even under the Moghuls its extent was very limited.

In analysing the adequacy or otherwise of the provision of a particular level of irrigation by surface-water (or for that matter ground-water) sources, estimates of the water response functions (i.e. the increase in yield per acre made possible by increasing the water supply at different stages in plant growth) for the relevant crops in the particular agro-climatic conditions of the area are required. Unfortunately, to this date, the estimation of water response functions for different crops and different regions is a grossly neglected area of research.[34] As a result, surface irrigation schemes in both the pre- and post-Independence periods have been designed on the basis of engineers' rather than economists' predilections.[35] Also, it would be too much to expect nineteenth century British irrigation engineers to be *au fait* with modern techniques of social cost–benefit analysis—which was not invented until the 1950s and 1960s. The schemes drawn up were thus essentially engineers' schemes which did not take account of all the possible direct and indirect economic effects, so that, instead of adding to real national income through high social rates of return, it is possible that at least some of them might have had negative or very low and thence very marginal social rates of return.

This presumption is buttressed by analyses of the effects of two large-scale surface-water irrigation schemes, both based on plans drawn up, and in one case executed, by British irrigation engineers, which we briefly discuss below. Before doing so, however, two points need to be stressed. As is evident from the above remarks, there is an important distinction between the technical (engineering) irrigation potential in different regions and its economic counterpart. The technical irrigation potential of the country has been estimated by the 1972 Irrigation Commission. On engineering criteria the fact that at Independence only a fraction of India's potential technical irrigation potential had been exploited might, as many commentators have stressed (see Maddison (1971, p. 50)) be taken to be a major failing of the Raj. But no such presumption follows as far as the utilization of the economic potential is concerned. Though the issue cannot be clinched in the absence of a proper social cost–benefit analysis of the various surface irrigation schemes developed during the British Raj, we would hypothesize that, given the available technology and knowledge of plant–soil moisture relationships and agro-climatic conditions at that time, it is likely that any further extension of public investment in large-scale surface irrigation would have been counter-productive.[36]

In support of this we cite evidence of the likely economic effects of two large-scale irrigation schemes on which some detailed information is available. The first are the great canal engineering works in the Doab, starting[37] with the East

Jumna Canal in the 1820s, and continuing with the Ganges Canal in 1847, the Lower Ganges Canal in 1868, and the Agra Canal in 1868. By 1877–8 the completed network of canals in the British North-west Province (modern-day Uttar Pradesh) consisted of 5,601 miles of channels and distributaries, irrigating an area of nearly 1.5 million acres. The system had cost (excluding interest payments) over £4 million of money borrowed from England.[38]

This system was begun during the pre-mutiny reforming phase of the British enterprise in India, and was motivated by the desire of the British, like Mohammed Tughlaq in years gone by (see ch. 4) to promote agricultural development by inducing farmers to shift to high-value, water-intensive and thence (in the absence of irrigation) risky crops such as cotton, indigo, sugar cane and wheat, from their traditional crops of millets (jowar and bajra) and pulses. In this they succeeded but with side-effects which the engineers designing the system had not foreseen.[39]

Whitcombe (1971) has documented how, side by side with the shift to this more profitable cropping pattern, canal irrigation also induced under-manuring, over-cropping, salination, the destruction of wells, and the creation of malaria-breeding swamps in the region. The traditional cropping pattern was based on the widespread use of shallow wells as a form of supplemental irrigation. In 1848–9 Baird-Smith estimated that there were 72,523 masonry wells (of a total of 137,337 for the North-west Province) each with a capacity of irrigating about 4.5 acres per season, and 280,000 temporary wells with an irrigating capacity of 1.5 acres each per season in the Doab. This yields a figure of about 1.5 million acres irrigated by wells in the Doab in 1847–8[40]—an area almost equal to that irrigated by the canal system in 1877–8.

But whereas the well irrigation provided supplemental irrigation, which presumably did not markedly increase the overall water intensity of the traditional crops grown (given their relatively lower marginal returns in terms of yields), canal irrigation enabled the overall water intensity per acre to be raised and hence induced the switch to higher-value, higher-yielding, fully irrigated crops. This higher water intensity was also promoted by keeping the charges for canal water relatively low. The rise in water intensity had predictable effects on the water-table, in increasing salinity and the consequent destruction of a substantial part of the cropped area. In 1891 Dr J. A. Voelcker in his famous report on agricultural conditions, found that in the North-west Province, nearly 4–5,000 square miles of land was affected by Reh.[41]

Nearly a hundred years later, similar effects were to result from the implementation in independent India of a large-scale surface irrigation scheme drawn up by colonial engineers for the Purna district in Central India,[42] but dusted off and implemented in the early 1960s. The major features of this scheme which need concern us are the complete variance between the planned and realized cropping patterns, and the resulting extreme under-utilization of the irrigation potential that was provided. As a result, the realized social return was only 5.5 per cent, as compared with the planned rate of return of about 16 per cent if the outcome projected in the appraisal report had actually occurred. The major reasons for this divergence between prospect and performance were the following. As the water-table in the command area is generally very high, great care had to be taken not to over-irrigate. This meant that the project planners laid down a cropping pattern in which water-intensive and highly privately profitable crops like sugar-cane, bananas, and other perennial cash crops were confined to well-drained areas near the river/canal beds. For the rest of the command area the scheme was meant to provide supplementary water to the natural rainfall in the region for the production of its traditional drought resistant crops like jowar (sorghum). How-ever, without any data on the water response function of sorghum, the project planners assumed that this supplemental irrigation would raise kharif (monsoon) sorghum yields from 187 kg/acre to 671 kg/acre, and rabi (winter/spring) sorg-hum yields from 187 kg/acre to 597 kg/acre. In practice, kharif yields were almost stationary at about 500 kg/ha though rabi yields rose from 250 kg/ha to 790 kg/ha. However, as the farmers normally grew an extended kharif sorghum crop which was not harvested until well into the rabi season and for which the water supply from natural rainfall is normally adequate (hence the lack of impact on these yields of irrigation), there was no demand for irrigation for sorghum in the rabi season, as the extended kharif season crop was traditional and gave high yields. The irrigation water was therefore used illegally to produce water-inten-sive crops, with the expected water logging effects and the destruction of a sub-stantial part of the cropped area in the command.

Whilst these two baleful stories underline the importance of the distinction between the technical and economic irrigation potential of major parts of India, and the factors—agronomic, climatic, and demographic—which are the deter-minants in translating the one into the other, there are obviously parts of the sub-continent where there is a more direct relationship between the two which is in large part dependent on the pattern and size of the water supply from natural rainfall. Thus the public development of surface irrigation schemes in north-western India (the Punjab and Sind) was obviously productive, whilst the schemes in our two woeful stories were not, because they overestimated the benefits from surface irrigation in areas where natural rainfall supplemented by wells was adequate to meet the water requirements of the traditional crops grown. The shift to more water-intensive crops resulting from the provision of additional water was socially disastrous because it led to waterlogging and the leaching of soils.

(iii) Conclusions

Our conclusions from this rather long excursus on irrigation can be brief. Irriga-tion is undoubtedly the major input in the development of agriculture. But the optimal form and level of provision of irrigation facilities depend upon climate, hydrology, and agronomy. It cannot be assumed that, because it is technically possible to tap surface or ground water, it would also be economic to do so. Nor can conservative peasant attitudes be blamed for the low irrigation intensities in the more heavily populated but higher-rainfall regions of India. The marginal returns (both private and social) to large-scale irrigation schemes in these regions are likely to be low, and certainly lower than those on the more intra-marginal projects designed to irrigate the relatively drier lands of the west. Even here, it cannot be assumed that the public execution of major irrigation schemes is socially more advantageous than the execution of small-scale minor irrigation works. Social cost–benefit analyses (until recently so rare in the design of public irrigation works in India) are essential to determine the relative desirability of the two types of scheme.

Nevertheless, there is clearly one area in which public investment was essential in optimizing potential social returns from irrigation, namely a hydro-geological survey of the ground water resources of the vast Deccan trap region. Even post-Independence India has neglected this task until fairly recently.

Judged by the above standards, the British record in promoting the one clear leading input for transforming traditional agriculture was very far from reprehensible. It is doubtful whether in the current state of technology and agro-economic knowledge any greater public investment in surface irrigation would have been socially justifiable—it being noted that, until the fairly recent arrival of the tube well, small-scale public irrigation works were unnecessary. That cultivators were keen and able to extend minor irrigation works themselves is shown by the large increase in the acreage irrigated by wells during British rule. The major constraints on the adoption of irrigation were ecological and partially demographic but not financial.

4. COMMERCIALIZATION OF AGRICULTURE

During the nineteenth century and as a direct result of various aspects of British rule, there was a steady commercialization of agriculture. There were two major factors. First, the creation, definition, and enforcement of saleable and mortgageable land rights under the different land revenue systems established by the British. Secondly, the improvement in internal communications primarily through railways, whose construction integrated the Indian economy into the world economy.

Nationalist and contemporary radical writers have seen a whole set of delete-rious effects flowing from this commercialization of agriculture. It has been argued that the combination of the new revenue system and its attendant crea-tion of a market in land and the integration of rural India into the world economy led to the exploitation of the peasantry by landlords, money-lenders, merchants, and the State. Rack-rented, crushed under the burden of mounting debt, newly proletarianized, and increasingly subject to famine because of the shift away from foodgrains to cash crops promoted by the integration into the world economy, the average Indian peasant suffered progressive immiserization during the British Raj, whilst the process of subinfeudation (particularly in eastern India) resulting from the creation of a land market and the high initial exactions of revenue by the British, provided a powerful brake on the advance of new technology in the agrarian sector.[43]

(i) Subinfeudation, technical change, and tax burdens

On the above canonical view, the beginnings of the deleterious effects of British rule on the agrarian economy are usually dated to the establishment of the new revenue systems and their accompanying creation of saleable land rights and thence a market in land. It is undoubtedly the case (see Chapter 5) that these changes, together with the heavy initial revenue demands made by the British, did lead to the growth of subinfeudation, as represented by the highly variegated 'patni' tenures in West Bengal.[44] Most nationalist and radical authors, however, have seen little economic virtue in these changes in tenure.[45] However, as we show in a formal model in the next section, it pays a risk-averse zamindar in conditions of climatic and hence income certainty to sub contract to other agents who are less risk-averse. This shifting of risk-bearing to those better able or more willing to bear it will be favourable for agricultural productivity.

* (a) The economics of subinfeudation   First it is necessary to provide some economic rationale for the process of subinfeudation.[46] This will allow us to assess whether or not it retarded rural development, *as compared with the Moghul system of land tenure it replaced*. There were two separate aspects of early British land policy—in particular the Permanent Settlement—which promoted subinfeudation. The first was the creation of clearly defined and saleable property rights of various forms in the rental shares of land. The second was the substitution of a fixed but permanent revenue settlement for the traditional Indian practice of collecting revenue as a share of a particular year's output.[47] To see the economic effects of these two changes, we consider a very simple two-period model of the agrarian economy (i) before and after the institution of legally enforceable land rights and (ii) before and after the permanent settlement of a fixed land revenue sum.

Because of climatic conditions the output on the landlord's farm, and hence his gross income—which we assume is a constant share (s) of the output[48]—is uncertain. In pre-British days, the landlord would *ex hypothesi* have had to pay a fixed share of the output (r) as revenue to the State, or its revenue agent. Suppose that there are only two weather-dependent states of nature, 'good' and 'bad' years which yield output Y^g in good and Y^b in bad years. The probability of occurrence of a good year is (p), and thence that of a bad year is ($1 - p$).

The expected net income (NYT) of the landlord under this traditional system will then be:

$$NYT = (s - r)(pY^g + (1 - p) Y^b) \qquad (4.1)$$

Assume that the landowner is risk-averse, so that his expected utility in the traditional system, given a utility function $U = U(NYT)$, is:

$$EUT = pU((s - r)Y^g + (1 - p) U((s - r) Y^b) \qquad (4.2)$$

Under the traditional system his tax-farming and thus his proprietary rights to a share in peasant output are either customary or else the gift of the State, and are not saleable. In that case, given his degree of risk aversion, the supply of labour and land, and the crop technology, there will be a particular value of s, for given r, which will maximize his expected utility.[49]

Suppose now that under the new British legal system his tax-farming rights become saleable, but the State's revenue demand *remains a fixed proportion* r *of the output of the land*. If existing and potential landowners are homogeneous except for differences in their degrees of risk aversion, a land market in tax-farming rights will develop. For suppose that, at an extreme, there is someone else apart from our risk-averse landowner who is risk-neutral. The current utility levels of the traditional landlord in the two states of nature are then represented by U_o^g in good and U_o^b in Fig. 7.1. Given the value of p, say this represents an expected utility level U_o, where R_o is the expected net income from the zamindari (the area under a zamindar). He would be indifferent in utility terms between the existing gamble of a net income of R_o^g in good and R_o^b in bad years, and a certain income of $\bar{R}_o$ which yields the some expected utility level U_o. Moreover, a risk-neutral purchaser of tax-farming rights from the original zamindar would find it possible to pay the zamindar the fixed income $\bar{R}_o$, and still earn a profit, as the expected net income which he would receive would be $R_o (> \bar{R}_o)$. A new tax-farming subtenant would thus arise, obtaining the share from the

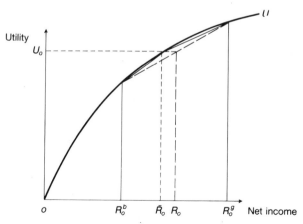

FIG 7.1 Expected Utility and Tax-farming

cultivator in the output, and paying out a fixed 'rent' to the zamindar of $\bar{R}_o$, and a variable rent equal to a share r of the output to the State.

What would be the effects, of this subinfeudation *ceteris paribus*, on agricultural output? This would depend upon whether or not landlords are involved in providing inputs (albeit on a cost-sharing basis) to their tenants. If they do, then the substitution of a risk-neutral (or, less stringently, less risk-averse) sub-tenant tax-farmer for the risk-averse zamindar in the actual production process will imply that *ceteris paribus* the intensity of cultivation and thence expected output should rise.

Next we incorporate the effects of the permanent settlement of revenue at a fixed annual level T, instead of the traditional share r in output. We also assume that the Government does not raise the average tax burden, as it fixes its permanent annual revenue T at the mean revenue it received under the traditional system, that is

$$T = r\left[p \cdot Y^g + (1 - p)Y^b\right] \tag{4.3}$$

The expected *net income* after the Permanent Settlement (*NYP*) of the original zamindar is then the same as under the traditional system, for

$$NYP = p(sY^G - T) + (1 - p)(sY^b - T) \tag{4.4}$$

which substituting for T from (4.3) yields

$$NYP = (s - r)(pY^g + (1 - p)Y^b) = NYT \tag{4.5}$$

However, the expected utility of the zamindar with the Permanent Settlement (*EUP*) will be

$$EUP = p \cdot U(sY^g - T) + (1 - p)U(sY^b - T) \tag{4.6}$$

as (i) $(sY^g - T) > (s - r)Y^g$ (by substituting for T from (4.3))[50]

(ii) $(sY^b - T) > (s - r)Y^b$

The zamindar's utility level U_1^g in *good* years under the new settlement will be *higher* than under the traditional system (which was U_0^g), whilst in *bad* years it will be *lower* at U_1^b than the level U_0^b under the old system. This is depicted in Fig. 7.2. As the expected net income (and hence mean net income) has remained unchanged but the variance of the net income has increased, the effect of the postulated Permanent Settlement implies an increase in the mean preserving spread of the distribution of net income and hence, if as we have postulated the zamindar is risk-averse, a decline in his expected utility level to U_1.

As before, suppose that there is a risk-neutral potential purchaser of the tax-farming rights of the zamindar. Being risk-neutral, he can offer the zamindar a fixed and certain annual rent $\bar{R}$ which yield him the same expect utility U_1 as the variable net income (R_1^b, R_1^g), or he can offer the zamindar a variable share contract in which he receives a share s' less than s in net output, so that the distribution of net incomes of the zamindar, has a reduced variance but from

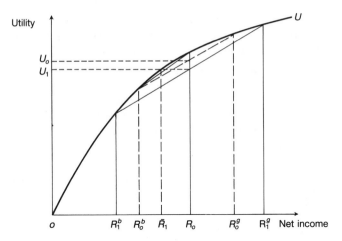

FIG 7.2 Expected Utility and the Permanent Settlement

which the expected utility (*EUS*) is at least equal to $U_1 = EUP$. Thus, the share s' for which the zamindar will be willing to settle will be such that his net income with a subtenant tax-farmer (*NYS*)

$$NYS = s'(pY^g + (1 - p)Y^b) \geq U_1 \qquad (4.7)$$

What about the tax-farming subtenant? Being risk-neutral, his net income (NYF) and expected utility will be

$$NYF = (s - r - s')(pY^g + (1 - p)Y^b) \qquad (4.8)$$

As long as s' is less than $(s - r)$ he will be willing to offer to become a subtenant. Moreover, he will be willing to pay a sum equal to the present value of the net income stream represented by (4.8), discounted at his private rate of time preference, say i. Assuming for simplicity that this is considered to be a perpetuity, he would be willing to purchase the subtenant tax-farming right for the sum V.

$$V = NYF/i = (s - r - s')\overline{Y}/i \qquad (4.9)$$

where

$$\overline{Y} \equiv (pY^g - (1 - p)Y^b)$$

The only question which remains, therefore, is whether there will be a feasible contract such that the original zamindar can be offered a share s' which satisfies both (4.7) and (4.8). Clearly there will, as the risk-averse zamindar will in effect be willing to accept a reduced mean income (which is what $s' < (s - r)$ in (4.8) entails)[51] for the reduction in its variance from (R_1^b, R_1^g).

Thus we have shown that there will be a contract under which the relatively *less* risk-averse purchaser of subfeudatory rights will take over the collection of the share from the cultivators as well as paying the zamindar a portion of this share, and the Government the fixed revenue demand. Again, given that he is less risk-averse than the zamindar who was previously involved in managing the estate, and if there is any cost-sharing of inputs with the cultivators, total output will increase.

This conclusion is exactly the opposite reached by Bhaduri (1976). The reason is that Bhaduri does not postulate any rational economic process giving rise to subinfeudation.[52] As we have argued above, different degrees of risk aversion amongst the old and the new tax-farmers closest to the peasants is necessary to generate this process, which therefore, by substituting a less risk-averse principal in the principal–agent problem of the 'landlord–tenant' contract, should lead to a rise in output.

(b) Tax burdens Finally we can consider the changing fiscal burden under British rule. Though the nationalist writers D. Naoroji and R. C. Dutt stressed the heavy tax burden of British rule, it should be emphasized[53] that given the 'relatively low and unchanging rate of revenue demand' there was a decline in the tax burden under the British compared with Moghul times. Maddison estimates that the tax system the British inherited from the Moghuls provided about 15 per cent of national income as land revenue, 'but by the end of the colonial period land tax was only 1 per cent of national income and the total tax burden was only 6 percent'.[54]

This declining tax burden was in fact responsible for the rising land prices for which data is available for eastern India (see Table 7.9). From equation (4.9) above, the path of land prices is explicable in terms of both the changing productivity of land (which at least in eastern India was unlikely to have altered by much in the nineteenth century) and the falling real revenue (r). The collapse in land prices with the institution of the Permanent Settlement was due both to a high level of revenue demand relative to the depressed prices of agricultural output prevailing at the time and also, if our model is correct, to the excess supply of estates for sale which must have resulted both from the establishment of legal, saleable land rights and from the conversion of the revenue demand from a variable share of output to a fixed annual sum.

Moreover, there is more direct evidence from the United Province (Uttar Pradesh) (see Tables 7.10 and 7.11) which suggests that both the real tax burden and the rent burden (of so-called 'stable' tenants) were declining in that region over the 1840–1929 period of British rule. Thereafter there is a fall in agricultural prices and some rise in the real tax burden. But Neale notes that during the Great Depression, 'after the first blow of the crisis, the government reduced rents to the levels existing at the beginning of the century'.

(ii) Concentration of land, proletarianization, and distribution

Part of the nationalist and more recent radical demonology is that the

TABLE 7.9(A). Land Prices, 1793–1935 (Sale Price as the Multiple of the Jumma)

Year	Sale price	Year	Sale price
1793–4	—	1814–15	5.67
1794–5	—	1815–16	3.85
1795–6	1.57	1816–17	6.85
1796–7	1.26	1817–18	4.22
1797–8	.94	1818–19	2.98
1798–9	.62	1819–20	4.88
1799–1800	.84	1820–1	4.41
1800/1–1802/3	—	1821–2	7.05
1803–4	.96	1822–3	4.49
1804–5	—	1823–4	5.13
1805–6	.95	1824–5	1.55
1806–7	1.34	1825–6	3.16
1807–8	1.44	1826–7	2.91
1808–9	2.46	1827–8	—
1809–10	2.78	1828–9	—
1810–11	4.38	1829–30	3.23
1811–12	5.14	1830–1	4.28
1812–13	4.49	1831–2	3.23
1813–14	7.08	1832–3	4.31

Source: Based on the data contained in the Revenue Letters from Bengal to the Court of Directors, derived in Chaudhri (1975, p. 19, table 2).

TABLE 7.9(B). Land Prices in the Bengal Presidency 1848/9–1910/11

Period	Sale price (annual average during each 5-year period)
1848/9–1852/3	3.41
1853/4–1857/8	8.77
1859/60–1863/4	10.25
1864/5–1868/9	10.16
1869/70–1873/4	7.72
1874/5–1878/9	8.79
1879/80–1883/4	6.91
1884/5–1888/9	6.10
1889/90–1893/4	6.64
1898/9–1902/3	6.36
1903/4–1907/8	4.90
1909–10	7.11
1910–11	6.06

Source: Compiled from the statistical appendices of the Reports on the land Revenue Administration in Bengal and Bihar, derived from Chaudhri (1975, p. 27, table 4).

TABLE 7.9(C).   Annual Average of Land Prices during four- to five-year Periods,
1918/19–1937/8

	Bihar and Orissa	Bengal
1918/19–1922/3	16.63	3.63
1923/4–1927/8	16.16	3.67
1928/9–1932/3	11.10	1.91
1934/5–1937/8	4.73	1.90

Source: The Statistical Appendices of the Reports on the Land Revenue Administration in Bengal and Bihar, derived from Chaudhri (1975, p. 33, table 7).

TABLE 7.9(D).   Average of Prices, 1938/9–1940/1

Bihar and Orissa	Bengal
5.29	2.02

Source: Chaudhri (1975, p. 33, table 8).

TABLE 7.9(E).   Movement of Prices in Bihar, 1928/9–1940/1

Year	Prices	Year	Prices
1928–9	15.70	1935–6	6.79
1929–30	17.89	1936–7	4.06
1930–1	8.26	1937–8	6.14
1931–2	9.64	1938–9	5.59
1932–3	4.04	1939–40	3.32
1933–4	3.92	1940–1	6.98
1934–5	2.76	—	—

Source: as for Table 7.9(*c*).

commercialization of agriculture and the legal changes facilitating the alienation of land led to its concentration. The bulk of the self-sufficient peasant proprietors thus had to live in worsening tenurial conditions, some of them being reduced to landless labourers. As land is the major asset in rural India, it is also argued, at least implicitly, that the distribution of rural income worsened under British rule.

(*a*) *Concentration of land*   Recent research has led to a questioning of all these assertions, as well as the slim evidence, if any, on which they were based. It is false to assume (as is often done implicitly) that land was relatively equally distributed amongst peasant proprietors in pre-British India. Moreover, a number of

TABLE 7.10.   Burden of Rent and Revenue in Muzaffarnagar District

	1840	1924	% change 1840/1924
Value of output per acre (Rs)	8.1	81	+ 900
Rent per cultivated acre (Rs)	2.6	10.8	+ 315
Rent as % of output	32	13	− 59
Population per cultivated acre	0.89[a]	1.31[a]	+ 47
Estimated size of an average holding (acres)	17.0	11.5	− 22
Value productivity per person, i.e. value per acre divided by population per acre[a] (Rs)	9.1	61.0	+ 580

a. Assuming the same ratio of cultivators to total population in 1840 as existed in 1924.
Source: Neale (1962, p. 164, table 8).

TABLE 7.11.   Index of Prices, Rents, and Revenues in United Provinces

Years	Wholesale prices	Rents of stable tenants	Rents of ordinary tenants	Revenue demand
1901–5	100	100	100	100
1920–4	221	115	137	108
1924–9	220	120	149	109
1930–4	122	121	163	112

Source: Neale (1962, p. 177, table 13).

regional studies have shown that there was barely any change in the concentration of landownership under the British. Dharma Kumar[56] has used the revenue data from Madras presidency to calculate Gini coefficients for landholdings district by district for 1853–4 and 1950–1. The Lorenz ratios for Madras presidency as a whole are reported in Table 7.12. These show that there was remarkably little change in the concentration of ownership over nearly a century of British rule, 'and indeed concentration was even reduced in a few districts, such as Tiruchirapalli, Tirunelveli, Coimbatore and Malabar. There are, of course, errors and biases in the data, but in the absence of land reform there was no reason for deliberate underestimation of large holdings. Moreover these findings are supported by individual village surveys.'[57] The reason why concentration did not grow was that 'both large and small holdings have been subdivided as

TABLE 7.12. Landownership in Madras Presidency: Lorenz Ratios, 1853/4–1945/6

Period	Registered holdings (pattas)	Owners[a]
1853–4	0.63	—
1890–1	0.59	0.54
1900–1	0.62	0.59
1930–1	0.63	0.63
1945–6	0.62	0.60

a. Where holdings were jointly held, separate calculations have been made to take account of inequalities in individual ownership.

Source: Kumar (1975, p. 242).

population grew, and in some districts the holdings of the rich appear to have been broken up faster, especially after 1900'.[58]

Even for Greater Bengal, as Ray and Ray (1973) note, there is no evidence of any increasing concentration of landholdings and worsening of tenurial conditions or increasing proletarianization of the peasants, in part because land was already very unequally distributed at the beginning of the nineteenth century (see Table 7.13). Ray and Ray (1973) show that 10 per cent of the population owned 50 per cent of the land in 1808 in Dinajpur, and agricultural labourers formed 18 per cent and sharecroppers with no land 34 per cent of the total cultivating population. Moreover, as Table 7.14 shows, the percentage of landless sharecroppers and agricultural labourers declined in both Dinajpur and Rangpur between 1808 and 1961. This remains true even if we count the number of small cultivators who own some land, rent some, and also hire out their family labour services as members of the landless class.

Similarly, a study for Gujarat shows no change in the Gini coefficients for landholding over the century of British rule.[59]

Finally, Stokes's[60] detailed analysis of agrarian change in United Provinces shows that population pressure led to the fragmentation of holdings but not to any large increase in pure landlessness. There was a large increase in the number of small landowners, but the number of great zamindars at the top of the pyramid who were protected by primogeniture remained stable. It was the smaller non-cultivating landlords who lost ground because of the tenancy legislation protecting the rights of tenants instituted in the later period of British rule. The main beneficiaries of the commercialization of agriculture were the middle peasants. Stokes estimates that nearly three-quarters of the total area was cultivated by peasants owning 8–10 acres. These were the 'kulaks' who, with the abolition of zamindari in post-Independence India, were to become the rural élite of the Hindu heartland.

TABLE 7.13.   Land Distribution among Cultivators in Dinajpur, Bengal, 1808

Category of cultivators	% cultivating population	% land
'Principal farmers' holding 165 bighars[a] on average	1.5	16.5
'Great farmers' holding 75 bighars on average	2.0	10.0
'Comfortable farmers' holding 60 bighars on average	2.5	10.0
'Easy farmers' holding 45 bighars on average	4.5	13.5
'Poor farmers' holding 30 bighars on average	12.5	25.0
'Needy farmers' holding 15 bighars on average	24.9	25.0
Sharecroppers with no land	34.0	0
Agricultural labourers with no land	18.1	0
TOTAL	100.0	100.0

a. 2 Dinajpur bighars = 1 acre.
Source: Ray and Ray (1973, p. 116).

TABLE 7.14.   Landless Agricultural Classes in Dinajpur and Rangpur (% of Total Cultivating Population)

	1808	1938	1961
Dinajpur:			
Sharecroppers	34.0	13.8	9.2
Agricultural laborers	18.1	23.5	16.0
Cultivators owing part, renting part, working for hire	—	—	21.4
Total landless	52.1	37.3	46.6
Rangpur:			
Sharecroppers	39.4	19.1	6.0
Agricultural labourers	11.6	12.9	14.8
Cultivators owning part, renting part, working for hire	—	—	17.4
Total landless	50.0	32.0	38.2

Source: Ray and Ray (1973, p. 1119, table 4), derived from Buchanan, *Geographical Description of Dinajpur*, pp. 236, 244; Buchanan Hamilton Manuscripts, Mss. Eur. G. 12, Account of Rangpur, vol. ii, table 36; Government of Bengal *Report of the Bengal Land Revenue Commission*, vol. ii, table 8(*d*) Alipore (1940); Census of Pakistan 1961, vol. ii, p. V-16. The figures for 1808, 1938, and 1961 are not strictly comparable, as the definition of the classes as well as the boundary of the districts differed on each occasion.

(b) Distribution of consumption   Nor is it likely that there were any marked changes in the distribution of income and consumption in the rural countryside. Thus Bhattacharya and Roy have used the data from Francis Buchanan's survey in 1810–13 of the districts of Bhagalpur, Patna–Gaya, and Shahabad, and the data from the National Sample Surveys (22nd round) for 1967–8 for the same districts, to estimate Lorenz curves for the pooled data of the three districts. The resulting Lorenz curves are shown in Fig. 7.3. The concentration ratio is 0.336 for 1811–13 and 0.308 for 1967–8. The small improvement in the distribution of consumption was due to an improvement in the condition of those in the middle of the distribution at the expense of those at the top, with the position of the bottom 30 per cent remaining virtually stationary over these 150 years.

(c) Proletarianization   Finally, it has been argued, following the work of S. J. Patel,[61] that the process of commercialization of agriculture under the British led to the creation of a new class of landless agricultural labourer. For the pre-1870 period, Patel had based his claim on various comments by either nineteenth century observers or other writers. In particular he cited[62] R. P. Dutt's statement that 'in 1842, Sir Thomas Munro as Census Commissioner reported that there were no landless peasants in India (an undoubtedly incorrect picture, but indicating that the numbers were not considered to require statistical measurement).'[63] Dharma Kumar (1965), apart from a detailed statistical critique of this view, devastatingly retorts: 'It does not strengthen one's confidence in this view to recall that there was no all-India census until 1871, that there was no Madras census in 1842, that Sir Thomas Munro was never Census Commissioner, and that in 1842 he was dead.'

More seriously, Kumar's study seeks to examine the robustness of the classical thesis as adumbrated by Patel and others.[64] If the classical thesis is correct, she argues, the best place to seek evidence for its confirmation is in Madras. The new ryotwari system was enforced most rigorously in this area in the nineteenth century, the revenue rates were highest, and land transfers easiest, so that it was in Madras that the village communities should have been hardest hit. Also, as south India had the highest proportion of landless labour to total population in the twentieth century, it would seem that the link between the commercialization of agriculture and proletarianization would have been strongest in this region. She estimates that 'the five main castes which were definitely "agricultural labor" castes. . . . together formed 12%, 13.1%. 12.9% and 12.5% of the total population in 1871, 1881, 1891 and 1901 respectively'.[65] As she estimates that at the beginning of the nineteenth century the landless agricultural labour force amounted to 10–15 per cent of the total population,[66] there was apparently no marked growth of landless labour in the region in the nineteenth century. Thus Kumar's study shows that 'long before Indian agriculture was involved in the international economy, a significant proportion of the agricultural population was effectively landless, and second, that the rate of growth (if any) of this landless class was certainly not very significant'.[67]

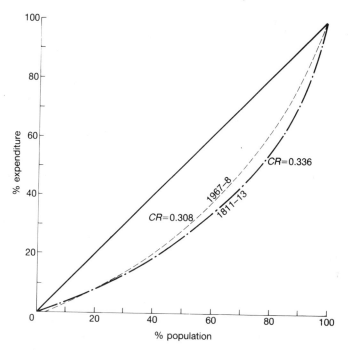

FIG 7.3   Lorenz Curves on Consumer Expenditure in Bihar, 1811–1813 and 1967–1968
(*CR* = Concentration Ratio)
Source: Bhattacharya and Roy (n.d.)

More seriously, Patel's claim that during the course of the six decades from
1871 to 1931 the proportion of agricultural labourers to the agricultural population in India increased from a meagre one-seventh 'to more than ⅓',[68] based on
the censuses from 1871 to 1931, has been questioned by Krishnamurthy. He
shows that 'this conclusion was reached by Patel on the basis of a serious
misunderstanding of the census data'.[69] Patel failed to take account of the
changes in the relevant coverage and definitions during the various censuses.
Once this is done, and using Patel's own methods, Krishnamurthy shows 'no
sustained upward trend in the share of agricultural labour in the agricultural working force'. This share was roughly (with fluctuations around the average) 25 per
cent for males and 30 per cent for females.

(iii) Railways, cash crops, and famines

There were a number of major famines, particularly in the later part of the nineteenth century (see Table 6.2). The processes leading to the commercialization of
agriculture have been blamed for the increasing incidence of famine in India.[70] It
has been argued that the development of the railways and the integration of the

rural economy into the world economy led to a shift in cropping patterns away from foodgrains in the interior portions of India. This diminished local food supplies and thus accentuated the endemic problem of famines resulting from the periodic monsoon failures to which India was prone.

McAlpin (1975) has examined the data for the relative shifts between foodgrains and cotton for major parts of India, as cotton is often cited[71] as the most important crop replacing foodgrains. She finds that

Railroad construction in India does not appear to have been accompanied by a decrease in either the absolute amount of land planted with foodgrains. Nor do exports of foodgrains appear to have been large, relative to production. The simple explanation for the poverty of many Indians at the end of the 19th century—that less food was being grown—is not supported. Attention must be directed instead to more complex explanations for starvation in 19th century India. The distribution of income appears more likely than the size of food production to have produced starvation.[72]

This latter point has been stressed more recently by A. K. Sen in his work on famines.[73] He argues that in exchange economies famines are rarely caused by a decline in food availability. Thus the increased commercialization and improvements in communication should have limited the incidence of famine if these were caused merely by a decline in food availability. Instead, argues Sen, it is the shift in 'exchange entitlements' of the vulnerable sections of the population which leads to famine. These exchange entitlements, for most rural communities, are the relative price of the wages landless workers receive for their only asset—labour—and the price at which they have to purchase food. A monsoon failure, say, by drastically reducing the demand for landless labour, will lead to a fall in the money wages for the given supply of labour, and thence to a reduction in its 'exchange entitlement' in terms of food, which if extreme enough could lead to famine. Clearly, producers of agricultural output—whether owners or tenants—would be partially protected against such a disastrous fall in exchange entitlements when their output falls, for the price of these outputs will rise, and hence their real incomes will probably not alter significantly as compared with landless labour.

If British rule had led to a marked increase in landless labour (the class most likely to suffer from a fall in its exchange entitlements in years of monsoon failure), some credence might have been given to the argument that the commercialization of agriculture led to an increase in landless labour, and thence to a greater incidence of famine. As from the evidence cited in the previous section there is no basis for assuming the validity of the first step in the argument, the rest cannot obviously be sustained.

(iv) Usury, growing indebtedness, and peasant ruin

Once again recent research contradicts the factual basis of the cononical view on the ruin of the peasant owing to a growing burden of debt incurred in response to tenurial changes and the commercialization of agriculture. Stokes (1978) has examined the role of indebtedness 'as the chief cause of the absence of effective agricultural improvement and dynamic growth in Indian agriculture',[74] in parts of central India. As he emphasizes, it is not merely nationalists and Marxists who viewed the role of the money-lenders with concern. Many believed that money-lenders reduced the 'mass of agriculturalists to cultivators working for the lowest subsistence return under a form of debt—peonage'.[75] This was also the view of the British officials in the latter half of the nineteenth century.

However, as Stokes shows, this view cannot be sustained. First, 'in central India, the moneylenders' grip predated British rule and sprang from the tax system rather than the credit needs of market-oriented agriculture.'[76] More importantly landlords had traditionally been money-lenders, grain traders, and cultivators, and the non-rural money-lenders merely took on the same role, so that in practice there was no real distinction between the agricultural and non-agricultural classes.[77] Neither were the agriculturally less advanced regions, nor the poorest cultivators, the most heavily indebted. Rather,

the most heavily indebted areas or classes were the good soil tracts and the middle rank of comfortably off peasant cultivators. . . . A high level of debt under such circumstances signified not so much distress as the absence of continuous growth in the agricultural economy and high consumer spending relative to productive investment. Yet, as a flourishing district like Hoshangabad (CP) showed, it was a burden that could periodically be worked off and then renewed as harvests and prices moved through their mysterious cycles of boom and slump.[78]

Furthermore Ghatak (1976) has done a detailed statistical analysis of the all-India rural credit data for 1950–1 and 1961–2.[79] If peasants had been immiserized by debt this would surely be apparent after a century of British rule. Ghatak found, however from his econometric exercises on post-Independence data that it was the need for capital rather than family expenditure on consumption that was the statistically significant explanatory variable explaining the demand for credit. Nor was there any evidence of monopoly profits charged by rural money-lenders in the average rural rate of interest of about 17–15 per cent in 1950–1 and 1961–2. 'The analysis of the cost side of interest rates showed that such rates could largely be explained by risk and uncertainty and the administrative costs involved in lending to agriculture.'[80]

The continuing mythology of the crushing burden of rural debt, and of debt peonage spread through the malign power of the monopolistic, usurious money-lender–trader unleashed by British rural policy, can only be explained by the traditional social opporbrium heaped on the merchant class—an attitude shared by the Platonic Guardians who ruled British India.[81]

NOTES

1. Heston (1973, p. 304).
2. The estimates (in the form of index numbers of the capital/labour ratio) cited for the pre-Independence years are due to Shukla (1965). However, as Ram N. Lal (1977) notes; 'Her estimates are based mostly on the inventory approach depending on data available from quinquennial livestock censuses and Rural Credit Survey. Since the publication of ''All-India Rural Debt and Investment Survey 1961–1962'' in 1965, most of the results have become obsolete mainly because the Rural Credit Survey results stand questioned by the Reserve Bank of India itself. They have been found to err on a very high side' (ibid., 128, para. 4). As, presumably, this upward bias affects all Shukla's estimates of the capital stock equally, the overall trends in the capital/labour ratio she estimated might still not be too erroneous. Her estimated capital/labour ratio declines marginally between 1900 and 1960/1 (from 100 to 96—see Shah (1974)) and we have assumed that it was probably roughly constant between 1901 and 1950/1. In any case, its trend (if any and if valid) is in marked contrast to the marked upward trend in this ratio in the post-Independence period, as can be seen from Table 7.4(*b*).
3. This can be seen by comparing the growth of total crop area (Table 7.4(*a*), row 5) and the growth of the percentage of the net sown area irrigated (Table 7.4(*a*) row 5). These are equal in each of the two periods, suggesting that multiple cropping (which accounts for the difference between net and total crop area) grew *pari passu* with irrigation.
4. See Ishikawa (1967, ch. 2).
5. See Government of India (1976, vol. i, pp. 122–3).
6. Ibid.
7. Nanavati and Anjaria (1965, p. 166).
8. Voelcker (1893, pp. 39–42).
9. Government of India (1976, p. 209).
10. Blyn (1966, p. 195).
11. Ibid., 201.
12. Ibid., 201.
13. Nanavati and Anjaria (1965, p. 45).
14. Ishikawa (1967, p. 69).
15. Narain (1965, ch. 8).
16. Ibid., 107.
17. Ishikawa (1967, pp. 71–3).
18. Ibid., 77 remarks that this switch is the first landmark in the development of land productivity in Asian rice economies.
19. Ibid., 70.
20. Ibid., 186 ff.
21. Ibid.
22. The reason why the incremental benefits from the (cheaper) irrigation systems in relatively drier areas is higher is that, without irrigation, these areas would typically be growing low-value, drought-resistant cereals such as millets. The substitution of a high-value crop of rice yielding 2.3 tonnes/ha. will yield a higher incremental value of output, therefore, than in the 'wet' areas, where the incremental benefit is merely and extra 1 tonne/ha. of rice.
23. See Blyn (1966, p. 138 ff.)
24. Ibid., 197–9, and Narain (1965, pp. 126–32).
25. Blyn (1966).
26. Narain (1965, p. 132).
27. Narain (1965, pp. 146–7). See also C. Prabha (1969) and Krishna (1964) on the growth performance of Punjab being largely due to the irrigation works provided.
28. Minhas *et al.* (1972) have provided an ingenious scheme for combining ground and surface water systems for the multi-purpose Bhakra system to optimize the competing uses of water at certain seasons, between irrigation and power generation.
29. See Lal (1972, ch. 4).
30. Ibid., 110.

31. Ibid., ch. 9.
32. See Narain (1965) for the remarkable expansion of cotton acreage, in particular in the 'dry zones' of the Deccan plateau, when world prices of cotton shot up during the American Civil War, and the subsequent shrinking of the cotton acreage when they equally dramatically collapsed in the 1890s.
33. See Lal (1972, ch. 4).
34. Thus the present author's estimation (Lal (1972a)) of a water response functions for jowar and sugar-cane (albeit by fairly crude methods) in Ahmednagar is one of the few such estimates available. Minhas *et al.* (1972), in their attempt to design an optimal schedule of operations for the post-Independence Bhakra system, found they were only able to provide a cost-effectiveness schema of evaluation because they were unable to 'measure the economic worth of this water without having proper water response functions for the crops grown in the Bhakra command' (p. 61).
35. See Lal (1973c) on how even the latest Irrigation Commission Report (in 1972) fails to take account of simple economics in its analysis and recommendations.
36. Thus Thavaraj (1955, 1963) shows that half of the gross public investment in irrigation was concentrated in the Punjab; Madras and Orissa accounted for a further 10%. 'Which,', Dharma Kumar asks, 'raises the further question, why did rice output fail to increase in Orissa?' (Kumar (1972, p.86)). The answer is that this investment was unproductive and hence of the protective variety in British irrigation terminology, and was classified as such (see Anstey (1952, p. 616, table x, b)) in the official statistics. This attests to the difficulty of using irrigation water to raise productivity in eastern Indian climatic conditions. Thus Bagchi (1972, p. 106) notes that 'in Central Provinces, Western Bengal and in Southern Bihar and Northern Orissa there was no easily accessible subsoil water which could be exploited by private means; there were also no rivers with gentle slopes which could be blocked to produce artificial reservoirs without considerable expenditure. In other words, costly public irrigation works on a large scale would have had to be constructed for an effective supply of water on a permanent basis.'
37. Which we saw in ch. 4 was also the area between the Jumna and the Ganges, where Mohammed Tughlaq attempted to raise agricultural productivity by administrative means.
38. Whitcombe (1971, p. 66).
39. The following account is based on ibid., 64–91. Whitcombe does tend to gild the lily (or should it be weed?) in her catalogue of the abuses that can be adduced to the canal system! Some of her points are well taken and are mentioned in the text above. She also does not provide any quantitative estimate of these indirect deleterious effects of the canal system, so it is not possible to form any judgement on the net economic effects, taking account of the undoubted gains from the canals in raising the net value of agricultural production in the region. For a more balanced, qualitative discussion of these net effects see Stone (1979).
40. Ibid., 67–8.
41. Ibid., 79. 'In the midst of this desolated Usar land, patches of "valuable" crops—opium, sugar cane, wheat, castor-oil plant and cotton—stood out like oases in the salt covered desert around them' (Voelcker Report 73, p. 55, cited in Whitcombe (1972)).
42. This account is based on Lal and Duane (1972).
43. See Thorner and Thorner (1962, pp. 54–7) for the most explicit statement of these deleterious effects of colonial rule on agrarian India. However, the Thorners were merely extending to all India a thesis which has a long lineage in the writings on the Permanent Settlement in Bengal. See e.g. Dutt (1901) and Mukherjee (1957, 1971). For an even more recent version of this thesis see Bhaduri (1976). A critique of the historical and factual basis of this thesis for Bengal is provided in Ray and Ray (1973).
44. See Chaudhri (1975) on the development of the land market in Bengal as a result of these changes. Patni tenures were under-tenures of a proprietary nature.
45. See for instance Bhaduri (1976), who does however recognize that this process of subinfeudation was a response by the zamindars to insure themselves against the risk of the rise in the revenue demand. However, as we argue below, this was only one of two separate factors leading to subinfeudation.
46. Thus Raychaudhuri (1969) asks: 'why did the tenure-holding talukdar not try to skip all the intermediary layers of interests and settle directly with the under-ryot, whenever possible, and

thus hog the surplus? I do not have any answer to this riddle and would very much welcome some analytical light on this problem' (p. 169).

47. This stark contrast in pre- and post-British tenurial arrangements is only made for analytical purposes. As the historians of the Permanent Settlement have emphasized, there was greater continuity between pre- and post-British tenurial forms. Thus the demand of a fixed revenue was also to be found in Mughal times, during which there were also some markets in tenancy rights. However, analytically the two aspects of the Permanent Settlement can be taken to have increased the coverage of these pre-British forms of land arrangement in eastern India.

48. We do not deal with the determination of this crop share, but see Newberry (1977), Jaynes (1979), Bardhan (1980a), Braverman and Srinivasan (1981), Braverman and Stiglitz (1981) for the modern theory of share-cropping which takes account of both problems in monitoring 'effort' as well as in risk-sharing and the ensuing second-best optimality of the interlinking of land, credit, and labour contracts, which are entailed in the 'principal agent' type of problem in highly uncertain rural environments.

49. Various complications suggested by the interlinked markers literature cited in the previous note could be incorporated in determining the 'optimal' s.

50. Thus $sY^g - T(s - r)Y^g = r[Y^g - (1 - p)Y^b]$, and as $Y^g > [pY^g + (1 - p)Y^b]$, as $Y^g > Y^b$ and $1 > p > 0$. $[sY^g - T - (s - r)Y^g] > 0$ and thence the inequality (i) follows. Moreover as $sY^b - T - (s - r)Y^b = r[Y^b - (pY^g + (1 - p)Y^b)]$ and as $Y^b < [pY^g + (1 - p)Y^b]$, $[sY^b - T - (s - r)Y^b] < 0$, and thence the inequality (ii) follows.

51. It being noted that the mean income with the subinfeudation of the zamindari will no longer be $(s - r)Y$ but $s'Y$.

52. Though he sees that the process was a form of insurance (Bhaduri 1976, p. 47), he fails to follow through the implications of this of the changes in the relative degree of risk aversion of those closest to managing the production decisions of the farms.

53. See Raychaudhuri in Frykenberg (1969, p. 162).

54. Maddison (1971, p. 45).

55. Neale (1962, p. 177).

56. Kumar (1975) and also Kumar and Krishnamurty (1981).

57. Kumar and Krishnamurty (1981).

58. Ibid.

59. Kumar and Krishnamurty (1981).

60. Stokes (1975, 1978). Also see Neale (1962), Metcalf (1979), Cohn (1969).

61. Patel (1952; 1965, pp. 3–32).

62. Patel (1965, p. 9).

63. Dutt (1940, p. 198).

64. See also Morris's (1966) review of Kumar's book which presents a succinct summary of her thesis, and on which the following account is in part based.

65. Kumar (1965, p. 59).

66. Ibid., 190–1.

67. Morris (1966).

68. Patel (1952, p. 9).

69. Krishnamurty (1972, p. 327).

70. See Bhatia (1963), Dutt (1901, p. 366), Chandra (1968, pp. 35–75).

71. Bhatia (1963, pp. 33–4).

72. McAlpin (1975, p. 58). Moreover as Maddison (1971) points out, 'It is noteworthy that the decades in which famines occurred were ones in which the population was static rather than falling. In the 1920's and 1930's there were no famines, and the 1944 famine in Bengal was due to war conditions and transport difficulties rather than crop failure. However the greater stability after 1920 may have been partly due to a lucky break in the weather cycle rather than to a new instability of agriculture' (p. 53). See also Harnetty (1970), who argues that the cotton exports of 1861–70 stimulated agricultural production so that there was no substitution of commercial for food crops.

73. Sen (1976a, 1977).

74. Stokes (1978, p. 12).

75. Ibid., 242.

76. Ibid., 245.

77. Ibid., 256–7. Recent theoretical work has shown that these so-called inter-linked contractual relationships' are a second-best optimal response in conditions where problems of risk-sharing and the provision of incentives in the absence of perfect monitoring of the agents' actions by the principal are prohibitively expensive. See Braverman and Srinivasan (1981), Braverman and Stiglitz (1981).
78. Stokes (1978, p. 13).
79. Ghatak (1976, ch. 3).
80. Ibid., 212 and ch. 4.
81. Thus M. L. Darling (1925, p. 176) writes of the money-lending castes: 'the Bania, being the most timid of the three, is the most subtle and insidious. "Heel ropes of silk and a bridle of munjh" is his motto, and the former always comes first!' However, Darling, whilst reacting with distaste to the character of the bania, nevertheless recognizes his utility. In an agricultural country like India, which is subject in a singular degree to pestilence and famine, the money-lender could always command a certain tolerance. 'Financing the village, marketing its produce, and supplying its necessities, the money lender in India frequently stood between the cultivator and death; and as Sir William Hunter remarks, he represents the one thrifty person among an improvident population "without whose help the cultivator would have had nothing to depend upon but the harvest of a single year". Whenever, therefore, we are tempted to revile him, we should remember that by his assistance to agriculture for 2,500 years he has made life possible for millions who must otherwise have perished or never been born' (p. 168).

8

The Economy under the Raj, III: Trade and Industry

INTRODUCTION

We have seen in the last chapter that, despite nationalist assertions to the contrary, the Raj at its best did something to promote agricultural development in which the expansion of the irrigated area, particularly in the drier western areas of Punjab and Sind, provided an impetus to agricultural growth which is still not spent (see pt. III below). But the vast, 'wet', paddy-growing regions of eastern India did not feel any warm breath of progress. Their rural problems, however, as we have argued, are more intractable, caused as they are by their ecological conditions—high though variable rainfall and great rivers which flood annually—which paradoxically, though bountiful in terms of the subsistence agriculture established in ancient India, makes it more difficult to move to the next higher stage of agriculture. The capital requirements for the creation of a vast irrigation-cum-flood-control system were clearly beyond the financial means of the Raj, and in any case, if our argument in the last chapter is correct, the irrigation developments undertaken in western India were clearly intra-marginal as compared with those in the 'wetter' east. The major charge of neglecting Indian agriculture has more substance when the promotion of agricultural research, education and extension are considered. But, as we shall see in this chapter, as the Raj was hobbled by financial problems the distribution of its available public resources was probably not too senseless.

We have also argued that there is little basis for concluding that the Raj accentuated Indian rural problems by the land tenure systems it created and the commercialization of agriculture it promoted. Rather, the crucial question which we examine in the first part of this chapter is why the commercialization of agriculture and the integration of the Indian economy into the world economy did not lead to a greater spurt in the development of cash crop agriculture and exports in India as compared with other colonial tropical countries. For it would seem that, even in this form of archetypal imperialist exploitation, India had been a laggard!

Having examined the relatively disappointing role of tropical exports in markedly raising the demand for labour in rural India, the second part of the chapter examines the record of Indian industry under the Raj. For if agriculture and tropical trade did not provide, or could not have provided, that vital impulse to move labouring India out of the Hindu equilibrium, the new-fangled spirit of industralism, on which much of the power and wealth of the West has been based, probably could—or so it has been thought by nationalists, not only in India but in most developing countries. Unfortunately, once again, the historical record is clouded by passion and ideology, and a canonical tradition, again both nationalist and radical, has developed, which sees the Raj as not only hindering India's modern industrial progress through its twin policies of free trade and *laissez-faire*, but actually 'de-industrializing' India by the wanton destruction of its traditional industries following in the wake of the imposition of free trade. As this vision is commonly shared by a large part of the Indian intelligentsia and more seriously (as we see in the next part) has provided, if not the driving force, certainly the ballast of post-Independence economic policy, we deal with these issues in some detail in the second part of this chapter.

1. THE GROWTH OF TROPICAL EXPORTS

The motive force behind the East India Company's acquisition of an Indian empire was commerce. The company's traditional trade consisted of exporting cotton goods from the north and Madras, spices from the south, indigo from Gujarat, and saltpetre from Bengal.[1] 'At the same time a private or 'country trade' developed between India and the Far East in the private hands of the company's merchants.'[2] It was the threat to its commercial interests from the impending anarchy in India which persuaded politicians like Pitt and Dundas in Britain to support Wellesley's attempt at unifying India by British arms. 'If there had been no money in it, they would certainly have withdrawn. The company's trade in India was no longer profitable, for its profits, instead of being augmented by the revenues of Bengal, were in fact absorbed by the costs of administration.'[3] Instead, the company promoted a highly profitable trade with China, whereby it paid for its tea imports from China by exports of opium from India. This trade, which was repeatedly banned and resisted by China, ultimately led to the Opium Wars, the opening up of China, and the carving up of the Chinese melon. It was the basis of the East India Company's commercial prosperity. 'Here was something which could not be given up, something which was made more profitable by political control. Without the control it would have declined and might have withered altogether. A cogent economic argument for the hegemony of India was the preservation of the China trade.'[4]

Opium was by the mid-nineteenth century the biggest export of India, and remained so till the 1880s, when its relative and absolute importance began to decline.[5]

We discuss in the next section the causes of the decline of Indian handicrafts and the attendant decline in Indian exports of manufactured goods, as part of the decline and rise of Indian industry. However, it should be noted that for a long time after the British victory at Plassey in 1757, cotton manufactures continued to be India's main export—until the end of the Napoleonic wars.

Maddison states[6] that they probably reached their peak in 1798 and, according to figures given by R.C. Dutt, even in '1813 Calcutta exported to London £2 million of cotton goods. However, in 1830 Calcutta imported £2 million of British manufactures. The first import of British cotton twist into India was in 1823, in 1824 it was 121,000 lbs; in 1828 it rose to 4 million lbs.'[7]

In order to transfer their revenues to Britain, the British had to generate an export surplus by promoting other exports. The export promotion of primary products such as sugar, silk, saltpetre, and indigo, and later cotton, tea, and jute, during the course of the British century can therefore, on one view, be looked upon as the classical colonial pattern of imperialism either keeping or, as is asserted in the case of India, converting subject peoples into hewers of wood and drawers of water.[8]

But from 1813, when British India was thrown open to free trade, these 'new exports' would only have been viable if India had a comparative advantage in their production. Until 1913, Indian exports grew about ninefold—that is, a compound rate of growth of over 3 per cent p.a.—according to Maddison's estimates[9] (see Table 8.1). But this growth was slower than of most other tropical countries, particularly in the 1870–1913 period when world trade boomed.[10] In this period (see Table 8.2), none of India's agricultural exports except for tea grew at the average rate of growth for agricultural commodities of 3 per cent per annum.[11] Thus, unlike other tropical countries in the period, and countries like Japan which were increasing agricultural exports by over 4 per cent p.a. over the period,[12] India's agricultural exports were only growing by about 1.4 per cent p.a.

Thus, though the commercialization of agriculture had by the 1870s led to a substantial expansion in agricultural exports, neither their size (relative to the

TABLE 8.1. Level of Asian Exports f.o.b., 1850–1950 ($ million)

	1850	1913	1937	1950
Ceylon	5	76	124	328
China	24	294	516	(700)
India	89	786	717	1,178
Indonesia	24	270	550	800
Japan	1	354	1,207	820
Malaya	24	193	522	1,312
Philippines	—	48	153	331
Thailand	3	43	76	304

Note: Trade figures refer to customs area of the year concerned. In 1850 and 1913 the Indian area included Burma. The comparability of 1937 and 1950 figures is affected by the separation of Pakistan.

Source: Maddison (1971, p. 59, table iii–1).

TABLE 8.2. Principal Agricultural Exports, 1911–1913

	Ratio	Growth rate
Jute	21.4	2.3
Cotton	21.3	1.1
Foodgrains (excluding rice)	15.3	2.7
Hides and skins	10.6	2.3
Oilseeds, cake, and oil	10.4	2.5
Tea	9.3	6.8
Opium	5.0	− 3.6
Remainder[a]	6.7	0.4
	100.0	1.4

a. In order of value: wool, lac, coffee, spices, dyes, dyestuffs, bones, rubber, tobacco, and sugar.

Source: Lidman and Domrese (1970, p. 311, table 12.1).

economy) nor their rate of growth was sufficient to impart any marked dynamic impulse to the economy as a whole. It should also be noted that from the 1850s, just about twenty years after the decimation of India's traditional textile exports, manufactured exports of cotton yarn from India, based on the establishment of modern cotton mills, began to expand.[13] With the later expansion of jute textiles, by 1913 20 per cent of Indian exports were manufactured goods.[14] Finally, by 1913, as a result of the past half-century's expansion of foreign trade (which took place in the free trade and *laissez-faire* environment imposed by the British), Maddison estimates that exports 'were 10.7% of national income, probably a higher ratio than has been reached before or since'.[15] As we shall see, for both manufacturing output and exports India's performance in the latter half of the nineteenth century was not below par. It was in the growth of agricultural exports that India lagged behind the rest of the tropical world and other late developers like Japan.

Lewis (1970, 1978) believes that the relative sluggishness of the Indian response to the opportunity presented by the growth of world trade in agricultural exports can be explained by the relative scarcity of wetlands for expanding the cultivation of these crops. In a sense this is right, but not for the reasons adduced by Lewis: 'Overpopulation, lack of water and lack of roads combine to explain the low level and slow growth of the Indian economy at this time.'[16] He also asserts:

Some parts developed as rapidly as anywhere else These were the wetter regions, which could grow jute, tea or rubber; or irrigated areas, like the Punjab, which developed a large export of wheat. In the second place, more irrigation would have brought even wider development. This was India's most urgent problem. . . . According to the Census Commissioner, population and cultivated acreage grew at the same rate between 1890 and 1911, but thereafter population grew faster than cultivated acreage and by 1951 the acreage cultivated per head had fallen by a quarter. In these cirumstances even land that could have grown commercial crops for export tended to be kept for growing food, since the peasant farmer still at that time gave highest priority to producing food for his own family.'[17]

Most of the inferences in these statements are false. As we have argued in the previous chapter, and as have others,[18] India before the population explosion dating from 1921 was not over-populated in any meaningful economic sense: in fact it was the mild expansion of population in the nineteenth century which enabled a labour supply to be organized for the plantations producing the new tropical export crops such as tea in the 'frontier areas' such as Assam (see volume II of this work).

Nor, as argued in the last chapter, could the development of irrigation (without flood control) in eastern India have had high social rates of return. Paradoxically, it was the existence of wetlands—which had already acquired a viable equilibrium (albeit at a relatively low subsistence level of living by modern standards) over centuries, in one of the first three stages of Ishikawa's patterns of rice culture (see ch. 7, sect. 3)—which prevented any marked shift of cropping patterns towards the water-intensive crops constituting tropical exports.

However, even in these regions, as attested by the development and fluctuations in jute acreage in eastern India, relative prices of rice to jute were the primary determinants of what must be considered to be a rational peasant response.[19] What India lacked were unoccupied wetlands—apart from those in Assam—which were not already given over to the cultivation of paddy. Most of the new crops would have found it difficult to displace paddy purely on economic grounds, and not because of any preference for foodgrain production amongst subsistence farmers *per se*. That is the half-truth in the Lewis position.

As regards irrigation (see ch. 7), its marginal returns were highest in the drier regions where as the work of Dharm Narain and Raj Krishna (1963) has shown, the relative prices of cash and foodgrain crops did lead to the predicted changes in cropping pattern. Thus it was not a failure of public policy nor the non-responsiveness of peasant farmers, as Lewis implies, which was the cause of the failure of the Indian economy to respond to the opportunities for tropical trade presented by the expansion of the world economy between 1880 and 1913, but ecological constraints. Given these, the Indian rural economy probably responded fairly optimally to the opportunities presented. To put the same point in another way, given these ecological constraints, India's comparative advantage has probably never been in any massive expansion of tropical exports, and its failure to match the performance of other tropical countries in this respect is merely a reflection of these factors.

2. THE DRAIN

Nevertheless, agricultural exports did expand, and moreover (see Figure 8.1) India's barter and income terms of trade, far from declining over the 1861–1939

FIG 8.1   Income Terms of Trade

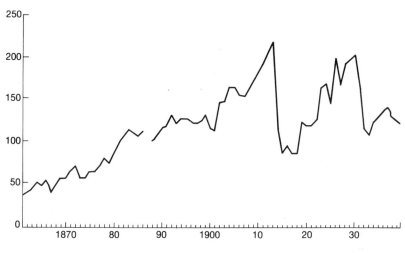

Source: Bhatia (1969)

period, actually improved except for the unusual periods during the First World War and the Great Depression. Thus, no immiserizing effects from the growth resulting from this free-trade period can be adduced. Even though foreign trade was not an engine of growth, it did not lead to any immiserization of Indians. It has been argued, however, that the so-called 'drain' of Indian resources to pay for the 'home charges' of the Raj limited the gains from trade to India. Both the size and the effects of this drain are a matter of controversy and not strictly relevant to our argument.[20]

Nevertheless, a few points may be noted. It is undoubtedly true that the home charges did imply a capital transfer from India, which India had to finance by running an export surplus during most of the British Raj. Maddison estimates that this transfer of resources accounted for about 1.5 per cent of GNP between 1921 and 1938. Mukerjee (1972) estimates that the 'unnecessary home charges' which alone could constitute a drain were between 0.04% and 0.07 of total national income between 1870 and 1900. In a desperately poor country this transfer is not trivial. The obvious retort that this transfer was paying for administrative and military services which India would have had to provide in any case is rather weak, because, if these public services had been provided by Indians, at least part of these home charges would have been spent on indigenous non-traded goods, with obviously stimulating effects on the domestic economy.

Nor did India, by the late nineteenth century, need to import foreigners to perform these higher-level administrative and military functions. For with the introduction of Western education in mid-century, India, unlike many parts of Africa, had the necessary skilled personnel to man its bureaucracy—particularly as the number of British civil servants in India was never very large. Maddison (1971) citing various census estimates, notes:

There were only 31,000 British in India in 1805 (of which 22,000 were in the army and 2,000 in civil government). The number increased substantially after the Mutiny but thereafter remained steady. In 1911, there were 164,000 British (106,000 employed, of which 66,000 were in the army and police and 4,000 in civil government)[22] In 1931, there were 168,000 (90,000 employed, 60,000 in the army and policy and 4,000 in civil government). They were a thinner layer than the Muslim rulers had been (never more than 0.05% of the population).[23]

Moreover, as Curzon himself admitted, by 1900 there were sufficient numbers of Indians able to replace the British at all levels of the bureaucracy. Thus he wrote[24] that 'the greatest peril with which our administration is confronted' was 'the system under which every year an increasing number of the 900 and odd higher posts that were meant and ought to have been exclusively and specifically reserved for Europeans are being filched away by the superior wits of the Native in the English examinations'. Various barriers, including for example the necessity of sitting for the Indian Civil Service (ICS) exam in England, were placed on Indian entry into these upper reaches of the bureaucracy.[25]

Thus the opportunity cost to India of employing foreigners, and imperious ones at that, was high! The resulting 'political drain' in the home charges should certainly be counted amongst the debits of the balance sheet of the Rja.[26] For the British, unlike earlier conquerors and rulers of India, never became a truly Indian power. Part of the tribute which rulers of India have always exacted from the Indian populace thus leaked out of the economy, and in conventional Keynesian terms must have constituted a depressive effect on the level of economic activity in the economy.

3. INDUSTRIAL DEVELOPMENT

If agricultural growth was sluggish during the Raj, the only other way of raising the demand for labour in India, and thence the standard of living of its inhabitants, was rapid industrial growth. Assuming there was no shortage of labour, capital, entrepreneurship, and technology, this would depend upon the overall demand from both home and foreign sources for domestically produced manufactures.

From Chapters 2 and 4 we know that even in ancient times India had produced handicrafts which supplied the demands of the urban aristocracy. This home luxury demand for domestic industrial products was supplemented by export demand, again presumably of the luxury type. No quantitative data is available on the size either of the total domestic production and/or of the exports of handicrafts from India at the time of the British conquest. However, Maddison's guess is that 'the home market for these goods was about 5% of Moghul national income. The export market was probably another 1.5% of national income.'[27]

(i) The decline of handicrafts

One of the indirect consequences of the establishment of British rule and with it the new systems of land tenure was the destruction of the old Muslim aristocracy who were the chief patrons and consumers of luxury products. Nor did India's new rulers and their Indian collaborators, who moved into the upper layers of Indian society, acquire the tastes of their predecessors, as had happened invariably in India's past. The new Indo-British bureaucracy—both its European members and imitative Indian collaborators—had European tastes. As a result, Maddison guesses that about three-quarters of the domestic demand for luxury handicrafts was destroyed.[28]

Between 1813 and 1830 (as noted above) cotton manufactures which had been India's main export produce were destroyed by competition from Lancashire. It has been alleged that this destruction of Indian textile exports to the UK was due to the high 'infant industry' protection offered to Lancashire in the early part of the nineteenth century. R. C. Dutt, citing the 'impartial verdict of H. H. Wilson, historian of India', states that in 1813 import duties of 70 and 80 per cent or total import bans protected Lancashire against imports of cotton and silk goods which could be sold at prices 50–60 per cent lower than the alternative British costs of production.[29]

It is unlikely, however, that the strong protection afforded to Lancashire affected UK textile import demand for any length of time. There was a rapid lowering of the costs of production in the new Lancashire textile mills, and as Little (1982a) notes, despite the substantial reduction in British import duties between 1824 and 1832, Indian exports fell steeply during this period. The decline of the Indian trade in textiles was inevitable in the face of the technological revolution taking place at that time in the West.

(ii) De-industrialization

While this new technology inevitably led to the destruction of some industry-specific factors of production in the indigenous textile industry, nevertheless within about twenty years (by the 1850s) India had set up her own textile mills, as a result of indigenous entrepreneurship, and from 1875 it began to export modern textiles once again.[30] The nature and composition of this trade and the changing balance between the handloom and modern sector need not concern us,[31] except to note that with the development of a modern indigenous textile industry, domestic producers increasingly captured both the domestic and foreign markets they had lost in the mid-nineteenth century to the technologically advanced industry in Lancashire. Thus for instance in the domestic market, 'in 1896, Indian mills supplied only 8% of total cloth consumption; in 1913, 20%; in 1936, 62%; and in 1945, 76%. By the latter date there were no imports of piece goods.'[32]

Thus, as we saw in Chapter 6 (Table 6.4 and 6.5), the decline in the relative importance of handicrafts in both industrial output and employment was matched broadly speaking by a rise in the importance of modern manufacturing industry (of which, until the First World War, cotton textiles was the major component). Moreover, as we saw in the previous section, in order to restore balance of payments equilibrium in the face of the collapse of traditional handicraft production, the British promoted the development of new 'commercial agricultural crops' which must also have had an expansionary effect on the overall demand for labour in the economy. For the later 1901-51 period, Krishnamurty (1967) has shown that while the ratio of workers in manufacturing to total employment did not vary very much (see Table 6.5), nevertheless capital intensity and hence output per unit of labour in industry as a whole was probably rising. Moreover, this was in part due to a structural shift in the composition of industrial output and employment away from the lower capital-intensive 'household' industry sector to the higher capital-intensive modern industrial sector. The overall expansion in industrial output, however, meant that there was no appreciable change in total industrial employment, but a relatively larger share was (as compared with the nineteenth century) provided by modern industry. Employment in the new-factory sector grew, while employment in the non-factory sector declined between 1901 and 1951.

However, there is a thesis first adumbrated by R. C. Dutt (1901), repeated by Dutt (1940), and given some statistical support by Colin Clark (1957)[33] which purports to show that in the later part of the nineteenth century the share of industrial employment in total employment was declining, so that whereas the West had an Industrial Revolution, India was being progressively de-industrialized.[34] This thesis has been questioned by Thorner[35] and to some extent by Krishnamurty (1967). More recently, however, Bagchi (1976) has sought to breathe fresh life into the thesis by using data from Buchanan-Hamilton's survey of Gangetic Bihar in the early nineteenth century. According to Bagchi, between 1809-13 and 1901, in the districts of Patna, Gaya, Bhagalpur, Purnea, Shahabad, and Monghyr, the proportion of industrial to total population fell from 18.6 to 8.5 per cent (see Table 8.3). His estimates (as well as the quality of the data) and the assumptions made have been questioned.[36] Krishnamurty has revised Bagchi's estimates (in particular for an overestimate of spinners and artisans) and finds that 'in 1807 there were about 902 thousand people supported by industry; the corresponding figure for 1901 is 1,231,000. Their percentage of the total population, however, declines from 12.4 to 10.5 over the period. So the evidence for Bihar suggests some *relative* decline in manufacturing but an *absolute* increase. One cannot however assume that this reflects the all-India situation in any way.'[37]

Thus, though the thesis of the 'de-industrialization' of India over the British century does not seem sustainable, it is undeniable that the impact of the influx of cheap textiles after the 1820s must have had deleterious effects on the levels of living of Indian handloom workers. The extent of the distress caused is more

TABLE 8.3(A).   Population Dependent on secondary Industry in Gangetic Bihar around 1809–1318

District	No. of spinners	No. of industrial workers or artisans other than spinners	Total population dependent on secondary industry	% industrial workers, of total population
Patna–Gaya	330,396	65,031	655,551	19.5
Bhagalpur	168,975	23,403	286,080	14.2
Purniya	287,000	60,172	587,860	20.2
Shahabad	159,500	25,557	287,285	20.2
TOTAL	945,871	174,163	1,816,776	18.6

TABLE 8.3(B).   Population Dependent on Secondary Indsutry, 1901

District	Total population	Industrial population	% industrial workers of total population
Patna	1,624,985	179,695	11.1
Gaya	2,059,933	187,016	9.1
Shahabad	1,962,696	228,051	11.6
Monghyr	2,068,804	155,439	7.5
Bhagalpur	2,088,953	115,618	5.5
Purnea	1,874,794	121,933	6.5
TOTAL	11,680,165	987,752	8.5

Source: Bagchi (1976, pp. 139–40, tables 1, 2).

difficult to assess—by anecdotal evidence, for instance: Sir William Bentinck's famous remark that 'the bones of the cotton weavers were bleaching the plains of India' points to widespread distress. It is not however clear to what extent the Indian handloom industry was wiped out by the influx of cheap imports. That there was a relative decline but probably no absolute decline is borne out by the fact that this is still a substantial industry in India, and no one has suggested that it has arisen only in the last twenty years, after its demise in the 1920s, because of post-Independence government policy! More seriously, Borpujari (1973) has argued, on the basis of an 1862 survey of the old cotton textile industry, that after the introduction of free trade, 'the spinning of cotton yarn by the old Indian methods was continuing at a considerable scale even after nearly half a century of competition from the yarn produced by the new methods developed in Britain'.[38] In weaving there was a switch to 'the weaving of coarse cloths with old Indian yarn'.[39]

'The relative strength of the old Indian spinners and weavers in the coarsest range of spinning and weaving asserted itself in the Indian market causing an expansion of this variety of old spinning and weaving sometimes at the expense of British products.'[40] The old fine cottons were no longer produced, and though some were woven with imported yarn in the 1850s the cotton famine of 1860–5 killed this luxury end of the handicraft industry off completely. After 1865 'what remained now of Indian spinning and weaving remained almost wholly an industry of the poor for the poor of India'.[41]

It is difficult to estimate whether the earnings of weavers declined as a result of this fall in demand for their labour. From some dubious data cited in Dutt (1901) it appears that in the early nineteenth–century weavers, particularly of coarse cloth, did not probably earn much more than common labourers. Bagchi (1972) states that in the early twentieth century 'before the First World War, generally speaking, weavers were just a cut above common laborers in urban centers as regards wages; while the lower limit of weavers' wages was reached by common laborers, the upper range was not.'

It seems likely therefore that there must have been some decline in earnings of weavers during the mid-nineteenth century, which could have been eased by some form of adjustment assistance if this were feasible—as it clearly was not, given the *laissez-faire* policy of the Government. Whether protection was justifiable instead is more debatable—even for that period.

The decline of the traditional cotton textile industry and its replacement by a modern one can be looked upon as an example of the working out of the principles of Ricardo's chapter 'On Machinery',[42] in which the substitution of fixed for working capital (as in the move from handicraft to modern methods in textile production) can be looked upon as first reducing or slowing down the growth in the demand for labour (as the machine initially displaced labour) but eventually leading to a higher demand for labour and growth of output. While we can regret the costs of the transition, and the fact that they were not mitigated by some form of adjustment assistance, these short-term costs of change are a necessary part of the price to be paid for the enormous long-term benefits of economic progress through industrialization.

If, moreover, following Hicks (1969), we consider the hallmark of the industrial revolution to be the substitution of fixed for working capital in industrial production as we move from the mercantile, handicraft, putting-out type modes to the fully fledged industrial, mechanical, and factory-based modes of industrial production, India had begun to experience the first stirrings of this revolution by 1851. Thus, far from being a century of de-industrialization, the British century marked the beginning of modern industrialization in India.

(iii) The growth of modern industry

Much of this industrialization was based on Indian enterprise and capital.[43] The resulting growth of Indian industry can be briefly charted before we turn to examine the central question of whether, as a result of alternative public policies, this growth could have been faster?

The first modern textile factory was set up by Parsi enterprise and capital in Bombay in 1851. The first jute mill whose output was exported was set up in 1854 by British (Scots) enterprise and capital in Calcutta. The first Indian steel mill was set up by the Tatas in Jamshedpur in 1911. Various other industries followed suit, especially with the introduction of discriminatory protection to various industries under the aegis of a newly established tariff board, and the gradual raising of the general *ad-valorem* tariff rate from 5 per cent in 1896 to 15 per cent in 1922, largely in pursuit of fiscal solvency.

The resulting industrial growth in India was better than in most other tropical countries in the period 1880–1913[44] as well as many in the West (see Table 8.4). Even in the 1913–38 period, Indian industrial growth was above the world average, and only lower than that in South Africa, USSR, Japan, Greece, and Finland (see Table 8.5). Yet India did not achieve industrial take-off like, say, Japan. Why?

It has been held that the failure of industry in India to develop even faster was due to the free-trade policies followed by the British in India from 1813 until the end of the First World War.[45] Some have seen an imperialist conspiracy in the policy of free trade as well as in the failure of British capital to invest and develop indigenous industries in which India clearly had a comparative advantage, most notably cotton textiles, before the late nineteenth century.[46] There is little evidence that can be adduced in favour of such conspiracy theories. The major reason, as Ray (1979) and Morris (1974, and *CEHI*) have emphasized, was the highly risky nature of industrial investment in India.

TABLE 8.4.   Industrial Growth: Cotton Textiles Industry, 1880–1914[a]

Year	No. of mills	No. employed (000)	No. of looms (000)	No. of spindles (000)	Yarn exports (lb. m.)
1880	58	39.5	13.3	1,408	26.7
1885	81	61.6	16.5	2,037	79.3
1890	114	99.2	22.1	2,935	170.5
1895	144	139.6	34.2	3,712	186
1900	194	156.4	40.5	4,942	118
1905	206	196.4	47.3	5,196	298
1907	227	225.4	66.7	5,763	216
1914	264	260.8	96.7	6,620	198[b]

a. Figures in the table are for cotton textiles. Overall comparative rates of growth of modern industry p.a.: India, 4–5%, Germany, 4.2%, Japan, 7% (Lidman and Domrese (1970, pp. 320–1)).
b. 1913–14.

Sources: Gadgil (1971), Lidman and Domrese (1970, p. 323).

TABLE 8.5(A).   Index of Manufacturing Production, 1938 (Base 1913 = 100)

Country	Index	Country	Index
South Africa	1,067.1	Romania	177.9
USSR	857.3	Norway	169.2
Japan	552.0	Canada	161.8
Greece	537.1	Latvia	158.0
Finland	300.1	Germany	149.3
India	239.7	Czechoslovakia	145.5
Sweden	232.2	Hungary	143.3
New Zealand	227.4	USA	143.0
Chile	204.2	Austria	127.0
Netherlands	204.1	UK	117.6
Denmark	202.1	France	114.6
Italy	195.2	Poland	105.2
Australia	192.3	Belgium	102.1
World	182.7	Switzerland	82.4
		Spain	58.0

Source: Ray (1979, p. 16, table 3).

TABLE 8.5(B).   Annual Indices of Manufacturing Production, 1913–1938

Year	Japan	India	Chile	Italy	Germany	Canada	USA	World
1913	100	100	100	100	100	100	100	100
1920	176.0	118.4	—	95.2	59.0	99.1	93.2	93.2
1921	167.1	112.6	—	98.4	74.7	89.4	81.1	81.1
1922	197.9	116.3	72.7	108.1	81.8	99.0	99.5	99.5
1923	206.4	116.5	77.9	119.3	55.4	108.3	104.5	104.5
1924	223.3	133.0	77.9	104.7	81.8	106.4	111.0	110.0
1925	221.8	132.0	89.6	156.8	94.9	116.5	120.7	120.7
1926	264.9	144.7	111.0	162.8	90.9	132.2	126.5	126.5
1927	270.0	151.5	115.8	161.2	122.1	141.0	134.5	134.5
1928	300.2	133.0	127.7	175.2	118.3	153.5	141.8	141.8
1929	324.0	157.3	156.3	181.0	117.3	162.7	153.8	153.3
1930	294.9	144.7	156.7	164.0	101.6	147.5	137.5	137.5
1931	288.1	155.3	116.3	145.1	85.1	128.2	122.5	122.5
1932	309.1	155.3	132.4	123.3	70.2	108.5	108.4	108.4
1933	360.7	167.7	146.2	133.2	79.4	108.5	121.7	121.7
1934	413.5	190.2	159.4	134.7	101.8	127.7	136.4	136.4
1935	457.8	205.4	183.6	162.2	116.7	141.0	154.5	154.5
1936	483.9	216.6	188.6	169.2	127.5	154.2	178.1	178.1
1937	551.0	234.9	196.6	194.5	138.1	174.8	195.8	195.8
1938	552.0	239.7	204.2	195.2	149.3	161.8	143.0	182.7

Source: Ray (1979, p. 17, table 4).

Most critics of British imperial industrial policy have identified the policies of *laissez-faire* and free trade with each other, and held them jointly to blame for the failure to promote Indian industrial development to the socially optimal degree. But the modern theory of trade and welfare has shown that the two need not and should not be looked at together. Given the well-known deviation of any actual market economy from the theoretical ideal of perfect competition, a case for various forms of government intervention and thence against *laissez-faire* can be readily constructed.[47] However, the case for free trade stands even when that for *laissez-faire* breaks down. Most arguments for protection turn out to be arguments for *domestic* taxes and subsidies,[48] and *not* for taxes and subsidies on foreign trade.[49] Thus the case for or against free trade stands independently of that for *laissez-faire*.

As far as commercial policy is concerned, the British Raj from 1813 can be roughly divided into two periods. The first, up to the First World War, was the period when free trade ruled. The subsequent period has been one where successively greater protection was provided to Indian industry. The remarkable feature of the first period from 1850 to 1914 was that a number of industries, both import-substituting as well as export-based, grew up—viz. cotton and jute textiles, steel, paper, sugar. Protection would clearly have been irrelevant in further promoting export industries such as jute textiles, but could obviously have induced further import substitution in the other industries. Whether or not that would have been socially desirable depends upon the reasons for granting protection.

It seems likely that manufacturing industry, particularly that producing engineering and heavy industrial goods such as steel, was in part hampered by the shortage of an adequately trained labour force. Thus for instance Tata Steel found that it took them from 1918–23 to 1935–9 to raise output per man from 5.52 tons to 36.32 tons![50] This process was facilitated both by replacing the higher-wage foreign supervisory staff by newly trained Indian personnel, and by the establishment of an apprentice school in 1927 for training fitters, welders, machinists, blacksmiths, pattern-makers, etc.[51]

It is well known that the private provision of such human skills leads to the creation of economies external to the firm but internal to the economy, and hence there is a case either for public provision of such industrial training or else the subsidization of the private firms' training costs. Furthermore, even for unskilled labour, there is the well-known consequence of dualism that, particularly for peasant farmers taking up industrial employment, their supply price in their new jobs is likely to be higher than their social opportunity cost—as the former is likely to be determined by their average product, the latter by their marginal product in agriculture.[52] Estimates for the 1970s suggest that the shadow wage rate for unskilled industrial labour in India was likely to be between 0.6 to 0.7 per cent of the market wage paid by industry. These features of the labour market provide a justification for some promotion of industry through some form of domestic tax subsidy system rather than for protection.

Similarly in the capital market, there were likely to have been various 'distortions' which required some public action. The provision of social overhead capital, in the form of power, transport, and education, though begun during the British Raj, was clearly inadequate for the needs of more rapidly growing industrial sectors. The differences in the levels of provision of social overhead capital during the last century of British rule and the first decades after Independence are highlighted by the data in Table 8.6.

Lack of complementary facilities means that the entrepreneur typically had to provide his own power and his own repair and replacement facilities and inventories. Thus, he needed not only more fixed capital but more working capital than the same enterprise would require in a developed system. Yet the businessman faced a situation where capital was typically more costly than in developed regions. Because local credit systems were badly underdeveloped, capital would flow only in fitful fashion. . . . All this suggests that the entrepreneur encountered higher real costs that needed the promise of higher rates of return if a gamble were to be taken. The great areas of uncertainty combined with the obvious objective obstacles to inhibit rapid expansion of modern industry.'[53]

For these reasons the private rate of return in industry could be expected to have been below the social rate. But protection was at most a second-best method and, as we shall see, in practice not even that for bringing the two together. It has also been argued by Bagchi (1972, 1976), that the development of Indian industry, in particular in the free trade period from 1850 to 1914, was hampered by limitations of demand. All observers seem to agree that there was no shortage of indigenous entrepreneurship, even though the lack of Bengali entrepreneurs in the nineteenth century remains somewhat of a puzzle.[54] Nevertheless, despite the large size of the population but given its poverty, there would not have been an expanding domestic market for industrial products. However, it is argued that from the 1850s onwards protection would have enabled the import substitution of the backwards linkage type (see Hirschman (1958))—that is, in earlier stages of production—to proceed at a much faster pace than was possible under free trade. The post-1914 industrial growth based on a diversification of the industrial structure is therefore considered to have been desirable, and the only lament is that this did not happen earlier.

In order, therefore, to judge whether protection did aid industrial growth, and more particularly whether it helped to counteract the various distortions in the 'capital' and 'labour' markets which hampered Indian industry, it is useful to compare Indian industrial growth performance in the free-trade and protection periods. Using Heston's (1983) estimates, the rate of industrial growth was fastest in the 1868–1900 period. This, however, was from a low base (see Table 6.4 and 8.7). Ian Little, using Sivasubramoniam's estimates, compared the growth-rate in value added (at constant domestic prices) for various aggregates and industries for the two periods 1900–13 and 1919–39 (see Table 8.7). From these and the run of Sivasubramoniam's figures it appears that the overall rate of

TABLE 8.6.   Pre-war and Post-war Trends in Public Investment

Pre-war years	Gross public investment (Rs m.)	% national income	Annual change in public investment (Rs m.)	Annual change in railway investment (Rs m.)
1925–6	644	—	+ 88	+ 58
1926–7	735	—	+ 91	+ 81
1927–8	827	—	+ 92	+ 81
1928–9	750	—	– 77	– 84
1929–30	814	—	+ 64	+ 69
1930–1	670	—	– 144	– 173
1931–2	488	3.0	– 182	– 96
1932–3	338	1.5	– 150	– 86
1933–4	334	1.6	– 4	– 4
1934–5	350	1.4	+ 16	+ 30
1935–6	436	2.2	+ 86	+ 28
1936–7	359	1.8	– 77	– 36
1937–8	358	1.7	– 1	+ 4

Post-war years	Gross public investment (Rs m.)	% net national income	% gross national investment	Gross fixed investment in railways (Rs m.)
1948–9	2,100	2.3	25	361
1949–50	2,570	2.9	28	374
1950–1	2,620	2.7	28	256
1951–2	2,860	2.9	25	654
1952–3	3,035	3.1	29	637
1953–4	3,375	3.2	30	701
1954–5	4,300	4.5	34	846
1955–6	5,700	5.7	38	1,271
1956–7	6,900	6.1	39	1,505
1957–8	8,300	7.3	46	2,159
1958–9	8,600	6.8	44	2,226
1959–60	7,800	6.1	—	1,346
1960–1	9,600	6.6	—	2,590

Sources: Estimates of gross public investment in undivided India: Thavaraj (1960, pp. 215–30). These figures refer to investment (real asset creation) undertaken by all the public enterprises and State trading organizations belonging to the central, provincial, other local governments and other public bodies, except the port trusts.

National income and gross public investment in new India were obtained from Government of India (1961b) and *Papers on National Income*, pp. 122–34. These figures cover investment by the central and State Governments, port trusts, improvement trusts, municipal corporations, district and local boards, and village panchayats. It also includes railways, post and telegraphs, forests, road transport, irrigation, and electricity departments of the central and State Governments but certain public corporations (e.g. Indian Airlines) are not included. Estimates of gross national investment are given by S. J. Patel in the *Economic Weekly* (annual no.), Jan. 1960. Railway investment figures from the Ministry of Railways, Government of India, *Reports of the Railway Board* (annual).

Derived in Healey (1965, p. 8, table 1).

TABLE 8.7. Manufacturing Growth-rates: Value Added (Constant Prices), 1900–1939

	1868–1900	1900–13	1919–39
1. Factory manufacturing	10.36	6.0	4.8
2. Small-scale manufacturing	—	4.7	2.3
3. Total of 1 and 2	—	4.7	3.3
4. Cotton	—	6.5	3.9
5. Sugar	—	2.8	8.5
6. Paper	—	1.5	6.4
7. Wool	—	3.6	4.2

Source: Little (1982), derived from Sivasubramonian (1977, tables 6, 10, 12, 13, 19) and from Heston (1983) for 1868–1900.

TABLE 8.8. Imports of Industrial Machinery and Mill-work into India, 1900–1940

Year	Value of imports of machinery and mill-work excluding agricultural machinery (Rs 000)	Index nos. of textile machinery prices (not comparable between panels)	Index nos. of textile machinery prices on a comparable basis (1904 = 100)	'Real' value of machinery and mill-work imported into India (Rs 000)
1899–1900	24,094	—	—	—
1900–1	20,554	—	—	—
1901–2	27,305	—	—	—
1902–3	30,130	—	—	—
1904–5	36,429	100.00	100.00	36,429
1905–6	45,919	98.29	98.29	46,718
1906–7	53,445	93.51	93.51	57,454
1907–8	62,940	95.41	95.41	65,968
1908–9	61,223	102.09	102.09	59,970
1909–10	44,901	100.68	100.68	44,598
1910–11	41,784	109.29	109.29	38,232
1911–12	41,021	107.54	107.54	38,145
1912–13	50,627	107.34	107.34	47,165
1913–14	72,524	103.67	103.67	69,957
1914–15	55,886	100.00	109.10	51,225
1915–16	43,926	110.14	120.16	36,556
1916–17	50,728	158.30	172.71	29,372
1917–18	41,037	218.28	238.14	17,232
1918–19	46,879	277.90	303.19	15,462
1919–20	84,155	265.42	289.57	29,062
1920–1	202,322	300.29	327.62	61,755
1921–2	315,205	339.23	370.10	85,168

Year	Value of imports of machinery and mill-work excluding agricultural machinery (Rs 000)	Index nos. of textile machinery prices (not comparable between panels)	Index nos. of textile machinery prices on a comparable basis (1904 = 100)	'Real' value of machinery and mill-work imported into India (Rs 000)
1922–3	218,172	289.45	315.79	69,088
1923–4	171,816	223.96	244.34	70,318
1924–5	126,448	210.28	229.42	55,116
1925–6	126,776	194.40	212.09	59,775
1926–7	116,453	210.61	229.78	50,680
1927–8	131,738	222.05	242.26	54,379
1928–9	163,761	184.70	201.51	81,237
1929–30	161,677	180.88	197.34	81,928
1930–1	126,676	186.52	203.28	62,316
1931–2	95,888	100.0	216.68	44,253
1932–3	98,213	87.82	190.29	51,612
1933–4	119,948	84.70	183.53	65,356
1934–5	113,915	83.38	180.67	63,051
1935–6	125,311	98.64	213.73	58,631
1936–7	126,281	111.92	242.51	52,072
1937–8	170,414	112.47	243.70	69,928
1938–9	189,083	121.67	263.63	71,723
1939–40	144,761	136.44	295.64	48,965

Source: Accounts relating to the sea-borne trade of British India, derived from Bagchi (1972, p. 80, table 3.2).

growth of manufacturing industry slowed down in the inter-war period, and this was largely the result of the slowing down in the growth of the cotton textile industry. Of course, as Little rightly notes, 'the fact that Indian industrial output grew faster in the free trade period than in the inter-war period does not of course prove that industrial protection is bad for *industrial* growth. Although this is not impossible in the long run, it could hardly be so in a period when simple import-substitution could take place.'[55]

But industrial growth must be judged by the realized social returns to the investments made; it cannot be taken as a sensible criterion of economic performance in itself. No estimates of social rates of return are available for the industries which grew under protection in the inter-war period. But from a detailed cost–benefit study of sugar,[56] the fastest-growing industry in the inter-war period, for the late 1960s, it does appear that social losses occurred. It would have been better to have grown other crops on the land taken up by the promotion of sugar-cane production because of the protection offered to sugar. Similarly, as we shall see in the next part, when the logic of promoting industrial growth through protection, and without any regard to social costs and benefits, was followed in the post-Independence period the effects, if not disastrous, have certainly been disappointing. More seriously for our purposes, the relative stagnation of Indian industry in the mid-1960s and its limited success in raising the levels of employment and incomes in the economy can be directly traced to the policy of discriminatory protection which began in the 1920s and was given such a powerful impetus by the coalescing of economic and political nationalism and the construction of a highly differentiated and socially enormously costly system of protection in post-Independence India.

Consider some simple contrasts between the 1900–1913 free-trade and the 1919–39 protection periods. First in Table 8.8 we can get a rough idea of the magnitude of industrial capital formation. For in the absence of any domestic production of machinery, industrial capital formation would depend upon imports of machinery, excluding agricultural machinery. In this table it appears that there was no marked increase in the buoyancy of industrial investment as a result of protection.[57]

Nor was employment growth promoted by protection. Table 8.9 gives Sivasubramonian's estimates of numbers employed in factories in India by different industries. This shows that for the 1900–13 period and 1919–1939 periods, total factory employment grew nearly twice as fast in the first than the second period. Moreover, the rate of growth of employment was slowing down in the inter-war period, from 2.4 per cent between 1919 and 1929 to 2.2 per cent between 1930 and 1939. Further, the inter-war (1919–39) rate of growth of 2.29 per cent p.a. was not much below the growth-rate of factory employment of 2.9 per cent between 1961 and 1971. Taken together with the growing capital stock in industry over the period since 1914, this implies that the capital labour ratio has been steadily rising since 1914. This rise, which became such a marked feature of post-Independence industrial growth, was a trend set in the period when India switched from free trade to protection.

None of this is surprising. Much of the earlier protection offered was defensive, it was rarely justifiable, by modern standards, on 'dynamic' and 'infant industry' grounds. Instead of infants being promoted, industries were protected against technical change occurring elsewhere, thus dampening the incentives for domestic producers to adapt to these changes. An example would be cotton textiles. Instead of adapting to technical change occurring abroad, Indian textile producers (mainly in Bombay[58]) who had so triumphantly turned the tables against Lancashire in the second half of the nineteenth century, sought protection in the twentieth. Or else industries such as sugar, in which India had no long-run comparative advantage, were promoted through protection. Nor was the policy of discriminating protection a sensible one, even granting that, because it was not feasible to offset the obvious distortions in labour and capital

TABLE 8.9(A). Average Daily Number of Workers Employed in Factories in India, 1900–1947 (thousands)

Year	Government and local fund factories	Textiles	Metals and minerals excluding mines	Engineering	Food, drink and tobacco	Chemicals	Paper and printing	Wood, stone, and glass	Miscellaneous	All industries
1900–1	—	—	—	—	—	—	—	—	—	584
1901–2	—	—	—	—	—	—	—	—	—	617
1902–3	—	407	20	73	14	10	17	10	91	642
1903–4	—	427	23	75	15	12	16	10	88	666
1904–5	—	460	24	85	15	12	17	17	136	766
1905–6	34	492	25	88	15	13	17	18	101	803
1906–7	42	526	29	94	16	12	19	21	134	893
1907–8	72	426	30	86	19	38	15	29	156	871
1908–9	73	445	28	74	21	55	22	28	148	894
1909–10	66	454	26	82	20	68	18	28	166	929
1910–11	67	456	28	82	24	62	18	39	181	957
1911–12	68	441	28	87	27	50	18	47	167	933
1912–13	78	476	21	97	32	41	20	38	200	1,003
1913–14	72	484	24	108	36	30	21	38	210	1,023
1914–15	108	508	31	103	40	26	26	42	205	1,089
1915–16	97	534	24	90	37	25	20	47	199	1,073
1916–17	112	557	28	103	47	23	23	42	208	1,141
1917–18	115	559	29	102	47	22	22	48	219	1,163
1918–19	128	577	35	103	48	25	23	50	224	1,213
1919–20	121	598	67	106	50	27	24	62	248	1,303

Table 8.9(A). *contd*

Year	Government and local fund factories	Textiles	Metals and minerals excluding mines	Engineering	Food, drink and tobacco	Chemicals	Paper and printing	Wood, stone, and glass	Miscellaneous	All industries
1920–1	127	623	54	123	56	32	25	80	269	1,389
1921–2	134	648	57	113	71	39	26	98	281	1,467
1922–3	123	698	76	152	67	34	25	35	209	1,419
1923–4	123	704	58	148	107	32	26	45	215	1,458
1924–5	109	720	49	170	126	36	26	40	230	1,506
1925–6	152	732	43	146	128	42	26	42	236	1,547
1926–7	155	728	41	151	133	48	28	68	233	1,585
1927–8	159	733	40	153	140	50	28	49	236	1,588
1928–9	172	720	29	146	146	49	30	45	239	1,576
1929–30	164	751	41	152	153	52	31	55	258	1,657
1930–1	156	755	41	139	143	54	32	59	245	1,624
1931–2	144	725	36	125	139	51	30	55	236	1,541
1932–3	137	731	33	111	162	48	30	50	220	1,522
1933–4	131	704	35	114	177	51	31	50	233	1,526
1934–5	148	736	52	127	242	58	34	66	243	1,706
1935–6	147	814	46	133	213	60	34	68	244	1,759
1936–7	159	818	48	131	227	60	36	72	268	1,819
1937–8	177	904	55	138	244	65	39	61	275	1,958
1938–9	171	954	57	147	259	67	44	73	265	2,037
1939–40	171	935	62	154	269	69	46	86	258	2,050
1940–1	199	948	73	165	288	73	50	88	260	2,144

1941–2[a]	221	953	76	204	280	73	48	78	223	2,156 (2,492)
1942–3[a]	299	965	82	224	284	74	49	82	223	2,282 (2,638)
1943–4[a]	356	1,002	93	254	293	84	51	90	213	2,436 (2,816)
1944–5[a]	420	993	91	265	295	91	53	96	310	2,614 (2,916)
1945–6	496	1,028	155	291	365	122	62	141	461	3,121
1946–7	394	1,156	94	240	375	123	61	134	267	2,844

a. Figures for 1941–2 to 1944–5 relate to British India only. Figures in brackets in the last column indicate adjusted figures, including native States.

Source: Sivasubramonian (1977, pp. 433–4, table 2).

TABLE 8.9(B).   Rates of Growth of Employment in Manufacturing, 1900–1939

	1902–13	1919–39
Textiles	1.59	2.25
Metals	1.67	– 0.39
Engineering	3.62	1.89
Food, drink, and tobacco	8.97	8.78
Chemicals	10.50	4.80
Paper and printing	1.94	3.31
Wood, stone, and glass	12.90	1.65
Miscellaneous	7.90	0.20
All industries	4.33	2.29

Source: Table 8.9(*a*).

markets, some protection of manufacturing made sense on 'second best' grounds. For these considerations would have merited protection of manufacturing in general. Instead, the policy of discriminatory protection created a multiplicity of effective protective rates in the traded goods sector without any economic rationale. Most seriously, by implicitly raising the domestic relative price and thence profitability of import substitution to that of exporting manufacturers, protection introduced a bias against the establishment of export industries, and thereby condemned Indian industry to the limits set by the size of the Indian market. The belief that industrial growth during the free-trade period was retarded by a lack of demand thus became a self-fulfilling prophecy once the nationalist solution—protection—was adopted.

All these points can be illustrated by the changing fortunes of India's largest industry—cotton textiles—which had grown up without any protection in the latter half of the nineteenth century.[59] The increasing protection granted to the industry in the inter-war period was a defensive measure against the growing efficiency of the Japanese in textile production. The lower Indian wages relative to Japan were in large part offset (by the 1930s) by the increased number of looms per worker and the higher productivity of workers in Japan (see Table 8.10). This lower labour efficiency also meant that 'the use of automatic looms in India was considerably delayed in relation to Japan. Millowners argued that without an increase in the number of looms handled by each worker in India, it was not profitable to use automatic looms.'[60]

A relatively large home market, increasingly protected against imports, reduced the incentives for Indian producers to improve efficiency. In the post-Independence period, investment in the cotton-textile industry was discouraged, on the grounds that existing capacity was sufficient to meet home demand, and investments to produce for exports were discouraged or made difficult by the trade control system erected from 1956 onwards. As a result India, which had established the first cotton-textile industry in the developing world,

TABLE 8.10. Comparative Labour Efficiency in Japan, India, and Britain for Low-count Cotton Manufacture, 1932

Source	Looms per weaver	Average efficiency per loom (%)	Working hours index (Britain = 100)	Wages (Rs per worker per day)
Ordinary looms (Japan)	5.5	—	—	—
Japan average	6	95–6	250	2–4
Toyoda looms	50	—	—	—
Britain	4	85	100	4–8
India	2	80	125	2

Source: Ray (1979, p. 66, table 17).

lost out in the markets for ready-made clothing and textiles in North America which boomed in the decades following the Second World War. The opportunity that India lost was taken up by the young upstarts on the Pacific rim—Hong Kong, Korea, and Taiwan—who used the opportunities provided by these export markets to transform the living conditions of their peoples within a decade to levels which for the mass of Indians still lie at the end of a rainbow!

4. FISCAL AND MONETARY POLICY

The damage done by the policy of protection, from the 1920s onwards, to the prospects of growth of Indian manufactured exports was compounded by the exchange rate policy followed by the Raj. The intricacies and twists and turns of fiscal and monetary policy are beyond the scope of this book. However, there are a number of points which are relevant.

The first point to note is the obvious one:

British rule was not maintained for the benefit of the Indian, nor simply for the sake of direct British interest in India; the Raj was there to keep firm the foundation on which much of the structure of formal and informal empire rested. For London the twin imperatives of Indian policy were that the Indian empire should pay for itself and that Indian resources should be available in the Imperial cause.[61]

But since 1857, to avoid a nationalist revolt of the whole populace, the Government of India had learnt to keep the domestic tax burden within bounds. It had continually to balance London's needs against those of its Indian subjects. Each imperial crisis, for example, the two World Wars, led to an increased demand for resources from London. To meet these without provoking Indian resistance the Raj made political concessions to Indian collaborators which effectively eroded its powers to tax in subsequent imperial crises. Thus over time the ability of the Raj to meet London's demands was gradually whittled away.

These twin sets of pressures meant that the Government of India had to tax its subjects lightly, and a large part of the resulting revenues were committed to maintaining an Indian army to subserve imperial ends. 'The greatest, because the only irreplaceable, advantage which the British derived from India was the use of the Indian army. In 1880 the Indian taxpayers supported 130,000 Indian troops and 60,000 British troops; in Lord Salisbury's words "India was an English barrack in the Oriental seas from which we may draw any number of troops without paying for them" '[62]

Hence military expenditure accounted for about 40 per cent of the Government of India's gross expenditure (see Table 8.11). This meant that on the one hand, the balance available for developmental work in India—for instance in the development of the social overhead capital which the country undoubtedly needed—was severely limited, while on the other, given the precariousness of its finances, any exogenous shock like a monsoon failure or a fall in India's terms of trade, or a depreciation in the rupee's external value (resulting in a rise in the

TABLE 8.11(A). Percentage of Revenue and Expenditure by Major Heads: Central Government, 1919–1940

	1919–20	1924–5	1929–30	1934–5	1939–40
Revenue:					
Land	12.5	0.3	0.3	0.2	0.1
Opium	3.5	2.8	2.3	0.6	0.4
Salt	4.4	5.4	5.1	6.6	8.6
Stamps	4.3	0.2	0.2	0.3	0.3
Excise	4.2	0.3	0.4	0.3	0.2
Customs	17.1	33.3	38.6	43.1	41.7
Income tax	13.6	11.6	12.6	14.4	13.2
Posts	7.0	0.8	0.01	1.0	1.3
Railways	24.0	27.1	28.0	26.5	27.1
Irrigation	3.1	0.1	0.1	0.01	0.01
Other	6.3	18.1	12.39	6.99	7.09
Expenditure:					
Direct demands	5.0	4.2	3.1	3.3	3.1
Interest	5.9	14.2	12.5	10.9	9.5
Posts	5.1	0.2	0.6	0.7	0.6
Civil departments	5.7	7.7	9.6	9.1	8.8
Railways	7.0	23.1	23.4	26.6	23.6
Irrigation	2.3	0.2	0.2	0.05	0.1
Civil works	1.2	1.3	1.9	2.0	2.1
Military	65.1	45.2	44.6	40.8	40.0
Other	2.7	3.9	4.1	6.65	12.2

Source: Governments of India Revenue and Expenditure Accounts, 1919–20 to 1934–5, Statistical Abstract for British India 1930–31 to 1930–40, derived from Tomlinson (1979, pp. 155–6, table 4.4).

TABLE 8.11(B).   Percentage of Revenue and Expenditure by Major Heads: All Provincial
                 Governments (excluding Burma), 1924–1940

	1924–5	1929–30	1934–5	1939–40
Revenue:[a]				
Land revenue	37.5	33.2	36.6	30.7
Excise	22.7	22.2	18.6	13.6
Stamps	15.7	15.7	15.1	11.1
Forests	4.5	4.5	3.5	3.2
Registration	1.5	1.5	1.5	1.3
Irrigation	8.4	9.2	10.1	11.9
Other	9.7	13.7	14.6	28.2
Expenditure:				
General administration	13.5	12.3	11.8	11.7
Justice	6.8	6.0	5.9	5.3
Jails	2.6	2.5	2.4	2.2
Police	14.2	12.7	13.6	12.6
Education	13.1	14.1	14.2	14.0
Medical	3.8	4.1	4.1	4.1
Public health	1.9	2.2	1.8	1.9
Agriculture	2.2	2.8	2.6	2.9
Industries	0.8	1.0	0.9	1.3
Cooperatives	—	—	—	1.0
Civil works	8.6	10.9	8.6	8.7
Debt services	3.8	3.7	3.8	2.2
Direct demands	10.7	10.7	9.3	10.5
Other	18.0	17.0	21.0	21.6

a. Excluding contributions from Central Government.

Source: As for Table 8.11(*a*).

rupee cost of financing the home charges fixed in sterling) could tumble the
Government of India into insolvency.

It was in response to these periodic financial crises that the gradual departure
from free-trade principles was made, and (see Chapter 5) the gradual devolution
of political and accompanying fiscal powers to the representative regional and
local legislatures became necessary.

Thus after the fall in the gold price of silver (from the 1870s onwards) and the
ensuing instability in the exchange markets in the 1890s, the silver rupee depre-
ciated against the gold-based pound. This caused a severe transfer problem for
the Government of India in meeting its home charges—denominated in
sterling—out of its relatively inelastic revenues—denominated in Rupees. Apart
from abandoning the silver standard, the currency committee of 1893 recommended a revenue tariff as the best solution for the Government of India's need

to increase its rupee resources. For any rise in direct taxation (including land revenue) would have led to dangerous political agitation, and increases in most of the feasible indirect taxes would either be unpopular (as on sugar or tobacco), yield diminishing revenues (opium), or hurt India's export trade and thus the balance of payments (export taxes).[63]

The same dilemma had to be faced at every financial crisis, of which there were many more in the twentieth than there had been in the second half of the nineteenth century. Each time, the solution adopted was to increase government income through raising import duties. Thus 'by the 1920's revenue tariffs were the largest single source of governmental income in India.'[64] Besides being fiscally expedient, this creeping protectionism was politically popular with both the political and the economic nationalists, who viewed the previous half-century's free-trade policies as damaging Indian interests, particularly those of its industry—even though, by hindsight and in the light of the modern theory of trade and welfare, we can now see that protection did more harm than good to Indian industry.

Equally serious for the efficient growth of Indian industry was the exchange rate policy that the Government followed after the First World War. During the period when sterling was floating, the rupee appreciated. In 1925, when sterling assumed an overvalued fixed parity, the rupee exchange rate was fixed at its pre-war parity, at a clearly overvalued level. To validate this overvaluation, which helped the Government of India in its tranfer of the home charges but on the other hand weakened the balance of payments, a deflationary monetary policy was followed during a large part of the inter-war period.[65]

Increasing protection, an overvalued currency, and general monetary deflation did not provide the most propitious circumstances for the growth of a healthy modern manufacturing sector. Taken together they tended to reduce the openness of the economy, a trend which was to be accentuated by the intensification of the first two prongs of the above policy by the Government of independent India. Most seriously, they turned Indian industry away from export markets on which alone a dynamic industrial sector could be built, given the natural limits faced by import-substituting industrialization to meet a home demand naturally limited by the poverty of the country and the inherent difficulties in transforming its traditional agricultural base.

Thus, from the end of the First World War, cheered on by the nationalists and by those increasingly impressed by the autarkic forced industrialization of Stalin's Russia (rather than the more open-economy-oriented but more spectacular industrial development of Japan), but motivated primarily by the exigencies of imperial finance, India was set on that disastrous road to an inward-looking, increasingly inefficient, and capital-intensive form of industrialization which was to culminate in industrial stagnation after the 1960s, when the limits of import substitution (both of the easy mass-consumer goods and the more difficult intermediate and capital goods) had been reached. In the process India built a monument to the vanity of its newly Westernized élite, for whom the domestic replication of the full panoply of industries in fully developed economies (irrespective of their social profitability) became a symbol of national pride. But their diagnosis of India's economic ills had been wrong from the start. For it was not free trade but *laissez-faire* that had arguably retarded industrial growth during the first half of the British Raj. By providing these Indians the poisoned chalice of protection, albeit for their own selfish ends, the British, unbeknownst to them or them successors, left their worst and bitterest legacy to Indian's labouring millions.

NOTES

1. Spear (1965, p. 112).
2. Ibid.
3. Ibid., 113.
4. Ibid.
5. Maddison (1971, p. 58).
6. Ibid., 56.
7. Dutt (1901, p. 202).
8. Baran (1957, pp. 277–85).
9. Maddison (1971, p. 59, table iii:1). He estimates that, in 1850, Indian exports were US$89 m. and US$786 m in 1913.
10. See Lewis (1978) and Lidman and Domrese (1970).
11. Lidman and Domrese (1970, p. 311).
12. Ibid., 312. They also note that in 1913 India's agricultural exports were about $1.70 per head. Japan's agricultural exports, starting from a much lower base some 40 years earlier, were now about 60% larger per head and were growing by 4% p.a.
13. The Indian cotton industry in the 19th century was largely a spinning industry, producing yarn rather than finished cloth. 'Of all the cotton mills in existence in 1903–4, just over half were entirely devoted to spinning but only 6 exclusively to weaving' (Charlesworth (1982, p. 38).
14. Lewis (1978, p. 169, table 7.4) presents the following estimates of Indian exports per head in 1913: primary, $2.0; manufactures, $0.5; total, $2.5. The annual rate of growth of total exports between 1883–1913 was 3.0%.
15. Maddison (1971, p. 59).
16. Lewis (1978, p. 205).
17. Lewis (1978, p. 205). Thus up to 1921 area under cultivation outpaced population, but the situation was reversed after 1921. According to Blyn, between 1891 and 1921 population grew at 0.84% p.a.; from 1921 to 1947 population grew at 1.12% p.a. while acreage grew at 0.35% p.a. (Kumar and Krishnamurty (1981)).
18. See Raychaudhuri (1968), Kumar and Krishnamurty (1981).
19. See Narain (1965, p. 5).
20. McLane (1963) estimates the annual average export surplus was £15 m. between 1899–1900 and 1908–09 (p. 23). The total home charges which India had to pay England were about £18.5 m. on average over the same period. The balance of these charges over and above the export surplus was financed by borrowing in England. These home charges amounted to more than quarter of the total expenditure of the Government of India (ibid., 25). Not all the home charges, however, constituted payments which would not otherwise have been incurred on economic grounds. The payments on account of interest payments on its foreign borrowings, to finance railway construction during the 19th century, were the largest part of this 'economic portion' of the home charges—though it is arguable whether the social returns to India from these borrowings matched the effective cost of borrowing (see ibid., 29 ff. for the various points of view). The best economic estimates of the drain are by Mukerjee (1972).

21. Maddison (1971, p. 65).
22. In 1911 (see Tables 6.1 and 6.8) the total population of India, including the native States, was 303 m. and thet total labour force was 122 m.
23. Maddison (1971, p. 44).
24. Curzon to Hamilton, 23 Apr. 1900, MSS, Eur. D.51015, cited in McLane (1963, p. 38).
25. That this was motivated by pure racial arrogance rather than by any apparent differences in productivity between the British and the educated Indians is borne out by the following uncompromising stand taken by Curzon in the communication cited above. While Curzon was willing to let a few Indians who could afford to go to England and pass the ICS exam into the superior positions in the British bureaucracy coveted by the new Westernized Indian élite, he was clear that 'the highest ranks of civil employment in India . . . must nevertheless, as a rule, be held by Englishmen, for the reason that they posses, partly by heredity, partly by upbringing, and partly by education, the knowledge of the principles of Government, the habits of mind and the vigour of character which are essential for the task and that, the rule of India being a British rule and any other rule being in the circumstances of the case impossible, the tone and standard should be set by those who have created and are responsible for it' (ibid).
26. McLane estimates that in 1901 'the economic charge was £10.4 million and £6.98 million "the political charges" ' (1963, p. 28)—the latter being the payments India made to foreigners.
27. Maddison (1971, p. 55).
28. Ibid. See Gadgil (1971, pp. 38–45), who states that the most important causes for the decline of handicrafts under British rule were '(1) the disappearance of the native Indian courts; (2) the establishment of an alien rule with the influx of the many foreign influences that such a change in the nature of Government meant; (3) the competition of a more highly developed form of industry' (p. 38).
29. Dutt (1901, p. 180).
30. See Morris D. Morris (*CEHI*, vol. i).
31. But see Bagchi (1972), Ray (1979), Harnetty (1972).
32. Maddison (1971, p. 57). See also Morris (*CEHI*, vol. i).
33. Clark (1957, pp. 499, 515).
34. This also became part of the nationalist dogma. See e.g. Nehru (1956, pp. 315 ff.), Dutt, op. cit. states: 'the real picture of modern India is a picture of what has been aptly called 'de-industrialization'—that is the decline of the old handicraft industry without the compensating advance of modern industry. The advance of factory industry has not overtaken the decay of handicraft. The process of decay characteristic of the 19th century has been carried forward in the 20th century and in the post-war period' (p. 165); and this, Nehru argued, 'is the real funda-mental cause of the appalling poverty of the Indian people, and it is of comparatively recent origin' (p. 316). Nehru, of course, was to seek to redress this when he came to power by putting India on the road of forced industrialization.
35. Thorner and Thorner (1962, ch. 6).
36. See Vicziany (1979) and Bagchi's (1979) reply.
37. Kumar and Krishnamurty (1981, p. 11).
38. Borpujari (1973, p. 41).
39. Ibid., 48.
40. Ibid., 49. It should also be noted that during the period of the cotton famine the survey reported 'a migration of weavers into agriculture, unskilled labor and beggary'. (ibid., 44).
41. Bagchi (1972, p. 225).
42. See Hicks (1969, pp. 151–4 and appendix).
43. See Ray (1979, pp. 240–1), Morris (*CEHI*, vol. ii).
44. See Lidman and Domrese (1970, p. 320–1): 'The rate of growth of large-scale industry was higher than in most other tropical countries at this time. An index of industrial production based on six large-scale manufacturing industries (Meek (1973)) more than doubled from 1896 to 1914. . . . By 1914 the Indian economy had developed the world's fourth largest cotton textile industry and the second largest jute manufacturing industry.'
45. See Bagchi (1972, 1976).
46. Sen (1965) has given this a more sophisticated twist in terms of a 'social ethos' of British capita-lists who would have felt it unpatriotic to invest in India. However, as Ray (1979) rightly notes: 'No social ethos against "unpatriotic" conduct was strong enough to deter Lancashire machi-nery manufacturers from helping the infant Bombay textile industry to its feet. Nor was that

ethos sufficiently powerful to check progressive British involvement in the cotton mill industry of Bombay' (p. 32).

47. For the application of this modern theory of optimal governmental intervention to India, see Lal (1980a).

48. Except for the so-called 'optimum tariff' argument, when a country has monopoly or monopsonistic power in foreign trade.

49. See Corden (1974) for an excellent summary of this modern theory of trade and welfare.

50. Ray (1979, p. 91).

51. Ibid., 91.

52. For estimates of the shadow wage rate of industrial labour in India in the early 1970s see Lal (1980a).

53. Morris (1974), cited in Ray (1979, p. 232).

54. See Kumar (1972, p. 80) for a review of the studies which seek to explain the relative weakness of Bengali entrepreneurship. One major thesis is that the longer the British contact with a region, the lower its entrepreneurial *élan*. But this does not explain why the Parsis, who had as long a history of contact with the British as the Bengalis, became India's first industrial entrepreneurs (see Kulke (1974)). It seems more likely that the Westernized Bengalis belonged to the traditional literary Hindu castes, and found it congenial to identify themselves with the contemptuous attitude toward commerce of the British bureaucracy based in imperial Calcutta. By contrast the Parsis and Marwaris were traditional trading communities. Moreover Bombay, which the Westernized Parsis increasingly made their home, came closest to being a mercantile city State in India. The Parsi merchants (see Kulke) were in the forefront not only of commercial but also of civic and political life of Bombay. At least in Bombay politicians and bureaucrats did not look upon commerce with the contempt it was accorded in the rest of India, as well as by the British rulers. On the Marwaris, see Timberg (1978).

55. Little (1982, p. 364).

56. See Lal (1972).

57. As Little (1982) remarks 'The average annual figure for 1904/05 to 1913/14 was Rs 50.4 billion, 22% higher after an average lapse of 20½ years, showing a growth rate of less than 1% per annum—less than of real national income. It appears that investment was no more buoyant in the protection period than it was before 1914.'

58. The Bombay mill-owners sought protection in the 1920s, but not the Ahmedabad ones, who were technologically better adapted. The Bombay Mill-owners Association took a pro-British stance while the Ahmedabad ones were nationalist.

59. The Indian textile industry was largely a spinning industry, and there were substantial cotton-piece good imports from Britain in the 19th century. Also, as Charlesworth (1982) notes, 'There is no evidence that the historical shift towards complete free trade during the late 19th century directly harmed Indian industry. Farnie (1979) points out that Indian cotton mills enjoyed boom conditions in the years immediately following the complete abolition of the cotton duties in 1882' (p. 64).

60. Ray (1979, p. 67).

61. Tomlinson (1975, pp. 338–9).

62. Ibid.

63. Tomlinson (1975, p. 334).

64. Ibid., 345.

65. See Tomlinson (1979), Ray (1979).

9

The Evolution of Labour Markets[1]

INTRODUCTION

Hicks (1969) writes:

the Market, as a form of organization, is the creation of traders and subsequently financiers, not (or not at all to the same extent) of farmers or of artisans. The commodity markets and the financial markets are the places where the market system is at home; when it proceeds to the formation of factor markets, land and labor markets, it is penetrating, or 'colonizing', relatively refractory territory. This was territory where its principles did not fit, or could only with difficulty be made to fit. Thus there was a struggle, which begins very early, and continues (though in forms which are undergoing significant changes) into our own day.[2]

The labour market would be closest to a commodity market, and thence to the textbook model of a perfectly competitive factor market, if all labour were of the casual labour type.[3] By contrast, in the pre-mercantile phase of development, and in much of traditional agriculture, we would expect that, though labour was exchanged (as it has been for millennia in Indian villages and in urban handicraft industries) directly in agricultural operations, or through the provision of various village-level services (provided by barbers, priests, blacksmiths), and of course indirectly through the exchange of the commodities that it produced, the spread of a modern labour market would be limited. We therefore examine the evolution of the labour market during the Raj in rural and urban India in turn.

1. RURAL LABOUR

The traditional exchange of labour services within the village community was · undertaken within the framework of the jajmani system (see Chapter 3, which also provides an economic rationale). If our earlier a priori arguments have any merit, this system depended both upon relative village autarky and upon relative demographic stability for its perpetuation. These major parameters of the Hindu equilibrium would need to have changed to alter this system of direct exchange of rural labour into a more overt mercantile transaction, closer to exchange in a pure (casual) labour market.

The period of British rule eroded the long-standing bases for the continuation of the jajmani system with its increasing commercialization of agriculture, its at first slow but steady rise in population (which became a gallop after 1921), and the creation of a land market with the definition and legal enforcement of a myriad of different types of right in land. It appears from more recent sociological evidence that, though the system has not completely disappeared, it is dying. Thus cash payments have increasingly replaced payments in kind, and even in areas where the jajmani system has not disappeared it covers a smaller portion of the village and a smaller number of castes. But patron–client relationships between the landed and the landless persist despite the decline of the formal caste system.[4]

The major reason for the decline of the jajmani system is probably demographic. For with an expansion of rural labour supply the danger of a labour shortage (as we argued in ch. 3), which led to this system of tying down labour, would be less serious: the pattern of labour demand and the form of payments to labour would alter.

Nineteenth- or early twentieth-century evidence to clinch this argument is rare. Atchi Reddy (1979) shows how the demographic situation in Nellore altered drastically between the two periods 1871–1921 and post-1921. In the earlier period there was hardly any increase in the population of Nellore district, and the numbers of male agricultural labourers actually fell; but the net sown area increased by 7 per cent. There was a complete change in the fifty years after 1921. Population increased by 68 per cent, and the number of agricultural labourers by 150 per cent, as mortality declined and emigration channels became clogged. Meanwhile gross sown area increased by about 21 per cent.

The major effects of this increase in the district's rural labour supply were twofold. First, attached labourers (i.e. those who were contracted to work for a year or more) fell from around 20 per cent of the work-force in 1921 to under 10 per cent in 1971, even in irrigated villages (where the demand for labour could be expected to be high). Also, the wages of annual labourers fell much faster than the daily wage rates.

The second form of adjustment was a decline in the traditional perquisites (like evening meals) of labourers, which implies a cut in the real wage. More importantly, the length of the working day declined. Employers when questioned stated that a labourer's efficiency falls off towards the end of the day, and so they preferred in effect to have a higher effective labour supply with a lower real wage payment (because of the cut in perquisites) by employing a larger number of workers for shorter hours.

By 1951, nearly 70 per cent of the hired labour in the farms was provided by casual daily labour, who participated in an active day-to-day labour market. They bargained as a group during busy seasons on a daily basis—with employers too acting as a group. The wage-rate depended upon the urgency of the task to be completed. Usually in these bargains no perquisites like meals were provided. The links between the employers and employees were now weak, and ended at the end of the day. Another result of this weakening of the traditional relationships is that the employer no longer feels morally bound to support labour families in distress through advancing wages, low interest loans, and gifts.

Another sign of the breakup of traditional relationships—the result mainly of demographic changes—is the marked decline in debt bondage which, as it did not contravene the slavery provisions of the Indian penal code, supposedly flourished all over India throughout the nineteenth century. But from the most recent NSS data it appears that in 1977 only about 1.5% of agricultural labourers were bonded.[5]

2. INDUSTRIAL LABOUR

The industrialization which began in the 1850s and the growth of mining and plantations led to the second major departure from the traditional labour market through the evolution of an industrial labour market, with pure wage-earning labourers. Employment in these 'modern' occupations was nevertheless fairly small (see Table 6.5), and as such did not constitute a radical change in the overall situation of labour in India. Nevertheless, it may be useful briefly to review various institutional changes which emerged in the use and conditions of urban labour during the last half-century of British rule in india, as they have set the framework within which the employment and wages of industrial labour have since been determined. This will also be of importance in judging whether these institutional and legal changes in the form of trade union organization and the legislation of various labour 'rights' is helpful or harmful for industrialization and economic development in India.

(i) Labour and factory legislation

One of the paradoxical features of labour legislation in India is that an imperial colonial Government was seemingly so concerned with the condition of industrial labour that it sought to protect it from various abuses by legislation which was only just being introduced in the metropolitan centre. It was not benevolence, however, but the protectionist sentiments of Lancashire which led to the institution of the first Factories Act of 1881, which has been described 'as the result of agitation by "ignorant English philanthropists and grasping English manufacturers" '.[6]

The act arose from the repeated representations made by the cotton-textile interests of Manchester to the Secretary of State for India 'to apply British factory legislation *en bloc* to India so as to neutralise the "unfair" advantages which the Indian mill industry was enjoying because of its large-scale employment of child labor and long hours of work'.[7] This was a variant of the 'pauper labour' argument for protection which has been constantly raised, most recently against the so-called 'Gang of Four'—Hong Kong, Taiwan, Korea, and Singapore—by the demand of the International Confederation of Labour Unions (ICLU) to introduce a minimum labour standard clause in the GATT articles, which would allow countries to discriminate against those who did not have the full panoply of so-called labour 'rights' granted to industrial workers in developed countries. The objective, then as now, is to raise the effective price of the abundant factor of production in these countries, and thence reduce their competitiveness in the production of labour-intensive exports—thus damaging the prospects of raising their standards of living.[8]

Various Factory Acts followed which, by limiting hours of work and laying down better conditions of work and various minimum labour standards recommended by the International Labour Organization (ILO), though subserving humanitarian sentiments, had the economic effect of raising the effective price of labour to producers.[9] That the resulting economic effects were not trivial becomes apparent when one of the major causes of the uncompetitiveness of Indian textiles relative to Japan in the inter-war period is considered. As we remarked in the last chapter (see Table 8.10), Indian textiles were becoming uncompetitive, despite lower wages, because the efficiency of Indian labour was lower. In explaining this divergence Ray remarks: 'The predominantly female textile labor in Japan had proved both pliable and skilled. Two shifts, made possible by adequate dormitory housing near the shed, had considerably increased working hours and had proved particularly economical. The use of female labor on such a scale was inconceivable in Bombay, nor did the prevailing labor laws permit such long working hours.'[10]

UK labour laws, instituted after the Industrial Revolution had transformed Britain, were now foisted on India with its completely different economic circumstances. They were responsible for creating a dualistic urban labour market, and for reducing the contribution that industrialization could make to labour absorption, and thence to the raising of real wages and incomes of labouring Indians. This was because, first, they raised the effective supply price of labour to the producer and gave him an incentive to choose less labour-intensive techniques of production than he otherwise would. The increasing capital intensity of Indian industry (see Part III) is in part due to this relative rise in the effective cost of labour induced by British labour legislation.

Secondly, the labour laws applied only to relatively large-scale industries, or else could only be enforced on them. This led to a fragmentation of industrial structure, as any small-scale producer would now face an added barrier in the labour market if he sought to move from being a small to a medium-scale producer. It has thus led (together with other more recent public policies to be discussed in Part III) to the evolution of an industrial caste system, in which there are finely graded and variously protected segments of the labour force as well as amongst the population of firms.

Thirdly, by raising the effective wage of a portion of the labour force, and thereby reducing the level of industrial employment that could be generated with any given level of industrial investment, this creation of an urban labour aristocracy meant not only that other labour incomes were directly worsened but, more heinously, that the larger interests of the non-industrial labour force in a more rapid growth of industrial employment, and the higher living standards that would have been entailed, were damaged.

(ii) The rise of trade unions

In the early part of the twentieth century another major development was the rise and growth of a trade union movement. This was in part due to the obvious political benefits to the nationalist movement of organizing industrial labour as a political force to fight alien rule. But in part it was the result of rational economic responses to problems of industrial relations in any modern industry. Though this last point is developed in greater detail in Volume II, an illustration of it may be provided here by the origins of trade unionism in India's first steel mill—the Tata Iron and Steel Company (TISCO).

Most early so-called 'unions' were little more than strike committees,[11] usually formed to bargain over wages or to fight to redress particular grievances, which disbanded once these issues were dealt with. In the early part of the twentieth century, various political parties attempted to organize workers under their party political flags. As a result there were (and still are) long-standing political rivalries amongst rival unions which plagued industry. Most plants would have their work-force divided into these rival unions. TISCO promoted the formation of a single, company-wide union in 1937, motivated in part by the high cost to the company of a strike in 1928.[12] They also introduced a bonus incentive scheme to win labour co-operation in increasing production.

Another notable example where the organization of a trade union provided the essential lubricant (rather than irritant) in smoothing industrial relations was the so-called 'Ahmedabad experiment'. Gandhi persuaded mill-owners and an association of workers (the Textile Labour Association) to agree to a voluntary scheme of arbitration of labour disputes, which except for one brief strike in 1923[13] has prevented other strikes in the Ahmedabad textile industry for nearly half a century.

Trade unions have flourished despite fluctuations in their fortunes caused by the varying industrial conditions in the country and internecine political warfare between the affiliation of unions called the All India Trade Union Congress (AITUC) controlled by the communists and later the socialists, and the non-communist Indian National Trade Union Congress (INTUC), and their various splinter groups. In 1926 there were about sixty trade unions affiliated to AITUC with nearly 150,000 members; by 1940–1 the number of registered trade unions had risen to 727 and their membership to over 500,000; by 1950–1 there were 3,766 registered trade unions, with over 1.5 million workers.[14] An indication of strike activity, and the man-days lost through industrial action, can be gleaned from Table 9.1. It will be apparent that there seems to be a marked decline in the man-days lost as a proportion of the industrial man-days available since the great strike of 1928.

TABLE 9.1.   Industrial Disputes in India, 1921–1980.

Year	No. of stoppages	No. of workers involved	Man-days lost
1921	396	600,351	6,984,426
1922	278	435,434	3,972,727
1923	213	301,044	5,051,794
1924	133	312,462	8,730,918
1925	134	270,423	12,578,129
1926	128	186,811	1,097,478
1927	129	131,655	2,019,970
1928	203	506,851	31,647,404
1929	141	531,059	12,165,691
1930	148	196,301	2,261,731
1931	166	203,008	2,408,123
1932	118	128,099	1,922,437
1933	146	164,938	2,160,961
1934	159	220,808	4,775,559
1935	145	114,217	973,457
1936	157	169,029	5,358,062
1937	379	647,801	8,982,257
1938	399	401,075	9,198,708
1939	406	409,075	4,992,795
1940	322	452,539	7,577,281
1941	359	291,054	3,330,503
1942	694	772,653	5,779,965
1943	716	525,088	2,342,287
1944	658	550,015	3,447,306
1945	820	747,530	4,054,499
1946	1,729	1,961,948	12,717,762
1947	1,811	1,840,784	16,562,666
1948	1,259	1,059,120	7,837,173
1949	920	605,457	6,600,395
1950	814	719,883	12,806,704
1951	1,071	691,321	3,818,928
1952	963	809,242	3,336,961
1953	772	466,607	3,382,608
1954	840	477,138	3,372,630
1955	1,166	527,767	5,697,848
1956	1,203	715,130	6,992,040
1957	1,630	889,371	6,429,319
1958	1,524	928,566	7,797,585
1959	1,531	693,616	5,633,148
1960	1,583	986,268	6,536,517
1961	1,357	511,860	4,918,755
1962	1,491	705,059	6,120,576
1963	1,471	563,121	3,268,524

TABLE 9.1. *contd*

Year	No. of stoppages	No. of workers involved	Man-days lost
1964	2,151	1,003,000	7,725,000
1965	1,835	991,000	4,470,000
1966	2,556	1,410,000	13,846,000
1967	2,815	1,490,000	19,148,000
1968	2,776	1,669,000	17,014,000
1969	2,627	1,827,000	19,048,000
1970	2,889	1,827,000	20,563,000
1971	2,752	1,613,000	16,546,000
1972	3,243	1,737,000	20,544,000
1973	3,370	2,546,000	20,626,000
1974	2,938	2,855,000	40,262,000
1975	1,943	1,143,000	21,901,000
1976	1,459	737,000	12,746,000
1977	3,117	2,193,000	25,320,000
1978	3,187	1,916,000	28,340,000
1979	3,048	2,874,000	43,854,000
1980	2,856	1,900,000	21,925,000

Source: Karnik (1978, appendix ii, pp. 409–10), and Government of India (1980, Table 55).

3. MIGRATION

In charting the evolution of the labour market in India, we may next consider migrations flows, as these are important in integrating otherwise compartmentalized and localized labour markets, and in determining to what extent and at what speed any expansion of labour demand at one or other of the newly emerging industrial, mining, or plantation centres was transmitted to a wider area. For, *ceteris paribus*, the more fragmented and localized the various sub-labour markets, the more would any growth impulse lead merely to increased quasirents of participants in the submarket where the increased labour demand originated.

There has always been rural–rural migration in India, but no systematic data even for the British period are availabe to check its magnitude. Despite the fact the even in 1951 only about 3.5 per cent of the work force was in the modern sector, the latter's growth in the British century did lead to some specific labour flows which could have been important, at least to the catchment areas from which they arose. This evidence is reviewed in Volume II. These migration flows would have reduced regional, urban–rural, and skilled–unskilled wage differentials which would otherwise have existed. As regards the latter, the evidence presented in Volume II shows some decline in the urban skilled–unskilled wage differential from about 3 to 2 towards the end of the period, but an unchanged rural–urban wage differential of about 0.75.

TABLE 9.2. Employment in the Public Sector, 1901–1978

	1901	1911	1921	1931	1951[a]	1960[b]	1978[b]
Police (other than village watchman)	241,892	239,319	222,529	240,532	379,721 (449,344)[d]		
% Percentage	10.2	9.6	8.9	8.7	12.6		
Village officer and servants (including village watchmen)	773,397	689,828	531,400	384,177	237,180 (286,935)[d]		
Percentage	32.8	27.6	21.4	13.9	8.0		
Employees of municipalities and district boards	107,976	66,381	82,546	116,487	224,249 (269,560)[d]		
Percentage	4.6	2.7	3.3	4.2	7.6		
Army, Navy, Air Force, employees of State Government, Union Government, and non-Indian Governments	795,651	717,430	793,890	707,140	1,320,967 (1,823,122)[d]		
Percentage	33.7	28.7	31.9	25.7	51.3		
TOTAL	1,918,916	1,712,958	1,630,365	1,448,336	2,162,117 (2,828,961)[d]	5,498,000[c]	12,943,000[c]

a. No figures are available for 1941.
b. For 1960 and 1978 figures are not available for different categories of public employees.
c. These figures refer only to civilian employees, and are exclusive of public-sector employment in railways and manufacturing.
d. These figures refer to both India and Pakistan, the successor states of the Raj.

Sources: Mukerji (1965, p. 74, table E); Government of India (1980, table 57).

TABLE 9.3. Salaries of Civil Service Officers, 1887–1913

Officers' drawing per month	Europeans	Anglo-Indians	Indians and Burmans	% of Indians and Burmans to total no. of officers
Rs 200 and over:				
1887	4,836	1,001	3,003	34
1913	4,898	1,593	4,573	42
Rs 500 and over:				
1887	3,163	83	426	12
1913	3,691	351	942	19
Rs 800 and over:				
1887	1,637	7	77	4
1913	2,153	106	242	10

Source: Bagchi (1972, p. 168, table 6.2).

4. PUBLIC EMPLOYMENT AND EARNINGS

Table 9.2 gives data on employment in the public sector under British rule, and Table 9.3 the structure of earnings in Government service. It is clear from these that the upper layers of the revenue economy did just as well as their predecessors in Indian history, even though in absolute numbers they were probably smaller.

NOTES

1. A fuller discussion of Indian labour markets is presented in Vol. II of this work.
2. Hicks (1969, p. 101).
3. Ibid., 123.
4. See Srinivas (1962, 1966); Beteille (1969).
5. Bhaduri (1977) has argued that where the landlord has an opportunity to enter into a bonded-labour contract with his tenant, the landlord's incentive to introduce yield-raising innovations is blunted. However, Srinivasan (1979) has shown that in a simple two-period model, where the landlord can offer a bonded-labour contract, the tenant's borrowing from his landlord *ceteris paribus* will not decline as a result of the introduction of yield-increasing innovations, even though the probability of his rendering bonded labour to the landlord declines. For this lowered probability lowers the real cost of borrowing to the tenant, while as long as consumption in the first period (before the harvest) is a normal good, the raising of the expected yield in the period by the innovation will lead to larger borrowing by the tenant to finance increased first-period consumption.
6. Bhattacharya (1979, p. 171).
7. Ibid.
8. See Lal (1981) for a critique of this not-so-modern variant of the pauper labour argument for protection.
9. 'Generally speaking, India had, by 1950, built up one of the most comprehensive labor codes to be found in any country at India's level of economic development. The standards laid down by the ILO had been accepted and measures were being worked out to attain these standards' (Bhattacharya, (1979, p. 186)).

10. Ray (1979, p. 67).
11. See Karnik (1978).
12. Ray (1979, p. 92) notes that the strike 'cost the company Rs 220 lakhs as against the loss of only Rs 28 lakhs due to collapse of prices and markets in the Great Depression'.
13. See Karnik (1978, ch. 8).
14. Bhattacharya (1979, pp. 193, 195) and Karnik (1978, appendix i).

10
The Effects and Legacy of the Raj

INTRODUCTION

It is time to sum up the legacy of the Raj. Did India's new colonial masters succeed in altering the parameters of the Hindu equilibrium established in ancient India? The Muslims, as we saw in Chapter 4, succumbed to native ways and traditions. Surprisingly, as we have seen, except for the legal and educational systems set up through the early reforming zeal of those inspired by radical and utilitarian ideals, the British too succeeded far less in changing the ultimate parameters than has been conceded either by nationalist historians glorifying a pre-British past destroyed by imperialism or by vainglorious British proconsuls and sentimental historians of the Raj. The most radical changes were in the establishment of an institutional, particularly legal and economic, framework through which an escape from the ancient equilibrium into the modern world was possible. But subsequent developments showed that this movement into a new era was rather half-hearted, and its effects very thinly spread over the sub-continent. Nevertheless, the Raj left legacies which have profoundly moulded the perceptions and actions of the Indian political and bureaucratic élite concerning Indian economic problems. We summarize our conclusions on these aspects in the next section, before assessing the impact of the Raj on Indian society and politics.

1. THE ECONOMIC LEGACY

Broadly speaking, we can divide its legacy in terms of the Raj's contribution to rural and industrial development and to the evolution of labour markets. We deal with these in turn.

(i) Rural development

India's current rural poverty was clearly not the creation of the British. Its causes, we would argue, lie in the relative success of the traditional Indian agrarian system in adapting to the existing and long-standing environmental constraints and uncertainties in a 'second-best' optimal fashion. The major changes in the Indian rural economy required changes in these underlying parameters of the Hindu equilibrium—the variability of climate, endemic political instability, a relatively stagnant population.

By their public health measures the British succeeded in changing the traditional growth-rate of India's population—whose consequences for the Hindu equilibrium have only become apparent in the post-Independence period.

By extending irrigation into the dry zones of western India, in particular Punjab and Sind, the British created new productive agriculture in these regions by sensibly undertaking the most socially productive form of available public investment at the time. Given the varying ecological and hydrological conditions in the rest of India, we have argued that the extension of large-scale flood cum irrigation works to eastern India, which alone (in the absence of a breakthrough in rice technology) can make a marked difference to agricultural productivity in these regions, would have been premature, as the social rates of return to such public investments would most likely have been marginal. More could, however, have been done to promote ground water development in the Deccan trap region if a publicly financed hydro-geological survey of the region had been undertaken. But this is a massive task, which even independent India has scarcely begun to tackle.

More could also have been done in promoting the use of improved seeds, fertilizers, and better cultural practices through extension. The technical agro-climatic knowledge required for such extension needs to be publicly provided because of the obvious externalities involved in the production of new knowledge. But even in this area, as experience in post-Independence India attests (discussed more fully in Part III), although some gains could have been made in raising rural productivity, particularly in the stagnant eastern Gangentic belt, no spectacular advance could have been expected without the development of new high-yielding seed varieties. It should also be noted that this 'leading inputs' approach to rural development was first begun with Dr Voelcker's report at the turn of the century, whose proposed solutions to the Indian agrarian problem have since formed the basis of most attempts to transform traditional Indian agriculture.

Dr Voelcker (and other British officials since the heyday of *laissez-faire*) as well as Indian nationalists and the radicals of today have stressed changing land tenure conditions as a prime mover in agrarian change. Although for a country with India's land/man ratio and labour-intensive cropping techniques there are good theoretical as well as empirical reasons for arguing that the ideal system of land tenure from the viewpoint of both equity and efficiency would be small, family labour-based and family-owned peasant farms,[1] it does not follow that when we compare the alternative tenures extant in Moghul India and those created by the British, the failure to promote the ideal system necessarily means that the alternative adopted was worse than the system it actually replaced. We have cast doubt on the nationalist view that the creation of a land market, as well as the permanent settlement of the land revenue in eastern India, was either inimical to technical change in agriculture or promoted concentration of land or increased rural proletarianization and poverty, *as compared with the system it replaced*. The new system was obviously not an ideal one, but on the whole it held promise of progress, not least because of its insidious long-run effects in promoting the change-over from custom to contract in economic relationships—a change-over which is central to the development of a developed modern market economy[2] and which, if generalized throughout India, would be the single most important means of dissolving the customary indirect modes of control through which the caste system has been maintained.

Nor can it be inferred, from the obvious correlation between the areas of the Permanent Settlement and agricultural stagnantion and those with the ryotwari system and agricultural progress, that the one caused the other. For as Stokes rightly notes: 'There seem grounds for believing that Ryotwari tenures through-out India were the tenurial form natural to regions of insecure agriculture where land was plentiful and hands few, just as landlord forms, whether zamindari, pattidari, or 'landed mirasi', were the products of regions of secure agriculture where population pressed on land and generated a quasi-rental surplus.' Thus, as we have argued, the ultimate causes of the divergent regional performance in agriculture must be found in the underlying demographic and ecological deter-minants of the pattern of agriculture established in the subcontinent over millennia rather than in their varied and epiphenomenal tenurial forms.

(ii) Industrialization and trade

Though nationalist and radical writers have emphasized the deindustrialization of India resulting from the decline in handicrafts (particularly of traditional cotton textiles) after the introduction of free trade in 1813, there is little evidence in support of this view. There was some decline in handicraft production, but over time this was counterbalanced by the growth of modern industry, which introduced both new technology and the hope that by creating new labour market forms, and by providing new and more productive avenues of employ-ment, a means could be found (in the long run) for India to break out of the 'Hindu equilibrium' in the countryside.

The relative speed with which indigenous entrepreneurship and capital were organized to establish a modern textile industry under a regime of free trade and *laissez-faire* suggests that neither, in itself, held back Indian industrializa-tion—though obviously there were areas, such as industrial training for the social promotion of industry, which were grossly neglected by the colonial authorities. But it should be noted that colonial policies were not entirely *laissez-faire*: for example, government promotion led to the establishment of the first tea planta-tions in Assam in the mid-nineteenth century; Tata's steel mill in the early part of the twentieth century was promoted by government commitments to purchase its output. Nevertheless it is undeniable that *laissez-faire* in industrial policy was not socially justifiable.

Equally harmful to the prospects of rapid and efficient industrialization was the slow and inadequate provision of social overhead facilities. But this was due to the persistent fiscal problems of an alien Government worried about the dangers of provoking nationalist revolts through a rising tax burden, and hobbled on the expenditure side by a high and rising commitment to finance an

Indian army, which was increasingly the strong arm maintaining the empire east of Suez.

Though industrial promotion was thus neglected, it is the lack of protection offered to Indian industry that was and is the major nationalist complaint, which identified free trade with *laissez-faire* (as much Indian opinion does to this day). However, as is by now well known to economists, even though a case for industrial promotion can be made, no similar case for protection follows.[4]

In fact, despite the non-optimal degree of promotion, free trade did not harm Indian industrial development.[5] Its performance in the free-trade era was well above the world average, and better than nearly all other countries except Japan. India also succeeded in raising the rate of growth of its manufactured exports, and thus became a modern exporter of manufacturers rather than of traditional handicrafts as it had been in the past.

By contrast, the creeping protection offered to Indian industry in the twentieth century, though instituted for reasons of fiscal expediency by the colonial power, began that process of inward-looking industrial development which was to reach its zenith as well as its limits within a decade of India achieving its independence. This industrial protection was popular with the nationalists, as well as with Indian businessmen, who had wrongly assumed that Indian industrial progress under free trade was niggardly and that the solution to faster industrialization was protection. Even considering the rate of growth of industry, which in itself is a poor index of performance as it says nothing about the social efficiency of the industrialization that occurred, the rate of growth of industrial output, and more seriously of employment, slowed down in the inter-war period.

The overvaluation of the rupee led to problems for the colonial Governments in transferring the home charges, whose large political component for 'services' provided by imperious foreigners certainly constituted a drain of Indian resources. In order to generate the necessary export surplus at the overvalued exchange rate, the economy was run at deflated levels of overall demand, which obviously lowered the home demand for indigenous industrial output, whilst exports were being directly hit by the high exchange rate.

The increases in discriminating protection began the process of creating a highly diversified and high degree of effective protection of Indian industry which has damaged its long-run efficiency. It has prevented an industrial take-off in the country which began the process of industrialization over a century before the upstart south-east Asian Gang of Four. Even though the latter lack an industrial structure as diversified as India's, they have succeeded in using industrialization based on their comparative advantage in producing labour-intensive manufactures to transform the living conditions of their populace.

For the crux of the industrialization problem for India remains as follows. Given its population size and relatively rich natural-resource base, a much higher degree of import-substituting industrialization is likely to be socially efficient in

India than in the small natural resource, poor economies of the Gang of Four. Nevertheless, given the low per capita income in the country, the limits of home demand in most lines of import-substituting manufacturing are likely to be reached fairly rapidly.[6] The transformation of domestic agriculture is thus doubly important, both in itself (as most Indians have earned and continue to earn their living from that sector) and in providing a growing home market for Indian industry. But Indian industrialization did not and does not have to wait on agricultural transformation, which for essentially ecological reasons is likely to be slow and difficult. The world market provides another outlet. The most serious long-run damage that the policy of protection of Indian industry (begun under the Raj, and intensified to an undreamt-of degree under its successor regime), had done to the prospects of India's poor has been through the bias such protection created against the development of labour-intensive manufactured exports from India.

It was protection and the introduction of various forms of factory legislation, rather than free trade, we have argued, which were the most harmful ingredients in the partly poisoned chalice that the Raj left its successors.

2. THE IMPACT ON SOCIETY

The major social changes wrought by the colonial impact can be briefly summarized. The Muslim aristocracy was decimated. 'The social pyramid was truncated because the British lopped off most of the top three layers of the Moghul hierarchy, i.e. the Moghul court, the Moghul aristocracy and quasi-autonomous princes (a quarter of these survived), and the local chieftains (zamindars who survived in about 40% of India).'[7]

This loss of status was matched by the rise in status of the new Westernized urban élites that were the product of British educational policy. By destroying the dominance of the Brahmins, their intellectual monopoly over Indian society was threatened. But with their traditional agility and penchant for parasitic government service, they were among the pioneering converts to the new Western ways. These Westernized Brahmins, along with members of certain other upper castes, particularly the Kayasthas, were the main beneficiaries of the opening up of jobs in the newly created civil service, first at its lower and increasingly, during the course of British rule, at its higher levels.[8] Other members of Westernized groups benefited from the growth in commerce and litigation that followed in the wake of British rule.

In the countryside the new tenurial arrangements instituted by the British, while bringing in a whiff of new ideas by (*a*) altering rights based on custom into those based on contract and (*b*) making these rights divisible, tradeable, and legally enforceable, nevertheless did not alter rural society in its essentials. However, the destruction of local autonomies, and the conversion of some of the rising urban mercantile and Westernized classes into 'landowners' in different parts of India, did provide some potential for altering the local social parameters which had governed the village communities for millennia. This potential was not however substantially realized because of the British need for local collaborators, who tended to be the newly Westernised but traditional literary castes. This gave rise to a class of professional politicians able to speak the language of the different levels of politics (local, provincial, and national),[9] and to mediate the often divergent interests of their clients with the authoritarian bureaucratic structure that was in place by the 1870s. With the gradual institution of representative legislative bodies at various levels, however, a long-term process for dissolving the social stratification of the past had been put in place.

The resulting social structure, and the percentage of the population in different occupations as well as their shares in national income, have been estimated by Maddison and his results are shown in Table 10.1. From this it appears that it was the new urban and Westernized capitalist and professional classes who were the main beneficiaries of British rule—it being noted that the professional classes should include both the new professional politicians as well as the indigenous bureaucrats. Though imbued to varying extents with the Western ideas

TABLE 10.1.   Social Structure at the End of British Rule

	% labour force	% national income
Non-village economy:	18	44
British officials and military		
British capitalists, plantation owners, traders, bankers, and managers	0.06	5
Native princes		
Big zamindars and jagirdars		3
Indian capitalists, merchants, and managers	0.94	3
The new Indian professional class		3
Petty traders, small entrepreneurs, traditional professions, clerical and manual workers in government, soldiers, railway workers, industrial workers, urban artisans, servants, sweepers, and scavengers	17	30
Village economy:	75	54
Village *rentiers*, rural money-lenders, small zamindars, tenants-in-chief	9	20
Working proprietors, protected tenants	20	18
Tenants-at-will, sharecroppers, village artisans and servants	29	12
Landless labourers, scavengers	17	4
Tribal economy	7	2

Source: Maddison (1971, p. 69, table 3-4).

implanted by Macaulay's educationald reforms, their influence was predominantly at the higher levels of Government and in the urban economy of the Raj.
The parameters of rural society were not markedly altered. The structure of caste
and the patron–client relationships forged over centuries still held sway.

One final social consequence of the administrative and political structure
created by the British needs to be noted. This is the gradual co-option of Westernized upper-caste Indians into the higher reaches of the bureaucratic 'steel
frame', the Indian civil service. By the end of the nineteenth century, with the
final conversion of the British from nabobs to sahibs, the British increasingly
became an upper caste, on the traditional Indian form—endogamous, occupationally specialized, pollution-conscious (though its polluting objects were different), and with hierarchically arranged subcastes. The Viceroy and his court came
to resemble the Moghul emperors in its splendour, and the Platonic Guardians[10]
who formed the 900 odd member ICS became the top caste, looking down upon
the other layers—military, service subcastes (such as teachers and doctors), and
below them the commercial subcaste (the British merchants and planters). On
the lowest rung of the Anglo-Indian ladder were the Eurasians.[11] The British
must appear to an unjaundiced eye as having succumbed, despite their earlier
intention of reforming Hindu society, to the traditional Indian social and political pattern.[12] Meanwhile, during the inter-war years of the twentieth century, the
idea of *laissez-faire* dominant throughout most of the later part of the nineteenth
century, which while probably hampering Indian economic development had
nevertheless held the growth of Leviathan in check, were increasingly coming
into question both in British and among India's Westernized intelectuals,
bureaucrats, and politicians. The growth of socialist ideas was to provide both the
ideological justification as well as, through their implementation, the means for
a vast extension of the revenue economy in the post-Independence period. The
resulting social and economic effects are the subject of the next part of this book.
But as an interim judgement, the conclusions of the major historian of the Indian
middle classes is worth quoting:

Since India's tradition of caste authoritarianism fitted in well with the imperial scheme of
things, Indian bureaucrats, who usually belonged to higher castes, were quick to step into
the shoes of the British who left India in 1947. Bureaucracy thus continued to retain its
hold over business in India and is increasing its hold with the extension of the state's
economic function. This may be beneficial to the educated middle classes, since as officers
of Government they step in as controllers of nationalized industries without any personal
stake in them. But it is no gain to the country as a whole. The system of state control in fact
stifles the growth of entrepreneurial elements which India has in past badly needed to
speed up production. Traditionally recruited from the literary classes, with no business
acumen, civil servants are most unsuited to accelerate production in Indian conditions,
especially within the framework of law and legislative authority.'[13]

The British had left a thin crust of professional politicians and administrators,
and a representative and legal institutional structure. In principle, these were

important legacies which could have finally displaced the Hindu equilibrium by replacing the revenue economy and the socio-economic attitudes it engendered by a more modern and efficient society and an industrial market economy on which alone the hopes of raising the levels of living of the Indian masses ultimately depend. Whether the hopes so eloquently expressed by Nehru on the stroke of midnight on 14 August 1947, when India achieved independence,[14] were to be achieved is the subject of the final part of this volume.

3. THE POLITICAL LEGACY

Although the British, through their development of a layered bureaucratic and legislative structure, had created a new institutional form which forced politicians to put together national coalitions of diverse local- and political-interest groups, it is less certain whether they succeeded in altering basic Indian political attitudes. Established as an expedient to squeeze more revenues without incurring the accompanying political and administrative costs, the representative institutions they erected were to be used by people less moved by the spirit of John Stuart Mill than the old Indian political tradition of feuding faction leaders fighting for a share of the regional or national spoils of a potentially imperial revenue economy.

The legal system is the one legacy and bulwark against the resurgence of the Asiatic despotism the early English liberal reformers saw and were so keen to bury. It is not altogether surprising, therefore, that as Indian politicians have lost their nationalist aura and sought to move back to some form of traditional, dynastic, quasi-monarchical rule they have found the system of law and lawyers erected by the British to be a hindrance. The assaults on the judiciary in the 1970s which attempted to reverse the major British legacy to the Indian polity—the separation of the judiciary and the executive—can be taken as signs both of the current desire (of at least some of the politicians) to return to an older Indian tradition of politics and of the shallowness of the seeming transformation in values wrought by the introduction of new political institutions on the participants in the Indian political game.

Finally, as a counterweight to these tendencies, there has however been a more widespread diffusion of the notion of nationhood, fed equally by Western ideas and by the political and (more importantly) economic unification of the subcontinent that was wrought by India's colonial masters. The most salient feature of the brief survey of the new histriography of the nationalist movement (in Chapter 5) (and the attendant explosion in the revenue economy in twentieth century, to be detailed in later chapters), is however, that, as far as the political parameters of the Hindu equilibrium are concerned, the British success in altering them was at best limited, and the future must remain uncertain. A new institutional structure (admittedly less bloody than in the past) for ambitious politicians to wield imperial authority had been created, but the ancient Indian notion that the State is the personal (possibly hereditary) jagir (fief) of those who control its central levers does not seem to have been eradicated from the minds of either the rulers or the ruled—minds which the crusading liberals of the first half of the nineteenth century so earnestly but hopelessly sought to change.

NOTES

1. The basic reason is that, theoretically, as large farms have to hire labour, the marginal product of labour on large farms is likely to be equated to the wage-rate. The latter is likely to be determined by the opportunity cost of peasant labour, which for labour used on family farms is equal to the average product of labour. Thus the marginal product of labour on large farms will be greater than that on small farms and hence, *ceteris paribus*, output per acre will be lower on large than on small family-based farms. A conversion of large into small peasant-based farms would therefore lead to an increase in agricultural output, along with obvious improvements in equity. For the empirical evidence on the inverse relationship between farm size and productivity see Sen (1975, appendix C). Most (or nearly all) economists would now accept this conclusion. We have to say 'most' because of the curious paper by Rudra and Sen (1980)—two of the most distinguished contributors to the empirical and theoretical literature—which has shown that both in theory and practice family-based peasant farms are the most efficient and equitable form of agrarian structure for countries with low landman ratios. In the above paper, however, Rudra and Sen take issue with the obvious policy implication that most people have, in my view rightly, drawn from their work, that such a peasant family-based agriculture should therefore be promoted. They state, however, that as co-operative and collectivist forms of agrarian structure have not been tried in India, no such conclusion is warranted. Moreover, in their view these co-operative forms of agriculture would have the same advantages as family-based farms, but on a larger scale. Hence, they argue, the debate on different agrarian systems in India should continue to include consideration of these alternative forms. Given the large literature demonstrating the inefficiency of socialist agriculture in both theory and practice (see Nove (1969, 1977)) and its abandonment on essentially pragmatic grounds whenever changing ideological predilections or the loosening of the grip of the ideologues allows, (for instance, most recently in China), this view would seem at the very least to be eccentric. But perhaps, more charitably, Rudra and Sen can be looked upon as being willing to sacrifice the demonstrable gains from promoting the embourgeoisement of the countryside for the moral value they attach to the co-operation (as opposed to competition) which they hope to promote through 'socialist' agrarian forms! More recent work by Bhalla and Roy (1987) has however led to a questioning of the above inverse relationship between farm size and productivity, once appropriate adjustments are made for differences in land quality. This would seem to undermine the traditional case for land reform in India.
2. Of course, those addicted to the promotion of a 'command economy' might not be too keen to promote a market economy, but to take issue with them and to deal with the economic, political, and moral issues involved in the great debate between 'command' and 'market' economies would require another book—though in the last chapter of this book I do provide some of the political and economic arguments for promoting a market economy in India, while Lal (1980a) deals with the more technocratic arguments for promoting a 'controlled market' as opposed to a 'command' economy.
3. Stokes (1978, p. 237).
4. See Little *et al.* (1970) for the theory and practice of efficient industrialization, and Bhagwati and Desai (1970) and Lal (1980a) for applications to India.
5. See Macpherson (1972, pp. 171–2), who also argues that high tariffs before 1914 would not have benefited the Indian economy.
6. Thus it might be noted that in 1981, after three decades of State-led import-substituting industrialization, value added in India's manufacturing industry was slightly lower than in Sweden and Belgium. It was 64% of Australia's and 56% of Spain's. I am indebted to Gary Pursell for these figures.

7. Maddison (1971, p. 67). See also Mishra (1961).
8. Thus Mishra notes: 'The Indian Public Service Commission reported in 1887 that of 1866 Hindu members of the judicial and executive services as many as 904, or nearly half were Brahmins, and 454, or nearly a quarter were Kayasths who were called Prabhus in Bombay. The number of Kshatriyas or Rajputs was 147; of Vaishyas 113; of Shudras 146, and of others 102. The Brahmins were especially dominant in Madras with 202 of a total of 297, and in Bombay, with 211 out of 328.' Whilst on government employment the 1901 Census reported that 'the Brahmins, though forming less than 1/13th of the total number of Hindus, hold 8 appointments out of 11, and the Prabhus, Baniyas, and "Sindhi Hindus" many of whom doubtless belong to the above castes, all but 4 of the remainder. The return contained no entry for lower castes' (Mishra (1961, pp. 322–3)).
9. On the continuing importance of the differing languages of politics (with the addition of the 'saintly') in Indian politics, see Morris-Jones (1971).
10. For a hagiographic account of the Indian civil service see Woodruff (1953, 1954), the second volume of whose book is called *The Guardians* and explicitly relates the training and attitudes of the ICS to Plato's Guardians (see vol. i, p. 15 and vol. ii, pp. 16 ff.). Woodruff also notes that by the end of the 19th century the 'contrast was at its clearest between on the one hand the ideal of a liberal empire, an India held in trust, and on the other the reality of despotic power wielded by Platonic Guardians in the interest of order and tranquility. . . . It was a despotism tempered by the despot's liberal upbringing and by the knowledge of Parliament's usually liberal attitude. But despotism it was all the same, as any system must be in which people are given what is good for them instead of what they want' (ibid., vol. ii, p. 17).
11. See Edwardes (1969, chs. 2, 5, 6): 'If anything, the opening up of the Company's dominions to unrestricted immigration intensified the disdain with which the army and civil service looked upon the other members of English society in India. As in England, people engaged in trade were beyond the pale. That paragon of Victorian chivalry, Henry Lawrence, summed up the view in a note in his journal about a Calcutta chemist and his wife, who were fellow-passengers on Lawrence's first journey home. The man he said was "a forward, vulgar, ignorant, malicious and pertinaceously obstinate fellow", and his wife was "much of a muchness. . . . Of course, they were in no society in Calcutta." Eurasians were regarded with as little favour, having the additional—and insulting—disability of mixed parentage and guilty liaisons. There was, of course, no doubt about who were the leaders of society. Whatever it said in public, the army (on which British dominion depended) never had any doubt in its heart that it was "infinitely inferior in every respect" to the civil service in rank and rewards' (p. 13).
12. See also Naipaul (1964) for a sensitive account of the charade of Englishness that the British played in India, and which was an important legacy of the Raj. 'They left no noble monument behind and no religion save a concept of Englishness as a desirable code of behavior—of chivalry, it might be described, tempered by legalism—which in Indian minds can be disassociated from the fact of English rule, the vulgarities of racial arrogance or the position of England today. . . . This concept of Englishness will survive because it was the product of fantasy, a work of national art; it will outlast England . . . the Raj was an expression of the English involvement with themselves rather than with the country they ruled. It is not, properly, an imperialist attitude. It points, not to the good or evil of British rule in India, but to its failure' (p. 212). Naipaul is also very perceptive in delineating the quality of fantasy and insecurity in the social pretensions of the British in India. He looks upon Kipling, quite rightly, as 'a poetic chronicler of Anglo-India. . . . His work is of a piece with the architecture of the Raj; and within the imperial shell we find, not billiard room cartoons or a suburban taste in novels, as in the district clubs, but Mrs. Hauksbee, the wit, the queen, the manipulator and card of Simla. How she suffers from the very generosity which sought to bestow on her the attributes she desired! Her wit is not wit; and to us today the susceptibility of her admirers is a little provincial, a little sad. . . . Mr. Somerset Maugham has already disposed of the pretensions of Mrs. Hauksbee. She once said of the voice of another woman that it was like the screech of the brakes of an underground train as it came into Earl's Court station. If Mrs. Hauksbee were what she claimed to be, Mr. Maugham commented, she had no business to be in Earl's Court; and she certainly oughtn't to have gone there by underground. There is much in Kipling that can be dealt with in this way. He genuinely saw people bigger than they were; they, perhaps less securely, saw themselves bigger than they were. They reacted one on the other; fantasy hardened into conviction. And to us they are now all betrayed' (p. 203).

13. Mishra (1961, p. 340).
14. Nehru stated: 'Long years ago we made a tryst with destiny, and now the time comes when we shall redeem our pledge, not wholly or in full measure, but very substantially. At the stroke of the midnight hour, when the world sleeps, India will awake to life and freedom. A moment comes, which comes but rarely in history, when we step out from the old to the new, when an age ends, and when the soul of a nation long suppressed finds utterance.'

Part III

The Independent Decades, 1947–1980

11

The Economy under Planning

INTRODUCTION

The establishment of a Congress Government in 1947 with Nehru at its head as Prime Minister did not mark as clear a break with the Raj as might have been expected. For with the rapport established between the new Prime Minister and the Viceroy turned Governor-General, Lord Louis Mountbatten, there was considerable continuity with the Raj—with the brown sahibs replacing the white! The country was still governed by the 'steel frame', the Indian civil service which, in the latter part of the inter-war period, had recruited a fairly large number of Indians.

Following the appalling distress caused by the mass migration and communal slaughter involved in the exchange of populations resulting from the partition of the subcontinent, the first task of the Government of independent India was to establish law and order. This having been done, there was the secondary problem of mopping up the various native States which owed paramountcy to the Raj, but whose future in independent India (and Pakistan) was left ambiguous at the time of the transfer of power. As a result of the ruthless diplomacy of the Home Minister, Sardar Patel, most of these native States were incorporated into the Indian Union, and independent India could begin the task of economic reconstruction.

The diagnoses by Congress and Nehru (in particular) of the Indian economic problem and its remedies were based partly on a misreading of the record of the Raj, as well as an emerging consensus amongst both Indian businessmen and intellectuals (and, it may be said, economists in the West) that *laissez-faire* was the root of all evil and central planning the new panacea.

With the gradual erosion of the commitment to both free trade and *laissez-faire*, essentially on grounds of expediency, the twilight of the Raj (towards the end of the Second World War) saw a marked rise in *dirigisme* in the running of the Indian economy. The rationing, price controls, and various other aspects of a bureaucratic command economy, which might have been a necessary expedient during wartime, provided the bureaucrats with fresh avenues to assert their power, as well as a faith in *dirigisme* which was to outlast the circumstances in which it arose.

The nationalists, who now ran independent India, moreover, were committed to government intervention on a massive scale. Once Gandhi had officially designated Nehru as his political heir, it was inevitable that the latter's views would condition the course of economic policy in post-Independence India.

Nehru's views were however by no means eccentric for the times, and commanded widespread support from the intelligentsia as well as from indigenous business groups. It may be instructive to examine these very briefly, as they have coloured Indian thinking on economic policy for decades. They are also a continuing reminder of Keynes's dictum: 'Practical men who believe themselves to be quite exempt from any intellectual influences are usually the slaves of some defunct economist. Madmen in authority, who hear voices in the air, are distilling their frenzy from some academic scribbler of a few years back. Sooner or later, it is ideas, not vested interests, which are dangerous for good or ill.'[1]

1. GANDHI AND 'HIND SWARAJ'

But before examining the set of ideas which came to determine independent India's economcic policy, it is necessary to briefly examine the views and work of Mahatma Gandhi, as it represents the most recent attempt to refurbish Hindu society and thereby perpetuate the ancient Hindu equilibrium. Politician or saint—Gandhi was and remains an enigma in Indian politics unless, as Judith Brown (1972) cogently argues, it is recognized that Gandhi's entry into the political arena was only a means to his unwavering end of maintaining the traditional Hindu socio-economic system—albeit cleansed of some aberrations.

The ex-barrister who spent twenty years of his adult professional life in South Africa, chiefly fighting racial discrimination, arrived in India in 1915 at the age of forty-six, with the aim of promoting his ideal of 'swaraj' (self-rule). He was gradually drawn into politics to pursue this end. After the success of the Rowlatt 'Satyagraha' (passive resistance) he organized, he saw he could use this instrument of non-violent terrorism he had forged in South Africa to reconcile the use of political means for spiritual ends. The history of Gandhi's political career, and his vital role in bringing a number of regional and local non-Western educated political sub-contractors into an all-India association, need not concern us. What is more important are the ends of his periodic forays into politics. These were most clearly expressed in a booklet he wrote in 1909 called *Hind Swaraj.*[2] This work is an uncompromising attack on Western civilization, and an agenda for maintaining the traditional, albeit refurbished Hindu socio-economic system. Gandhi saw swaraj 'not as a question of who held the reins of government; he saw swaraj, self-rule, as a quality or state of life which could only exist where Indians followed their traditional civilization, uncorrupted by modern innovations. . . . The means to this end was truth-force, satyagraha.'[3] He was implacably opposed to Western education, industrialization, and all those other 'modern' forces which could undermine the ancient Hindu equilibrium. Above all even though he was unequivocally against untouchability, he nevertheless upheld the caste system and its central feature of endogamy.[4] He wished to see a revival of the ancient and largely self-sufficient village communities which were an essential part of the Hindu equilibrium.

It is surely not accidental that, in Hind Swaraj, Gandhi launches a diatribe against the three major agents of Western civilization destroying India—railways, lawyers, and doctors. The railways, of course, destroyed village autarky; the lawyers symbolize the rule of law, which led to the replacement of custom by contract; whilst the doctors were the major agents reducing the mortality which led to the population expansion of the twentieth century. Thus all three agents were (in our terms) changing the basic parameters of the Hindu equilibrium. Small wonder that Gandhi should have been opposed to them!

In his attempt to vindicate and maintain the caste system, Gandhi was following a line of Hindu reformers who had reacted to the onslaught on caste and Hindu society launched by the early Christian missionaries and the utilitarian reformers in the nineteenth century, by seeking to reform certain abuses in the caste system whilst preserving its essence.[5] The most prominent amongst these were Swami Vivekananda and Dayananda Saraswati. Like them, Gandhi sought to affirm the caste system whilst purging it of certain evils.[6] But for him, even the great curse of untouchability was a matter which Hindu society had to deal with internally and in which the other communities had no business! By redefining untouchables as Harijans, Gandhi effectively co-opted and annexed these groups into Hinduism![7]

The Westernized Indians who formed an important part of the polity, whilst showing some sympathy with Gandhi's desire to uphold the traditional system, did not however accept his wholesale attack on Western civilization and education. As long as Gandhi's novel methods of mass mobilization were seen to be a successful method of challenging the Raj, his socio-economic views were tolerated. However, with time, 'as non-cooperation penetrated the localities the clash of interests, particularly of caste and community was sharpened rather than softened by Gandhi's tactics'.[8] The double-edged nature of Gandhi's mass mobilization political technique became apparent. As the political leaders discarded his technique of satyagraha, Gandhi's hope of achieving his ideals through political action faded. As Judith Brown aptly sums up:

The idealist created in South Africa became a political failure, ousted by the pragmatists among his compatriots from the arena of politics in which he felt bound to pursue his ideals after 1919. The wheel came full circle, and in the last months of his life the Mahatma reverted to that political isolation and practical philanthrophy which had marked his earliest years as an exile returned to his homeland.[9]

But whilst Gandhi's attempt to maintain the traditional Hindu equilibrium failed, ironically many of the social attitudes and ideas underpinned by the caste system found a new lease of life because of a modern ideology espoused by secular Western-educated Indians. Their major representative was Nehru. He felt the caste system was doomed because of the inevitable and rapid economic change that would emerge with Independence. This may have been right for the long run. But in the short run the Hindu equilibrium was not to be so easily shattered, partly because of Nehru's ideas.

2. THE RISE OF PLANNING

The interesting aspect for our purposes is the continued resonance, in the views of Nehru and of the new Westernized classes, of the ancient Indian casteist feeling about commerce and merchants. For, as we noted in the last chapter, the Raj did not succeed in altering this particular, and most important, parameter of the Hindu equilibrium. Not all Indian politicans who were the inheritors of the Raj showed this 'aristocratic' contempt for business and commerce. Gandhi, a Vaishya (merchant caste) by birth, certainly did not, but after designating Nehru as his successor he had withdrawn into the spiritual shadows, and within six months of having achieved Independence he was dead at the hands of an assasin.

Nehru was a towering personality and an intellectual—but also a Brahmin! He professed to being a socialist, and was much impressed by the *dirigiste* example of the Soviet Union in transforming a backward economy into a world power within the life-time of a generation. He had imbibed the Fabian radicalism of the inter-war period and, with so many British intellectuals, was an ardent advocate of planning—which was identified with some variant of the methods of government control instituted in the Soviet Union.

But this was not just a fantasy dreamt up in an intellectual ivory tower. Many businessmen, who identified their relative success during the last half of the Raj with the gradual erosion of the policies of *laissez-faire* and free trade, also advocated planning as a panacea for India's economic ills. It was nationalist businessmen who produced the early precursors of post-Independence Indian plans, in their so-called 'Bombay plan'. Whilst Nehru certainly, but the nationalist businessmen more doubtfully, admired the Soviet model, Nehru baulked at the suppression of liberty that the Stalinist model of development entailed. He hoped instead, as a good Fabian socialist, to combine the 'order' and 'rationality' of central planning with the preservation of individual and democratic rights in India. Moreover, he was, at least in his own mind, a socialist. But it is interesting to see what socialism meant for him. In his *Autobiography*, he writes:

right through history the old Indian ideal did not glorify political and military triumph, and it looked down upon money and the professional money-making class. Honour and wealth did not go together, and honour was meant to go, at least in theory, to the men who served the community with little in the shape of financial reward. Today [the old culture] is fighting silently and desperately against a new and all-powerful opponent—the *bania* [Vaishya] civilization of the capitalist West. It will succumb to the newcomer. . . . But the West also brings an antidote to the evils of this cut-throat civilization—the principles of socialism, of cooperation, and service to the community for the common good. This is not so unlike the old Brahmin ideal of service, but it means the brahmanisation—not in the religious sense, of course—of all classes and groups and the abolition of class distinctions.[10]

A more succinct expression of the ancient Hindu caste prejudice against commerce and merchants would be difficult to find. The British unfortunately, as we saw in the last chapter, had in their later years, and despite the commercial origins of their rule in India, taken over most of the Indian higher-caste attitudes to commerce. The brown sahibs, who like Nehru belonged to these upper castes, found these attitudes traditional. 'Socialism' merely provided them with a modern ideological garb in which to clothe these ancient prejudices. Commercial success, as in the past, was to be looked down upon and the ancient Hindu disjunction between commercial power (and, increasingly, political power) and social status was to continue.

This identification of socialism with a contempt for commerce and business and, by association, that prime symbol of the mercantile mentality—the market—was to colour economic policy-making in the newly independent India, to the cost, as we shall see, of its poor labouring millions. 'Socialism' in India has merely provided the excuse for a vast extension of the essentially feudal and imperial revenue economy, whose foundations were laid in ancient India, and whose parameters successive conquerors of India have failed to alter.[11]

Thus, Nehru identified socialism with bureaucratic modes of allocation, with all that it implies in terms of the power and patronage afforded to the ancient Hindu literary castes which formed much of the bureaucracy. But in this Nehru was merely echoing the views of his Fabian mentors. Thus, in *The Discovery of India*, he quotes with approbation a statement of R. H. Tawney's that 'the choice is not between competition and monopoly, but between monopoly which is irresponsible and private and a monopoly which is responsible and public'. He then expresses the belief that public monopolies will eventually replace private monopolies under his preferred economic system which he labels 'democratically-planned collectivism'. Under such a system, he notes: 'An equalization of income will not result from all this, but there will be far more equitable sharing and a progressive tendency towards equalization. In any event, the vast differences that exist today will disappear completely, and class distinctions, which are essentially based on differences in income, will begin to fade away.'[12]

That he envisages this socialist Utopia to be established by the supplanting of the price mechanism, whose essential lubricant is private profit and utility maximization, is evident from the following continuation of the above passage: 'Such a change would mean an upsetting of the present-day acquisitive society based primarily on the profit motive. The profit motive may still continue to some extent but it will not be the dominating urge, nor will it have the same scope as it has today.'

We need not go into the details of the *dirigiste* system of controls and planning that was progressively set up.[13] But a brief summary may be in order, and we will have something to say, of course, about the consequences of this system in what follows.

Officially, planning was inaugurated in India with the establishment of a planning commission in March 1950. This has since produced seven five-year plans.[14] Its primary function has been to take decisions on two basic questions: the overall level of savings and investment, and hence growth, desired by the Government, and the pattern of this investment. The first problem has led to endless debate during the formulation of each plan, about the desirable and feasible size (in terms of investment) of each plan, whilst the second has led to continuing and acrimonious debate about the appropriate sectoral allocation of the planned investment. There have been large discrepancies between the planned and realized patterns of investment and growth rates in successive plans (see Lal (1980a)).

The instruments used by the Government to legislate the investment and output targets laid down in each plan were a complex system of industrial licensing and foreign exchange, price, and distributional controls. As direct control of agricultural investment production decisions was not sought, most detailed target-setting was confined to the large-scale industrial sector, which felt the full weight of the legislation of these targets through bureaucratic controls.

But as the plan determined the allocation of inter-sectoral public investment, including that on infrastructure (and that in the private sector which could be controlled through the credit controls of the nationalized banking sector), it influenced the inter-sectoral resource allocation between agriculture and industry.

An expansion of the public sector to man the commanding heights of the economy in producing 'basic goods' and infrastructure became a corner-stone of public policy with the Industrial Development and Regulation Act of 1951 and the Industrial Policy Resolution of 1956. The latter demarcated the spheres in which industries were (*a*) to be solely developed by the State—broadly infra-structure industries, (*b*) to be progressively State-owned but with private enterprise expected to supplement State efforts—these were primarily 'basic' industries such as non-ferrous metals, coal, bulk drugs, fertilizers and other petrochemicals, and a wide range of engineering industries producing capital goods, and (*c*) all other industries, mainly producing consumer goods, which were to be left to the private sector.

The methods of setting plan targets need not concern us, except to note that the planning models used could by no stretch of the imagination be said to yield anything resembling an 'optimal' plan.[15] But the problem as we have discussed elsewhere (Lal (1980a)) lies deeper, in the informational and incentive compati-bility requirements in devising an 'optimal' plan.

These issues were aired in a famous debate between Oskar Lange, Abba Lerner, Ludwig von Mises, and Friedrich Hayek during the 1930s and 1940s.[16] The planners (Lange and Lerner) argued that (*a*) because of the ubiquitous imperfections in most markets, no market economy could ever in practice attain the Utopian norm of perfect competition, but that (*b*) by using computers to stimulate the outcome of a perfectly competitive economy and legislating to compel the production of the resulting quantities of inputs and outputs (or their relative prices), a planned economy could achieve Utopia. Hayek and Mises pointed out that though such a form of planning might be theoretically feasible in a world where information about resources, technology, and the myriad actual and possible production processes and tastes of consumers could be costlessly acquired by the central planning authority, in the real world it would be impossible. Moreover, even if it were possible to acquire the information, it would be impossible speedily to solve the resulting system of millions of simultaneous equations.

Experience with planned economies, particularly that of the Soviet Union, provided factual corroboration of the Mises–Hayek position.[17] Economic theorists[18] soon demonstrated that, whilst the planners might acquire the relevant information by, in effect, playing a game with truthful producers which elicited their profit-maximizing combinations of inputs and outputs at different (hypothetical) relative prices, the game would converge to a unique and optimal outcome only if the technological conditions were identical with those required for a market economy to be perfectly competitive. That this should be so is not surprising, since the planners are envisaged as playing a game identical to that played by the so-called 'Walrasian auctioneer' in a perfectly competitive economy. But if the real world conformed to the technological assumptions of the perfect competition model, we would observe perfect competition in a market economy and the planners would be redundant! Conversely, if the technological features of the real world are such that perfect competition cannot exist, omnipotent but not omniscient planners will be unable to simulate such a condition in a planned economy.

Further, there can be no assurance that the producers tell the truth; it may be in their interest to lie systematically to the planners in order to obtain, for example, a larger share of inputs (say, leather) to produce the planned output (say, shoes). In this instance, even if the world met the technological requirements for perfect competition, because of this so-called 'incentive incompatibility' the planned economy would not attain Utopia—whereas by utilizing the universal human incentive of self-interest (or greed, as it is emotively labelled), a market economy could.

Whilst the economic rationale for the detailed planned targets that were set is highly questionable, as these were not (as they could not be) detailed enough, the resulting evolution of controls to enforce them led to what can only be described as 'epiphenomenal' planning.

All private industries were required to be licensed under the Act of 1951 for (*a*) setting up a new unit, (*b*) substantial expansion of an existing unit, and (*c*) changing the product mix of an existing unit.

The objectives to be subserved by industrial licensing were (*a*) to enforce the planned pattern of investment, (*b*) to counteract trends towards monopoly and the concentration of wealth, (*c*) to maintain regional balance in locating industries, (*d*) to protect the interests of small-scale producers and encourage the entry of new entrepreneurs, and (*e*) to foster improvement in industry by ensuring the optimum scale of plants and the adoption of advanced technology.

There were various bureaucratic hoops to subserve these multiple objectives which a prospective investor had to surmount before an industrial licence was granted. As most industrial investment also required inputs of capital or intermediate (maintenance) goods, the prospective producer also had to run the gauntlet of the trade control system. The public sector, though not subject to industrial licensing, nevertheless was subject to the same import control procedures as the private sector.

As the plan did not specifically lay down targets for *all* industries, it proved virtually impossible to provide any rational criteria to subserve the multiple objectives desired. Moreover, even when there were explicit industry level targets in the plan, there were no criteria for deciding the intra-industry allocation of investment amongst different firms. In practice a 'first come first served' rule came to be followed in issuing licences within an industry. As there was no follow-up or provision for speedy utilization of licences, this led to a pre-emption of targeted capacity by a few producers who had no intention of establishing the licensed capacity. As a counter-measure the authorities began to issue licences beyond targeted capacities. This eroded any possibility of legislating for the planned pattern of investment.

As industrial licensing was in effect a negative instrument for channelling investment, the gradual erosion of even this function has meant that, even from a planner's viewpoint, licensing now merely has 'costs' (of delay, arbitrariness, and the corruption it engenders) and no 'benefits' (the desired investment pattern).

Thus, despite the intentions of the planners and the official rhetoric, the pattern of investment has ultimately been determined by the relative private profitabilities of different industries. These in turn have been affected primarily by the trade control system and the various price and distributional controls on a large number of commodities. The resulting pattern of incentives bore little relationship to that required for promoting the planned pattern of investments, nor to the pattern required for equalizing the relative private with the relative social (from a broad economic viewpoint) profitability of industrial investments.

The Indian control system as it emerged was thus at best based on the predilections of engineers and not economists. This inappropriate intellectual perspective has continued to plague discussions of economic policy in India, not least those concerning various aspects of labour market performance, such as unemployment. An engineer is trained to think in terms of essentially a fixed-coefficients world—that is, one where the inputs required to produce the output of each good are constant. The problem of trade-offs, and the consequent notion of opportunity costs, which is central to an economist's thinking, is alien to the conventional engineer's thought processes.[19] If coefficients are really fixed, then of course prices do not matter, and the system of planning without prices, based on quantitative targets to meet fixed 'needs', becomes rational. Oddly enough, because this happens for historical reasons to be the implicit method underlying the material balance type of planning in the Soviet Union, many socialists, seeking to achieve their Valhalla by imitating the Soviet Union, have just assumed that the world has little substitutability in production and consumption, and hence that the Soviet type of planning method is economically rational. It is beyond the scope of this book to show the unworldliness and folly of this view, although I have expounded on this theme in the Indian context elsewhere.[20] But we will return to this theme toward the end of this book. For the moment, we need only note that Nehru's socialism, instead of ushering in a brave new world, was in his own words (quoted above) a harking back to a bygone world and to attitudes that had perpetrated the Hindu equilibrium for millennia.[21]

3. OVERALL TRENDS

Dirigisme, as opposed to the *laissez-faire* policies (however modified in its dying phase) of a colonial regime, has the virtue that it does do something about the provision of public goods in the form of social overhead investment—a necessary precondition for development. Starved, as the Indian economy had been even under the British (who in this respect at least were likely to have been better than many of India's past rulers), of the optimal level of such investment—essentially because of an alien power's difficulties in raising the necessary revenue or diverting funds from military uses to finance such expenditure—it would not be surprising if independent India were to do better at least in this respect.

The two major achievements of post-Independence India have been in raising the level of infrastructural investment and in the rate of savings and capital formation in the economy, as compared with the century of alien rule. This is in part responsible for the seemingly marked divergence in trends in per capita output and agricultural and industrial growth, which we briefly discuss in this section. But in discussing these trends a pertinent question must always be kept in mind: could more have been done, and were the increased investment resources spent wisely?

Table 11.1 provides some summary statistics on the growth of per capita consumption and net national product. It is evident from this table that on these indicators of performance there appears to have been an acceleration of growth in the three post-Independence decades, as compared with the record under the Raj. However, from Table 11.2 it is apparent that the structure of output and employment does not seem to have changed markedly over this period, as compared with the last half of the Raj (for which we had data, see Tables 6.4 and 6.5). As we have already seen in Table 6.7, nearly 75 per cent of the increase in the labour force, which itself increased by about 87 million in the twenty years between 1951 and 1971, was absorbed in agriculture.

TABLE 11.1(A).   Gross National Product and Net National Product (i.e. National Income)

Year	GNP at factor cost (Rs crores)		NNP at factor cost		Per capita NNP (Rs)		Index no. of NNP		Index no. of per capital NNP	
	At current prices	At 1970–1 prices	At current prices	At 1970–1 prices	At current prices	At 1970–1 prices	At current prices	At 1970–1 prices	At current prices	At 1970–1 prices
1950–1	9,157	17,469	8,833	16,731	246.0	466.0	100.0	100.0	100.0	100.0
1951–2	9,515	17,841	9,156	17,086	250.8	468.1	103.7	102.1	102.0	100.4
1952–3	9,324	18,483	8,935	17,699	240.2	475.8	101.2	105.8	97.6	102.1
1953–4	9,993	19,660	9,601	18,854	253.3	497.5	108.7	112.7	103.0	106.8
1954–5	9,174	20,190	8,745	19,328	226.6	500.7	99.0	115.5	92.1	107.4
1955–6	9,720	20,854	9,272	19,953	235.9	507.7	105.0	119.3	95.9	108.9
1956–7	11,209	21,988	10,723	21,046	267.4	524.8	121.4	125.8	108.7	112.6
1957–8	11,237	21,593	10,701	20,587	261.6	503.3	121.1	123.0	106.3	108.0
1958–9	12,650	23,413	12,023	22,329	287.6	534.2	136.1	133.5	116.9	114.6
1959–60	13,090	23,802	12,429	22,676	291.8	532.3	140.7	135.5	118.6	114.2
1960–1	13,999	25,424	13,263	24,250	305.6	558.8	150.2	144.9	124.2	119.9
1961–2	14,799	26,293	13,987	25,039	315.0	563.9	158.3	149.7	128.0	121.0
1962–3	15,727	26,834	14,795	25,414	325.9	559.8	167.5	151.9	132.5	120.1
1963–4	17,978	28,210	16,977	26,746	365.9	576.4	192.2	159.9	148.7	123.7
1964–5	21,113	30,399	20,001	28,808	422.0	607.8	226.4	172.2	171.5	130.4
1965–6	21,866	28,791	20,637	27,103	425.5	558.8	233.6	162.0	173.0	119.9
1966–7	25,250	29,081	23,848	27,298	481.8	551.5	270.0	163.2	195.9	118.3
1967–8	29,612	31,590	28,054	29,715	554.4	587.3	317.6	177.6	225.4	126.0
1968–9	30,293	32,460	28,607	30,513	552.3	589.1	323.9	182.4	224.5	126.4
1969–70	33,521	34,518	31,606	32,408	597.5	612.6	357.8	193.7	242.9	131.5

1970–1	36,452	36,452	34,235	632.8	632.8	387.6	204.6	257.2	135.8
1971–2	38,972	37,000	34,715	660.2	626.6	414.0	207.5	268.4	134.5
1972–3	42,939	36,599	34,191	711.5	604.1	455.9	204.4	289.2	129.6
1973–4	53,501	38,486	36,033	870.1	621.3	572.7	215.4	354.4	133.3
1974–5	63,051	38,958	36,590	1,003.5	617.0	675.3	218.7	408.8	132.4
1975–6	66,227	42,694	40,170	1,024.0	661.8	705.3	240.1	417.1	142.0
1976–7	71,432	43,076	40,429	1,079.4	652.1	759.5	241.6	439.7	139.9
1977–8[a]	80,665	46,823	44,043	1,193.6	694.7	858.8	263.2	486.2	149.1
1978–9[a]	87,170	49,573	46,546	1,254.7	717.2	924.1	278.2	511.1	153.9
1979–80[a]	95,627	47,180	44,085	1,339.3	663.9	1,009.2	263.5	545.5	142.5
1980–1[a]	114,319	50,824	47,507	1,563.7	699.7	1,204.9	283.9	636.9	150.2
1981–2[a]	130,576	53,166	49,631	1,740.7	715.1	1,370.9	296.6	709.0	153.5
1982–3[a]	143,712	54,084	50,437	1,868.4	711.3	1,503.3	301.5	761.1	152.6
1983–4[a]	172,739	58,113	54,276	2,201.4	748.6	1,811.1	324.4	896.7	160.6

a. Quick estimates.

Source: Economic Survey, 1984-5.

TABLE 11.1(B).   Annual Growth-rates

	GNP at factor cost (Rs crores)		NNP at factor cost (Rs crores)		Per capita NNP (Rs)	
	At current prices	At 1970–1 prices	At current prices	At 1970–1 prices	At current prices	At 1970–1 prices
First plan period	1.2	3.6	1.0	3.6	– 0.8	1.7
Second plan period	7.6	4.0	7.4	4.0	5.3	1.9
Third plan period	9.3	2.5	9.2	2.2	6.8	—
Three annual plans period						
(1966/7–1968/9)	11.5	4.1	11.5	4.0	9.1	1.8
Fourth plan period	12.0	3.5	'12.0	3.4	9.5	1.1
Fifth plan period	10.3	5.2	10.0	5.3	7.6	2.9
1974–5	17.9	1.2	17.9	1.5	15.3	– 0.7
1975–6	5.0	9.6	4.5	9.8	2.0	7.3
1976–7	7.9	0.9	7.7	0.6	5.4	– 1.5
1977–8	12.9	8.7	13.1	8.9	10.6	6.5
1978–9	8.1	5.9	7.6	5.7	5.1	3.2
1979–80	9.7	– 4.8	9.2	– 5.3	6.7	– 7.4
1980–1	19.5	7.7	19.4	7.8	16.8	5.4
1981–2	14.2	4.6	13.8	4.5	11.3	2.2
1982–3	10.1	1.7	9.7	1.6	7.3	– 0.5
1983–4	20.2	7.4	20.5	7.6	17.8	5.2

Source: Government of India, *Economic Survey, 1984–5*.

4. AGRICULTURAL GROWTH

The three post-Independence decades can conveniently be broken down into two periods, 1949/50–1964/5 and the period since 1967–8. The latter period is that of the so-called 'green revolution', to be promoted by the provision and encouragement of the use of the 'leading inputs' in areas of high agricultural potential. The former was a period when more eclectic and co-operative solutions to the agrarian problem were tried.[22]

The two intervening years, 1964–5 and 1965–6, were years of severe drought, and their inclusion as the end- or base-period in determining trends could lead to biased estimates. Although there has been much talk of a green revolution since 1965, the studies which have estimated trends in agriculture for the two periods[23] show no marked change in the trends of output or yields for the country as a whole.

A study which provides estimates of trends and includes the data up to 1977–8

TABLE 11.2(A)   Estimates of Net National Product by Industry of Origin (% Distribution, 1970–1971 Prices)

Industry group	1970–1	1971–2	1972–3	1973–4	1974–5	1975–6	1976–7	1977–8	1978–9	1979–80
Agriculture, forestry and logging, fishing, mining, and quarrying	50.6	49.5	47.2	48.1	46.6	47.9	44.8	45.7	44.0	40.6
Manufacturing, construction, electricity, gas, and water supply	19.8	20.1	21.1	20.5	20.6	19.8	21.5	21.2	22.2	22.7
Transport, communications, and trade	15.9	16.2	16.7	16.4	17.3	17.2	17.9	17.7	18.2	19.4
Banking and insurance, real estate, and ownership of dwellings and business services	4.9	5.1	5.4	5.3	5.1	5.1	5.5	5.4	5.6	6.0
Public administration and defence and other services	9.6	10.0	10.5	10.4	10.7	10.2	10.5	10.2	10.2	11.4
Net domestic product at factor cost	100.8	100.9	100.9	100.7	100.3	100.2	100.2	100.2	100.2	100.1
Net factor income from abroad	– 0.8	– 0.9	– 0.9	– 0.7	– 0.3	– 0.2	– 0.2	– 0.2	– 0.2	– 0.1
Net national product at factor cost	100.0	100.0	100.0	100.0	100.0	100.0	100.0	100.0	100.0	100.0

Source: Government of India, Economic Survey, 1980–1.

TABLE 11.2(B).   Structure of Work-force as at 31 March, 1978

Category	No. (m.)	%
Wage and salary earners:	100.54	38.5
Organized sector	24.83	9.5
Public	15.00	5.7
Private	9.83	3.8
Unorganized sector	75.71	29.0
Agricultural workers	58.34	22.3
Non-agricultural workers[a]	11.41	4.4
Others	5.96	2.3
Self-employed:	160.38	61.5
Cultivators	128.13	49.1
Non-cultivators[a]	32.25	12.4
TOTAL	260.92	100.0

a. Derived from of National Sample Survey, 29th round.
Source: Draft Five-year Plan 1978–83, pt. ii.

is that by Srinivasan (1979). His estimated trends, as well as *F* ratios to test for differences in trend lines for the two periods, are given in Tables 11.3 and 11.4. These show that (*a*) there has been a decline in the rate of growth of gross sown area, particularly that under non-food crops in the second, post-1967 decade, as compared with the earlier period; (*b*) output and yield per unit area of food crops and all crops has grown uniformly with no evidence of either acceleration or deceleration since 1967–8;[24] (*c*) the post-1967 slow-down in the growth of crop area was shared by nearly all the crops except *wheat* and the coarse grains—jowar, bajra, and maize—suffered an *absolute loss* in area in this later period; (*d*) wheat is the only crop in which there has been an acceleration in the growth of output and yield per unit area in the post-1967 period, as compared with the earlier post-Independence period. No similar change in trends is exhibited by any other crop, with the possible exception of jowar, whose yields seem to have grown faster in the second period. Thus, despite talk of a green revolution, India has so far merely witnessed a wheat revolution. 'The overall trend in growth rates of food, non-food and all crops hovers around 3 % per annum, the first two being a shade under and the last a shade over 3 %. The growth rate of wheat output in the decade since 1967–68 is, on the other hand, over 5 ½ % per annum.'[25]

The acceleration of agricultural growth in India after Independence has been due to the intensification of agriculture in terms of an increase both in the labour and in the capital input per unit land (see Table 7.4). These, as we emphasized in Chapter 7, are the Boserupian responses to the acceleration in the growth of population after 1921. The increases in labour supply provided both an incentive and the means to raise the labour input in agriculture both directly and indirectly, through minor irrigation works which have constituted the bulk of

TABLE 11.3(A)   Comparison of Trend Lines: Period I, 1949/50–1964/5; Period II, 1965/6–1977/8

	Log-linear		Log-quadratic	
	$F(2, 25)^a$	$F(1, 25)^b$	$F(1, 25)^a$	$F(1, 25)^b$
Area:				
Food	10.38**	11.01**	3.77*	2.50
Non-food	27.36**	35.40**	5.56**	2.97
All crops	20.89**	23.10**	6.64**	3.04
Production:				
Food	3.13	1.34	3.41*	2.25
Non-food	9.10**	2.50	4.06*	0.31
All crops	4.46*	0.37	3.81*	1.39
Yield:				
Food	5.75**	9.11**	3.32*	2.61
Non-food	4.48*	8.62**	2.58	2.82
All crops	5.95**	9.03**	3.41*	2.27

Notes:
Null hypothesis:
a. Regression lines same in both periods.
b. Slopes of time and (time)^2 same in two periods.
Significance level:
  * 5%.
** 1%.

both total and new irrigated acreage. But there was also an increase in the provision and use of Ishikawa's 'leading inputs'—fertilizer, better seeds, and increases in surface irrigation. The provision and marked productivity-enhancing effects of those leading inputs were largely confined to the west—Punjab, Rajasthan, and Uttar Pradesh—and Andhra Pradesh and Tamil Nadu. As in the past, the well-watered rice-growing belt of eastern India did not show any signs of a marked break with the old, near-subsistence framework of traditional agriculture.

(i) The Boserupian process and the Ishikawa curve

To illustrate the continuance of the Boserupian process in India, except for certain regions where the 'wheat revolution' has taken root, we make use of what we have labelled the 'Ishikawa curve'.[26] This is a relationship between land productivity and per-farm holding of cultivated land. Ishikawa hypothesizes that, in traditional subsistence cultivation of rice, this is a rectangular hyperbola so that, roughly speaking, increases in total output keep pace with rural labour supply (which is the force reducing farm size). He presents evidence from a number of countries (see Fig. 11.1) which also shows the countries which have suceeded in escaping from this low-productivity trap.[27]

TABLE 11.3(B)   Comparison of Trend Lines, Excluding 1965–6:
Period I, 1949/50–1964/5; Period II, 1967/8–1977/8

	Log-linear		Log-quadratic	
	$F(2, 23)^a$	$F(1, 23)^b$	$F(3, 21)^a$	$F(2, 21)^b$
Area:				
Food	11.90**	14.79**	2.08	2.54
Non-food	25.73**	18.79**	5.16**	1.32
All crops	21.18**	21.82**	4.47*	3.63*
Production:				
Food	0.48	0.52	0.43	0.61
Non-food	8.01	3.40	2.46	0.62
All crops	1.94	1.30	0.60	0.45
Yield:				
Food	0.78	1.10	0.17	0.24
Non-food	1.67	2.47	1.56	2.34
All crops	0.71	1.24	0.33	0.48

Notes:
Null hypothesis:
a. Regression lines same in both periods.
b. Slopes of time and (time)^2 same in two periods.
Significance level:
  * 5%.
 ** 1%.

Source: Srinivasan (1979).

TABLE 11.4.   Slopes of Trend Lines: Period I, 1949/50–1964/5;
Period II, 1965/6–1977/8; Period III, 1967/8

Period				Pooled		Pooled with dummy	
	I	II	III	I and II	I and III	I and II	I and III
Rice:							
Area	.0132	.0087	.0074	.0100	.0101	.0116	.0118
Production	.0343	.0332	.0219	.0247	.0252	.0339	.0313
Yield	.0211	.0245	.0145	.0147	.0151	.0223	.0195
Jowar:							
Area	.0098	− .0137	− .0173	− .0005*	− .4292*	.0016*	.0032*
Production	.0247	.0163*	.0152*	.0117	.0118	.0218	.0224
Yield	.0149	.0300	.0324	.0122	.0125	.0202	.0192
Maize:							
Area	.0263	.0109	.0019*	.0236	.0236	.0209	.0203
Production	.0380	.0116*	− .0005*	.0306	.03306	.0288	.0286
Yield	.0117	.0007*	− .0023*	.0070	.0070	.0079	.0083*
Bajra:							
Area	.0108	− .0089*	− .0139	.0060	.0058	.0039*	.0048*

Period	I	II	III	Pooled		Pooled with dummy	
				I and II	I and III	I and II	I and III
Production	.0232	.0145*	.0001*	.0241	.0242	.0201	.0175*
Yield	.0124*	.0234*	.0140*	.0181	.0184	.0162	.0128
Wheat:							
Area	.0265	.0409	.0306	.0277	.0281	.0315	.0275
Production	.0391	.0806	.0557	.0567	.0577	.0536	.0432
Yield	.0126	.0397	.0252	.0291	.0296	.0221	.0157
Cereals:							
Area	.0143	.0072	.0033*	.0101	.0101	.0118	.0116
Production	.0318	.0394	.0264	.0287	.0292	.0345	.0305
Yield	.0175	.0322	.0230	.0187	.0191	.0226	.0189
Gram:							
Area	.0165	− .0006*	.0029*	− .0040*	− .0040*	.0105	.0132
Production	.0262	.0149*	.0009*	.0028*	.0035*	.0223	.0201
Yield	.0098*	.0155*	− .0097*	.0068	.0075	.0118	.0069
Pulses:							
Area	.0188	.0047*	.0074*	.0042	.0042	.0139	.0161
Production	.0138	.0128*	.0020*	.0022*	.0027	.0135	.0109
Yield	− .0050*	.0082*	.0055*	− .0020*	− .0015*	− .0004*	− .0051
Foodgrains:							
Area	.0140	.0064	.0038*	.0084	.0085	.0113	.0115
Production	.0287	.0365	.0237	.0252	.0257	.0314	.0275
Yield	.0147	.0300	.0199	.0168	.0172	.0200	.0160
Ground-nuts:							
Area	.0393	− .0048	− .0031*	.0188	.0185	.0239	.0288
Production	.0424	.0212*	.0112*	.0222	.0225	.0350	.0348
Yield	.0031*	.0260	.0148*	.0034*	.0040*	.0111	.0059*
Oilseeds:							
Area	.0264	.0006*	.0004*	.0131	.0130	.0174	.0200
Production	.0314	.0224	.0139*	.0213	.0216	.0282	.0271
Yield	.0049*	.0219	.0136*	.0082	.0086	.0108	.0070
Cotton:							
Area	.0244	− .0063	− .0064*	.0060	.0059	.0137	.0168
Production	.0446	.0228	.0201	.0249	.02050	.0370	.0386
Yield	.0202	.0292	.0266	.0189	.0191	.0233	.0217
Jute:							
Area	.0296	− .0058*	− .0023*	.0072*	.0070*	.0173	.0218
Production	.0345	.0063*	.0068*	.0116	.0116	.0246	.0277
Yield	.0049*	.0121*	.0091*	.0044	.0046	.0074	.0059*
Fibres:							
Area	.0255	− .0062	− .0057*	.0060	.0059	.0145	.0179
Production	.0436	.0191	.0174*	.0216	.0217	.0351	.0372
Yield	.0180	.0253	.0231	.0156	.0158	.0206	.0193
Sugar:							
Area	.0303	.0203	.0303	.0225	.0224	.0268	.0303
Production	.0442	.0374	.0422	.0339	.0340	.0418	.0437
Yield	.0138	.0171	.0120	.0114	.0116	.0150	.0134
Tea:							
Area	.0055	.0061	.0058	.0080	.0080	.0057	.0055
Production	.0197	.0333	.0315	.0241	.0242	.0244	.0234
Yield	.0142	.0272	.0293	.0161	.0162	.0187	.0179

TABLE 11.4. *contd*

Period	I	II	III	Pooled I and II	Pooled I and III	Pooled with dummy I and II	Pooled with dummy I and III
Tobacco:							
Area	.0165	.0116*	.0054*	.0087	.0113	.0113	.0112
Production	.0273	.0210	.0159*	.0203	.0087	.0251	.0245
Yield	.0108	.0194	.0213	.0116	.0116	.0138	.0133
Non-food crops:							
Area	.0249	.0081	.0100	.0139	.0139	.0191	.0213
Production	.0348	.0289	.0266	.0267	.0269	.0327	.0328
Yield	.0098	.0208	.0166	.0128	.0130	.0137	.0115
All crops:							
Area	.0161	.0070	.0055	.0096	.0096	.0129	.0135
Production	.0307	.0339	.0247	.0257	.0260	.0318	.0293
Yield	.0147	.0269	.0192	.0161	.0164	.0189	.0158

* not significant at 5% level.

Source: Srinivasan (1979).

FIG 11.1 Relations between Land Productivity and Per-farm Cultivated Area, Selected Asian Countries

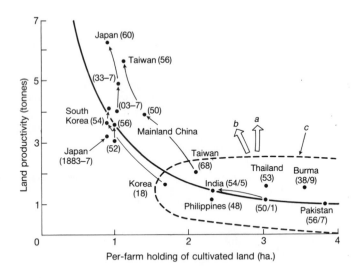

Notes:
1. Land productivity is defined in this chart as (per-crop-ha. yield of paddy) × (multiple cropping index).
2. Circle *c* indicates the location of countries with per-crop-ha. yield of paddy less than 2.3 tonnes.
Source: Ishikawa (1967, p. 78).

In Table 11.5(*a*), we provide data for 1970–1 on the output of foodgrains per hectare (kg/ha) for the different States in India (*Y*), as well as on the average size of *operational* land holdings in each State (*X*). The hypothesized subsistence relationship is a rectangular hyperbola given by:

$$Y = A + \frac{1}{X} B \tag{11.1}$$

We know that the prime wheat revolution areas, Punjab and Haryana, at least, have moved out of the traditional low-level subsistence trap. So we estimate (11.1), without Punjab and Haryana, by an OLS regression, from the data in Table 11.5(*a*). The estimated relationship is:

$$Y = 553.26 + \frac{1}{X} 660.76 \qquad R^2 = 0.70 \qquad (R.11.1)$$
$$\quad (82.88) \quad (119.93) \qquad\qquad F = 30.33$$
$$\qquad\qquad\qquad\qquad\qquad n = 15$$

(Figures in brackets are standard errors.)

The relationship is statistically significant and the data provide a fairly good fit. The estimated curve and the observations for each State, *including* those for Haryana and Punjab, are plotted in Fig. 11.2(*a*). This shows that, apart from Haryana and Punjab, Gujarat and Tamil Nadu might also be moving out of the subsistence agriculture trap. With the expansion of population the rest of the States seem to be crawling up the Ishikawa curve.

Further support for the hypothesis is provided for the 1980s by the data on State-wide foodgrain yield per hectare for 1981–2 and the average size of holdings for 1976–7, summarized in Table 11.5(*b*). As the latter is not for the same year as the yield data, and also is not for *operational* holdings, the results are not likely to be as good as for the earlier period. Again excluding Punjab and Haryana, our estimate of the Ishikawa curve for 1981–2 for the data in Table 11.5(*b*) was:

$$Y = 0.783 + 0.423 \left(\frac{1}{x}\right) \qquad (R.11.1(a))$$
$$\quad (0.113) \quad (0.137)$$

$R^2 = 0.42$
$F = 9.52$
$n = 15$
(Figures in brackets
are standard errors. $x = X/1000$)

Finally, we pooled the data for 1970–1 and 1980–1 in Tables 11.5(*a*) and (*b*) and our estimate of the Ishikawa curve was:

$$Y = 0.676 + 0.521 \left(\frac{1}{x}\right) \qquad (R.11.1(b))$$
$$\quad (0.071) \quad (0.093)$$

TABLE 11.5(A). Various Statistics of Indian Agriculture, by State, 1970–1980

State	Foodgrain output/ha. 1970–1 (kg/ha.) (1)	Average size of operational holdings (ha.) (2)	Fertilizer nutrients per cropped hectare 1978–9 (kg) (3)	Net irrigated to net sown area 1975–6 (%) (4)	Expected major and medium irrigation potential 1982–3 to ultimate potential (%) (5)	Expected minor irrigation potential 1982–3 to ultimate potential (%) (6)	Normal annual rainfall (mm) (7)	Area irrigated by private sources to net Irrigated area (%) (8)
Andra Pradesh	781	2.51	46.3	31	65	52	975	0.52
Assam	973	1.47	2.5	22[a]	15	26	2,348	0.88
Bihar	795	1.52	17.2	33	44	60	1,280	0.65
Gujarat	864	4.11	31.4	15	43	89	823	0.86
Haryana	1,235	4.11	37.4	48	62	88	646	0.42
Himachal Pradesh	1,156	1.53	—	—	—	—	1,806	1.00
Jammu and Kashmir	1,220	0.94	—	—	—	—	1,084	0.70
Kerala	1,426	0.70	33.4	10	59	34	2,824	0.51
Madhya Pradesh	648	4.00	9.0	10	32	50	1,208	0.59
Maharashtra	433	4.28	19.4	10	43	55	673	0.80
Mysore	830	3.20	32.3	13	60	60	777	0.62
Orissa	883	1.89	9.3	17	44	43	1,475	0.35
Punjab	1,861	2.89	94.8	75	78	86	593	0.56
Rajasthan	686	5.46	7.7	17	71	78	531	0.67
Tamil Nadu	1,342	1.45	68.1	43	82	86	997	0.64
Uttar Pradesh	998	1.16	45.5	46	55	81	975	0.71
West Bengal	1,224	1.20	30.6	24	78	53	1,482	0.58

a. 1973–4.

Sources: (1) Government of India (1973b, p. 78, table 5.2, and p. 88). (2) Government of India (1974b, p. 41, table 9.1). (3)–(6) Krishna (1980, table 3).
(7) Government of India (1980, p. 38, table 13). (8) Ibid., 77, table 33.

TABLE 11.5(B)   Data for Ishikawa Curve, 1975–1982

State	Average size of holdings, 1976–7 (ha.) (1)	Average yield foodgrains/ha. 1981–2 (tonnes/ha.) (2)
Andhra Pradesh	2.34	1.24
Assam	1.37	0.97
Bihar	1.11	0.87
Gujarat	3.71	1.07
Harayana	3.58	1.39
Himachal Pradesh	1.63	1.24
Jammu and Kashmir	1.07	1.53
Karnataka	2.98	0.98
Kerala	0.49	1.54
Madhya Pradesh	3.50	0.72
Maharashtra	3.66	0.74
Orissa	1.60	0.91
Punjab	2.74	2.67
Rajasthan	4.65	0.55
Tamil Nadu	1.25	1.52
Uttar Pradesh	1.05	1.19
West Bengal	0.99	1.07

Sources: Col. 1: Ezekiel (1984, table 30). Col. 2: Government of India (1983).

$$R^2 = 0.53$$
$$F = 31.35$$
$$n = 30$$

The scatter diagram for this pooled regression and the computed Ishikawa curve (II) are shown in Fig. 11.2(*b*).

There seems to be little evidence, apart from Punjab and Haryana, of the other States escaping the traditional agricultural equilibrium. Most of the States seem to be crawling up the Ishikawa curve with population expansion.

(ii) Irrigation

Irrigation and fertilizers are the two major leading inputs which can transform traditional agriculture, thereby greatly increasing the demand for labour and thence the real labour incomes in the countryside for any given level of labour supply. Table 11.5(*a*) also shows the fertilizer applied per cropped hectare and the ratio of net irrigated to net sown area in each of the States of India in the 1970s. It also provides data on the expected ratio of utilization to estimated potential of major and minor irrigation works by 1982–3. As we saw in Chapter 7, the distinction between major and minor irrigation corresponds broadly to

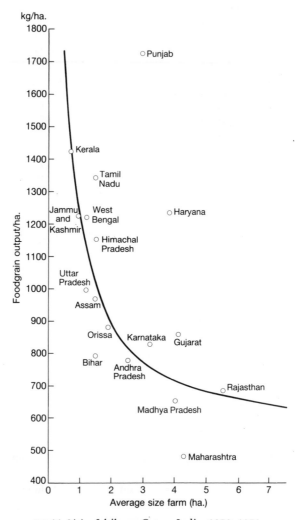

FIG 11.2(*a*)   Ishikawa Curve, India, 1970–1971

that between surface and ground water sources of irrigation and to the public versus private provision of these services.

We had also hypothesized in Chapter 7 that the economic utilization of irrigation water would be likely to vary with the pattern of rainfall. The productivity, and hence the private incentives for utilizing irrigation (particularly from surface sources), would be greatest in the relatively drier regions. Table 11.5(*a*) also provides the normal annual rainfall in each of these States. As by and large minor irrigation is financed and organized privately, we would expect that the ratio of utilization of the potential of this source across the States would vary with rainfall. By contrast, the publicly provided surface irrigation systems would be

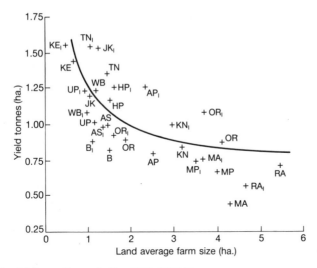

FIG 11.2(*b*)   Ishikawa Curve, India, 1970–1981/2

AP = Andhra Pradesh; AS = Assam; B = Bihar; G = Gujarat; HP = Himachal Pradesh; JK = Jammu and Kashmir; KN = Karnataka; KE = Kerala; MP = Madhya Pradesh; MA = Maharashtra; O = Orissa; R = Rajasthan; TN = Tamil Nadu; UP = Uttar Pradesh; WB = West Bengal. For each State, the unindexed observation is for 1970, the observation indexed by 1 is for 1980.

unlikely to show such a relationship. We therefore ran OLS regressions of the ratio of utilization to potential of the two major sources of irrigation (I_1, I_2) and rainfall (R). The estimated equations were:

Minor irrigation:

$$I_1 = 87.3 - 0.019R \qquad R^2 = 0.48; F = 12.00 \qquad (R.11.2)$$
$$ (7.48)\,(0.0056) \qquad\qquad n = 15$$

Major and medium irrigation:

$$I_2 = 58.85 - 0.00096R \qquad R^2 = 0.0017; F = 0.022 \qquad (R.11.3)$$
$$ (8.53)\,(0.006) \qquad\qquad n = 15$$

(Figures in brackets are standard errors.)

As expected, there is a statistically significant negative relationship between the ratio of utilization to potential of minor irrigation but no similar relationship for major irrigation, although the coefficient of the rainfall variable is of the right sign. This highlights a point emphasized in Chapter 7, that there is likely to be a marked divergence between the economic and technical irrigation potential of the different regions. As much of minor irrigation is privately financed, its development is likely to be based on economic considerations, which in the absence of detailed social cost–benefit studies may not be the case with publicly provided large-scale irrigation schemes.

In order to provide some evidence on the relatively low return from surface irrigation schemes in areas outside the obvious 'dry zones' of the west, we also provide data in Table 11.5(*a*) on the ratios of privately and publicly irrigated to net sown areas for the different States. We first ran an OLS regression on the data on foodgrain output/ha. (*F*) against that for the ratio of total net irrigated acreage to net sown area (*I*), with and without the Punjab and Haryana, the latter two States being clearly ones where the returns to irrigation (both private and social) are known to be high. The estimated equations were:

All States:

$$F = 615.5 + 13.59I \qquad R^2 = 0.48 \qquad (R.11.4)$$
$$(130.1) \quad (3.89) \qquad F = 12.00$$
$$n = 15$$

All States except Punjab and Haryana:

$$F = 733.6 + 7.82I \qquad R^2 = 0.12 \qquad (R.11.5)$$
$$(164.4) \quad (6.31) \qquad F = 1.5$$
$$n = 13$$

(Figures in brackets are standard errors.)

These suggest that the positive relationship between irrigaton and foodgrain yields is a phenomenon largely confined to the dry western zones where, besides the above direct effects, irrigation also provides the necessary precondition for the use of the new seeds and fertilizers which enhance land productivity.

We ran regressions on the data in Table 11.5(*a*) for foodgrain output/ha. (*F*) as the dependent, and fertilizers/ha. (*N*) and irrigation percentage of sown area (*I*) for all the States, and then without Punjab and Haryana. The results were:

All States:

$$F = 599.73 + 7.89\,N + 5.21\,I \qquad (R.11.6)$$
$$(119.46) \quad (4.50) \qquad (5.97)$$
$$R^2 = 0.59$$
$$F = 8.63$$
$$n = 15$$

All States Except Punjab and Haryana:

$$F = 692.63 + 7.51\,N + 0.79\,I \qquad (R.11.7)$$
$$(158.16) \quad (5.08) \qquad (7.75)$$
$$R^2 = 0.28$$
$$F = 1.9$$
$$n = 13$$

(Figures in brackets are standard errors.)

These again show that the positive relationship between fertilizers and foodgrain output is, as we would expect, largely confined to the western, dryer but irrigated areas of the country. What is more, the productivity of the privately provided (mainly ground water) irrigation is low, and is only high in the dry zone, where its development and use are complementary with that of the major surface water schemes. This can be seen from the following regressions that we ran, again with and without Punjab and Haryana, for the foodgrain output per hectare (F) and the ratio of privately irrigated, and publicly irrigated to net sown area (I_3, I_4), from the data in Table 11.5(a):

Private irrigation—all States:
$$F = 666.22 + 19.28I_3 \qquad R^2 = 0.35$$
$$(148.7) \quad (7.3) \qquad F = 7.00$$
$$n = 15$$

Private irrigation—without Punjab and Haryana:
$$F = 786.3 + 8.46I_3 \qquad R^2 = 0.080$$
$$(153.4) \quad (8.7) \qquad F = 0.96$$
$$n = 13\,\raisebox{1ex}{.}$$

Public irrigation—all States:
$$F = 696.41 + 27.56I_4 \qquad R^2 = 0.48$$
$$(111.2) \quad (7.90) \qquad F = 12.00$$
$$n = 15 \qquad\qquad\qquad (R.11.8)$$

Public irrigation—without Punjab and Haryana:
$$F = 746.3 + 21.03I_4 \qquad R^2 = 0.13$$
$$(149.2) \quad (16.1) \qquad F = 1.64$$
$$n = 13$$

Private (I_3) and public (I_4) irrigation—all States:
$$F = 637.94 + 7.12I_3 + 21.70I_4 \qquad R^2 = 0.51$$
$$(9.01) \quad (10.9) \qquad F = 6.25$$
$$n = 15$$

Private (I_3) and public (I_4) irrigation—without Punjab and Haryana:
$$F = 720.09 + 3.67I_3 + 17.37I_4 \qquad R^2 = 0.15$$
$$(10.37) \quad (19.72) \qquad F = 0.85$$

(Figures in brackets are standard errors.)

Whilst, however, at this aggregate level it might appear that irrigation is less than productive, for rice irrigation *is* productive, as is shown by a regression we have run on the data in Table 11.6 on average rice yields per hectare (R and the percentage of the area under irrigation (I).

All States:
$$R = 844.07 + 9.36I \qquad R^2 = 0.65$$
$$(103.99) \quad (1.79) \qquad F = 27.86$$
$$n = 17$$

All States—except Punjab and Haryana:
$$R = 852.36 + 9.04I \qquad R^2 = 0.57 \qquad (R.11.9)$$
$$(114.9) \quad (2.20) \qquad F = 17.23$$
$$n = 15$$

(Figures in brackets are standard errors.)

TABLE 11.6. Average Yields in Rice Cultivation, by State, 1970–1971[a]

State	% irrigated area	Average yield (kg/ha.)
Tamil Nadu	93	1,974
Jammu and Kashmir	92	1,785
Punjab	94	1,765
Haryana	88	1,710
Karnataka	55	1,684
Kerala	41	1,484
Andhra Pradesh	93	1,359
West Bengal	20	1,239
Maharashtra	21	1,227
Gujarat	26	1,223
Himachal Pradesh	54	1,178
Rajasthan	62	1,126
Assam	11	1,006
Orissa	20	962
Madhya Pradesh	14	843
Uttar Pradesh	18	811
Bihar	33	788
ALL-INDIA	36	1,145

a. States have been arranged in the descending order of the extent of average yield rates.

Sources: *Estimates of Area and Production of Principal Crops in India, 1971-2* (Ministry of Agriculture, Government of India); *All-India Report on Agricultural Census, 1970-1*, p. 62.

The productivity-enhancing effect of irrigation on rice yields seems robust even outside Punjab and Haryana. However, in the eastern Gangetic plain, as discussed in Chapter 7, as irrigation (without flood control) does not enable farmers to switch to the more productive form of rice cultivation, the marginal returns from irrigation are not likely to be as high as to irrigated wheat in the dry western zones. Some evidence on this is presented in Table 11.7(*a*), which shows that, in the traditional autumn rice cultivation, irrigation raises yields between 0 and 80 per cent. By contrast, irrigated wheat yields are 30–130 per cent above unirrigated ones in the dry States of Rajasthan, Haryana, and Punjab, but not as high in Bihar (see Table 11.7(*b*)).

Thus it is not surprising that in the 1963/4–1973/4 period, when rice output increased by 6.7 million tonnes over the 1963–4 level of 37 million tonnes, Tamil Nadu and Andhra Pradesh, with their assured irrigation, higher crop intensity, and heavy use of fertilizers, accounted for over a third (2.7 million tonnes) of the increased output.

It appears from the above evidence that, as we would expect, the much-touted high productivity of irrigation in India is really a phenomenon of the dry lands of the west and of the relatively drier regions of Tamil Nadu and the deltaic region

TABLE 11.7(A)   Irrigated and Unirrigated Yields of Rice, eastern States and Madhya Pradesh

State	Average yield (kg/ha.)			
	Irrigated		Unirrigated	
	1969–70	1968–9	1969–70	1968–9
Assam:				
Autumn	764	—	776	—
Winter	1,368	1,284	1,000	1,156
Bihar:				
Autumn	873	884	467	458
Winter	772	822	670	652
Summer	1,424	—	628	—
Orissa:				
Autumn	644	637	481	438
Winter	1,154	1,104	925	924
Summer	1,406	1,204	787	910
West Bengal:				
Autumn	—	2,170	—	1,243
Summer	—	2,366	—	1,778
Madhya Pradesh	1,267	1,162	708	628

Source: *All-India Report on Agricultural Census 1970–1*, p. 62.

TABLE 11.7(B)   Irrigated and Unirrigated Yields of Wheat (kg/ha.)

State	1968–9		1969–70	
	Irrigated	Unirrigated	Irrigated	Unirrigated
Madhya Pradesh	1,040	616	1,103	620
Bihar	970	795	1,139	717
Uttar Pradesh	—	—	—	—
Rajasthan	1,080	700	1,108	655
Haryana	1,764	1,019	2,004	1,503
Punjab	2,397	1,043	—	—

Source: *All-India Report on Agricultural Census 1970–1*, p. 62.

of Andhra Pradesh—the core of the ancient south Indian variant of the Hindu civilization. With the growth of population and labour supply, most of the rest of the country, and in particular the well-watered eastern Gangetic plain, has merely seen an extension of irrigation of the traditional protective type. Without the massive public investments in irrigation-cum-flood-control measures (and the development of appropriate new rice seeds) which we discussed in Chapter 7, there is unlikely to be any marked change in the conditions which have established and maintained the Hindu equilibrium for millennia in the region. But whether, from a national viewpoint, the social returns for such public investment are likely to be as high as from the promotion of labour-intensive industrialization in the region is more debatable. For, as we have argued in the last part, it is likely that the dynamic comparative advantage of the region does not lie in tropical agriculture. However, without the necessary social cost–benefit studies, this is at best a conjecture.

5. SAVINGS, CAPITAL INFLOWS, INVESTMENT, AND THE GROWTH OF THE PUBLIC SECTOR

The most dramatic change in the post-Independence economy has been the rise in the savings rate. Table 11.8 gives the data on net domestic savings, foreign capital inflows, and net domestic capital formation in India. The savings rate rose from about 5.5 per cent of net domestic product at Independence to about 15.4 per cent in 1975 and, according to the most recent estimates of the Central Statistical Organization (SO), to 18.75 per cent in 1982, whilst the Reserve Bank has offered a tentative estimate for 1978–9 of 20 per cent of the net national product.[28] Equally important, despite the considerable passion expended in India on the issue, foreign capital inflows have, since the late 1960s, made a marginal contribution to the rate of investment in the economy.[29]

India's continuing economic stagnation cannot therefore be laid at the door of a shortage of capital. It is the productivity of the investments India has made, as well as their relatively capital-intensive nature, which has lowered the actual below the potential rate of growth of both output and demand for labour. As we have seen in the last section, this was not because of an undue neglect of agricultural investment[30] but rather because of the pattern of industrialization promoted, and the proliferation of a vast, unwieldy, and inefficient public sector.

Table 11.9 gives the proportion of total investment absorbed by the public sector. Reflecting Nehru's and the Indian intelligentsia's ancient Hindu caste prejudices against private trade and commerce, the public sector was promoted to mount 'the commanding heights of the economy'. Undoubtedly a rational case for the promotion of public enterprise can be made (see Lal (1980b)), but the cancer-like growth of the Indian public sector cannot be justified on any of these rational grounds.[31]

Statistics on the size of the public sector in India refer only to those enterprises which are wholly owned by the State with no private participation in equity or management.[32] Thus, following the practice of many other countries where the public sector includes enterprises in which the Government holds the majority of shares directly or indirectly, in India many private enterprises (including the steel-making pioneer Tata Iron and Steel Company—in which the State now

TABLE 11.8. Domestic Saving and Domestic Capital Formation

Year	% gross domestic product at market prices		% net domestic product at market prices		
	Gross domestic saving	Gross domestic capital formation	Net domestic saving	Net domestic capital formation	Net foreign capital inflow
1950–1	—	—	5.5	5.5	0.0
1960–1	13.7	16.9	9.3	12.7	3.4
1961–2	13.1	15.3	8.4	10.7	2.3
1962–3	14.5	17.1	9.6	12.3	2.7
1963–4	14.4	16.6	9.8	12.1	2.3
1964–5	13.6	16.2	9.2	12.0	2.8
1965–6	15.7	18.2	11.2	13.8	2.6
1966–7	16.3	19.7	11.8	15.4	3.6
1967–8	13.9	16.5	9.6	12.3	2.7
1968–9	14.1	15.4	9.5	10.8	1.3
1969–70	16.4	17.1	11.8	12.5	0.7
1970–1[a]	16.8	17.8	12.0	13.0	1.0
1971–2[a]	17.3	18.4	12.4	13.6	1.2
1972–3[a]	16.2	16.9	11.3	11.9	0.6
1973–4[a]	19.3	20.0	15.0	15.7	0.7
1974–5[a]	18.2	19.1	13.8	14.8	1.0
1975–6[a]	20.0	19.9	15.4	15.2	– 0.2
1976–7[a]	22.0	20.4	17.4	15.7	– 1.7
1977–8[a]	21.6	20.0	17.0	15.3	– 1.7
1978–9[a]	23.9	23.7	19.2	19.0	– 0.2
1979–80	21.2	21.8	16.1	16.6	0.5

a. Revised.

Source: Central Statistical Organization.

owns 71 per cent of the shares) would also be part of the public sector. Moreover, the centrally run railways and the power utilities run by the States are also not included in the official statistics on the public sector. Furthermore, there are enterprises owned by the States which even on the narrow definition are not usually included in the statistics.

Bearing those qualifications in mind, in 1951 there were by official definitions only five public enterprises (as defined above); by 1984 there were 214. By 1979 the gross fixed assets of the central public sector exceeded that of the private sector by over 16 per cent (viz Rs 117.8 billion and Rs 101.1 bilion respectively). In basic industries (see Table 11.9*b*)) the public sector had a near monopoly of domestic production. In addition, as the State owns 100 per cent of power

TABLE 11.9(A)   Public- and Private-sector Investment

Sector	First plan	Second plan	Third plan	Fourth plan[a]	Fifth plan[a]	
					Draft	Revised
Value (Rs 10 m.):						
Public-sector outlay	1,960	4,672	8,577	15,902	37,250	39,288
Public-sector investment	1,560	3,731	7,180	13,655	31,400	36,703
Private-sector investment	1,800	3,100	4,100	8,980	16,161	27,048
TOTAL	3,360	6,831	11,280	22,635	47,561	63,751
% distribution:						
Public sector	46.4	54.6	63.6	60.3	66.0	57.6
Private sector	53.6	45.4	36.4	39.7	34.0	42.4
TOTAL	100.0	100.0	100.0	100.0	100.0	100.0

a. These figures are targets: the others are actual.

Source: Plan documents derived from Lal (1980a, table 1.1(g)).

TABLE 11.9(B).   Share of Public-sector Output in Basic Industries, 1983–1984

Industry	%
Coal	96.97
Lignite	100.00
Crude petroleum	100.00
Saleable Steel	74.50
Aluminium	27.90
Copper	100.00
Lead	100.00
Zinc	89.30
Nitrogenous fertilizer	47.70
Phosphatic fertilizer	27.30
Telephones	100.00
Teleprinters	100.00

Source: Jha (1985).

generation, has a monopoly of rail and air transport, life and general insurance, and has 95 per cent of the banking sector, the broadly defined public sector has a dominant influence on the economy.

In the 1970s the promotional role of the public sector in developing new basic industries was extended through nationalization and bail-outs for declining and/or sick industries (e.g. some 145 textile mills, for example), many in the consumer goods sector, as well as in coalmining. Thus not only was industrial entry prevented by industrial licensing and the attendant bureaucratic controls, but increasingly exit also was ruled out by this practice of absorbing sick industries into the public sector.

Judged by conventional accounting criteria, the performance of the public sector has been abysmal compared with the the private sector. The latter's performance in itself is not particularly noteworthy if we judged them by their social profitability. But for three industries in which there are both private and public enterprises, some estimates of social profitability (at world prices) by Jha (1985), summarized in Table 11.9(*c*), show the relatively poor public-sector performance.

Elsewhere I have dealt in detail[33] with the defects of the industrial planning system used to foster the public sector, and outlined reforms required in the light of modern second-best welfare economics to make planning more rational. These issues need not detain us, although we will return to them in the concluding chapter. However, one important point needs to be noted. One of the official reasons given for promoting the public sector was its purported role in raising the savings rate of the Indian economy. In fact, the increased savings rate as well as the bulk of national savings has been provided by the private 'household sector'. Thus, Raj (1979) states that in 1979, when a very high rate of savings was reached, savings in the public sector had gone up between 1966–7 and 1978–9 from about 1.5 per cent of net national product (NNP) to about 4 per cent, whilst savings of the household sector rose from about 10 per cent of NNP in 1966–7 to nearly 15.75 per cent in 1978–9. For the defenders of the public sector, such as Raj, 'the consequent reversal [from the planned pattern] in the relative importance of private- and public-sector saving in the growth process poses naturally some problems'. As well it may!

For us, however, it is time to turn to a quick evaluation of the industrial development in which the public sector was supposed to have played such a major part, and to see what returns Indians received for the very large investments made in their name by public sector-led industrialization.

TABLE 11.9(C)   Relative Profitability of the Public Sector, 1974–1975

Industry	Ratio of value added to GCE[a] at market prices		Ratio of value added to GCE at border prices	
	Public	Private	Public	Private
Engineering	11.42	23.12	10.57[b]	18.95[b]
Chemicals	6.26	21.26	4.01[b]	10.07[b]

a. Gross capital employed.
b. No attempt has been made to calculate gross capital employed at border prices. These figures are valid therefore only for intra-sectoral comparisons.

Source: Jha (1985, table 2).

6. INDUSTRIAL DEVELOPMENT

Table 11.10 gives the data on industrial output, employment, and net fixed capital stock during the post-Independence decades. Table 11.11(*a*) summarizes some relevant industrial statistics for India since the mid-nineteenth century, and also provides some comparative data on South Korea and Taiwan. In order to examine the trends in growth of industrial output, employment, and capital (although this refers to the whole non-agricultural sector), we have fitted Gompertz curves of the form:

$$Y_t = k.a^{b^t}$$

to the data.[34] The results are reported in Table 11.11(*b*), which also reports the fitted curves to the pre-Independence data. From this, it is apparent that:

(i)   while, in the pre-Independence period, industrial output was accelerating, in the post-Independence period it has been decelerating;
(ii) in both the pre-Independence and post-Independence periods, the growth of industrial employment has been decelerating, and the underlying (average) growth-rate has been much lower in the post- as compared with the pre-Independence period;
(iii) there has been a massive increase in the non-agricultural-sector capital stock, which has been growing at a high and accelerating rate.

Table 11.12 provides further proof, if this were needed, of the very large increase in the capital labour ratio during the planned post-Independence decade. This increasing capital intensity has been due to the socially inefficient pattern of industrialization engendered by the heavy industry-biased, public sector-oriented industrialization promoted in India, through a plethora of inefficient investment and import controls. These inefficiencies, and the damage, both direct and indirect, that has as a result been done to the prospects of India's poor, have been documented in detail elsewhere,[35] and we need only provide a brief summary of the effects of the major instruments of *dirigisme*—industrial licensing, import controls, and, more recently, export incentives.

After the first serious foreign-exchange crisis in independent India in 1956–7, a complex system of quota restrictions on imports was instituted. All requests to import were subjected to administrative scrutiny, and even the most petty imported items required a licence. Moreover, import licences were not available for goods which could be produced within India. This led to effective rates of protection which exceeded 200 per cent on average, with a high variability of rates around the average.

In Table 11.13(*a*), we present estimates from an earlier work (Lal (1980a)) on the social rate of return on manufacturing industry during the 1958–68 period (derived using Little and Mirrlees (1974), methods). These show, as we would

Table 11.10. Industrial Output, Employment, and Capital Stock, 1948–1979

Year	Index of industrial production (1960 = 100) (1)	Industrial employment (m.) (2)	Net fixed capital stock at constant prices, non-agricultural sector (3)
1948	—	—	5,098
1949	—	—	5,447
1950	—	—	5,780
1951	56.0	3.07	6,145
1952	58.2	3.11	6,386
1953	59.7	3.15	6,643
1954	63.8	3.16	7,091
1955	70.6	3.11	7,799
1956	76.8	3.33	8,357
1957	80.0	3.53	9,286
1958	82.7	3.43	10,142
1959	89.8	3.57	10,972
1960	100.0	3.65	11,842
1961	109.2	3.74	12,751
1962	119.7	4.02	13,776
1963	129.7	4.20	15,071
1964	140.9	4.53	16,516
1965	153.8	4.69	18,088
1966	152.6	4.76	19,714
1967	151.4	4.72	21,113
1968	161.1	4.80	22,526
1969	172.5	5.04	—
1970	180.8	5.22	—
1971	188.8	5.44	—
1972	200.0	5.49	—
1973	200.9	5.82	—
1974	204.5	6.02	—
1975	215.5	6.38	—
1976	241.7	6.65	—
1977	250.1	—	—
1978	267.2	—	—
1979	270.7	—	—

Sources: Col. 1: to 1971, Dey (1975, table A.29); after 1971, the series with base 1970–1 from *Economic Survey 1980* (Government of India, Ministry of Finance, New Delhi, 1981), p. 93, has been linked. Col. 2: Satyanarayana (1981), based on data from Annual Survey of Industry and Sample Survey of Manufacturing Industry. Col. 3: Dholakia (1974).

TABLE 11.11(A)   Summary Statistics on Manufacturing

	Period	% p.a.
India:		
Manufacturing growth-rates-value added[a]	1868–1900	10.36
(constant prices)	1900–13	6.00
	1919–39	4.80
	1956–65	6.9
	1966–79	5.5
Rates of growth of employment in manufacturing[b]	1902–13	4.43
	1919–39	2.29
	1959–65	3.60
	1966–79	3.50
Rates of growth of capital stock in manufacturing[c]	1959–65	13.6
	1966–79	6.8
South Korea:[d]		
Mining and manufacturing growth-rate-net value of	1910–40	9.7
commodity product (constant price)	1953–60	11.1
	1960–76	18.4
Incremental capital output ratio	1953–60	2.59
	1960–74	1.33
Growth-rate of employment in manufacturing	1963–76	12.1
Taiwan:		
Rate of growth of manufacturing output[e]	1930s	6.0
	1953–8	8.9
	1958–63	12.6
	1963–8	19.7
	1968–72	23.1
	1972–5	7.1
Average marginal capital output ratios[e]	1952–60	1.68
	1960–6	1.97
	1966–73	2.20
	1975–80	3.96
Percentage growth in industrial employment[f]	1952–60	69
	1960–6	41.6
	1966–75	116.7

Sources:
a. Derived from data in Heston (1983) and Sivasubramonian (1977); post-Second World War growth-rate from the national accounts.
b. Pre-Independence: Sivasubramonian (1977); post-Independence: Ahluwalia (1985, tables A5.2 and 3).
c. Ahluwalia (1985).
d. Mason *et al.* (1980).
e. EPD, *Taiwan Statistical Data Book.*
f. Galenson (1979).

TABLE 11.11(B) Parameters of Gompertz Curve Fitted to Trends in Various Industrial-sector Variables (Y = $k(a)^{bt}$)

	k	a	b
Industrial production:			
1882–1900	506.13	1.07	1.17
1900–45	368.67	1.32	1.04
1953–79	457.09	0.11	0.95
Industrial employment:			
1902–46	11,511.4	0.058	0.986
1953–76	2,200.1	0.001	0.995
Capital stock in the non-agricultural sector:			
1948–67	185.13	25.15	1.02

Note: In interpreting these results, note that (i) if $a < 1$, and $b < 1$, the Gompertz curve is increasing at a decreasing rate of growth, with an upper asymptote; (ii) if $a > 1$ and $b > 1$, the curve is increasing at an increasing rate of growth, with a lower asymptote.
Source: Data in Heston (1983) and in Tables 11.10 and 7.4.

TABLE 11.12. Capital/Labour Ratios in Indian Manufacturing, (1970–1971 Prices)

	Fixed capital per worker (Rs)			Annual average growth-rate (%)		
	1950–1	1960–1	1970–1	1950–71 (20 yrs.)	1950–61 (10 yrs.)	1960–71 (10 yrs.)
Registered	4,662[a] (6,359)	12,711	20,056	—	—	4.67
Unregistered	790	2,024	2,402	5.72	9.86	1.73
TOTAL	1,583	4,508	7,670	—	—	—

a. Not comparable, as the employment figures include workers in electricity. The figure in brackets is for the capital/labour ratio for registered manufacturing-cum-electricity.
Source: Choudhury (1983, table 6, appendices ii and iii).

TABLE 11.13(A) Average Social Rates of Return in Indian Manufacturing, 1958–1968

Year	SWR = W[a] (%)	SWR = 0 (%)	SWR = 0.6 W (%)
1958	1.6	36.0	15.4
1960	1.6	39.0	16.6
1961	2.4	37.0	16.2
1962	0.9	29.0	12.1
1963	1.9	29.0	12.7
1964	1.4	26.0	11.2
1968	– 6.1	22.6	5.4

a. SWR: shadow wage-rate
W: market wage
Source: Lal (1980a, p. 44).

TABLE 11.13(B)   Total Factor Productivity Growth Estimates, Indian Manufacturing,
(1959/60–1979/80)

	% p.a.
India	– 0.2– – 1.3
Korea	5.7
Turkey	2.0
Yugoslavia	0.8
Japan	3.1

Source: Ahluwalia (1958, pp. 132–5). The estimates other than for India are Ahluwalia's of Nishimizu and Robinson's (1983) estimates based on a gross production function to a value-added production function as for India.

expect, declining social rates of return, irrespective of the shadow wage-rate assumptions made. Furthermore, Ahluwalia (1985) has estimated total factor productivity in Indian manufacturing for the 1960s and 1970s. Her estimates, and equivalent ones for Korea, Turkey, Yugoslavia, and Japan, are all summarized in Table 11.13(*b*). This table shows the growing absolute and relative inefficiency of Indian industry.

At various stages during the 1960s and early 1970s these harmful effects of the existing trade control system—particularly on exports—had begun to be acknowledged, even in India. Export incentives, aimed at redressing the bias against exports, were introduced. Not surprisingly the partial removal of this bias led to a spurt in exports, as economists who were not mesmerized by foreign-exchange bottle-necks had always predicted.[36] In many instances, however, the *dirigiste* impulse was not stifled. India matched its highly complex and bureaucratic system of import allocation with an equally complex system of export incentives. The major instrument used was an import entitlement for exporters in the form of import licences whose premium provided the exporter with a subsidy. The effect was to create a host of new distortions in the export sector.[37] A simple policy of export maximization was pursued; any producer wishing to export found a Government willing to grant him an import entitlement whose premium was sufficient to equalize the relatively high domestic costs and low foreign prices of his product. Since the entitlements were usually tied to the import content of exports, these schemes subsidized import-intensive exports rather than those with a high domestic value added. The widespread practice of over-invoicing exports, coupled with different effective exchange-rates for exports and imports, meant that a number of goods with a high import content were exported for a lower foreign-currency return than the foreign-currency cost of the imports embodied in them! India thus ended up by pursuing import substitution and export promotion without reference to economic costs, guided only by the belief that 'India should produce whatever it can and India should export whatever it produces'.[38] The inefficiency, waste, and corruption that the Indian trade control system has engendered are incalculable.

Moreover, the failure to industrialize by using the most abundant resource in the economy—unskilled labour—has meant that the large capital investment in modern industry has not yielded the feasible improvements in employment and poverty redressal. The policy of import-substitution, which began with the creeping tariff protection introduced by the Raj after the First World War and was greatly intensified by the system of quantitative import controls erected by India in the 1950s, is responsible. Despite the recognition in official circles of the deleterious effects of these trade controls on both equity and efficiency in the economy, these controls have not been dismantled.

In the 1950s and 60s there was an explosion of world trade in manufacturing and semi-manufacturing (see Table 11.14). Although it was one of the pioneering industrializing countries in the Third World, India steadily lost ground to various other developing countries, who followed more nearly optimal trade policies than post-Independence India—still haunted by its fear of free trade which, since the nineteenth century, the nationalists had misdiagnosed as the cause of India's continuing poverty. The trade control system that had evolved by the early 1960s created a bias against labour-intensive manufactured exports. When export promotion was undertaken it was inefficient, and the patterns of export subsidies were not based on rational economic grounds, as can be seen from estimates (see Table 11.15) of the social profitability of exports promoted in a sample of export industries. These show that the subsidy system has not in general succeeded in raising the implicit exchange-rate for goods with higher social export profitability, and that the relative divergences between private and social profitability have been altered in essentially arbitrary ways by the export subsidy system. Socially profitable exports did not grow by as much as they could have. India's lost trading opportunities were taken up by other developing countries, in particular the so-called 'Gang of Four'.[39] Perhaps as spectacular a redressal of poverty as occurred in these South-east Asian countries following from a policy of optimal trade may not have occurred in India. For it is likely that India, as compared with the Gang of Four, would have had (even under free trade) a lower share of trade in national product. Nevertheless, an opportunity for greatly increasing the demand for unskilled labour *was* lost.

The trade control system engendered a *dirigiste* cast of mind in the bureaucracy, amongst the populace, and in the politicians. It has also meant a vast extension of the traditional Hindu revenue economy. It is only a rare politician who would be willing to dismantle such a lucrative machine of patronage and power. We take up these political consequences of the industrial and trade controls set up in post-Independence India in the next chapter.

In concluding this section we need only note that, given the difficulties, in particular in eastern India, of raising agricultural productivity, the early Indian planners were right to think that rapid industrialization was required to raise labour incomes and cure Indian poverty. Their mistake was to base

TABLE 11.14. Structure and Growth of Exports for India and All Developing Countries, 1960–1978[a]

| Export | Composition of exports (%) | | | | Growth-rates of export volume (% p.a.) | | | | | |
| | Developing countries | | India[b] | | Developing countries | | | India | | |
	1960	1978	1960/61	1978/79	1960–78	1960–9	1970–9	1960/1–1978/9	1960/1–1969/70	1970/1–1978/9
Food[c]	42.4	28.7	32.8	27.6	2.8	2.6	2.1	3.0	0.3[d]	4.4
Raw materials[e]	37.4	18.6	18.7	9.3	2.9	2.8	0.7	3.3	4.3	1.3[d]
	(44.7)	(23.4)			(3.4)	(5.0)	(−0.2)			
Manufactures[f]	20.2	52.7	48.6	63.1	11.6	9.9	11.6	6.8	4.5	11.2
	(12.9)	(47.8)			(13.6)	(10.1)	(14.4)			
Total[g]	100.0	100.0	100.0	100.0	5.8	4.5	5.8	5.1	3.4	7.6

a. Errors due to rounding. All growth-rates are semi-logarithmic least squares trends. Petroleum is excluded throughout.
b. The indexes for India are those with 1968–9 weights.
c. Standard Industrial Trade Classification (SITC) 0 + 1.
d. The growth-rate is not significantly different from zero at the 0.5% confidence level.
e. SITC 2 + 4. For developing countries the figures in brackets show the addition of SITC 68 (refined metals), an insignificant element for India except in a few years when sales from private silver stocks are permitted. For developing countries, however, exports in SITC 68 are important (7.3% of exports in 1960) and fall naturally under raw materials.
d. SITC 5–9 for the composition of exports and SITC 5–8 for growth-rates. For developing countries the figures in brackets show the results of the exclusion of SITC 68.
g.

Source: Wolf (1981, table 2.6), derived from United Nations, Monthly Bulletin of Statistics, special table G; and UN Conference on Trade and Development, Handbook of International Trade and Development Statistics, table A.8 (New York, various years).

TABLE 11.15.   Estimates of Various Indices for Ten ICICI exporting firms[a]

Firm in industry	e_{di}[b] 1972	e_{di}[b] 1974	e'_{di}[b] 1972	e'_{di}[b] 1974	r^s (%)[c] 1972	r^s (%)[c] 1974	r_x^p (%)[d] 1972	r_x^p (%)[d] 1974	r_d^p (%) 1972	r_d^p (%) 1974	r_{xe}^p (%)[c] 1972	r_{xe}^p (%)[c] 1974
Light commercial vehicles	0.48	0.33	0.53	0.33	28	20	6	-9	49	41	44	13
Wire ropes	0.33	0.10	0.33	0.16	-27	26	35	6	42	28	-20	22
Textile machinery I	0.24	0.13	0.24	0.13	50	75	12	8	14	11	25	17
Textile machinery II	0.12	0.14	0.14	0.14	17	24	-8	-19	4	-3	-4	-11
Abrasives	0.04	0.13	0.04	0.13	-55	-38	-42	-31	16	15	-30	-26
Electrical equipment	0.08	0.18	0.08	0.18	20	23	-2	-8	3	-2	2	2
Castings and forgings	0.12	0.04	0.12	0.04	-10	34	-14	19	24	21	-9	22
Steel rubes and pipes	0.90	0.35	0.90	0.35	'-5	57	-22	14	14	22	-5	55
Textiles	0.05	0.24	0.05	0.24	-3	20	-21	-3	7	9	-19	25
Chemicals	0.00	0.00	0.00	0.00	108	32	51	-15	37	1	51	-15
Mean	0.24	0.16	0.24	0.17								
Standard deviation	0.28	0.11	0.28	0.11								

a. Derived from the ICICI (Industrial Credit and Investment Corporation of India) export firm survey data.

e_{di} = percentage excess of the implicit over the official exchange rate assuming the full capacity imported inputs are *not* provided to exporters.

e'_{di} = percentage excess of the implicit over the official exchange rate assuming the full capacity imported inputs *are* provided to exporters.

r^s = social rate of profit.

r_x^p = private rate of profit assuming all the output is exported, and there are no incentives.

r_d^p = private rate of profit assuming all the output is sold in the domestic market.

r_{xe}^p = private rate of profit assuming the output is exported and receives the same indirect and direct rate of subsidy as current exports of the firm.

b. Where no premia rates were available as no REP (Import Replenishment) was nominated, the two e_d values will be the same.

c. The social rates of profit has been derived from the data for each firm with the inputs being shadow priced on Little–Mirrlees lines by using the shadow price estimates in Lal (1980a). The capital data was from the balance sheets of the firms. The output was priced at f.o.b. prices. The resulting rates of profit are those which would accrue assuming the actual degree of capacity utilization if inputs and outputs were priced at 'border' prices.

d. This private rate of profit has been obtained by valuing the output at f.o.b. prices and the inputs at market prices. The capital figures were taken from the balance sheets.

e. This rate of profit was obtained by valuing the output at f.o.b. prices plus total subsidies on actual exports and inputs at market prices. The capital figures were taken from the balance sheets.

Source: Lal (1979a, table 3).

industrialization almost entirely on import substitution. India's industry then inevitably faced the limits of a home market which, though large in terms of numbers of people, was small in terms of purchasing power.[40] Carrying import substitution further and further back in the stages of production postpones, but does not eradicate, these limits of home demand for industrial products. Export markets which were buoyant throughout the post-war period (and which, despite some slowing down in the 1970s, still are) provided an elastic demand for a whole range of unskilled labour-intensive industrial products. With India's head-start in industrialization, an abundance of domestic entrepreneurs as well as technicians, the promotion of labour-intensive manufactures would have benefited Indian labour enormously.

Moreover, the shadow wage-rates of unskilled labour were much lower in the ancient Hindu heartland of India (Table 11.16). As these eastern regions have not found it easy to transform their traditional agriculture, footloose, labour-intensive industries provided with the required social overhead facilities would, under different policies, have been able to provide a considerable, if not a

TABLE 11.16.   Summary of Ratios of Social to Market Wage-rates for Rural and Industrial Labour, by States

State	Rural			Urban–industrial		
	k_I	k_{II}	k_{III}	k_I	k_{II}	k_{III}
Andhra Pradesh	1.04	1.02	1.04	0.66	0.66	0.66
Assam	1.05	1.04	1.04	0.70	0.70	0.70
Bihar	0.73	0.70	0.70	0.56	0.56	0.56
Gujarat	0.95	0.94	0.94	0.62	0.62	0.62
Jammu and Kashmir	1.08	1.08	1.08	0.65	0.65	0.65
Kerala	0.88	0.88	0.88	0.62	0.62	0.62
Madhya Pradesh	0.96	0.94	0.96	0.67	0.67	0.67
Maharashtra	0.77	0.76	0.77	0.63	0.63	0.63
Mysore	0.94	0.94	0.94	0.67	0.67	0.67
Orissa	0.97	0.96	0.96	0.73	0.73	0.73
Punjab and Haryana	0.94	0.94	0.94	0.76	0.76	0.76
Rajasthan	0.93	0.92	0.92	0.65	0.65	0.65
Tamil Nadu	1.07	1.05	1.05	0.71	0.71	0.71
Uttar Pradesh	1.00	0.99	0.99	0.74	0.73	0.73
West Bengal	0.70	0.70	0.70	0.57	0.57	0.57

Notes: *SWR*: social wage-rate
         w: market wage
         k =   *SWR/w*
         k_I: assuming no rural surplus labour
         k_{II}:   assuming maximal estimates of rural surplus labour valid
         k_{III}:   on 'best' estimates of rural surplus labour
Source: Lal (1980a, p. 203).

spectacular, rise in the local demand for labour and thence, by raising labour incomes, have ameliorated the poverty which still blights these regions (see Chapter 13 below). Instead, the new industries set up in these regions have been mainly of the capital-intensive variety, based on the mineral resource of the area, which have done little to provide extra employment and raise incomes in the region.

NOTES

1. Keynes (1936, pp. 383–4).
2. Gandhi (1958– , vol. x, pp. 6–68).
3. Brown (1972, p. 12).
4. Ibid., 46.
5. Forrester (1980).
6. Ibid.
7. 'Yet, if anything, it was this very unprecedented action itself, this annexation of untouchables into Hinduism, this arbitrary cooption by definition, which was to be so profoundly offensive to Ambedkar and other leaders of the Untouchables' (Frykenberg (1985, p. 326)).
8. Brown (1972).
9. Ibid., 360.
10. Nehru (1936, pp. 431–2).
11. See Lal (1980a) for a fuller discussion of the validity of identifying 'socialism,' with *dirigisme* and bureaucratic modes of allocation in India, and Lal (1985) for a fuller discussion of the origins and interconnections between 'nationalism', 'socialism', and 'planning'.
12. Nehru (1956, p. 555).
13. These are discussed in Lal (1980a), which also discusses the optimal forms of government intervention, given the well-known limitations of a policy of *laissez-faire*, and the consequent need to deal with various forms of 'market failure'.
14. With some annual plans in the years 1966/7–1968/9 and two versions of the sixth plan.
15. See Rudra's (1975) devastating critique and Lal (1980a) for the theoretical bases of Indian planning.
16. Lange and Taylor (1938), Lerner (1946), Hayek (1935), von Mises (1935).
17. Nove (1961).
18. Heal (1973) surveys this literature.
19. Although it should be said that economists, brought up on various fixed-coefficients planning models, have found it easy and natural to slip into this engineering frame of mind, even when they have explicitly been concerned with various economic trade-offs.
20. Lal (1980a). See also Lal (1983).
21. See Lal (1985) for a discussion of the atavistic impulses underlying nationalism, socialism, and planning.
22. See Dantwala (1979), Rudra (1978) for surveys of agricultural policy since 1950.
23. Dey (1975, 1977), Rudra (1978), Vaidyanathan (1977a), Srinivasan (1979).
24. These conclusions refute the assertions to the contrary made by various radical writers in India, of whom Sau (1981) may be taken as representative. He asserts, 'the pace of expansion in foodgrain output during this period (1960–61 to 1970–71) was slower than that in the earlier period, 1949–50/1959–60' (p. 6). As usual, by choosing arbitrary base- and end-points, conclusions based on preconceived notions can be readily derived.
25. Srinivasan (1979, p. 6).
26. See Ishikawa (1967, pp. 78–83). On the basis of the 1981 draft of this book manuscript this term has also been adopted by Reynolds (1983) (1985).
27. Another way of looking at the Ishikawa curve is that it is the macro-equivalent of the inverse relationship between farm size and productivity to be found at the farm level in Indian agriculture—on which see Sen (1975) and Saini (1979).
28. See Raj (1979). But Srinivasan, in a personal communication, has queried these latest

estimates. For the CSO estimates also show that per capita real consumption *fell* from Rs 543 (average for the triennium 1969/70–1971/2 at 1970/1 prices) to Rs 539 (average for the triennium 1975/6–1977/8) while per capita income *rose* from Rs 625 to Rs 669. This absolute decline in per capita consumption, whilst per capita income and the savings ratio rose, could be taken to imply that the poor in India (as the radicals have always insisted) have been impoverished *absolutely* and not just *relatively*. But before such a startling conclusion is accepted, it is worth pondering the following observations of Srinivasan, which of course cannot be tested until the NSS 32nd round consumer expenditure data confirm whether or not there has been an *absolute* fall in per capita consumption.

Srinivasan notes, 'The CSO treats foodgrain stocks in the hands of *producers* as consumption, i.e. changes in such stocks do not form part of savings or dissavings of households. This treatment is, in fact, because of data unavailability. Now, with Punjab–Haryana–Western UP increasingly dominant in production as well as in sales to Government of wheat *and* rice, it would appear that stocks that formerly would have been held by widely dispersed producers are now entering public stocks, the changes in which are duly reflected in CSO figures of savings. This could explain both the *apparent* fall in real consumption (because earlier consumption was artificially increased by stocks) and increase in savings.'

29. Whilst in the mid-1970s, largely fuelled by remittances from migrants to western Asia, India ran a large balance of payments surplus, and was thus a net *lender* to the outside world!
30. But see Lipton (1977) for a contrary view, and Byers (1979) for a counter-blast to Lipton.
31. These are based on the legislation of a second-best welfare optimum in the face of various forms of market failure, where the alternative instrument of using taxes and subsidies is either infeasible or else more socially costly than promoting the particular enterprise under public auspices.
32. The following is based on Jha (1985).
33. Lal (1980a).
34. See Rudra (1978), Dey (1975) for the reasons why this form of curve is to be preferred, as it enables one to judge whether growth is accelerating, decelerating, or constant over the relevant period.
35. For a critique of India's trade and industrialization policies, see Bhagwati and Desai (1970), Bhagwati and Srinivasan (1975) and Lal (1969, 1973a, 1980a).
36. Bhagwati and Srinivasan (1975).
37. Lal (1980a).
38. Bhagwati and Desai (1970, p. 466).
39. South Korea, Taiwan, Hong Kong, and Singapore. Bhagwati and Srinivasan (1975) have estimated (Table 3.4) that if India had maintained its 1948–50 volume share throughout the 1950s for its major traditional exports, viz. jute and cotton manufacturers, tea, tobacco, and oilseeds, its export earnings would have been Rs 5 b. greater over the period, that is, an increase of 16% over the actuals. From Table 11.14, moreover, it is evident that the 1960s were the really dismal period of Indian export performance, partly because this was the period when the import-substituting policies were at their height. After the 1966 devaluation, some of the biases against export were removed, and India export performance became closer to the LDC average. However, as many of the incentive schemes were inefficient, neither the composition or level of exports promoted was optimal—see Lal (1979a), (1980a) for a fuller discussion of these export incentive schemes.
40. Moreover, when the importance of exports was realized, various inefficient methods of export subsidization were used (see Lal (1980a)), when a policy of trade liberalization and a move to free trade was (and still is) required.

12

Contemporary Controversies: Poverty, Distribution, and Growth

INTRODUCTION

Perhaps the area of fiercest continuing controversy concerns the question of whether growth can be equitable and poverty redressing without institutional reform in the Indian context. Much of this debate obviously concerns labour market variables and performance. To clarify this debate some rather simple points can be made. First, as we saw in Chapter 11, India's growth performance in both agriculture (except for the wheat belt) and industry has been far from brilliant. Industrial growth has increasingly been capital-intensive, so that a large part of the incremental savings generated in the post-Independence period have not increased the demand for industrial labour by as much as would have been possible with a more labour-intensive form of industrialization. Moreover, the efficiency of factor use has been declining. In agriculture, by contrast (see Table 7.4), there has been an increase in the labour intensity of cultivation, but no marked increase in the demand for labour except in the wheat revolution belt. It would be extremely unlikely, given this dismal growth performance (compared with some other developing countries), to expect much alleviation of India's traditional poverty. Instead, given our review of the past, and arguments in support of the thesis of the continuance in the post-Independence period of the Hindu equilibrium, our maintained hypothesis would be that there is likely to have been little impact on either poverty redressal or income distribution in the country.

However, until very recently it was asserted, and purported to be established from the available statistical evidence, that the post-Independence decades had seen a steady immiserization of the poor and/or a worsening of their relative positions in a general worsening of the income distribution in the country.[1] More seriously it was argued that where growth did occur, as in the wheat revolution areas, this growth had led not merely to a relative worsening of the levels of living of the rural poor, but most heinously to absolute declines. In an earlier article[2] I had questioned both the empirical and the theoretical basis of these views, and had shown with the available data that no such conclusions were warranted. Since then there have been three more detailed studies, by Ahluwalia (1978) and Dutta (1980a), which (it is to be hoped) have nailed down the coffin of these 'new orthodox' views![3]

We briefly outline the results of the latest of these studies by Dutta (1980a) in the next section. We then consider the implicit model underlying the views of the 'new orthodoxy', and the ideological predilections of their proponents which enable them to distort or ignore evidence controverting their beliefs. This is of some importance, for it is—as we will argue—just another manifestation of the continued hold of the ideals of India's traditional casteist revenue economy which have been given a new lease of life clothed in the modern ideological garb of Fabian socialism.

1. FACTS

Dutta (1980a) has used the National Sample Survey (NSS) consumer expenditure data for the nine years between 1960–1 and 1973–4 to compute two different indices for rural and urban India: the head-count measure of the percentage of people below a fixed poverty line, and Sen's poverty index, which also takes account of the distribution of poverty amongst the poor and which gives more weight per unit of lower incomes. From the same data source he has also computed Gini coefficients to determine changes in the relative inequality of consumption in both urban and rural India. The measurement of trends in poverty and income distribution is bedevilled by the problem of the choice of the correct index number of prices to be used to determine 'real' consumption changes.[4] Ideally, expenditure class-specific price indices are needed. Dutta uses adjusted estimates made by Murty and Murty of fractile specific price indices to determine real consumption trends.[5] He makes use of Dandekar and Rath's (1971) estimate of Rs 15 per capita per month at 1960–1 prices as the rural poverty line, and Rs 20 per capita per month for urban areas. The urban figures have been derived by converting the rural into an equivalent urban poverty line by using the estimated rural–urban price differential of 20 per cent estimated by Chatterjee and Bhattacharya (1971), and adjusting upwards slightly to take account of 'certain imposed and induced needs in urban areas' (Dutta (1980a, p. 126)).

Dutta's estimates of the two poverty indices and the Gini coefficients of nominal per capital expenditure in urban and rural India are reported in Table 12.1. Table 12.1(c) also reports the computed linear time trends in these variables. The following conclusions emerge:

(i)   There is no evidence to suggest that there is any trend change in poverty in either the rural or the urban sector.[6]
(ii) There are, however, cyclical fluctuations in the incidence of poverty, with it rising in the 1960s and declining thereafter.
(iii) There has been a significant trend decrease in inequality (in terms of the Gini coefficient) in both sectors.
(iv) The decline in the Gini coefficient has been caused by an *absolute* fall in the living standards of the top 15 percent of the population in the two sectors, and not by a transfer of consumption from the rich to the poor. This is

TABLE 12.1(A). Estimates of Poverty in Rural and Urban India

Year	Rural		Urban	
	P_H^r	P_s^r	P_H^u	P_s^u
1960–1	38.03	.141	40.40	.156
1961–2	39.30	.133	39.36	.155
1963–4	44.50	.163	42.52	.161
1965–6	47.41	.181	46.43	.180
1967–8	56.20	.234	48.32	.188
1968–9	50.40	.199	45.53	.176
1969–70	49.20	.189	44.40	.168
1970–1	45.40	.170	41.50	.158
1973–4	44.30	.155	38.70	.130

Notes: $P_H^r(P_H^u)$ — rural (urban) poverty (% of population below poverty line)
   $P_s^r(P_s^u)$ — rural (urban) poverty (Sen index)
Source: Dutta (1980a).

TABLE 12.1(B). Gini Coefficients of Distribution of Per Capita Expenditure

Year	Rural: G_r	Urban: G_u
1960–1	.323	.348
1961–2	.310	.358
1963–4	.287	.351
1965–6	.297	.347
1967–8	.293	.341
1968–9	.305	.329
1969–70	.293	.340
1970–1	.283	.327
1973–4	.280	.301

Notes: $G^r(G^u)$ — Gini coefficient Rural (Urban)
   $R^r(R^u)$ — richness index rural (urban) given by the ratio of the mean income of the rich to the mean income in the sector.
Source: Dutta (1980a).

evident from Dutta's separate estimates of the trends in the mean real per capita consumption of the rich and the poor in the two sectors. He finds that, whilst the mean real per capita consumption of the poor shows no trend increase, that of the rich shows a statistically significant decline of 0.8 per cent p.a. in the rural and 0.7 per cent p.a. in the urban sector.

(v) Moreover, as Lal (1976a) and Ahluwalia (1978) have shown for inter-State data on poverty and agricultural growth, the latter aids rather than hinders poverty redressal, and is also good for equality.

TABLE 12.1(C)   Linear Time Trends in Distributional Variables[a]

Dependent variable[b]	Estimated coefficient			
	Constant	Time	R^2	F
P^r_H	41.47	.9245 (1.3504)	.270	1.824
P^r_s	.154	.0040 (.9795)	.121	.9598
G^r	.317	– .004[c] (3.3807)	.558[c]	8.837
R^r [d]	223.84	– .2487 (.2307)	.01	.063
P^u_H	42.72	.0486 (.1006)	.0016	.0112
P^u_s	.168	– .001 (.2614)	.036	.2614
G^u	.359	– .005[e] (3.6762)	.616[c]	11.229
R^u	253.16	.788 (.6012)	.049	.3611

a. Terms in brackets denote T ratios.
b. See notes to Tables 12.1(a) and (b).
c. Indicates that the coefficient is significantly different from zero at the 5% level of significance.
d. $R^r (R^u)$ — richness index rural (urban) given by the ratio of the mean income of the rich to the mean income in the sector.
e. Indicates that the coefficient is signicantly different from zero at the 1% level of significance.
Source: Dutta (1980a).

Thus, though about 40 per cent of the population appears to be poor in both urban and rural areas, there has been no marked impact for better or worse in this ratio over the post-Independence decades. If any immiserization has taken place, it is of those in the *top 15 per cent* of the income distribution in both rural and urban areas, and this has led to a lowering of the concentration ratio which, in any case, is low by historical standards. Essentially, as not much has changed in the parameters underlying the long established Hindu equilibrium, these results are hardly surprising.[7]

2. IDEOLOGY

How then does one explain the babel of voices asserting the contrary, and asserting that even the dismally low growth that has occurred has led to a worsening income distribution and increasing poverty? Their diagnosis of this assumed train of events consists of a standard demonology, namely that any growth which takes place within the so-called 'existing institutional framework' must immiserize the poor and worsen the income distribution. The purported distributional features retarding equitable and poverty-redressing growth processes are identified, in agriculture, as an increased concentration of land, proletarianization of rural labour, and increase in usurious rural debt; whilst in the industrial sector the demons are increased concentration in industry, the stranglehold of bloodsucking multinational companies, and the lack of political will amongst bourgeois politicians to implement full-scale planning on the Soviet model, which along with the development of collectivist agriculture is, of course, seen as the panacea for all the country's ills.[8]

As the purported trends in income distribution and poverty redressal under-lying these assertions have been shown to be false empirically, as have the assumptions they implicitly make about the functioning of labour markets in India (see Volume II), we may briefly attempt to exorcise the remaining demons in this radical demonology in the light of the factual evidence. We have to consider this evidence regarding each of the purported 'institutional' features preventing poverty redressal and equitable growth:

(i) Concentration of land

Raj (1976) purported to show that:

(i)   landlessness had increased sharply between 1953–4 and 1961–2;
(ii) that this was accompanied by a sizeable fall in the number of households with small-sized holdings and by significant increases both in total area operated by this category of households and in the average size of their 'operational holdings';
(iii) 'the average size of holdings among holders of small-sized holdings declined by as much as 15 per cent between 1961–62 and 1971–72'.[9]

Sanyal (1977a) soon showed that because of computational errors, and 'two interpretational errors', 'the first affected the estimate of the "landless" for all the time periods and the second vitiated all the estimates for the 8th Round'![10] The correct estimates of the distribution of the number of households and area operated by size of household operational holding from the three NSS rounds, derived by Sanyal, together with Raj's erroneous estimates, are shown in Table 12.2. Raj had interpreted landless households as those in the zero class of household *operational* holdings, which includes those who are truly landless in that they neither own nor operate land, but also includes a large subset of those households who *own but do not operate* the land. There is nothing to suggest that the latter, as Sanyal rightly notes, are swelling the rural wage labour supply, as Raj asserts. But more seriously, even if both sets of households are counted as 'landless', correcting Raj's error in interpreting the 8th round data leaves no grounds for his conclusion that there was a sharp increase in 'landlessness' between 1953–4 and 1960–1. Nor is any of his other conclusions valid (see Table 12.2).

TABLE 12.2.   Distribution of the Number of Households and Area Operated by Size of
Household Operational Holding

(*a*) Total numbers

	1953–4 (m.)	1960–1 (m.)	1970–1 (m.)
Households not operating land	17.2 (6.6)[a]	18.5 (18.6)	21.9 (21.9)
Holders of small-sized holdings (0.01–2.49 acres)	17.1 (27.6)	21.2 (21.0)	26.3 (26.3)
Holders of medium-sized holdings (2.50–9.99 acres)	17.8 (18.2)	21.2 (20.6)	23.5 (23.6)
Holders of large-sized holdings (10 acres and above)	8.9 (8.6)	8.6 (8.5)	8.3 (8.2)

(*b*). Size of household operational holding

	1953–4		1960–1		1970–1	
	Total operated area (m. acres)	Average size (acres)	Total operated area (m. acres)	Average size (acres)	Total operated area (m. acres)	Average size (acres)
Households not operating land	—	—	—	—	—	—
Holders of small-sized holdings	18.2 (19.9)	1.06 (0.72)	25.0 (31.8)	1.18 (1.51)	33.8 (33.8)	1.29 (1.29)
Holders of medium-sized holdings	96.1 (100.0)	5.40 (5.49)	119.2 (112.2)	5.76 (5.45)	137.2 (137.3)	5.84 (5.82)
Holders of large-sized holdings	221.4 (215.8)	24.96 (25.09)	208.8 (208.6)	24.39 (25.54)	194.7 (194.8)	23.46 (23.75)

a. Figures in brackets are quoted from Raj (1976, p. 1287, table 1). The years quoted indicate the reference periods of the 8th, 17th and 26th rounds.

Source: Sanyal (1977a).

TABLE 12.3.   Distribution of Rural Landownership of five States

	Andhra Pradesh	Bihar	Gujarat	Punjab and Haryana	West Bengal
Landless households (% of all rural households):					
1954–5	30.12	16.56	—	36.86	20.54
1961–2	6.84	8.63	14.74	12.33	12.56
1971–2	8.95	4.34	13.44	9.09	9.78
Households owning up to 2.5 acres (%):					
1954–5	40.38	50.71	—	22.73	52.93
1961–2	59.48	59.35	34.07	49.10	56.69
1971–2	59.35	67.44	38.81	56.93	67.84
Lorenz ratio of landownership (including landless households):					
1954–5	0.80	0.70	—	0.76	0.73
1961–2	0.76	0.70	0.68	0.75	0.66
1971–2	0.73	0.68	0.69	0.76	0.66
Lorenz ratio of landownership (excluding landless households):					
1954–5	0.72	0.64	—	0.62	0.66
1961–2	0.74	0.67	0.63	0.71	0.61
1971–2	0.71	0.66	0.64	0.74	0.61

Source: Sanyal (1977b).

In fact, from the data, the distribution of *operational* holdings given in Table 12.2, and that on *land ownership* available for four States for 1954–5, 1961–2, and 1971–2 periods and reported in Table 12.3, it is apparent that:

(i)   There has been a marked decrease in households not *owning* land, though a slight increase in the numbers of households not *operating* any land. But the proportion of rural households not *operating* land has declined marginally from 28 per cent in 1953–4 to 27 per cent in 1970–1. Thus no marked increase in 'landlessness' on any definition is supported by the evidence.

(ii)   There has been an increase in both the average size as well as in the number of small-sized holdings, unlike the largest-sized holdings, whose numbers and average size have declined over the twenty years!

(iii)   The concentration of land (including 'landless' labour households) amongst households has declined in all the five States for which Sanyal (1977b) has computed Lorenz ratios.

(ii) Increasing proletarianization

Once again, Raj (1976) has misinterpreted NSS and census data on the distribution of the rural work-force, purporting to show that there has been a large growth (*a*) of the 'employee' class, as he terms it (on the basis of NSS data) and (b) of agricultural labourers as shown by the 1961 and 1971 censuses. As Visaria (1977) soon pointed out, Raj failed to take account of the changed definition of the labour force between the 19th and 27th round of the NSS as well as certain problems with the 19th-round data which showed markedly different results in its 16th and 17th schedules. After making these adjustments, the percentage distribution of the rural male population by activity status from the NSS data is derived by Visaria, and is reported in Table 12.4 (which also shows Raj's estimates, viz. those for the 19th-round schedule 17, and the unadjusted 17th-round figures). Clearly no marked increase in the percentage of employees in the rural population is discernible.

Nor are the prima-facie inferences about a rise in the proportion of agricultural labourers in the rural population relative to cultivators from the 1961 and 1971 censuses supportable: again, changes of definition have made the two censuses non-comparable. Nevertheless (see Sundaram (1977), Krishnamurty (1972b), and Government of India (1980a)), there does appear to have been an increase in agricultural labour in the total working population over the 1960s and 1970s. But taken together with the decline in the landless (in terms of owned holdings—see Table 12.2), this increase in the proportion of agricultural labourers cannot be taken as a sign of proletarianization, but rather of the increasing interdependence and integration of the markets for leasing in and out of land and agricultural wage labour. A landed agricultural labourer can hardly be called a prole!

(iii) Increasing rural indebtedness and usury

We have already dealt with the evidence against this viewpoint in Chapter 7, and hence can move on to the industrial sector.

(iv) Constraints on industrial development

We can consider together all the interrelated assertions made about the reasons for the continuing industrial stagnation in India.[11] The broad thesis runs somewhat as follows: because of kulak power there has been a general tendency for the agricultural terms of trade to turn against industry, which has reduced the demand for industrial products. This was combined with a purported worsening of the income distribution which increased the demand for luxury goods; but as investment in luxury good production rose even faster, capacity utilization declined. Furthermore, the purported decline in rural and industrial wages meant that the demand for industrial mass-consumption goods fell. Meanwhile foreign capital was 'a highly effective mechanism of extracting surplus'

TABLE 12.4. % Distribution of the Rural Male Population of Round Figure (Based on NSS Estimates)

	Aug.–Sept. 1952 (4th round)	May–Aug. 1953 (6th round)	Oct. 1953–Mar. 1954 (7th round)	Sept. 1958–Aug. 1959 (14th round)	July 1960–June 1961 (16th round)	Sept. 1961–July 1961 (17th round)	July 1964–June 1965 (19th round, schedule 17)	July 1964–June 1965 (19th round,[a] schedule 16)	July 1966–June 1967 (21st round,[a] schedule 16)	Oct. 1972–Mar. 1973 (27th round)	Oct. 1972–Mar. 1973 (27th round) adjusted
Own-account workers	40.01	25.04	29.68	27.47	22.72	21.94	18.11	20.81	21.30	[30.36][b]	25.93
Unpaid family labour	—	14.72	11.97	11.24	8.82	7.96	5.95	8.34	8.85	11.83	10.11
Employers	1.20	0.74	1.09	0.80	5.79	4.52	13.83	7.81	5.32	—	—
Employees	18.13	17.55	16.02	15.30	16.60	15.83	13.69	14.27	17.32	21.92	18.73
Total gainfully employed	59.34	58.05	58.76	54.81	54.23	50.25	51.59	51.23	52.79	64.11	54.77
Unemployed	0.05	0.98	0.32	2.07	1.44	1.95	1.42	1.37	0.98	0.79	0.67
Total in the labour force	59.39	59.03	59.08	56.88	55.67	52.20	53.01	52.60	53.77	64.90	55.44
Not in the labour force	40.61	40.97	40.92	43.12	44.33	47.80	46.99	47.40	46.23	35.10	44.56
TOTAL POPULATION	100.00	100.00	100.00	100.00	100.00	100.00	100.00	100.00	100.00	100.00	100.00

a. Persons whose activity status was not reported have been distributed pro rata among other categories shown in the table. Such persons formed 1.76% of all males in the 19th round and 0.45% of all males in the 21st round.

b. The estimate given under 'own account workers' also covers 'employers'.

Source: Visaria (1977); the derivations are Visaria's.

from the host country. Finally, the big private capitalists, instead of investing in expanding productive capacity through capital accumulation, have been more concerned with growing by acquiring subsidiaries through mergers and take-overs.

The factual basis of nearly every one of the above claims is false. We have already provided evidence to show that the distribution of income has not worsened; real rural and industrial wages (see Volume II) have not fallen. Evidence on the other claims is given below.

Table 12.5 shows the terms of trade for agriculture and manufacturing

TABLE 12.5. Some Price Index Ratios, 1951–1979

Year	Agriculture/ manufacturing	Rice/ wheat	Cotton/ agriculture	Jute/ agriculture
1951	94.6	94.7	109.3	151.4
1952	87.7	94.0	109.0	108.5
1953	87.6	99.0	104.2	86.3
1954	82.1	98.1	117.3	99.2
1955	80.0	97.8	117.1	131.9
1956	82.9	97.1	117.7	116.0
1957	84.8	103.2	109.4	120.7
1958	86.0	100.4	98.4	104.0
1959	86.6	89.4	96.6	97.2
1960	83.4	107.5	101.6	141.4
1961	73.2	105.1	107.7	181.3
1962	82.8	111.2	96.1	94.4
1963	80.3	119.9	99.6	97.0
1964	89.1	101.3	89.8	95.0
1965	94.9	89.2	82.2	116.2
1966	97.0	102.8	75.6	139.4
1967	84.6	95.2	84.7	108.9
1968	97.1	101.3	81.5	107.5
1969	102.4	96.1	84.0	118.3
1970	101.9	97.3	91.8	99.9
1971	92.7	105.6	111.4	94.4
1972	89.2	106.5	84.5	99.1
1973	97.9	121.9	83.8	80.8
1974	101.2	106.6	98.5	59.8
1975	94.4	111.1	84.4	67.9
1976	88.9	102.9	117.9	81.5
1977	96.9	104.9	115.5	83.5
1978	96.9	102.7	100.4	86.8
1979	89.7	110.4	89.9	96.1

Source: Desai (1981).

between 1951 and 1979. There has been no continual improvement in agriculture's terms of trade. The famed power of the kulaks has certainly not been sufficient to raise agricultural prices above manufacturing ones. Mitra also asserts that, as a larger proportion of the marketed surplus of wheat is produced on large farms than on smaller ones, the kulaks have succeeded in raising the price of wheat relative to rice.[12] No such conclusion is warranted from the data presented in Table 12.5.

On luxury consumption, Desai notes: 'According to figures computed by Mitra (1977, p. 164) from Reserve Bank statistics, the weight of consumer durables in the index of industrial production rose from 2.21 per cent in 1956 to 5.68 per cent in 1960, 7.84 per cent in 1970 and 8.09 per cent in 1972. According to Reserve Bank of India (1977, p. 212), however, their weight was only 2.92 per cent in 1970.'[13] Any comment would be superfluous!

'The state of foreign capital in the Indian economy is quite significant. . . . The involvement of foreign capital in the manufacturing industries of India is increasing,'[14] Table 12.6 gives the ratios of outstanding foreign business investments in India between 1969 and 1973, and total fixed capital in the manufacturing sector (census sector of the Annual Survey of Industry). Private foreign investment has accounted for about 20 per cent of the fixed capital stock (based on book values) in Indian manufacturing, and this share is declining. Nor can any 'net drain' from this foreign investment be deduced. There is an obvious fallacy in computing this drain by comparing undiscounted sums of the inflows and outflows on the foreign capital account. For if the foreign investor is to get a positive rate of return on his investment, the undiscounted sums paid out on account of the repatriation of capital and dividends and interest must exceed the inflows which made the outflow possible (see Lal (1975a)). Yet the fallacy continues to be perpetrated (as in Sau (1981)). What is more, no overall deleterious effects from the foreign investment that has occurred can be deduced from social cost–benefit studies conducted in relation to these investments in India (see Lal (1975a), 1978b)). Where the social returns to India were low or

TABLE 12.6.   Foreign Investment in the Manufacturing Sector

Year	Foreign business investment outstanding (Rs crores) (1)	Fixed capital in the census sector (Rs crores) (2)	Ratios (1)/(2) (%)
1969	1,619	7,609	21
1970	1,641	8,324	20
1971	1,680	8,802	19
1972	1,756	—	—
1973	1,816	10,185	18

Sources: *Statistical Abstract of India* 1978, p. 101, table 96, p. 95, table 37.

negative, the major reason was the high effective protection provided by the system of import controls set up since the late 1950s (see Lal (1975a)).

On the concentration of industry, the 'new orthodoxy' fails to note that the most important cause of the concentration of industry is the growth of the public sector, whose share of output in organized manufacturing has grown from 8 per cent in 1960–1 to 30 per cent in 1975–6.[15] It is the growing dominance of an inefficient public sector which should worry those concerned about the evil effects of the concentration of industry, rather than any (highly debatable) tendency for concentration in private industry. In any case, as the continuing debate in developed countries shows, there is no clear economic reason to expect any increase in concentration of industry through mergers or take-overs to be necessarily detrimental in terms of economic welfare.[16]

(v) Trahisons des clercs?

We have, I hope, provided enough evidence to suggest that a fairly wide spectrum of Indian officials and economists have reached a consensus on the diagnosis of India's ills whose factual basis can be shown to be false. Why then do they still continue to proffer the same shop-worn panaceas based on these misdiagnoses?

The only explanation is the inordinate hold of a particular theoretical vision of the workings of the Indian economy which is a mixture of the ideas of Marx, Hobson, and W. A. Lewis, with a dash of P. C. Mahalanobis thrown in.[17] The essential feature of this vision is a suspicion of markets, merchants, and the profit motive. Vernon Ruttan may be right in stressing that these attitudes, apparent for instance in the criticisms of the green revolution, may have been ideologically motivated because the 'hope for the radicalization of the lower peasantry and landless labour has been viewed as dependent on the continuation of the process of "immissering growth" '.[18] Nevertheless, taking the body of Indian intellectuals as a whole, no 'trahison des clercs' can be adduced. After all, the author of this work is an Indian and a Hindu! Most of the authors we have cited to expose the 'new orthodoxy' are Indians. The more interesting question is why, despite the increasing factual evidence presented by Indians against the new orthodox views, these still command respect in India.

No better clue is provided than by considering the writings of a distinguished Indian economist whom not even his worst enemies would implicate in a 'trahisons des clercs'. He has done as much as most to dispel many of the sillier shibboleths propounded by the 'radical' presses.[19] He rightly discounts the more hysterical reactions about the failures of the so-called 'green revolution' and would probably deny most of the assertions made by the 'new orthodox' school, and yet he hankers after the same panaceas. The clue is to be found in his heartfelt objection to the Intensive Agricultural Development Plan's strategy of promoting the profit motive in agriculture:

the task of developing agriculture is being entrusted to the greed and the acquisitive spirit which motivates capitalists. *In traditional Indian agriculture greed was located and condemned in the professional money lender, the speculative trader, etc.* An important discovery of the proponents of the strategy is that the same greed, the same acquisitive spirit, may also be found latent in the cultivators; all the components of the strategy are aimed at further encouraging this spirit. . . . This clearly stated aim seems to have been achieved. The 'Holy Grail' which the richer famers are pursuing is the way of life of the urban middle class; the latter in their turn are craving the comforts of the consumption society of the West.[20]

Here is an obvious echo of Nehru's sentiments quoted earlier.

This then is the crux of the explanation why so many Indian intellectuals dislike markets and the price mechanism—that these depend upon, even if they do not promote, the greed and acquisitiveness which, as we have seen and as Rudra explicitly states, was looked down upon by the literary and politically powerful castes in India. It is this Brahminical attitude, today imbibed by a large part of the Westernized stratum of Indian society, which is at the root of that seeming 'trahison de clercs' which has apparently been taking place in India at least over the last two decades.[21]

3. THE ADMINISTRATIVE PHILOSOPHY

(i) Planning

The consequences of the continuing support for the bureaucratic mode of allocation can be briefly delineated. It is best considered by examining very briefly the content of that touchstone of the intellectual consensus outlined earlier, namely central planning. In India this has been automatically identified with the form of planning adopted in supposedly socialist countries such as the Soviet Union and China, and any departure from these forms is taken as a betrayal of socialist ideals. However, as I have argued in detail elsewhere, this is to confuse means with ends.[22] The fundamental socialist end is equity if not equality,[23] and there can be no a priori reason why planning of the Soviet or Chinese variety should necessarily promote equitable growth.

The case for planning—which is ultimately the devising of a rational set of public-policy interventions—depends upon purported departures of any real-world economy from that of textbook perfect competition. The rules for dealing with the resulting distortions, by either correcting or optimally adjusting to them, have been clarified and developed by modern second-best welfare economics.[24] These rules need not concern us. What should be noted, however, is that even if a prima-facie case for government *intervention* were established, it would still be an open question what form the requisite intervention should take, or whether in certain cases, taking account of 'bureaucratic failure', the only feasible second-best policy might be no goverment intervention at all.[25]

For the most pervasive cause of so-called 'market failure' is the existence of what economists call transactions costs, which prevent markets for particular goods and services from operating efficiently or, in more severe cases, from operating at all. These transaction costs in turn are generally due to the costs of acquiring the relevant information in an irreducibly uncertain world, and/or the difficulty of excluding non-buyers from enjoying the benefits of goods for which buyers in the relevant market may have paid a price.

It cannot be assumed if there is market failure that an alternative bureaucratic mode of allocation will not also suffer from the same problems of imperfect information and irreducible uncertainty, leading analogously to 'bureaucratic failure'. In fact, the costs of bureaucrats acquiring the necessary information in an imperfect world may be even higher than for those in an imperfectly functioning market economy. The outcome of the bureaucratic mode of allocation may turn out to be even worse than the workings of an imperfect market mechanism. When the best that can be achieved is a second-best outcome, bureaucratic allocations may lead to a fourth- or fifth-best compared with the second- or third-best outcome within the imperfect market system.[26]

What of planning? In my book the devising of a rational set of public policy interventions applying the canons of second-best welfare economics is what planning should consist of, and not the mechanical, material-balance type of target-setting which passes for planning in India. Though of some general interest in a country hooked on astrologers and forecasts, it is at best an irrelevance except perhaps for the design of the composition of public expenditure and investments.

The question of public investments in turn raises the whole set of issues regarding the rational choice of public-sector investments and their efficient management. Ultimately the choice of public-sector investments, as well as the criteria for judging their efficiency and setting their prices, is again a part of second-best welfare economics, and the principles for their design are readily available. The essential problem that remains is however of a different and primarily of a political nature. In a changing world, and one in which the future is inherently uncertain, it is inevitable that some mistakes in investment choices and/or declining social profitabilities in certain lines of production will occur. In a market system, bankruptcies which lead to the exit of inefficient firms are part and parcel of this essential dynamic process of change. One of the serious defects of the politicization of economic policy by supplanting the price mechanism through discretionary bureaucratic interventions is that this normal and healthy process of the exit of inefficient firms becomes well-nigh impossible. Sick mills are nationalized, subsidies are endlessly given to lame ducks, and good money is sent flowing after bad. It is essentially for this reason (aside from any political reasons flowing from the concentration of power in the hands of the Government) that in my view there is an almost built-in bias towards inefficiency in the operation of public enterprises, which provides the strongest argument against them.

(ii) Political and social consequences

But it is the political and social consequences of the pursuit of the administrative philosophy which are even more serious than the above economic inefficiences that it engenders. There is a type of conspiracy theory extant amongst the India intellegentsia which considers that past economic failures have been due to a lack of so-called 'political will' because the ship of State has been hijacked by this or that self-seeking interest group—kulaks one day,[27] something called intermediate classes[28] another, and most recently 'the petty proles'.[29]

These views overlook two important points, emphasized for instance in our earlier chapter on the evolution of the polity under the Raj. With the gradual development of representative institutions, a class of political brokers has arisen whose main function is to put together politically viable coalitions of a vast collection of heterogenous interest groups in a subcontinental polity. The great strength of the resultant democratic structure is that, as long as it is preserved, it is extremely unlikely that any single interest group can for very long hijack the State. Although the disturbing authoritarian trends exhibited in the 1970s suggest that the temptation to bypass the messy process of building such viable subcontinental political coalitions is ever-present, the political and legal system has proved surprisingly resilient.

Moreover, the perpetuation and vast expansion of the traditional Indian political form of a revenue economy by the extension of the Permit Raj has provided aspiring politicians with new means of building coalitions through the use of public patronage to generate private profits for various interest groups. But there was nothing inevitable about the rise of the Permit Raj. It was promoted, and continues to be perpetuated, in part because of the intellectual support provided by large sections of the Indian intellegentsia. Transfixed by Utopian modes of thought in which selfless politicians with 'political will' use near-perfect bureaucrats who are omniscient (even if not omnipotent) in their ideal world, they hanker after an economic system in which both efficiency and equity are always subserved to the optimal extent. Furthermore, confusing ends with means, they then consider any attack on the administrative philosophy as an attack on their cherished Utopia. The result is the perpetuation of the climate of opinion in which the 'organized plunder' cloaked in the populist rhetoric of the Permit Raj is tolerated.[30] This (in some ways noble) unworldliness of the intellegentsia is nothing but a modern-day variant of long-standing Brahminical attitudes towards both politics and commerce.[31] The real 'trahison des clercs' in India is not therefore the failure to recognize and broadcast the increasing divergence of their basic assumptions about the workings of the economy from reality, but their perhaps understandable failure to overcome the unworldliness and anti-business thinking of the ancient Brahminical tradition.

There are two dangers in this way of thinking. First, ignoring as it does the necessarily interest-group nature of politics in a subcontinental economy, it provides, through its advocacy and support of the administrative philosophy and its attendant apparatus, the means for the continuing corruption which has been such a large part (though not as blatant as in some other developing countries) of past economic policy. Secondly, when the unwholesome nature of the resulting spoils system becomes apparent, many intellectuals openly or secretly long for a set of Platonic Guardians, amongst whom they naturally expect to find themselves.

But if, as I believe, any such 'interest-free' state is impossible, and any long-term authoritarian solution to the country's problems infeasible, this desire for 'highly motivated', 'dedicated', or 'idealistic' cadres is a pipe-dream. We have to face up to the fact that democratic politics (no matter how unsavoury) are probably here to stay; that democratic politics must necessarily be interest-group politics; and that we must design our economic interventions accordingly. This will mean not only that many policies will be infeasible but, equally importantly, that the outcomes of many policies (based on the implicit assumption that they will be administered by omniscient Platonic Guardians) will often be the converse of those intended.

India's problems therefore are political and ideological. It is not difficult however to foresee, Cassandra-like, the consequence of the continuance of the hold of the administrative philosophy. But Cassandra is hoarse, and is due for a vocational change!

NOTES

1. See Bardhan (1973), Dandekar and Rath (1971), Dantwala (1973) and the papers collected in Bardhan and Srinivasan (1974). See Kumar (1974) for a survey of this literature and Lal (1976c) for a critical review of the larger distribution and development literature.
2. Lal (1976a), summarized in Ch. 8 of Vol. II of this work.
3. But that is too optimistic, as contrary assertions are still made on the basis of dubious statistical exercises. See e.g. Jose (1978), Sau (1981). But see also Ahluwalia (1985) for a more balanced view.
4. See the debate between Minhas (1970) and Bardhan (1970).
5. See Dutta (1980, pt. 2) for the details.
6. This is also Ahluwalia's conclusion (1978) for the rural sector to which his analysis is confined.
7. We should however note that there has been under-reporting of incomes in the higher categories which, with the development of the illegal economy over the Permit Raj, may have grown over time.
8. For a recent regurgitation of these views see Sau (1981).
9. Raj (1976, pp. 1286–7), on the basis of NSS data for 1953–4 (8th round), 1960–1 (17th round), and 1970–1 (26th round).
10. Sanyal (1977a, p. 147).
11. Desai (1981) provides a bibliography of the writings of what we can label the 'radical' school on industrial development. For a representative sample see Bagchi (1970), Chakravarty (1974), Sau (1981), Vaidyanathan (1977b), and Mitra (1977).
12. Mitra (1977, p. 131).
13. Desai (1981, p. 387).
14. Sau (1981, p. 57).
15. Government of India (1980a, p. 184).
16. See Allen (1969), Baumol *et al.* (1982).

17. I am not alone in noticing this consensus, expressed for example in the pages of the *Economic and Political Weekly* and its increasing disjunction from reality (Lal (1979a)). See e.g. Desai (1981) who has also noticed this disjunction.
18. Ruttan (1977, p. 16).
19. Thus there has been a scholastic and in my view futile debate in the pages of the *Economic and Political Weekly* about whether India agrarian relations are capitalist, semi-feudal, feudal, or colonial. Rudra has sensibly argued that most of this hair-splitting is not germane to any understanding of the Indian rural scene: see Rudra (1978, pp. 398–9).
20. Ibid., 387 (emphasis added).
21. Thus Raj (1979) states: 'so the answer lies not so much in restricting more severely the rate of growth of money supply (which can at best make only a small difference to the available fuel for feeding inflation) as in preventing such speculation becoming attractive. For this there is no more effective deterrent than large reserves of foreign exchange and of essential commodities such as foodgrain supported by an administrative machinery that could really make speedy and effective use of them for counter-speculative operations when needed.' The ancient Hindu suspicion of the trader and trading is once again displayed. It should be noted that there is no evidence in India that traders are non-competitive (see Lele (1971), or that the normal speculation which involves buying when prices are low and selling when they are high is necessarily destabilizing, in the sense that such speculation increases the amplitude of exogenous price fluctuations instead of reducing them as in the case of stabilizing speculation. For a critique of the critics of speculation see Henderson and Lal (1976) with reference to commodity speculation and Lal (1980e) for speculation on the foreign exchanges. For the atavistic impulses underlying these nationalist and socialist views of commerce, see Lal (1985).
22. See Lal (1980a, pt. 1).
23. Of course the pursuit of this end itself is not as transparently obvious as many economists seem to believe. See Lal (1976c) for a critique of the 'distribution and development' literature.
24. For its application to India, see Lal (1980a).
25. See Lal (1983).
26. See Lal (1983) for a fuller elaboration of this argument.
27. See Sau (1981), Bharadwaj (1974).
28. See Kalecki (1972), Raj (1973), Jha (1980).
29. See Desai (1981). It is particularly sad that Desai, who is clear-headed in seeing the factual poverty of the extant intellectual consensus, should succumb to this easiest of all mental escape routes for explaining the difference between India's promise and performance.
30. Estimates of the so-called 'black economy' in India vary widely. The latest estimates by the National Institute of Public Finance and Policy, which also reviews past studies, are 18–21% of GDP in 1980–1. See Kumar (1985) for a critique of these estimates.
31. These atavistic attitudes are of course common amongst many modernizing Third World élites—see Lal (1985) for a fuller discussion.

13

On Policy: From a Revenue to a Market Economy

The importance of the policy environment in promoting development is now widely accepted. A great deal of empirical work since the Second World War based on the varied experiences of a myriad developing countries has provided fairly robust guide-lines for the type of policy environment which best promotes growth.[1] Broadly speaking there is an emerging consensus of the importance of markets and incentives, and the limits of government intervention and central planning. But the role of Government in providing the essential physical and social infrastructure of the economy remains vital. The important question therefore does *not* concern the need for government intervention as compared with *laissez-faire*, but on the appropriate extent and form the intervention should take.

This chapter therefore seeks to outline first the major policy changes that are required to develop India and shatter the age-old Hindu equilibrium. But equally importantly, as these policies are well known it also attempts to explain why, for deep-seated 'ecological' reasons, the natural propensities of Indian rulers have made the adoption of these policies so difficult. This discussion in the second part of the chapter also allows me to provide a more explicit statement of the general theoretical perspective which underlies this book.

1. POLICIES

For a policy-oriented development economist, India presents an enigma. Amongst developing countries in the early 1950s its prospects for initiating a process of rapid economic development would have seemed to be amongst the brightest. It had a fairly varied natural resource base, no shortage of skills or entrepreneurs, a relatively incorruptible and efficient administrative structure, politicians who were committed to development and who by and large were not immune to technical advice. Yet by the late 1970s it is clear that, by comparison with various other countries, in particular in south-east Asia, India's development experience has been relatively disappointing (see Table 11.11 for some comparative statistics underlying this failure). What is more, with time the various obstacles supposedly hampering Indian economic development have been shown to have been shibboleths. The three 'commodities' whose shortage was conventionally identified as constraining Indian economic growth, namely food, foreign exchange, and saving, have (as we saw in chs. 11 and 12) been bountiful in the 1970s, particularly once policy-induced distortions causing their supplies to be constrained were partially removed (at least for foreign exchange). Yet there is no sign as yet of any marked break in the trends of agricultural and industrial output since the 1950s. It is of course true that, for a subcontinental economy, all-India trends mask important differences in regional ones: for instance, parts of the west and north-west, and the south, have performed well above the national average. The real stagnation has been in eastern and central India—the ancient Hindu heartland (see Table 13.1).

(i) The overall policy framework

In explaining the failure of performance to match promise it is natural to look at the sins of omission and commission of public policy, and a number of these have been identified in the preceeding chapters. The most serious of these in our view are not merely the failure to seize the opportunities available for labour-intensive industrialization, but the actual obstacles placed in the adoption of this most important means for raising the demand for Indian labour.

By contrast, many observers of the Indian scene have provided different explanations for the relative failure to raise Indian standards of living, such as the increased supply of labour and/or the failure to undertake radical institutional reforms, usually of a collectivist variety, in Indian agriculture, as well as the failure to deal with what are viewed as continuing sources of market failure in the development of Indian industry. We have been at pains to show that the evidence does not support these views. The undoubted acceleration of population growth in post-Independence India has not led to any increase in surplus labour and unemployment (both strictly defined—see vol. II). Nor is there any evidence for the malfunctioning of labour markets (see vol. II) or for the past growth process to have led to any cornering of its meagre rewards by the 'rich' at the expense of the poor (see ch. 12). If anything, the available evidence shows an immiserization of the top 15 per cent of Indians, rather than of the bottom deciles!

(ii) Labour market-related policies

Moreover, the recent rigorous econometric estimates that have been made of the elasticities of rural labour demand and supply suggest that, contrary to the beliefs engendered by surplus-labour models, increases in rural-labour demand can be expected to be reflected in comparable increases in labour earnings (see vol. II). The fear that, with infinitely elastic supplies of rural labour, any growth-induced shift in the labour demand curve would merely lead to a rise in profits and rents with no impact on wages and labour earnings can no longer be sustained on the existing evidence; whilst given the evidence on the primarily economic motivation of migration as well as its extent, the fear that there would be no spread effects of locally induced increases in the demand for labour—say through labour-intensive industrialization in various 'urban' centres—cannot be

TABLE 13.1. Regional Indices of Development

State	Farm output/rural population, 1975–6 (Rs)	Growth rate of grain production, 1961/2–1978/9 (% p.a.)	Value added by manufacturing per capita, 1976–7 (Rs)	% of workers engaged in manufacturing, 1971	Proportion of villages without an adequate water supply, 1977–8 (%)	Power consumption per capita, 1977–8 (kWh)	Literacy rate 1976 (%)	% of population below an all-India poverty line, 1972–3 (%)	% share in all-India poverty population (%)	Composite quality of life index, 1975–6 (Kerala = 100)	State domestic product per capita, 1977–8 (Rs) (constant 1970–1 prices)
Andhra	506	1.7	119	9	58	82	36	54.9	8.5	21	607
Assam	453	2.2	118	9	69	36	43	46.9	2.6	23	552
Bihar	341	1.8	78	5	24	89	31	54.9	11.5	23	434
Gujarat	607	4.2	322	12	18	207	54	41.1	4.0	24	786
Haryana	1,032	5.1	203	10	50	173	47	23.1	0.9	52	973
Karnataka	592	3.0	207	10	3	135	50	50.7	5.3	38	730
Kerala	479	1.1	140	16	36	100	86	56.9	4.4	100	584
Madhya Pradesh	459	0.9	111	7	10	95	36	58.6	8.9	15	494
Maharashtra	555	2.5	413	13	11	210	65	47.7	8.6	58	991
Orissa	515	1.4	98	6	23	116	38	68.6	5.4	35	501
Punjab	1,161	6.4	236	11	11	227	56	21.5	1.0	62	1,298
Rajasthan	600	2.5	94	7	52	87	32	46.0	4.3	31	542
Tamil Nadu	442	1.9	227	11	7	159	56	59.6	8.7	36	657
Uttar Pradesh	427	2.5	91	7	27	82	36	52.6	16.7	5	503
West Bengal	511	2.5	237	14	2	119	53	56.9	9.2	46	769
All-India	519	2.6	—	10	26	121	46	—	100.0	—	701

Source: Krishna (1980).

sustained either. Nor can the belief be sustained that most rural–urban migration in India represents one-way flows of human and physical resources. The role of urban–rural remittances, from the only detailed study available (vol. II), in financing rural development is by no means unsubstantial.

Even though trade unions were established very early in India, and as in some other developing countries have been nurtured in the past as much as for their political as for their economic uses, it does appear that the latter are not negligible (see vol. II). In much of modern industry, faced for technological reasons with various problems of monitoring the performance and providing incentives to the non-casual labour force, they are (and are seen to be) useful means for managing men. The same cannot be said, however, of the plethora of labour laws which continue to hobble Indian industry. Their origins lie (see ch. 9) in the attempt of Lancashire cotton textile interests to reduce the competitiveness of the emerging Indian textile industry by legislating the 'minimum labour standards' which Britain only instituted after it had achieved its own industrial breakthrough. The foisting of these labour laws on the nascent Indian industrial sector a few years after they were instituted in the UK has, over the years, reduced the incentives to deploy India's most abundant resource to full advantage in her industrialization. Along with protection, these labour laws are one of the major sources of the continuing bias against labour-intensive industrialization in India. A reconsideration of these so-called 'rights' (a colonial legacy) granted to only a minuscule proportion of the Indian labour force at the expense of the less fortunate majority of Indian workers, is in our view long overdue.

Finally we have argued, contrary to the contemporary consensus, that the population growth which has occurred since 1921, far from having damaged Indian economic prospects, has probably been a major stimulant to agricultural growth, and that the small increase in the rate of growth of per capita incomes in post- as compared with pre-Independence India is in part due to this alteration of one of the major parameters of the Hindu equilibrium.

(iii) Alleviating low-end poverty

Nevertheless, in the short run, even if the efficient growth-promoting impulses flowing from a dismantling of India's current revenue economy were to occur, there would still be a great amount of low-level poverty, in particular in rural areas. Recent Indian public policy debates have been much concerned with alleviating this poverty through the institution of public works programmes.

Various programmes for expanding rural employment and alleviating low-end poverty have been implemented in India during the 1970s. Between 1971 and 1974 there was the crash scheme for rural employment; other programmes included the small farmer development agency, the marginal farmers and agricultural labourers programme, and the drought-prone area programme. Sen (1975) provides a judicious evaluation of these schemes. It appears that whilst they did do something to raise the incomes of the poor, they did not attack the poverty of the poorest, nor was their aim of using the labour employed on productive works achieved, in part because no set of economic criteria was laid down to evaluate the various projects.[2]

More recently the two major schemes for using some form of rural public works to alleviate low-end poverty are the employment guarantee scheme (EGS) of Maharashtra and the Antyodaya scheme in Rajasthan. The schemes share common features. They are, as in earlier special-employment schemes, meant to both redress low-end poverty and generate income-earning assets. They also employ a work criterion, as in the old English Poor Law, to provide the public dole embodied in the schemes. The details of the schemes need not concern us.

Few detailed economic studies have been made of these schemes.[3] However, from partial evaluations the following points emerge.[4]

First, as with many similar schemes in the past, as no proper economic cost–benefit type of framework is used in either designing or evaluating the various projects on which the labour employed on the schemes is used, it is quite likely that the production 'gains' from these schemes have been minimal and, at least in the case of the EGS, the project managers are increasingly short of projects.[5] (see Abraham (1980). Secondly, both schemes do seem to have been effective in their dole aspects, as a substantial share of the project costs have gone towards raising the income levels of the poor.[6] Thirdly, the EGS's fiscal costs have mushroomed, and there is some dispute on whether taking its financing (through taxes and cesses, essentially on those in the urban organized sector) and production benefits (mainly to the landed in rural areas) together, the net effect—apart from the dole aspects—is not distributionally regressive. Fourthly, in principle the use of seasonally underemployed labour on collective village public works does make economic sense, despite the failure in practice to base the choice of these works on economic criteria.

Fifthly, the Antyodaya idea perhaps provides a more viable (as it is more decentralized) method of alleviating low-end poverty. Through decentralization of the scheme to the village level, many of the obvious defects of the EGS type of scheme (the dangers of corruption, and the likely unproductive aspects of the projects undertaken as well as their probably inegalitarian distribution of benefits) are avoided. On the other hand, as has been noted by the Indian Institute of Public Opinion (1979), the distribution of destitutes whose poverty is redressed by these village-level schemes will not be identical with the distribution of poverty in the States, as the scheme does not differentiate between the five poorest families in a 'rich' and those in a 'poor' village.[7] But given the other obvious defects in more centralized schemes which could overcome this problem, the Antyodaya scheme is probably the best second-best alternative available in the political and administrative conditions of rural India.

(iv) Conclusions

Apart from some means for putting an income floor under the really needy and distressed, the major aim of public policy should be twofold. First, and most important, is the provision of the social overhead capital which is still desperately needed (*a*) to remove the ecological constraints on rural development in the Hindu heartland (though it is important that its level of provision and design is tested by social cost–benefit analysis), and (*b*) to provide those essential non-traded goods which are complementary inputs in the development process, such as power, transport, and education, and whose private provision, for well-known reasons, is not likely to be socially optimal. The second goal is to dismantle the counter-productive and positively harmful system of controls and planning without prices that has been set up in India over the last few decades, and instead to allow the incipient market economy at last to develop in India. For in our long-run perspective the real failure over the years has been in the inability of the market economy finally to replace the traditional revenue economy of ancient India. To say this is not to eulogize markets, or to assume that a market economy in India would correspond to the perfectly competitive norm laid down in economic textbooks. As is well known, so-called 'market failures' of various kinds are likely to be ubiquitous in any real-world economy. However, the great error is to assume that public-policy interventions which supplant the market and its chief instrument, the price mechanism, will then necessarily yield more gains in terms of social welfare than the workings of an imperfect market economy. For *bureaucratic failures*, as India's experience during the post-Independence decades eloquently attests, is likely to be as ubiquitous as market failure. There are thus reasons, essentially of a second-best welfare-economic nature, in support of fostering a market economy, albeit one controlled through economically rational public policy interventions in the workings of the price mechanism.[8]

But there is a deeper and, for India, a much more important reason for creating a market economy. For if the traditional mould of Indian society and its economy is to be shattered, one of the most important changes required is to substitute for the traditional reliance on custom one of contract in the economic sphere. The revenue economy, through its bureaucratic mode of allocation, in fact perpetuates all those patron–client traditional ties which have maintained the ancient Hindu equilibrium for millennia. A market economy working within a clearly defined legal system provides a relatively impersonal and 'arm's-length' method of mediating economic and (indirectly) social transactions. It enables the diverse interest groups which must necessarily be present in a pluralistic sub-continental polity to coexist and put their energies to productive uses rather than use those energies in the 'rent-seeking' and attempted hijacking of the levers of the State power which must necessarily be induced by the enormous powers of patronage and profit to be found in a modern-day revenue economy. There is of course a third mode, a fully-fledged command economy of the Soviet or Maoist variety. This is not the place to debate the relative technical (economic) merits of a command versus a market economy. Though many Indian intellectuals have set their hearts on this mode as the panacea for Indian ills, I believe that, whatever its merits, its institution in India is infeasible. Both the Soviet Union and China have long histories of centralized Governments and at least incipient command economies. Stalin had a precursor in Peter the Great, and Mao Tse Tung in the Ching emperor whom he eulogized. In India the promotion of an authoritarian centralized command economy is, for the social and historical reasons adumbrated at length in Parts I and II of this book, more likely to degenerate into the traditional dynastic, and hence unstable, form of imperial polity. An Alauddin Khilji is at best what Indian collectivists can hope to foster!

2. THE POLITICAL ECONOMY OF THE PREDATORY STATE

A major theme underlying this book is a view of the nature of Government or the State which is at variance with that commonly assumed by development economists. It may be useful to provide an explicit statement of this alternative view, as it also allows us to relate our speculations concerning the 'Hindu equilibrium' to the historical experience of other countries.

A detailed typology of actual and possible forms of Government forms is beyond the scope of this book. But I have found it useful to think in terms of two polar types—the benevolent (Platonic Guardian) and the self-serving (predatory) State. The objectives of the former are well known, as they form the staple of every elementary economics textbook. The objectives of the latter are more murky but must, by analogy with biological predator–prey models, involve the self-serving extraction of the maximum continuing flow of resources (which includes intangibles such as power and prestige) for the members of the Government and its associates. Predators will share an interest in the enlargement of the incomes of their prey (say through economic growth, promoted by the provision of public goods—of which the most important is law and order) in so far as this raises the potential flow of their own income. Unlike the case of the benevolent State, the welfare of their subjects—as conceived by economists—may at best be only a very minor direct component of a predatory State's 'objective function'. More important, however, is the likely opportunistic nature of Government behaviour in the latter State, which implies that, compared with the more principled benevolent State, its orderings over social states are likely to be fickle. Most actual States will of course not fall into either of these extreme categories, but it is useful for clarificatory purposes to maintain this sharp contrast.

The economic advice usually offered to developing countries is based on an implicit model of a state run by Platonic Guardians. Whatever the merits of this view (in a descriptive sense) of the rulers of many Western democracies, it is particularly inappropriate if we consider the past or many of the present rulers of the Third World.

By contrast, the emerging 'new political economy'[10] has begun to substitute the notion of a 'predatory' State which maximizes the profits of Government for that of a benevolent State seeking to maximize the welfare—however defined—of its constituents. Many policy recommendations of the traditional analysis are overturned. Thus, the so-called 'Ramsey optimal-tax rules'[11] for commodity taxation are no longer optimal for the constituents if a revenue-maximizing Leviathan is sought to be controlled. Brennan and Buchanan have devised a public finance to control Leviathan through a constitution in which, behind a Rawlsian veil of ignorance, the constitution-makers decide on the base of taxation, leaving the predatory State to decide the rates. The applicability of their model to modern-day bureaucracies in Western democracies has been questioned by Usher, as 'the tyranny of the despot and the tyranny of the majority' are not identical. Behind a veil of ignorance citizens would limit the powers of a king more than that of majoritatian democracies, 'if only because they are less likely to emerge as a king than as members of the majority coalition'.[12]

We do not know whether a predatory or contractarian origin of the State is historically more valid.[13] But it is interesting to determine how groups 'with a comparative advantage in coercion produced a state which on the one hand devised a set of property rights to maximize the returns to the rulers and on the other hand, within that framework, developed a body of law and its enforcement aimed at promoting economic efficiency and hence, tax revenue'.[14]

Questions of *positive* political economy then arise: are there differences amongst States in the extent of their predation? If so, what type of predatory State is likely to emerge, and over what territorial area in different technical, economic, and ecological conditions? As these economic conditions are unlikely to be exogenous, the feasible forms of economic organization will also depend upon the type of property right a particular predatory State finds it profitable to establish. Many economic historians (Hicks, North, Jones, Baechler, Braudel) emphasize the rise of the market and its associated property rights as an essential element (historically) for sustained 'modern' economic growth (in Kuznets's terms). When, therefore, is a self-interested predatory State likely to institute an efficient set of property rights required for a market economy?

(i) The State, law and order, and natural monopoly

There is one essential aspect of a State which makes it inherently prone to predation: its monopoly of the use of violence within its territory. Moreover, this violence-using and violence-controlling 'industry' is a natural monopoly.[15]

But the resulting State can range from the 'protection' provided by the Mafia 'against a violence [it] itself threatens, and who actually supply a sort of "black market" protection in return, suppressing rival gangsters'[16] to the modern-day Western democracies which besides maintaining law and order also provide other public goods to their citizens. But even these democracies have evolved from nation-states which were similar to the Mafia in their operation.[17]

The services of this natural monopoly are paid for by revenues extracted from the newly protected prey. The natural interest of the monopoly's controllers would be to maximize their net revenue. But this need not lead to the establishment of an efficient set of property rights. As Hicks (1969) and North (1981) emphasize; 'efficient property rights may lead to a higher income in the state but lower tax revenues for the ruler because of the transaction costs (monitoring, metering and collecting such taxes) as compared to those of a more inefficient set of property rights. A ruler therefore frequently found it in his interests to grant a monopoly rather than property rights which would lead to more competitive conditions.'[18]

Most economic historians have noted the link between the rise of the market and mercantile economies. Geography was important for the rise of the first mercantile States and 'market' economies in Greece. In these city-states and democracies, the State was under the control of its citizens and enforced the property rights required for the existence of a market economy—the need for protection of property and the need for protection of contracts.[19] When, later, military technology made the Greek city-state unviable it was Venice, controlled by its merchants, which took up the torch of the mercantile and market economy, which then passed subsequently to the Hansa towns of the North Sea and the Baltic, then to Holland, and later to England. In all these cases the system of property rights required to sustain an efficient market system required for growth entailed the curbing of the inherent predatory power of the State by its citizens through various forms of taxation based on representation. By contrast, the 'revenue economies' of absolutist France and Spain did not create such rights. Why?

Relative barriers to entry in the national 'predation' monopoly is the answer usually given. This idea can be sharpened by applying the newly formalized theory of 'contestable markets'. The State at a minimum is a two-good, multi-product, natural monopoly, providing 'protection' and 'justice'. These goods are complementary, with substantial increasing returns to scale in their costs of production, and their joint cost function is likely to meet Baumol, Bailey, and Willig's (BBW) criteria for a 'sustainable equilibrium for a multi-product monopoly'.[20] This is defined as 'a stationary equilibrium set of product quantities and prices which does not attract rivals into the industry'.

BBW show that, for a multi-product natural monopolist, the sustainable equilibrium preventing entry involves pricing its services at the Ramsey prices[21] associated with the maximum profits allowed by barriers to entry, which are 'the annual equivalent of the discounted present value of the entry costs or barriers to entry facing new firms in the market'.[22]

* (ii) A model of a predatory State

These ideas from recent developments in the theory of industrial organization can be combined with those due to North, and formalized by Findlay and Wilson, which emphasize the social productivity even of predatory States. We outline such a composite model of a predatory State in this section. For simplicity we assume that the State is only a single-good natural monopoly, or else provides multiple public goods in fixed proportions, so that they can be considered to be a composite commodity.

As most current developing countries as well as developed countries in the past were primarily agrarian economies, we consider a simple model of a predatory State whose only source of revenue is a proportional tax on agricultural output (Y) at the rate t.

Suppose that the area controlled by the State is divided into M identical villages, each with a fixed labour supply of L working on a fixed supply of land in each village of N. For simplicity assume (as in much of the development literature) that there is equal work and income-sharing in each village, so that each worker receives the (net of tax) average product of labour ($y (1 - t)$) in agriculture (where $y = Y/L_A$, and L_A is the labour force in each village engaged in agriculture). The State uses part of the revenue it obtains to hire public servants from each village (L_g), to administer the village and provide any other public goods either at the national or local level, such as irrigation or police. The cost of hiring a marginal public employee will be equal to the supply price of rural labor, which in turn will be equal to the net of tax average product of labour. Moreover, following Findlay and Wilson (1987), we assume that the provision of these public goods raises the productivity of the economy above what would exist in the absence of the State—viz. under anarchy.

Thus in each of the M villages we have

$$L_g + L_A = L \tag{13.1}$$

$$\text{and } Y = A (L_g) F (L_A, N) \tag{13.2}$$
$$A' (L_g) > 0: A'' (L_g) < 0; A (0) = 1$$

with L and N fixed, we can using (13.1) write (13.2) as

$$Y = Y (L_g; L, N) \tag{13.3}$$

with $Y = Y^O > 0 = A(0) F(L_A, N)$ when $L_A = L$ and $L_g = 0$; and $Y = 0$, when $L_A = 0$ and $L_g = L$.

The total revenue (TR) the predator controlling the State earns is given by

$$TR = M.t.Y \tag{13.4}$$

The total variable costs (TVC) of the predatory State are

$$TVC = M.L_g. \, (1 - t) \, y \, (L_g) \tag{13.5}$$

$$\text{where } y(Lg) \equiv \frac{Y(Lg)}{L_A}$$

In addition to these variable costs, the incumbent predator controlling the State will have had to expend fixed capital costs of K to capture and maintain the State, of which we assume αK are sunk costs. So the 'effective' fixed costs of the incumbent (FC_I) will be $(1 - \alpha)K$.

$$FC_I = (1 - \alpha)K \tag{13.6}$$

The total cost curve (TC_I) of the incumbent will therefore be from (13.5) and (13.6):

$$TC_I = M.L_g \, (1 - t) y \, (L_g) + (1 - \alpha)K \tag{13.7}$$

By contrast, a new entrant seeking to control this natural monopoly and assumed to have access to the same military technology would incur the same variable costs as the incumbent, but will have to expend the full fixed costs (that is, inclusive of the sunk cost αK) in capturing and replacing the incumbent. The new entrant's total cost curve TC_E will therefore be

$$TC_E = TVC + K \tag{13.8}$$

and this will lie above the incumbent's total cost curve by the fixed amount αK, as in Fig. 13.1.

If the size of the territory to be controlled (M) lies within the decreasing average cost portion of the total cost curve, the incumbent will be able to find a tax rate t, and earn a 'monopoly' profit equal to the sunk cost αK, which makes his monopoly sustainable in the sense that the new entrant cannot charge a lower tax rate and break even. Thus, as in Fig. 13.1, for territory size M, the incumbent will charge a tax rate t, such that the total revenue line intersects the entrant's cost curve at C_E. As the incumbent's costs are C_I, he will make a profit of αK. The net revenue-maximizing predator State's profit π function will be:

$$\pi = TR - TC_I = \alpha K \tag{13.9}$$

Substituting for TR and TC_I from (13.4), (13.3), and (13.7), we can determine the optimum tax rate t and level of public employment L_g, by maximizing:

$$\pi = M[tY(L_g) - (1 - t) \, y(L_g) \, . \, L_g] - (1 - \alpha) \, K \tag{13.10}$$

with respect to L_g, that is setting $\dfrac{\delta \pi}{\delta L_g} = 0$, which yields

$$tY'(L_g) = (1 - t) \, [y(L_g) + L_g.y'(L_g)] \tag{13.11}$$

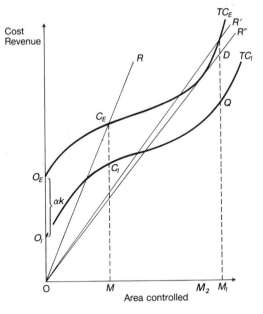

FIG 13.1   Determination of Area Controlled

namely, as is to be expected, the marginal revenue equals marginal cost of public employment, at which the profit from equation (13.9) equals αK. From (13.9), (13.6), and (13.5), the total surplus (S) between the total revenue (TR) and total variable costs (TVC) earned by the incumbent is

$$S = TR - TVC = K \qquad (13.12)$$

with the surplus per identical village being K/M.

The resulting general equilibrium of this agrarian predatory state can be depicted in Fig. 13.2.

The first quadrant depicts the total agricultural output curve of each identical village with respect to the given labour force OL working on the fixed acreage N. If there are no government employees—hence no State—then the whole of the village's labour force works in agriculture and produces output LY^O. This is the 'anarchy' level of output. With some government employees being hired to provide public goods, the agricultural labour force shrinks but total output increases, until the allocation of the labour force is such that there are $LL^*_A = L^*_g$ workers in public employment, and OL^*_A working in agriculture producing the maximal attainable output Y^* (higher than Y_0, because of the public goods provided by the L^*_g public employees).

For a given tax rate t on rural output, the vertical distance between the $Y(1 - t)$ Y curves in quadrant I, gives the total revenue available for a particular level of

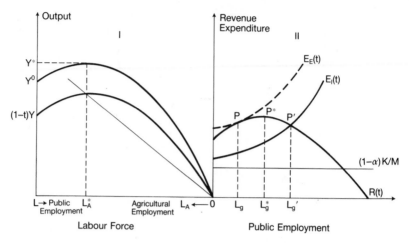

FIG 13.2   The Equilibrium of the Predatory State

public (L_g) employment. This per-village revenue function ($R(t)$) is plotted in quadrant II of Fig. 13.2. For any given tax rate (t) it reaches a maximum where $L^*_g = L - L^*_A$ workers are employed in the public sector. The competitive wage for public employees is equal to the supply price of rural labour, which *ex hypothesi* is the net of tax average product in agriculture, given by the slope of the ray Oy, when the level of rural agricultural employment is L^*_A and public employment is L^*_g.

Thus by a similar construction for each level of L_g, and for the given tax rate (t), the village-level variable-cost function $VC(t)$ can be derived in quadrant II. Adding the 'effective' fixed costs per village that the incumbent of the predatory State has to incur to maintain its natural monopoly of $(1 - \alpha)K/M$ yields the per-village public-expenditure function $E_I(t)$ of the incumbent, which is a vertical displacement by $(1 - \alpha)K/M$ of the variable cost ($VC(t)$) function. The per-village expenditure function of a potential entrant to this natural monopoly $E_E(t)$ will lie at a vertical distance equal to $\alpha K/M$ above the incumbent's expenditure function. The optimal tax rate for the net revenue-maximizing predatory State will be determined by the tangency of the entrant's expenditure function with the revenue function for this optimal rate, as at P in quadrant II of Fig. 13.2. For suppose the tax rate were higher ($t' > t$), then the incumbent's and entrant's expenditure function ($E(t')$) would shift downwards and the revenue function ($R(t')$) upwards (not drawn). The incumbent's monopoly would no longer be sustainable in the range where the new entrant's expenditure function ($E_E(t')$) now lies below the revenue function $R(t')$. Similarly, if the tax rate were lower ($t'' < t$), the revenue and expenditure functions would shift downwards and upwards respectively and the incumbent would not be maximizing net revenue. Thus we have shown that there will be a unique tax rate, and fiscal-cum-public-employment equilibrium, determined by the underlying production function and the net barrier to entry costs facing a new entrant. The net revenue-maximizing predatory State will choose a tax rate (t), and public employment level (L_g) (for each village) such that the vertical distance between the $E(t)$ and $R(t)$ function at its maximum equals the per-village sustainable rent it can charge of $\alpha K / M$. It is also obvious from the shapes of the production, revenue, and expenditure functions that the net revenue-maximizing public-employment level will be less than the socially optimal level L_g.[23]

Hitherto we have assumed that the size of the territory to be controlled lay within the decreasing average cost portion of the total cost curve of the State monopoly in Fig. 13.1, which yielded a sustainable equilibrium. Suppose, however, that either the size of the territory to be controlled was larger (say $M1$ in Fig. 13.1), or else the fixed costs were low enough so that the increasing average costs (for the given tax rate t) occurred within the range OM in Fig. 13.1. The incumbent may no longer be able to extract a sustainable rent equal to the maximum 'natural rent' given by his sunk costs αK. Thus, if for the cost curves depicted in Fig. 13.1 the area to be controlled is $M1$, setting a tax rate which yields total revenue given by points on the ray OR' would, while yielding the incumbent the 'natural rent' αK, make his monopoly unsustainable. For a new entrant can now set a slightly lower tax rate and still cover his total costs by controlling between M_2 to M_1 villages (in Fig. 13.1), where his total revenue curve (just slightly lower than OR') lies above his total cost curve. The incumbent can guard against this possibility by setting his tax rate at a level which yields a total revenue line OR'', tangent to the incumbent's total cost curve (TC_E). The incumbent's sustainable rent will then only be DQ which is less than αK.

However, depending upon the shape of the fixed-cost curve in controlling the given territory, it is possible (see Baumol and Willig (1981)) that there may be no tax rate which will be sustainable against entry, and political instability in the territory will be the norm. Moreover, if the territory is large enough (a large alluvial plain such as the Indo-Gangetic region in northern India) and the fixed costs required to establish a State are prohibitive for one sovereign to control the whole territory, there may be a number of States in an otherwise homogeneous region. Even if all their cost curves are identical, there may also not be a stable equilibrium in the *number* of States in the territory (see Baumol and Fischer, 1978)).

The above model emphasizes the importance of fixed costs (K) and the extent of sunk costs (αK) as barriers to entry in the 'optimal' fiscal and public employment equilibrium of the predatory State.

(iii) Barriers to entry

We need to distinguish between internal and external competitors to the rulers of a State, though of course there are many historical examples of claimants of both sorts combining to overthrow the incumbent natural monopolist.

For potential external predators the geography of the particular region and 'amalgamation costs'[24] are relevant in determining the barriers to entry. The early European city-states which first established a market system could exist independently because of their geography.[25] Later, with changes in military technology, the feasible territorial size of a State grew. The 'core areas' of the new European States were alluvial plains on which plough husbandry could be practised to yield the tax base for military control.[26] Though the intervening areas could be and were brought into polities linked to the core areas as communications and military technology improved, there were a number of natural barriers, like the sea which protected England, the Pyrenees, and the Alps and the northern marshes which defined the 'natural' defences of Spain, France, the Netherlands, and Italy.[27] These raised the entry cost for external predators.

Also, paradoxically, modern-day countries such as Switzerland and the Netherlands (the old United Provinces) found that economic disadvantages such as difficult terrain also proved to be their political strength, as external predators found it too costly (in terms of net returns) to control them.

In addition there were the amalgamation costs faced by external predators. Given ethnic, linguistic, and religious differences between the external predator and the peoples in an incumbent's territory—differences in Europe 'dating from early folk movements and settlement history'[28]—the incumbent could count on a form of 'loyalty' which the external predator could not.[29]

What of entry barriers to challenges from internal competitors? This depended upon military technology and the physical size of the 'naturally' defensible territory. *Ceteris paribus*, a physically smaller territory would be easier to take over than a larger one, whilst the changing technology of warfare which made large scale an advantage in the violence industry would tend to favour the incumbent. For instance, the development of the cannon in the mid fifteenth century removed the security of baronial fortifications in Europe and shifted the balance of advantages to an incumbent centralizing predator who could build larger and more expensive castles.[30]

Thus the resource base for extracting revenue and the geographical area 'naturally' defensible with available military technology would determine the 'optimal' territorial size of the State in a particular region as well as the stable sustainable 'natural' rent that could be extracted by the predator. But what shapes the system of property rights that these factors will tend to enforce?

North and Thomas argue that this will depend upon the relative 'bargaining strengths' of the rulers and constituents.[31] But this 'bargaining strength' has in effect been subsumed in the 'entry barriers' which determine the sustainable 'natural' rent the incumbent predator can extract.

The lower the entry barriers to internal rivals, the more likely it is that the reduction in natural 'rents' represented by the property rights required for an open market will be instituted. However, the effects of entry barriers facing external rivals may be more ambiguous. The higher these barriers, the smaller the incentive for the incumbent predator to come to terms with his prey, something he might have to do to increase their 'loyalty' and hence the 'amalgamation costs' faced by external competitors if external barriers were lower. But equally, to the extent that the constituents fear amalgamation by an external predator, they are less likely to press their case against an incumbent predator the lower the entry barrier, and vice versa.

The system of efficient property rights based on the relative bargaining strength of the prey is most likely to emerge in regions where geography and military technology allow the 'natural' territorial size of the State to be such that barriers to internal and external entry are high enough to prevent endemic political instability associated with internal baronial warfare or external invasions, but not so high as to make the incumbent secure enough to extract the maximum feasible revenue from his prey. It is the uniqueness of Europe, as Jones emphasizes, that it provided the ecological environment for the development of a 'States system' after the Renaissance, which bucked the historical trend towards organizing large regional populations into empires. In Europe no empire was built after the fall of Rome—overseas empires came later. Though Europe thereby lost some economies of scale, the predatory power of the individual States was lowered compared with an imperial monopoly over the region. The environmental characteristic was 'the scatter of regions of high arable potential set in a continent of wastes and forests'.[32]

A second factor, perhaps of equal importance, is the structure of the economy which determines the feasible set of taxes—their relative structure, if the monopoly is to be sustainable, being determined by the Ramsey Rules *à la* BBW. Here the important distinction (as Hicks notes) is the relative importance of internal versus external trade. As in pre-modern economies this is likely to depend upon natural-resource endowments, particularly the availability of rich arable land relative to the population, we would expect external trade to be more important for the *relatively* resource poor countries. The Greek city-states, the Netherlands, and England would successively classify as countries which fall in this category.

The self-interest of the predator in expanding the tax base of an economy dependent on external trade should induce him to set up the property rights for a mercantile economy.[33] The economic history of Britain and the Netherlands *vis-à-vis* France and Spain can (as North and Thomas show) be written in terms of the different systems of property rights that were established after the Renaissance, and there were good ecological and economic reasons why this should have been so.

If the incumbent predator is far-sighted he will charge Ramsey prices for the multi-product natural monopoly he owns, extracting the 'natural' rent equal to the present discounted value of the internal and external entry costs. However, even if these costs do not change over time (which is unlikely) they cannot be ascertained with any exactitude. Their estimates will be probabilistic. Depending upon differences in subjective probabilities and/or different degrees of risk aversion on the part of the incumbent and his rivals, what may 'objectively' seem to be a sustainable equilibrium may or may not turn out to be one. There may thus be sustainable equilibria in practice which involve extracting more or less than the 'natural' rent than is entailed by 'objective' entry barriers. There may then be long-run 'predatory' cycles[34] in which the *long-run* sustainable equilibrium is undermined over time by predators beginning to charge more than the Ramsey prices. The higher prices make entry profitable. This leads in the medium run (which of course could be more than a century!) to the eventual overthrow of the incumbent and the establishment of a fresh sustainable equilibrium by a new group of predators.

(iv) Cycles in fiscal predation

Military technology has obviously been important in determining the degree to which the natural monopoly that has been periodically established in the Indo-Gangetic plain is contestable by internal rivals. Once a new entrant established his dominance, the sustainability on a dynastic basis of the newly established monopoly depended upon his heirs being far-sighted enough not to extract more than the natural rent. If they did, then there would be an incentive for internal competitors to arise and attempt to provide a competitive supply. The rebellions at the edges of the empire (where, because of costs of transport and communication, rival entry would be easier) which have plagued (as they still plague)[35] India's imperial rulers would then become endemic. The ensuing breakdown of the empire would be followed by another period of chaos until one or other of the fueding chiefs succeeded in establishing his hegemony but refrained from over-charging for the natural monopoly he had acquired. If the underlying ecological, demographic, and economic conditions did not alter markedly—as they did not, until very recently—there would be cycles of growth and decay of empires linked to cycles in 'rents' that the predatory State sought to exact, with the 'stable' equilibrium corresponding to the sustainable 'natural' rents extractable under the rules of BBW!

We have little to go on in documenting the changing fiscal exaction of India's predators until about AD 1000. But the simple theory outlined above does seem to fit the case of at least two of the major Indian empires that have risen and fallen since then—the medieval Moghul empires, and the British Raj of the eighteenth to twentieth centuries.

The theory suggests that, given the large alluvial 'core area' of the Indo-Gangetic plain and the considerable entry barriers facing external rivals, the 'natural' rent that a stable predatory State could extract would be relatively high. Secondly, given the importance of internal relative to external trade, there would be little incentive for the predatory State to create the property rights required to establish a mercantile and thereby a market economy. These predictions are borne out by the account we have presented of India's 'revenue economy' in this book.

Summarizing the story of fiscal cycles we have presented: 'There now seems to be a consensus that the Moghul State claimed at least one third to half or more of the agricultural produce in cash.'[36] As we have noted, Maddison's estimate of the fiscal exaction by the Moghuls was about 15–18 per cent of national income[37] as compared with a tax burden in England in 1688 of 6.3 per cent of national income. As we would expect, England is a country which has a lower threshold of internal 'entry' costs and hence lower 'natural' rents. This tax burden was increased under Aurangzeb and his successors and contributed to the decline of the Moghuls (in line with the cyclical model of fiscal excess). The internal chaos and breakdown only came to an end with the gradual establishment and extension of British power over the subcontinent.

The British Raj, as we have noted (ch. 8) was relatively benign in its fiscal exactions, imposing a total tax burden (according to Maddison) of only 6 per cent of national income.[38] Unlike its predecessors, the Raj could not extract the 'natural' rent that past predatory States had extracted because of the lowering of the barriers preventing the entry of a rival. For, unlike most of India's other invaders, the British, after a brief initial period (which ended with the 1857 mutiny) in which they attempted to become a traditional Indian power, set themselves apart and above their subjects. This meant that, unlike the case with any of India's previous rulers, there was a possibility of a nationalist revolt *of the populace as a whole* against its rulers. This meant that the entry costs for internal rivals had been considerably reduced, and the British found that the 'secret of successful Indian government was low taxation',[39] whilst providing law and order more cheaply than had historically been possible.

But with the ending of alien rule and the accompanying reduction of the danger of an internal nationalist revolt, the 'natural' rent to be extracted once again rose to its historical levels. India's rulers did not miss this opportunity, and the economic history of India since Independence can, as we have noted, be looked upon as a vast extension of India's historical revenue economy permitted by these changed circumstances. The overt revenues extracted by the State in the late 1970s were running at over 20 per cent of national income, but this does not begin to take account of the rents that various public officials and those lucky enough to obtain various permits and licences were extracting from the mercantilist system of trade, industrial, and price controls that the post-Independence predatory State has established in India.

This I hope suggests that ecological factors have been important in shaping the long-run propensities which have shaped a particular form of predatory State in India, which, though recently garbed in representative clothes, has not changed its nature or essential purpose. In fact, the advances in what Hicks terms the 'administrative revolution' of the last 100 years have led to a huge expansion of the traditional Indian form of revenue economy, with dire consequences for its economic development.

(v) Precommitment and efficiency

Can these natural proclivities of large 'natural' rent-rich States to establish an inefficient set of property rights be stemmed? There is one important historical case where this has happened—the United States. It has been done by a form of precommitment[40]—a constitution—which tied the State, Ulysses-like, to the mast so that it was not ensnared by the sirens of its 'natural' rent-seeking proclivities. This was possible because, as North notes, 'The American colonies were in the extraordinary position of taking over from England not only the body of property rights (and common law) that had been evolving there, but also the deep distrust of a powerful state that emerged from the English Revolution.'[41] But, as he goes on to show, under populist pressure the controls that the framers of the constitution had instituted to control the State broke down. The reasons were concerns about the distributional justice of an unregulated market and demands for fundamental political and economic structural change to alter the distribution of income.[42] The resulting politicization of economic life and its consequences for the attenuation of the market system is another story. But for my purpose it is important to remember the hold of a similar public ideology—Fabian socialism—in modern India (see ch. 11). Thus when India got a constitution at Independence it legitimized the continuation of a grossly expanded version of the revenue economy in the name of 'social justice'. Thus precommitment in the form of a constitution is not enough if the ideology of the constitution-makers is not conducive to chaining Leviathan. Most inefficient predatory States need to be saved from themselves by some form of pre-commitment, but in devising and recommending the form of that pre-commitment we must be clear-headed.

If our model of the predatory State is to be believed, the need is to ensure that, in a State seeking to maximize the size of the bureaucracy, the tax rate is set so that only the optimal level of public goods is provided—that is, the rate which ensures that with a balanced budget L^*g of public employment is provided in terms of Figure 13.2. If such a precommitment can be obtained it could lead towards a welfare-optimal dynamic adjustment to a more developmentally orientated set of property rights. This brings us straight back to Brennan and Buchanan's fiscal constitutionalism—which is where we came in. How we get a reluctant Ulysses to tie himself (or herself) to the mast then becomes the really important question for political economy. But deriving *lasting* constitutional checks in most current developing countries will never be easy, for, as De Jasy has quipped about chaining Leviathan: 'With its key always within reach, a chastity belt will at best occasion delay before nature takes its course'![43]

NOTES

1. See Lal (1983), Little (1982b), for reviews of the findings of the economics of developing countries.
2. Also see Rudra (1978). Singh (1978) and Burki (1976) provide broad surveys of public works programmes in south Asia, whilst Lewis (1972) provides some arguments in their support as supplementary measures in an overall growth-with-equity package of public policies.
3. But see Dandekar (1980), Abraham (1980), and Sen (1975), who all provide some partial evidence that all is not as well as it seems, at least in the EGS and earlier 'crash employment schemes'.
4. See Reynolds and Sundar (1977), Dandekar (1980), Abraham (1980) for evaluations of the EGS, and Chopra (1981) and IIPO (1979) on the Antyodaya scheme.
5. See Abraham (1980).
6. See Dandekar (1980) and Chopra (1981).
7. This of course is similar to the charge levied against the similar system in Britain, in the form of the old English Poor Law.
8. See Lal (1980a) for a fuller discussion of these purely technical aspects.
9. Alauddin Khilji ruled between 1296 and 1316. In order to maintain a large standing army at low cost, he instituted price controls and grain rationing. A complex system of espionage was created, and draconian punishments meted out to transgressors. But the control system did not outlast him, and its effects on the economic health of the country are dubious. See Habib (*CEHI*, vol. i, pp. 86 ff.) and Majumdar *et al.* (1978, pp. 300–2).
10. See Alt and Chrystal (1983) and Colander (1984) for a review.
11. These broadly recommend the use of taxes on commodities in most inelastic demand, as this reduces the excess burden associated with distortionary taxation.
12. Usher (1983, p. 1022).
13. As North notes, 'whether the state originated as a predatory group attacking and exploiting a peasant village (a predatory origin of the state) or developed out of the communal needs for organisation of the peasant village (a contract origin of the state) cannot be resolved .' (North 1981, p. 64)).
14. Ibid.
15. 'There have been times when violence-using enterprises competed in demanding payments for protection in almost the same territory, for example, during the Thirty Years' war in Germany. But such a situation was even more uneconomic than would be competition in the same territories between rival telephone systems. Competing police forces were even more inefficient than competing fire companies. A monopoly of the use of force within a contiguous territory enabled a protection-producing enterprise to improve its product and reduce its costs' (Lane (1958), p. 402).
16. Ibid, 403.
17. North and Thomas (1973, p. 87) note of the emergence of European nation states in the 15th and 16th centuries: 'Born in expanding warfare, created by intrigue and treachery, the crowned heads appeared to have more the characteristics of Mafia bosses than the characteristics of kings envisioned a century later by John Locke.'
18. North (1981, p. 28).
19. Hicks (1969, p. 33).
20. Baumol *et al.* (1977, p. 350). These are that (*a*) the total cost function for the two products produced jointly by the firm have 'strictly decreasing ray average cost, that is, if a *proportionate* increase in *all of the firm's outputs* produces a less than proportionate increase in its total cost' (p. 354) and (*b*) the cost function is trans-ray convex, which 'requires, in essence, that complementarities in production outweigh scale effects along the relevant cross section' (p. 354).
21. If the vector of optimal outputs is denoted by y^*, $C(y)$, is the cost of producing the outputs (*excluding* entry cost) and MR_i and P^i the marginal revenue and price respectively of the *i*th product, the Ramsey conditions require for the 2 good case

$$\frac{MR_1(y^*) - C_1(y^*)}{MR_2(y^*) - C_2(y^*)} = \frac{P^1(y^*) - C_1(y^*)}{P^2(y^*) - C_2(y^*)}$$

22. It should be noted, however, that 'Ramsey pricing is sufficient but not necessary for substainability. Consequently, there may exist sustainable price vectors, perhaps even many of them that do not satisfy the Ramsey conditions' (Baumol *et al.*, (1982, p. 2)).

23. From Fig. 13.2 and equation (13.3) the output-maximizing public-employment level (L^*_g) is given by $Y'(L^*_g) = 0$, whereas from (13.11) the profit-maximizing public-employment level (L_g) is given by $Y'(L_g) > 0$. Hence $L_g < L^*_g$.

24. Jones (1981, p. 106).

25. See Hicks (1969, p. 39).

26. See Jones (1981, pp. 105–6).

27. Ibid.

28. Ibid., 106.

29. However, as McNeill emphasizes, in the Old World (from about 800 BC to the 14th century AD) there was a chronic conflict between the nomads of the steppes and settled agriculturalists. The nomadic pastoralists' 'rapidity of movement and superior diet gave them a clear military advantage over more sessile and (often) protein-deficient cultivators' (McNeill (1984, p. 2)). From the time when pastoral nomads first learned to shoot arrows from horseback till the Mughal and Manchu conquests of India and China in the 16th and 17th centuries, 'the political history of civilized Eurasia and Africa consists largely of intermittent conquest by invaders from the grasslands, punctuated by recurrent rebellions of agricultural populations against subjugation to the heirs of such conquerors' (McNeill (1983, p. 12)).

30. Bean (1973).

31. See North and Thomas (1973, p. 98).

32. Jones (1981, p. 105).

33. A fact which may be of importance in explaining the development of the mercantile economies amongst the contemporary south-east Asian NICs—the 'Gang of Four'—Korea, Taiwan, Hong Kong, and Singapore.

34. The growth-cycle model of Goodwin (1967) which is explicitly based on the biological predator–prey model of Volterra would seem to be applicable.

35. Consider e.g. recent events in Assam and Punjab, and the long-standing separatist movement in Tamil Nadu.

36. Bhattacharya (1983, p. 1708).

37. Maddison (1971, p. 22).

38. Ibid., 45.

39. Tomlinson (1975, p. 338).

40. The importance of 'precommitment' as an essential element in human rationality goes back to the discussion of akrasia by Aristtole, and appears in various modern guises in economics such as the 'isolation paradox' (Sen (1967)), inconsistent time preferences (Strotz (1955–6)), and endogenous changes in tastes (von Weiszacker (1971)). Elster (1979)) provides a splendid discussion and elucidation of this important facet of 'imperfect rationality'. Schelling (1984) is a recent economist's view of the subject.

41. North (1981, p. 187).

42. Ibid., 192.

43. De Jasy (1985, p. 187).

14

A SUMMARY

This has been a long book in which we have covered an enormous amount of ground. All that I can hope to do in this concluding chapter is to draw some of the major themes together.

1. THE PARAMETERS OF THE HINDU EQUILIBRIUM

The bedrock of our major thesis lies in the demographic, ecological, and political conditions in which the ancient Hindus fashioned a social and economic system that yielded a stable Hindu equilibrium which, despite various attempts at change, has scarcely altered over millennia. Its social expression was the caste system, for whose economic aspects in the form of occupational segmentation of the labour market, we have sought a second-best rationale in terms of simple models of decision-making under uncertainty. The major constraints faced by the ancient Hindus in creating a viable social and economic system were fourfold.

The *first* was the need to secure an uncertain labour supply for settled and (by the standards of the time) relatively labour-intensive agriculture. For India until very recently has been a labour-scarce country. Its demographic stability, with obvious downward deviations in times when the four horsemen of the Apocalypse ran riot, is one of the fundamental parameters which has shaped Indian society and its economy. The major change that has taken place in the twentieth century is the alteration in this parameter as a result of the population explosion which can be dated to the early part of this century, and whose cause was a reduction in mortality through the agency of modern medicine.

The *second* major constraint faced by the ancient Hindus was endemic political instability amongst their numerous feuding monarchies.[1] The loadstone of every petty Indian chieftain has been the establishment of a subcontinental empire—these centripetal tendencies being counterbalanced by the endemic centrifugal forces flowing from geography, and the ensuing difficulties of communication in holding the subcontinent together. Though the most prosperous and glorious periods of Indian history have been the periods of stability under dynastic imperial rule, the difficulty of maintaining the imperial unity of India has in its long history made such periods relatively infrequent. The great strength of the social and economic system set up by the ancient Hindus, therefore, was its highly decentralized nature, which provided specific incentives to warring chieftains to disturb the ongoing life of the relatively autarkic village communities as little as possible. This was done in part by making war the trade of professionals, and thus saving the mass of the populace from being inducted into the deadly disputes of India's changing rulers.

Equally important, however, was the creation of a local administrative and revenue structure, and a tradition of paying a certain customary share of the village output as revenue to the current overlord, which meant that any new political victor had a ready and willing source of tribute in place. It would be a foolhardy monarch who would seek to change these local arrangements, which greatly reduced the effort required on his part to finance his armies and court. The village communities in turn bought relative peace and quiet and could carry on their daily business more or less undisturbed beneath the hurly-burly of continuing aristocratic conflict over the millennia. This explains both the continuity of the village communities and the prima-facie surprising supineness Indians have shown in quickly buckling under the heel of any new ruler.

A consequence of this decentralized social system, with its primary loyalties to an intricate web of vertically and horizontally arranged subcastes, was that the idea of nationalism did not take root. When it did emerge, both the intellectual bases and political manifestations of Indian nationalism were a foreign import. Despite the hagiographers of the nationalist movement, to more dispassionate eyes it appears as a traditional Indian political response to new rules of the political game laid down in the latter phases of the British Raj (see chs. 5 and 10). The legal and representative institutions set up by the British embodying these new rules of the game did, however, provide both a less bloody alternative to the traditional military one for ambitious individuals to achieve political supremacy over the subcontinent and the hope that, over time, a more enduring framework for maintaining Indian unity and political stability than the traditional Indian form of unstable dynastic imperial rule would be established. It is early days yet to judge whether this last hope will be fulfilled, though the recent direct and indirect assault on these legal and representative institutions (during the Emergency in the mid-1970s) does suggest that a fundamental change in this political parameter underlying the Hindu equilibrium has not as yet been firmly established.

The *third* parameter underlying the social and economic systems set up in ancient India was ecological, mainly climatic. The uncertainty arising from the vagaries of the monsoon, as well as the uneven spread of natural rainfall, has meant that various expected utility-maximizng but not necessarily expected profit-maximizing agrarian systems became desirable. Numerous features of factor and product markets in the rural economy as well as seemingly uneconomic cropping patterns, which appear to entail sub-optimal departures from the marginal conditions underlying the theoretical perfectly competitive norm, make sense, however, as second-best Pareto efficient responses in spreading and pooling risks in the highly uncertain environment of Indian agriculture. It is in these terms that we have sought to provide explanations for the jajmani system and the process of subinfeudation that occurred in eastern India after the Permanent Settlement. This is also the line of research currently being explored very fruitfully in the literature of so-called 'inter-linked rural factor markets'.[2]

The *fourth* parameter consisted of a set of distinctive social attitudes and beliefs which have influenced the natural attitudes of Indian rulers towards trade and commerce. This is the Brahminical tradition which has looked down upon the vaishyas (merchants) and has been suspicious of the self-interested pursuit of profit which underlies their operations in markets. These atitudes were not dysfunctional over the wide sweep of Indian history covered in this book, as they were part and parcel of that more general system of beliefs comprising the Hindu socio-economic system. This, as we have argued, succeeded in maintaining an agrarian revenue economy which, though stagnant, was an efficient environmental adaptation for millennia. This intellectual or ideological parameter, as we have argued, has hardly been altered. Its continuance prevents that movement from a traditional agricultural revenue economy to a market-based industrial economy, so essential for ending India's economic stagnation. The *Western* ideology imported in the last phase of the British regime—Fabian socialism—has strengthened rather than weakened India's atavistic attitudes to commerce and the market.

According to our thesis, by the early years of the Christian era the population and agrarian system had become stabilized in a form which yielded on average a standard of living which, though low by current standards, was for millennia amongst the highest attained by contemporary countries and civilizations. It is this relative economic success of the system for nearly a thousand years (until about AD 1600) which explains both its relative imperviousness to change and its long survival. As, until fairly recently, there was no shortage of land the mild expansion of population that probably took place over the millennia (undoubtedly with many fluctuations) was easily accommodated by an intensification of agriculture, with little change in the basic technology and cropping patterns established in the early Aryan settlements.

2. RURAL DEVELOPMENT

The major changes required to break the mould of this traditional agriculture were (*a*) (on Boserupian lines) an expansion of population and (*b*) the provision of social overhead capital in the form of irrigation to free Indian agriculture from the vagaries of the monsoon. The first of these conditions was met by the population expansion after 1921 which, far from being a curse as is conventionally assumed on Malthusian grounds, was the one dynamic factor which has in part been responsible for the slight trend increase in agricultural growth in the post-Independence period. This improvement in agricultural performance was also in part due to the greater public provision of the second of the above elements, irrigation and the associated 'leading inputs'—fertilizers and high-yielding seeds.

But the expansion of irrigation has been uneven. As minor irrigation formed part of the traditional agricultural technology, it has expanded *pari passu* with the increasing intensification of agriculture accompanying the population expansion. But, not surprisingly, the marginal private and also social returns (on the basis of the few available cost–benefit studies) on such supplemental irrigation decrease with the increase in natural rainfall. Furthermore, as most of central India forms part of the Deccan trap rock formation, the lack of a hydro-geological survey for the region has meant that the siting of productive wells has been highly uncertain, thereby lowering the expected return from an expansion of minor irrigation.

The public provision of productive large-scale surface irrigation works, as well as the requisite information on the hydro-geology of the Deccan, was thus a pre-requisite for changing the ecological parameters underlying the Hindu equilibrium. Even for the public and primarily surface irrigation works, however, the social returns were likely to have been highest in the drier regions, which are broadly speaking to be found in the west, particularly the north-West.

Paradoxically, the ecologically richest part of the subcontinent, the central and eastern Gangetic plain and deltas, which are the best watered from natural rainfall and whose fertility is periodically renewed by the silt deposited in the flood-plains, are likely to be the most difficult to develop agriculturally. The famed wealth and prosperity in ancient times of eastern India, which was the site of the early Hindu empires, was largely due to its more favourable climatic and soil conditions. The resulting subsistence rice economy which has remained unchanged for millennia was highly productive by contemporary standards, in so far as it enabled a fairly large rural and urban population to be maintained from its agricultural surplus. But to alter this agrarian equilibrium in eastern India it is necessray to make massive public investments in not merely irrigation but also flood control. For the next higher stage of rice technology requires a *controlled* water supply. In an all-India context, the social returns on such investment are unlikely to be as high as to the pure surface irrigation works begun under the British and accelerated in independent India in the west, which have, together with new seeds and fertilizers, led to what has been labelled the 'green revolution' in these areas. It is these differing ecological conditions and the relative difficulties in altering them which, in our view, explain the relative agricultural stagnation and associated rural poverty in the Hindu heartland of the Gangetic plain.

3. FOSTERING EFFICIENT INDUSTRIALIZATION

We have argued that, if rural development of the Hindu heartland is difficult, the advent of modern labour-intensive industry nevertheless provides an alternative means for raising the demand for labour which still remains the only certain means for raising the levels of living of India's labouring millions. In this, despite nationalist cant and continuing attempts to denigrate the economic achievements of the British century, the Indian response to the new opportunities for industrialization up to the First World War was impressive. Despite the lack of promotion and protection, flowing from the twin policies of *laissez-faire* and free trade underpinning the nineteenth-century economic policy of the Raj, Indian enterprise and capital was able to turn the tables on Lancashire and set up a thriving and efficient modern textile industry. Similarly, with some promotional help from officialdom, plantations and a steel industry were begun. Indian industrialization thus began well before that of most other developping countries. Though it is undeniable that greater governmental promotion of industry, essentially through some form of subsidies to capital and labour training, was required, the oft-repeated charge that free trade hampered industrial development does not seem to be valid.

Instead, we have suggested that it was the combination of protective labour legislation and creeping and discriminating protection, instituted essentially on grounds of fiscal expediency during the last phase of the Raj, which set in motion those trends towards an inward-looking, import-substituting, capital-intensive form of industrialization whose apotheosis was reached in the 1950s and 1960s. The damage this has done to India's poor is one of the most serious outcomes of public policy of the last fifty years.

4. IDEAS AND IDEALS

Hicks (1969) has stressed that in the evolution of modern Western economies the rise of the merchant and the market were important preconditions for that phase of modern economic growth which, as Baechler has noted, 'began as a European accident, [but] has become an obligatory command for the whole world'[3]. At least since the sixth century BC, as we have seen in Parts I and II, India has had a substantial and prosperous mercantile class. Yet since its ideological vehicle, the republican anti-casteist sects of Buddhism and Jainism, lost out to caste in the early Christian era, the ideals and values of merchants have never had much appeal for India's rulers.

The contempt in which merchants and markets have traditionally been held in Hindu society was (as we saw in chs. 10 and 11) given a new garb by the Fabian socialism which so appealed to the newly Westernised but traditional literary castes of India. This contempt, moreover, has been allied with a breath-taking ignorance of mercantile activity amongst these castes. This is the result of the endogamous and occupationally segregated caste system. In more socially mobile societies there is always a fair chance that the rulers and their courtiers would have had some mercantile relatives who would have instructed them on the nature of trade and commerce, and the importance of risk-taking and entrepreneurship in the process of development. The caste system has, however, cocooned the Indian literary castes from any such influences. The danger this represented to the prospects of India's economy was masked until fairly recently when, as a result of the 'administrative revolution' which has greatly augmented the means whereby the Government can extend the hold of the revenue economy, these literary castes have increasingly intervened in spheres which were traditionally not their province. Their inbred contempt and ignorance of merchants and markets prevents them both from recognizing the failures of their past misguided interventions and from promoting that evolution of a market economy (albeit controlled through measures which supplement the price mechanism) on which to a large extent the future economic prospects of Indians now depends.

There are, however, some hopeful signs that this resulting unworldliness of Indian rulers concerning trade and commerce might be changing.[4] What scribblers cannot achieve, inflation and an excess supply of bureaucrats might at last engender. For, as is shown in volume II, one of the remarkable features of the changes in the relative wage structure in post-Independence India has been the decline in top civil-service salaries. The corresponding labour market signals have been received by the children of these literary castes who, from casual empiricism, seem to be turning towards non-traditional but more lucrative careers in business and politics. If this means that, in time, the so-called 'policy-makers' in India will become less contemptuous and ignorant of trade and commerce, then that substitution of Bania for Brahmin ideals, which Nehru so passionately decried (see ch. 11) but which is nevertheless essential for India's economic progress, might at last begin to dissolve the intellectual bulwarks of Indian economic stagnation.

Conclusions

We can thus end our long journey on a relatively hopeful note. Many of the parameters which have sustained the ancient Hindu equilibrium have decisively shifted during the past century: population growth has ended India's ancient demographic stability and the need to tie labour down to land; the green revolution has ended village autarky; even the modest industrial growth since Independence has meant that contract is replacing custom in many relationships—particularly in the labour market; whilst the growth of western education, social legislation—which has picked up where Bentinck left off—and the gradual movement of the literary castes into business and commerce are slowly changing long-standing casteist attitudes. It is to be hoped that the revenue economy will over time be replaced by a market economy. If this happens, the Hindu equilibrium will not only be threatened, as it is now, but will at last be undermined.

NOTES

1. 'Megasthenes in the 4th century BC heard of 118 kingdoms, and the actual number may well have been more. In all ages the crowd of principalities and powers has been almost past counting. From time to time a strong paramount power has arisen and succeeded for a few years in introducing a certain amount of political unity, but such occasions were rare. When no such power existed, the states, hundreds in number, might be likened to a swarm of free, mutually repellent molecules in a state of incessant movement, now flying apart, and again coalescing' (Smith (1981, p. 5)).
2. See Braverman and Srinivasan (1981); Bardhan (1980a); and vol. ii, ch. 7 of this work.
3. Baechler (1975, p. 108).
4. It is encouraging that the newest member of India's latest imperial family is not a professional politician. In fact he is the first member of his family in three generations to have earned a living outside politics. Moreover, many of his close associates seem to understand commerce much better than earlier Indian politicians, as they have made their living by it. These signs provide hope for the future.

BIBLIOGRAPHY

Abraham, A. (1980). 'Maharashtra's Employment Guarantee Scheme', *Economic and Political Weekly*, 32.

Adams, J., and Craig West, R. (1979). 'Money, Prices and Economic Development in India, 1861–1895'. *Journal of Economic History*, Mar.

Agarwala, R. (1965). 'Wages in the Early Stages of Economic Development', *Arthaniti*, July.

Ahluwalia, I. J. (1985). *Industrial Growth in India: Stagnation Since the Mid 1960s*, Delhi.

Ahluwalia, M. S. (1978). 'Rural Poverty in India: 1956–57 to 1973–74', *Journal of Development Studies*, 14.3.

Ahmad, I. (1966). 'The Ashraf–Ailaf Dichotomy in Muslim Social Structure in India', *Indian Economic Social History Review*, 3.3.

Akerlof, G. (1976). 'The Economics of Caste and of the Rat Race and other Woeful Tales', *Quarterly Journal of Economics*, 90.4

—— (1980). 'A Theory of Social Custom, of which Unemployment May be One Consequence', *Quarterly Journal of Economics*, 94.4.

—— and Miyazaki, M. (1980). 'The Implicit Contract Theory of Unemployment Meets the Wage Bill Argument', *Review of Economic Studies*, Jan.

Alchian, A., and Demsetz H. (1972). 'Production, Information Costs and Economic Organization', *American Economic Review*, Dec.

Allchin, B., and Allchin, R. (1968). *The Birth of Indian Civilisation*, London.

—— (1982). *The Rise of Civilisation in India and Pakistan*, Cambridge.

Allen, G. C. (1969). *Economic Fact and Fantasy*, 2nd edn., London.

Alt. J. E., and Chrystal, K. A. (1983). *Political Economics*, Berkeley, CA.

Anstey, V. (1952). *The Economic Development of India*, 4th edn., London.

Ardant, G. (1975). 'Financial Policy and Economic Infrastructure of Modern States and Nations', in C. Tilley (ed.), *The Formulation of National States in Western Europe*, Princeton, NJ.

Arrow, K. J. (1974). *The Limits of Organisation*, New York.

—— and Hahn, F. H. (1971). *General Competitive Analysis*, San Francisco.

Azariadis, C. (1975). 'Implicit Contracts and Underemployment Equilibria', *Journal of Political Economy*, Dec.

Bachler, J. (1975). *The Origins of Capitalism*, Oxford.

Bagchi, A. K. (1970). 'Long-term Constraints on India's Industrial Growth 1951–1968', in Robinson and Kidron.

—— (1972). *Private Investment in India: 1900–1939* Cambridge.

—— (1976). 'De-Industrialization in India in the 19th century: Some Theoretical Implications', *Journal of Development Studies*, 12.2.

—— (1979). 'A Reply', *Indian Economic and Social History Review*, 16.2.

Baran, P. A. (1957). *The Political Economy of Growth*, New York.

Bardhan, K. (1973). 'Factors Affecting Wage Rates for Agricultural Labour', *Economic and Political Weekly*, 8.

—— (1977). 'Rural Employment, Wages and Labour Markets in India: A Survey of Evidence', (pts.) i, ii, and iii, *Economic and Political Weekly*, 12.26–8.

Bardhan, P. K. (1970). 'On the Minimum Level of Living and the Rural Poor', *Indian Economic Review*, 5.1.

—— (1973). 'On the Incidence of Poverty in Rural India', *Economic and Political Weekly*, annual no.

—— (1979). 'Labour Supply Functions in a Poor Agrarian Economy', *American Economic Review*, 69.1.

—— (1980a). 'Interlocking Factor Markets and Agrarian Development: A Review of Issues', *Oxford Economic Papers*, Mar.

—— (1980b). 'Determinants of Supply and Demand for Labour in a Poor Agrarian Economy: An Analysis of Household Survey Data in Rural West Bengal', mimeo, ADC–ICRISAT conference, Hyderabad.

—— and Srinivasan, T. N. (eds.) (1974). *Poverty and Income Distribution in India*, Calcutta Statistical Publishing Society.

Basham, A. L. (1967). *The Wonder that was India*, London.

Basu, A. (1967). 'Technical Education in India, 1900–1920', *Indian Economic and Social History Review*, 4.4.

—— (1971). 'Indian Primary Education, 1900–1920', *Indian Economic and Social History Review*, 8.3.

Basu, S. (1974). 'Share of Labour in Manufacturing Industries', *Economic and Political Weekly*, 9.28.

Bauer, P. T. (1971). 'Economic History as Theory', *Economica*, 38.150.

Baumol, W. J., Bailey, E. E. and Willig, R. D. (1977). 'Weak Invisible Hand Theorems on the Sustainability of Multiproduct Natural Monopoly', *American Economic Review*, 67.3.

—— and Fischer, D. (1978). 'Cost Minimizing Number of Firms and Determination of Industry Structure', *Quarterly Journal of Economics*, 92.3.

——, Panzer, J. C., and Willig, R. D. (1982). *Contestable Markets and the Theory of Industry Structure*, New York.

—— and Willig, R. D. (1981). 'Fixed Costs, Sunk Costs, Entry Barriers, and Sustainability of Monopoly', *Quarterly Journal of Economics*, 96.3.

Bayly, C.A. (1983). *Rulers, Townsmen and Bazaars*, Cambridge.

Bean, R. (1973). 'War and the Birth of the Nation State', *Journal of Economic History*, Mar.

Beckerman, W. (1975). *In Defense of Economic Growth*, London.

Berlin, I. (1978). 'The Hedgehog and the Fox', in *Russian Thinkers*, London.

Berry, R. A., and Soligo, R. (1968). 'Rural–Urban Migration, Agricultural Output and the Supply Price of Labour in a Labour Surplus Economy', *Oxford Economic Papers*, 20.

Beteille, A. (1969). *Castes Old and New*, Bombay.

Bhaduri, A. (1973). 'Agricultural Backwardness under Semi-Feudalism', *Economic Journal*.

—— (1976). 'The Evolution of Land Relations in Eastern India under British Rule', *Indian Economic and Social History Review*, 13.1.

—— (1977). 'On the Formation of Usurious Interest Rates in Backward Agriculture', *Cambridge Journal of Economics*, 1.4.

Bhagwati, J. N., and Desai, P. (1970). *India: Planning for Industrialization*, London, Oxford University Press.

— and Srinivasan, T. N. (1974): 'On Reanalysing the Harris–Todaro Model', *American Economic Review*, 64.

— (1975). *Foreign Trade Regimes and Economic Development: India*, New York.

Bhalla, S., and Roy, P. (1988). 'Misspecification in Farm Productivity Analysis: The Role of Land Quality', *Oxford Economic Papers*, 40.

Bharadwaj, K. (1974). *Production Conditions in India Agriculture: A Study Based on Farm Management Surveys*, Cambridge.

Bhatia, B. M. (1963). *Famines in India, 1850–1945*, 2nd edn., Bombay.

— (1969). 'Terms of Trade and Economic Development: A Case Study of India—1861–1939', *Indian Economic Journal*, 16.4–5.

Bhatia, K. K., and Mukherjee, R. N. (1970). 'A Study of Wage Differences in India Industries', in Deshpande and Sandesara.

Bhattacharya, D. (1965). 'Trend of Wages in India: 1874–1900', *Artha Vijnana*, 7.3.

Bhattacharya, Dhires (1979). *A Concise History of the Indian Economy 1750–1950*, 2nd edn. New Delhi.

Bhattacharya, Durgaprasad and Roy, R. D. (n.d.). 'A Note on Agricultural Wages in Bengal and Bihar, 1793–1972', mimeo, Pre-Census Population Studies Unit, Indian Statistical Institute, Calcutta.

Bhattacharya, S. (1971). *Financial Foundations of the British Raj: Men and Ideas in the Post Mutiny Period of Reconstruction of Indian Public Finance, 1888–1872*, Simla.

— (1983). 'Towards an Interpretation of the Pre-Colonial Economy', *Economic and Political Weekly*, 1 Oct.

Binswanger, H., and Rosenzweig, M. (1981): 'Contractual Arrangements, Employment and Wages in Rural Labour Markets: A Critical Review', mimeo, Studies in Employment and Rural Development 67, Washington, D. C.

Blaug, M. (1976). 'Human Capital Theory: A Slightly Jaundiced Survey', *Journal of Economic Literature*, Sept.

—, Layard, R., and Woodhall, M. (1969). *The Causes of Graduate Unemployment in India*, London.

Bliss, C. J., and Stern, N. H. (1978): 'Productivity, Wages and Nutrition', pts. 1 and 2, *Journal of Development Economics*, 5.

Bloch, M. (1961). *Feudal Society*, London.

Blyn, G. (1966). *Agricultural Trends in India, 1891–1947, Output Availability and Productivity*, Philadelphia, Pa.

Borpujari, J. G. (1973). 'Indian Cottons and the Cotton Famine, 1860–65', *Indian Economic and Social History Review*, 10.1.

Bose, A. (1965). 'Six Decades of Urbanisation in India', *Indian Economic and Social History Review*, 2.1.

Boserup, E. (1965). *The Conditions of Agricultural Growth*, London.

— (1981). *Population and Technological Change*, Chicago.

Braudel, F. (1982). *Civilization and Capitalism*, vol. 2: *The Wheels of Commerce*, London.

Braverman, A., and Srinivasan, T. N. (1981). 'Credit and Share Cropping in Agrarian Societies', *Journal of Development Economics*, 9.3.

—— and Stiglitz J. E. (1981). 'Sharecropping and the Interlinking of Agrarian Markets', *American Economic Review*, 72.4.

Brennan, G., and Buchanan, J. M. (1980). *The Power to Tax*, Cambridge.

Brown, J. M. (1972). *Gandhi's Rise to Power: Indian Politics 1915–1922*, Cambridge.

—— (1977). *Gandhi and Civil Disobedience: The Mahatma in Indian Politics 1928–1934*, Cambridge.

Brown, N. M. (1964). 'The Sanctity of the Cow in Hinduism', *Economic Weekly*, 16.5–7.

Buchanan, D. H. (1934). *The Development of Capitalist Enterprise in India*, New York; reprinted 1966, London.

Burki, S. (1976). 'Public Works Programs in Developing Countries', mimeo, World Bank Staff Working Paper 224, Washington, DC.

Byers, T. J. (1979). 'Neo-populous Pipe Dreams: Daedelus in the Third World and the Myth of Urban Bias', *Journal of Peasant Studies*, 6.2.

Caldwell, B. (1982). *Beyond Positivism: Economic Methodology in the Twentieth Century*, London, 1982.

Cassen, R. M. (1978). *India: Population, Economy, Society*, New York.

CEHI—Cambridge Economic History of India: vol. i, see Raychaudhuri and Habib; vol. ii, see Kumar and Desai.

Census Commission, *Pocket Book of Population Statistics*, New Delhi.

Chakravarty, S. (1974). 'Reflections on the Growth Process in the Indian Economy', in Wadhwa.

Chakravarty, L. (1978). 'Emergence of an Industrial Labour Force in a Dual Economy: British India, 1880–1920', *Indian Economic and Social History Review*, July–Sept.

Chandok, H. L. (1980). *Wholesale Price Statistics India 1947–1978*, vol. 2, New Delhi.

Chandra, B. (1968). 'Reinterpretation of 19th century Indian Economic History', *Indian Economic and Social History Review*, 5.1.

Chandra, S. (1966). 'Some Aspects of the Growth of a Money Economy in India During the 17th century', *Indian Economy and Social History Review*, 3.4.

Charlesworth, N. (1982). *British Rule and the Indian Economy 1800–1914*, London.

Chatterjee, G. S., and Bhattacharya, N. (1971). 'On Rural–Urban Differentials in Consumer Prices and Per Capita Household Consumption in India by Levels of Living', *Sankhya*, series B.

Chaudhri, B. B. (1975). 'Land Market in Eastern India, 1793–1940', *Indian Economic and Social History Review*, 12.1–2.

Chaudhri, K. N. (1968). 'India's International Economy in the 19th Century: An Historical Survey', *Modern Asian Studies*, 2.1.

Chopra, P. (1981). 'Unto the Last', *Ceres*, Jan.–Feb.

Choudhury, U. D. R. (1983). 'The Behaviour of Capital–Labour Ratios in the Indian Economy, 1950–71', in Robinson *et al.*, vol. i.

Clark, C. (1957). *The Conditions of Economic Progress*, 3rd edn., London.

—— and Haswell, M. R. (1967). *The Economics of Subsistence Agriculture*, 3rd edn., London.

Cohn, B. S. (1969). 'Structural Change in Indian Rural Society, 1596–1885', in Frykenberg.

Colander, D. C. (ed.) (1984). *Neoclassical Political Economy*, Cambridge, Mass.

Colinvaux, P. (1983). *The Fates of Nations*, London.

Collier, P., and Lal, D. (1980). 'Coercion, Compassion and Competition: Wage and Employment Trends and Structures in Kenya 1800–1980s, mimeo, Washington, DC.

—— (1986). *Labour and Poverty in Kenya 1900–1980*, Oxford.

Corden, W. M. (1974). *Trade Policy and Economic Welfare*, Oxford.

—— and Findlay, R. (1975). 'Urban Unemployment, Intersectoral Capital Mobility and Development Policy', *Economica*, 42.

Cornwallis Correspondence, ed. C. Ross, 3 vols., London, 1859.

Coulborn, R. (ed.) (1956). *Feudalism in History*, Princeton, NJ.

Dairty, W. A. Jr. (1980). 'The Boserup Theory of Agricultural Growth: A Model for anthropological Economics', *Journal of Development Economics*, 7.2.

Dandekar, K. (1980). 'Employment Guarantee Scheme and Food for Work Programme', *Economic and Political Weekly*, 15.15.

Dandekar, V. M. (1954). *Second Report on the Poona Schedule of the National Sample Survey 1950–51*, Poona.

—— (1964). 'Problem of Numbers in Cattle Development', *Economic Weekly*, 16.5–7.

—— (1969). 'India's Sacred Cattle and Cultural Ecology', *Economic and Political Weekly*, 4.39.

—— (1970). 'Sacred Cattle and More Sacred Production Functions', *Economic and Political Weekly*, 5.12.

—— and Rath, N. (1971). *Poverty in India*, Poona, India School of Political Economy.

Dantwala, M. L. (1973). *Poverty in India Then and Now, 1870–1970*, New Delhi.

—— (1979). 'Agricultural Policy in India since Independence', in C. M. Shah and C. N. Vakil (eds.), *Agricultural Development of India*, New Delhi.

Darling, M. L. (1925). *The Punjab Peasant in Prosperity and Debt*, 4th edn., New Delhi.

Dasgupta, R. (1971). 'Estimation of Demographic Measures for India, 1881, Based on Census Age Distribution', *Population Studies*, 25.

—— (1976). 'Factory Labour in Eastern India: Sources of Supply 1855–1946,' *Indian Economic and Social History Review*, July–Sept.

Datta, J. M. (1962). 'Population of India about 320 BC', *Man in India*, 42.4.

Datta, K. L. (1914). *Report on the Enquiry Into the Rise of Prices in India*, Calcutta.

Davis, K. (1951). *The Population of India and Pakistan*, Princeton, NJ.

—— (1955). 'Social and Demographic Aspects of Economic Development in India', in Kuznets *et al.*

Day, W. M. (1949). 'Relative Permanence of Former Boundaries in India', *Scottish Geographical Magazine*, 65.3.

Deane, P., and Cole, W. (1964). *British Economic Growth 1688–1959* Cambridge.

de Jasy, Anthony (1985). *The State*, Oxford.

Desai, A. V. (1965). 'The Livestock Situation', *Economic Weekly*. 17.5–7.

—— (1972). 'Population and Standards of Living in Akbar's Time', *Indian Economic and Social History Review*, 9.1.

—— (1978). 'Population and Standards of Living in Akbar's Time: A Second Look', *Indian Economic and Social History Review*, 15.1.

—— (1981). 'Factors Underlying the Slow Growth of Indian Industry', *Economic and Political Weekly*, 16.10–12.

Desai, M., and Mazumdar, D. (1970). 'A Test of the Hypothesis of Disguised Unemployment', *Economica*, 37.

Deshpande, L. K. and Sandesera, J. (1970). *Wages Policy and Wage Determination in India*, Bombay.

Dey, A. K. (1975). 'Rates of Growth of Agriculture and Industry', *Economic and Political Weekly*, 10.25–6.

—— (1977). 'Green Revolution Contrasts: Rice and Wheat', *Economic and Political Weekly*, 4 June.

Dholakia, B. H. (1974). *The Sources of Economic Growth in India*, Baroda.

—— (1976). 'Determinants of Inter-Industry Wage Structure in India', *Indian Journal of Industrial Relations*, 12.

—— (1979). 'Wage Structure in Consumer Goods and Capital Goods Industries in India', *Indian Journal of Labour Economics*.

Dixit, A. (1973). 'Models of Dual Economies', in Mirrlees and Stern.

Doeringer, P., and Piore, M. J. (1971). *Internal Labour Markets and Manpower Analysis*, Lexington, Mass.

Dore, R. P. (1961). 'Function and Cause', *American Sociological Review*, 26; reprinted in A. Ryan (ed.), *The Philosophy of Social Explanation*, Oxford, 1973.

Dreze, J. (1979). 'Human Capital and Risk-Bearing', *Stanford Institute for Mathematical Studies in the Social Sciences*, Reprint Series 288, reprinted from *Geneva Papers on Risk and Insurance Association*, 12.

Dumont, L. (1970). *Homo Hierarchicus* London.

Durand, J. D. (1977). 'Historical Estimates of World Population', *Population and Development Review*, 3.3.

Dutt, R. C. (1901). *The Economic History of India*, vols. i and ii, 1st Indian Reprint, New Delhi, 1960; first published London, 1901.

Dutt, R. P. (1940). *India Today*, London.

Dutta, B. (1980a). 'Intersectoral Disparities and Income Distribution in India, 1960–61 to 1973–74', *Indian Economic Review*, 15.2.

—— (1980b). 'Industrial Wage Structure in India: A Survey', mimeo, Washington, DC.

Edwardes, M. (1967). *British India 1777–1947*, London, Sidgwick & Jackson.

—— (1969). *Bound to Exile: The Victorians in India*, London.

Elliot, J. H. (1961). 'The Decline of Spain', *Past and Present*, 20.

Elster, J. (1979). *Ulysses and the Sirens: Studies in Rationality and Irrationality*, Cambridge.

—— (1983). *Explaining Technical Change*, Cambridge.

Evenson, R. E., and Binswanger, H. P. (1980). 'Estimating Labour Demand Functions for Indian Agriculture', mimeo, ADC–ICRISAT conference, Hyderabad.

Ezekiel, H. (ed.) (1984). *The Economic Times Statistical Survey of the Indian Economy*, Bombay.

Fei, J., and Ranis, G. (1964). *The Development of a Labour Surplus Economy*, Homewood, Ill.

Fields, G. (1974). 'The Private Demand for Education in Relation to Labour Market Conditions in Less-developed Countries', *Economic Journal*, 84.

Findlay, R., and Wilson, J. D. (1987). 'The Political Economy of Leviathan', in A. Razin and E. Sadka (eds.), *Economic Policy in Theory and Practice*, London.

Flew, A. (1985). *Thinking about Social Thinking*, Oxford.

Fonseca, A. J. (1964). *Wage Determination and Organised Labour in India*, London.

Forrester, D. B. (1980). *Caste and Christianity*, New Jersey.

Friedman, M. (1968). 'The Role of Monetary Policy,' *American Economic Review*, 58.

Frykenberg, R. E. (ed.) (1969). *Land Control and Social Structure in Indian History*, Madison, Wis.

—— (1985). 'Caste, Morality and Western Religion under the Raj', *Modern Asian Studies*, 19.2.

Gadgil, D. R. (1971). *The Industrial Evolution of India in Recent Times, 1860–1939*, 5th edn., New Delhi.

Galenson, W. (1979). 'The Labour Force, Wages and Living Standards', in W. Galenson (ed.), *Economic Growth and Structural Changes in Taiwan*, Ithaca, NY.

Gallagher, J., Johnson, G. and Seal, A. (eds.) (1973). *Locality, Province and Nation: Essays on Indian Politics 1870–1940*, Cambridge.

Gandhi, M. K. (1958–). *The Collected Works of Mahatma Gandhi*, Delhi.

Ganguli, B. N. (ed.) (1964). *Readings in Indian Economic History*, Bombay.

Garraty, J. A. (1978). *Unemployment in History*, New York.

Gazetteer of India (1975). Vol. ii *Economic Structure and Activities*, New Delhi.

Geddes, W. R. (1954). *The Land Dayaks of Sarawak*, Colonial Research Study 14, London, HMSO.

Gersowitz, M., Diaz-Alejandro, C. F., Ranis, G., and Rosenzweig, M. R. (eds.) (1982). *The Theory and Experience of Economic Development*, London.

Ghatak, S. (1976). *Rural Money Markets in India*, New Delhi.

Ghosh, S. (1966). *Indian Labour in the Early Phase of Industrialization*, Calcutta.

Goodwin, R. M. (1967). 'A Growth Cycle', in C. Feinstein (ed.), *Socialism, Capitalism and Economic Growth*, Cambridge.

Gordon, D. (1974). 'A Neo-Classical Theory of Keynesian Unemployment', *Economic Inquiry*, Dec.

Govt. of India (1961a). *Census of India 1961: Household Economic Tables*, New Delhi.

—— (1961b). *Estimates of National Income, 1948–9 to 1959–60*, New Delhi.

—— (1965). *Gazetter of India*, vols. i, ii, and II, New Delhi.

—— (1969). *Report of the National Commission on Labour*, New Delhi.

—— (1970). *Report of the Committee of Experts on Unemployment Estimates* (Dantwala Committee Report), New Delhi.

—— (1971a). *Pocket Book of Population Statistics*, New Delhi.

—— (1971b). *Census of India 1971*, New Delhi.

—— (1972a). *National Sample Survey 25th Round (1970–71)*, provisional tables on Employment and Unemployment Situation in India, New Delhi.

—— (1972b). *Report of the Irrigation Commission*, New Delhi, Ministry of Agriculture.

—— (1973a). *Report of the Committee on Unemployment* (Bhagwati Committee Report), New Delhi.

—— (1973b). *Indian Agriculture in Brief*, 12th edn, New Delhi.

—— (1974a). *Statistical Abstract: India 1972*, New Delhi.

—— (1974b). *Agricultural Census 1970–71*, New Delhi.

—— (1976). *Report of the National Commission on Agriculture*, pt. 1, New Delhi.

—— (1978). *Draft Five Year Plan, 1978–83*, New Delhi.

—— (1980a). *Draft Sixth Five Year Plan 1978–83, Revised*, New Delhi.

—— (1980b). *Statistical Abstract: India 1978*, New Delhi.

—— (1980c). *Basic Statistics Relating to the Indian Economy 1950–51 to 1978–79*, New Delhi.

—— (1983). *Sixth Five Year Plan 1980-85: Mid-term Appraisal*.

—— (annual). *Economic Survey*, New Delhi.

—— . *Studies in the Economics of Farm Management*, various States and various years, New Delhi.

Gray, J. H. (1987). 'The Economic Approach to Human Behaviour: Its Prospects and Limitations', in G. Radnitzky and P. Berholz (eds.), *Economic Imperialism*, New York.

Guha, A. (1968). 'Colonization of Assam: Years of Transitional Crisis 1826–40', *Indian Economic and Social History Review*, 5.2.

Habib, I. (1963). *The Agrarian System of Mughal India*, Bombay.

—— (1980). 'The Technology and Economy of Moghul India', *Indian Economic and Social History Review*, 17.1.

Hahn, F. (1973). *On the Notion of Equilibrium in Economics*, Cambridge.

—— (1984). *Macroeconomics and Equilibrium*, Oxford.

Hanumantha Rao, C. M. (1969). 'India's "Surplus" Cattle: Some Empirical Results', *Economic and Political Weekly*, 4.52.

Harberger, A. (1971). 'On Measuring the Social Opportunity Cost of Labour', *International Labour Review*, 103.

Harnetty, P. (1970). 'Cotton Exports and Indian Agriculture', *Economic History Review*, 24 (2nd ser.).

—— (1972). *Imperialism and Free Trade: Lancashire and India in the mid 19th century*, Manchester.

Harris, J., and Todaro, M. (1970). 'Migration, Unemployment and Development: A Two Sector Analysis', *American Economic Review*, 60.

Harris, M. (1975). *Cows, Pigs, Wars and Witches: The Riddles of Culture*, London.

Hayek, F. A. (ed.) (1935). *Collectivist Economic Planning*, London.

—— (1967). *Studies in Philosophy, Politics and Economics*, London.

Heal, G. M. (1973). *The Theory of Economic Planning*, Amsterdam.

Healey, J. M. (1965). *The Development of Social Overhead Capital in India 1950-60*, Oxford.

Henderson, P. D., and Lal, D. (1976). 'UNCTAD IV, The Commodities Problem and International Economic Reform', *ODI Review*, 2.

Herdt, R., and Baker, E. A. (1972). 'Agricultural Wages, Production and the High Yielding Varieties', *Economic and Political Weekly*, 7.13.

Heston, A. (1971). 'An Approach to the Sacred Cow in India', *Current Anthropology*, 12.

—— (1973). 'Official Yields Per Acre in India, 1886–1947: Some Questions of Interpretation', *Indian Economic and Social History Review*, 10.4.

—— (1977). 'The Standards of Living in Akbar's Time: A Comment', *Indian Economic and Social History Review*, 14.3.

—— (1978). 'A Further Critique of Historical Yields Per Acre in India', *Indian Economic and Social History Review*, 15.2.

—— (1983). 'National Income', in *CEHI*, vol. ii.

Hey, J. D. (1979). *Uncertainty in Microeconomics*, New York.

Hicks, J. R. (1936). 'Mr Keynes's "Theory of Employment" ', *Economic Journal*, 46.2.

—— (1969). *A Theory of Economic History*, Oxford.

—— (1973). *Capital and Time: A New-Austrian Theory*, Oxford.

—— (1977). *Economic Perspectives*, Oxford.

Hirschman, A. O. (1958). *The Strategy of Economic Development*, New Haven, Conn.

Hirshleifer, J. (1977). 'Economics from a Biological Viewpoint', *Journal of Law and Economics*, 20.1.

—— (1982). 'Evolutionary Models in Economics and Law', *Research in Law and Economics*, 4.

Hocart, A. M. (1950). *Caste: A Comparative Study*, London.

Hutton, J. M. (1963). *Caste in India*, 4th edn., Oxford.

Indian Institute of Public Opinion (IIPO) (1979). 'An Analysis of Distortions of Destitution in Choosing Families for Antyodaya Relief', *Quarterly Economic Report of the Indian Institute of Public Opinion*, 96.

Ishikawa, S. (1967). *Economic Development in Asian Perspective*, Tokyo.

Jackson, D. (1972). 'Wage Policy and Industrial Relations in India', *Economic Journal*, 82.

de Jasy, A. (1985). *The State*, Oxford.

Jaynes, D. J. (1979). 'Economics of Land Tenure', mimeo, ADC–ICRISAT conference, Hyderabad.

Jha, P. S. (1980). *India: The Political Economy of Stagnation*, New Delhi.

—— (1985). 'The Public Sector in India: An Appraisal', mimeo, Washington, DC.

Johri, C. K. (1967). *Unionism in a Developing Economy*, Bombay.

—— and Agarwal, N. C. (1966). 'Inter-industry Wage Structure in India, 1950–1961', *Indian Journal of Industrial Relations*, 2.

—— and Mishra, V. K. (1973). 'Wage Payment Systems Wage Differentials and Incomes Policy', *Indian Journal of Industrial Relations*, 9.

Jones, E. L. (1981). *The European Miracle*, Cambridge.

Jorgenson, D. W. (1961). 'The Development of a Dual Economy', *Economic Journal*, 71.

—— (1967a). 'Surplus Agricultural Labour and the Development of a Dual Economy', *Oxford Economic Papers*, 19.

—— (1967b). 'Testing Alternative Theories of the Development of a Dual Economy' in I. Adelman and E. Thorbecke (eds.), *The Theory and Design of Economic Development*, Baltimore, Johns Hopkins University Press, reprinted in I. Livingstone (ed.), *Penguin Readings in Economic Development*, London, 1971.

Jose, A. V. (1973). 'Wage Rates of Agricultural Labourers in Kerala', *Economic and Political Weekly*, 8.4–6.

—— (1974). 'Trends in Real Wage Rates of Agricultural Labourers', *Economic and Political Weekly*, 9.3.

—— (1978). 'Real Wages, Employment and Income of Agricultural Labourers', *Economic and Political Weekly*, 13.12.

Kalecki, M. (1972). 'Social and Economic Aspects of "Intermediate Regimes" ', in his *Selected Essays: Socialist and Mixed Economy*, Cambridge.

Kao, C. H. C., Anschel, K. R. and Eicher, C. K. (1964). 'Disguised Unemployment in Agriculture', in C. K. Eicher and L. Witt (eds.), *Agriculture in Economic Development*, New York.

Karnik, V. B. (1978). *Indian Trade Unions: A Survey*, 3rd edn., Bombay.

Ketkar, S. V. (1909). *History of Caste in India*, reprinted 1979, Jaipur.

Keynes, J. M. (1936). *The General Theory of Employment, Interest and Money*, London.

Klass, M. (1980). *Caste*, Philadelphia.

Kosambi, D. D. (1981). *The Culture and Civilisation of Ancient India in Historical Outline*, New Delhi.

Krishna, R. (1963). 'Farm Supply Response in India: Pakistan', *Economic Journal*, 73.1.

—— (1964). 'The Growth of Aggregate Agricultural Output in the Punjab', *Indian Economic Journal*, July–Sept.

—— (1976). 'Rural Unemployment: A Survey of Concepts and Estimates for India', World Bank Staff Working Paper 234, Washington, DC.

—— (1980). *The Center and the Periphery: Inter State Disparities in Economic Development*, (G. L. Mehta Memorial Lecture), *Economic Times*, 10, 12, and 13 May.

Krishnaji, N. (1971). 'Wages of Agricultural Labour', *Economic and Political Weekly*, 6.39.

Krishnamurthy, J. (1967). 'Changes in the Composition of the Working Force in Manufacturing, 1901–51: A Theoretical and Empirical Analysis', *Indian Economic and Social History Review*, 4.1.

—— (1972a). 'Working Force in 1971 Census', *Economic and Political Weekly*, 15 Jan.

—— (1972b). 'The Growth of Agricultural Labour in India: A Note', *Indian Economic and Social History Review*, 9.3.

—— (n.d.). 'Population and Economic Activity', mimeo, New Delhi.

Kulke, E. (1974). *The Parsees*, Munich; Indian edn., New Delhi, 1978.

Kumar, A. (1985). 'Sizing Up the Black Economy: Some Issues Raised by the NIPFP Methodology', *Economic and Political Weekly*, 20.35.

Kumar, D. (1965). *Land and Caste in South India: Agricultural Labour in the Madras Presidency during the 19th century*, Cambridge.

—— (1967). Review of Blyn (1966), *Indian Economic and Social History Review*, 4.4.

—— (1972). 'Recent Research in the Economic History of Modern India', *Indian Economic and Social History Review*, 9.1.

—— (1974). 'Income Distribution and Poverty in India', *World Development*, 2.1.

—— (1975). 'Landownership and Inequality in Madras Presidency, 1853–54 to 1946–47', *Indian Economic and Social History Review*, 12.3.

—— and Desai, M. (eds.). *The Cambridge Economic History of India*, vol. ii, c. *1750–1970*, Cambridge.

—— and Krishnamurthy, J. (1981). 'The Evolution of Labour Markets in India 1857–1947', mimeo, Employment and Rural Development Division, Washington, DC.

Kuran, T. (1987). 'Preference Falsification, Policy Continuity and Collective Conservatism', *Economic Journal*, 97.

Kurve, M. B. S. (1948). 'Agricultural Wages and Systems of Payment in the Bombay Karnataka', *Indian Journal of Agricultural Economics*, Apr.

Kuznets, S. (1965). *Modern Economic Growth*, New Haven, Conn.

—— (1974). *Population, Capital and Growth*, London.

—— , Moore, S. W. E., and Spengler, J. J. (eds.) (1955). *Economic Growth: Brazil, India, Japan*, Durham, N.C.

Lal, D. (1969). *The Implications of Economic Controls and Liberalization*, UN ECAFE Growth Studies series 6, Bangkok.

—— (1972a). *Wells and Welfare: An Exploratory Cost-Benefit Study of the Economics of Small-scale Irrigation in Maharashtra*, Paris.

—— (1972b). 'Poverty and Unemployment: A Question of Policy', *South Asian Review*, 5.4.

—— (1973a). 'Disutility of Effort Migration and the Shadow Wage Rate', *Oxford Economic Papers*, 25.1.

—— (1973b). *New Economic Policies for India*, London.

—— (1973c). 'Economics of Irrigation Engineers', *Economic and Political Weekly*, 8.26.

—— (1974a). *Methods of Project Analysis: A Review*, World Bank Staff Occasional Paper 16, Baltimore, Md.

—— (1974b). 'The Structure of Earnings in India', mimeo, New Delhi.

—— (1974c). 'Rural–Urban Consumer Price Differentials—By States', mimeo, New Delhi.

—— (1974d). 'The Determinants of Wages, Migration, and Urban Unemployment in India', mimeo, New Delhi.

—— (1974e). 'The Anatomy of Migration in India', mimeo, New Delhi.

—— (1975a). *Appraising Foreign Investment in Developing Countries*, London.

—— (1975b). 'Private and Social Rates of Return in Indian Manufacturing', *Economic and Political Weekly*, 10.52.

—— (1976a). 'Agricultural Growth, Real Wages, and the Rural Poor in India, *Economic and Political Weekly*, 26.

—— (1976b). 'Supply Price and Surplus Labour: Some Indian Evidence', *World Development*, 4.10–11.

—— (1976c). 'Distribution and Development: A Review Article', *World Development*, 4.9.

—— (1977). *Unemployment and Wage Inflation in Industrial Economies*, Paris.

—— (1977a). 'Agricultural Growth and Rural Real Wages: A Reply', *Economic and Political Weekly*, 12.20.

—— (1978a). 'Shadow Pricing and Wage and Employment Issues in National Economic Planning', *The Bangladesh Development Studies*, Dacca, 1978, reprinted as World Bank Reprint Series 131, Washington , DC.

—— (1978b). 'On the Multinationals', *Overseas Development Institute Review*, 2.

—— (1979a). 'The Continuing Hangover', *Seminar*, 244.

—— (1979b). 'Indian Export Incentives', *Journal of Development Economics*, 6.1.

—— (1979c). 'Theories of Industrial Wage Structures: A Review', *Indian Journal of Industrial Relations*, 15.2, reprinted as World Bank Reprint Series 142, Washington, DC (n.d.).

—— (1980a). *Prices for Planning: Towards the Reform of Indian Planning*, London.

—— (1980b). 'Public Enterprises', in J. Cody, H. Hughes, and D. Wall (eds.), *Policies for Industrial Progress in Developing Countries*, Oxford.

—— (1980c). 'Do Keynesian Diagnoses and Remedies Need Revision?', in A. Maddison and B. S. Wilpstra (eds.), *Unemployment: The European Perspective*, London.

—— (1980d). 'Field Notes on Industrial Wages in India', Studies in Employment and Rural Development 65, Washington, DC.

—— (1980e). *A Liberal International Economic Order: The International Monetary System and Economic Development*, Princeton, NJ.

—— (1981). *Minimum Labour Standards: A Variant of the Pauper Labour Argument*, London.

—— (1983). *The Poverty of 'Development Economics'* London; American ed. Cambridge, Mass. 1985.

—— (1985). 'Nationalism, Socialism and Planning: Influential Ideas in the South', *World Development*, 13.6.

—— and Duane, P. (1972). 'A Reappraisal of the Purna Irrigation Project in Maharashtra, India', mimeo, Washington, DC.

Lal, R. N. (1977). *Capital Formation and Its Financing in India*, New Delhi.

Lambert, R. D. (1963). *Workers, Factories and Social Change in India*, Princeton, NJ.

Lane, F. C. (1958). 'Economic Consequences of Organised Violence', *Journal of Economic History*, 18.4.

Lange, O., and Taylor, F. M. (1938). *On the Economic Theory of Socialism*, University of Minnesota Press, Minneapolis.

Leibenstein, H. (1957). *Economic Backwardness and Economic Growth*, New York.

Lele, U. (1971). *Food Grain Marketing in India*, Ithaca, NY.

Lerner, A. P. (1946). *The Economics of Control*, London.

Letham, A. J. (1978). 'Merchandise Trade Imbalances and Uneven Economic Development in India and China', *Journal of European Economic History*, 7.1.

Lewis, J. P. (1972). 'The Public Works Approach to Low End Poverty Problems', *Journal of Development Planning*, 5.

Lewis, W. A. (1954). 'Economic Development with Unlimited Supplies of Labour', *Manchester School*, May.

—— (1969). *Aspects of Tropical Trade*, Stockholm.

—— (ed.) (1970). *Tropical Development 1880-1913: Studies in Economic Progress*, London.

—— (1972). 'Reflections on Unlimited Labour', in L. E. di Marco (ed.), *International Economics and Development*, New York.

—— (1978). *Growth and Fluctuations 1870-1913*, London.

——(1979). 'The Dual Economy Revisited', *Manchester School*, Sept.

Lidman, R., and Domrese, R. J. (1970). 'India', in Lewis.

Lipton, M. (1977). *Why Poor People Stay Poor*, London.

Little, I. M. D. (1982a). 'Indian Industrialisation before 1945', in Gersowitz *et al.*

—— (1982b). *Economic Development*, New York.

—— and Mirrlees, J. A. (1974). *Project Appraisal and Planning for Developing Countries*, London.

——, Scitovsky, T. and Scott, M. Fg. (1970). *Industry and Trade in Some Developing Countries: A Comparative Study*, London.

Luce, R. D., and Raiffa, H. (1966). *Games and Decisions*, New York.

Macaulay, T. B. (1898). *The Complete Works of Lord Macaulay*, 12 vols., London.

McAlpin, M. B. (1975). 'Railroads, Cultivation Patterns, and Foodgrain Availability: India 1860-1900', *Indian Economic and Social History Review*, 12.1.

McLane, J. (1963). 'The Drain of Wealth and Indian Nationalism at the Turn of the Century', in Raychaudhuri. (1963).

McNeill, W. H. (1976). *Plagues and Peoples*, New York.

—— (1983). *The Great Frontier: Freedom and Hierarchy in Modern Times*, Princeton, NJ.

—— (1984). 'Migration in Historical Perspective', *Population and Development Review*, 10.1.

MacPherson, W. J. (1972). 'Economic Development in India under the British Crown, 1858–1947', in A. J. Youngson (ed.), *Economic Development in the Long Run*, London.

Madan, B. K. (1977). *The Real Wages of Industrial Labour in India*, New Delhi.

Maddison, A. (1971). *Class Structure and Economic Growth: India and Pakistan since the Moghuls*, London.

—— (1985). 'Alternative Estimates of the Real Product of India 1900–46', *Indian Economic and Social History Review*.

Majumdar, R. C., Raychandhri, H. C., and Datta, K. (1978). *An Advanced History of India*, 4th edn., London.

Malinowski, B. (1927). *Sex and Repression in Savage Society*, New York.

Marx, K. (1867). *Capital*, English trans., 3 vols., Moscow, 1965, 1966, 1967.

Mason, E. *et al.* (1980). *The Economic and Social Modernisation of the Republic of Korea*, Cambridge, Mass.

Matsui, T. (1968). 'On the 19th Century Indian Economic History. A Review of a Reinterpretation', *Indian Economic and Social History Review*, 5.1.

Mazumdar, D. (1959). 'The Marginal Productivity Theory of Wages and Disguised Unemployment', *Review of Economic Studies*, 26.

—— (1973). 'Labour Supply in Early Industrialization: The Case of the Bombay Textile Industry', *Economic History Review*, 2nd series, 26.3.

Meek, D. B. (1937). 'Some Measures of Economic Activity in India', *Journal of the Royal Statistical Society*, pt. 3.

Mehra, S. (1966). 'Surplus Labour in India Agriculture', *Indian Economic Review*, Apr.

Mersch, W. (1975). 'The Formation of a Rural Proletariat on the Tea Plantations of Eastern India 1860–1921', paper presented at the conference on Indian Economic and Social History, 1975, Cambridge.

Metcalf, T. R. (1979). *Land, Landless and the British Raj: Northern India in the 19th century*, Delhi.

Minhas, B. S. (1970). 'Rural Poverty Land Redistribution and Development', *Indian Economic Review*, 5.1.

——, Parikh, K. S. and Srinivasan, T. N., with Marglin, S. A., and Weisskopf, T. E. (1972). *Scheduling the Operations of the Bhakra System*, Calcutta.

Mirrlees, J. A. (1975). 'A Pure Theory of Underdeveloped Economies', in Reynolds (1975).

—— (1979). 'The Optimal Structure of Incentives and Authority within an Organisation', *Bell Journal of Economics*, spring.

—— and Stern, N. H. (eds.) (1973). *Models of Economic Growth*, London.

von Mises, L. (1935). 'Economic Calculation in the Socialist Commonwealth', in Hayek 1935.

Mishra, B. B. (1961). *The Indian Middle Classes*, London.

Mishra, S. (1948). 'Agricultural Wages in Relation to Rural Cost of Living,' *Indian Journal of Economics*, July.

Mishra, S. N. (1970). 'Some Inferences from Compositional Changes in India's Livestock Population (1920–1966)', *Indian Journal of Agricultural Economics*, 25.4.

Mitra, A. (1977). *Terms of Trade and Class Relations*, London.

Mitra, A. and Mukherjee, S. (1980). *Population, Food and Land Inequality in India—1971*, New Delhi.

Moore, B., Jr. (1967). *Social Origins of Dictatorship and Democracy*, London.

Moosvi, S. (1973). 'Production, Consumption and Population in Akbar's Time', *Indian Economic and Social History Review*, 10.2.

—— (1977). 'Note on Professor Heston's "Standard of Living in Akbar's Time" ', *Indian Economic and Social History Review*, 14.3.

—— (1978). 'The Zamindar's Share in the Peasant Surplus in the Moghul Empire: Evidence of the Ain-i-Akbari Statistics', *Indian Economic and Social History Review*, 15.3.

—— (1987). *The Economy of the Muqhal Empire* c. *1595*, Delhi.

Moreland, W. H. (1920). *India at the Death of Akbar*, London.

—— (1929). *The Agrarian System of Moslem India*, Cambridge; 1929, revised edn., New Delhi, 1968.

Morris, M. D. (1965). *The Emergence of an Industrial Labour Force in India*, Berkeley, CA.

—— (1966). 'Economic Change and Agriculture in 19th century India', *Indian Economic and Social History Review*, 3.2.

—— (1967). 'Values as an Obstacle to Economic Growth in South Asia: An Historical Survey', *Journal of Economic History*, 27.4.

—— (1968a). 'Towards a Reinterpretation of 19th Century Indian Economic History', *Indian Economic and Social History Review* 5.1, reprinted from Journal of Economic History, Dec. 1963.

—— (1968b). 'Trends and Tendencies in Indian Economic History', *Indian Economic and Social History Review*, 5.4.

—— (1974). 'Private Investment on the Indian Sub-continent 1900–1939. Some Methodological Considerations', *Modern Asian Studies*, 8.4.

Morris-Jones, W. H. (1971). *The Government and Politics of India*, 3rd edn., London.

Mukerjee, T. (1972). 'The Theory of Economic Drain: The Impact of British Rule on the Indian Economy 1840–1900', in K. E. Boulding and T. Mukerjee (eds.), *Economic Imperialism*, Ann Arbor, Mich.

Mukerji, K. (1965). *Levels of Economic Activity and Public Expenditure in India*, Poona and London.

Mukherjee, M. (1969). *National Income of India: Trends and Structure*, Calcutta.

Mukherjee, R. (1967). *Economic History of India 1600–1800*, Allahabad.

Mukhia, H. (1981). 'Was There Feudalism in Indian History?', *Journal of Peasant Studies*, 8.3.

Myrdal, G. (1968). *Asian Drama*, New York.

Naipaul, V. S. *An Area of Darkness; An Experience of India*, London.

Nanavati, M. B., and Anjaria, J. J. (1965). *The Indian Rural Problem*, Bombay.

Naoroji, D. (1880). *The Poverty of India*, London.

Narain, D. (1965). *The Impact of Price Movements on Areas Under Selected Crops in India 1900–39*, Cambridge.

Nath, P. (1929). *A Study in the Economic Conditions of Ancient India*, London.

Nath, R. (1976). *Occupational Pattern and Wage Structure in Indian Industries*, Delhi.

Nath, S. K. (1974). 'Estimating the Seasonal Marginal Products of Labour in Agriculture', *Oxford Economic Papers*, 26.

National Council of Applied Economic Research (1976). *Wage Differentials in Indian Industries*, Delhi.

National Sample Survey (NSS), Reports, various subjects and years, Delhi.

Nayyar, R. (1976). 'Agricultural Growth and Rural Wages: A Comment', *Economic and Political Weekly*, 6 Nov.

Neale, W. C. (1962). *Economic Change in Rural India: Land Tenure and Reform in Uttar Pradesh 1800–1955*, New Haven, Conn.

Nehru, J. (1936). *An Autobiography*, 1st Indian edn., New Delhi.

—— (1956). *The Discovery of India*, 6th edn., Calcutta.

Newberry, D. M. G. (1977). 'Risk Sharing, Sharecropping and Uncertain Labour Markets', *Review of Economic Studies*, 44.3.

Nishimizu, M., and Robinson, S. (1983). 'Sectoral Productivity Growth in Semi-industrial Countries: A Comparative Analysis', Washington, DC.

North, D. C. (1981). *Structure and Change in Economic History*, New York.

—— and Thomas, R. P. (1973). *The Rise of the Western World: A New Economic History*, Cambridge.

Nove, A. (1961). *The Soviet Economy*, London.

—— (1969). *An Economic History of the USSR*, London.

—— (1977). *The Soviet Economic System*, London.

Nurkse, R. (1953). *Problems of Capital Formation in Underdeveloped Countries*, Oxford.

Palekar, S. A. (1962). *Problems of Wage Policy for Economic Development*, Bombay.

Pandey, S. M. (1973). 'Wage Determination in Indian Agriculture: An Empirical Analysis', Seminar on Incomes Policy and Industrial Relations, New Delhi.

Papola, T. S. (1970). *Principles of Wage Determination: An Empirical Study*, Bombay.

—— (1972). 'Inter-regional' Variations in Manufacturing Wages in India: Industrial Structure and Region Effects', *Indian Journal of Industrial Relations*, 8.

—— and K. K. Subrahmanian (1975). *Wage Structure and Labour Mobility in a Local Labour Market*, Ahmedabad.

Parkin, M., and Nobay, A. (eds.) (1975). *Current Economic Problems*, Cambridge.

Patel, S. J. (1952). *Agricultural Labourers in Modern India and Pakistan*, Bombay.

—— (1965). *Essays in Economic Transition*, New York.

Phelps, E. S. *et al.* (1970). *Microeconomic Foundations of Employment and Inflation Policy*, London.

Piggott, S. (1950). *Prehistoric India*, Harmondsworth.

Prabha, C. (1969). 'Disrict Wise Rates of Growth of Agricultural Output in East and West Punjab during the Pre-Partition Periods', *Indian Social Economic and Social History Review*, 6.4.

Prakash, I. (1964). 'Organisation of Industrial Production in Urban Centers in India During the 17th Century with Special Reference to Textiles', in Ganguli.

Raj, K. N. (1960). *Some Economic Aspects of the Bharkra-Nangal Project*, New Delhi.

—— (1969). 'Investment in Livestock in "Agrarian Economies" ' *Indian Economic Review*, 4.1.

—— (1971). 'Indian's Sacred Cattle: Theories and Empirical Findings', *Economic and Political Weekly*, 6.13.

—— (1973). 'The Politics and Economics of Intermediate Regimes', *Economic and Political Weekly*, 7.

—— (1976). 'Trends in Rural Unemployment in India', *Economic and Political Weekly*, 11.31–3.

—— (1979). 'Recent Economic Trends in India and Prospective Changes in Development Strategy', *Seminar*, 244.

Ranadive, K. (1970). 'Neglected Dimensions in Incomes Policy', in Deshpande and Sandesara.

Rao, V. M. (1972). 'Agricultural Wages in India: A Reliability Analysis', *Indian Journal of Agricultural Economics*, 27.3.

Rath, N. (1973). 'Regional Variation in Level and Cost of Living in Rural India in 1961–62', *Artha Vijnana*, 15.4.

—— and Joshi, R. V. (1966). 'Relative Movements of Agricultural Wage Rates and Cereal Prices: Some Indian Evidence', *Artha Vijnana*, 7.3.

Ray, R. K. (1979). *Industrialization in India: Growth and Conflict in the Private Sector 1914–47*, Delhi.

Ray, R., and Ray, R. (1973). 'The Dynamics of Continuity in Rural Bengal Under the British Imperium: A Study of Quasi-stable Equilibrium in Underdeveloped Societies in a Changing World', *Indian Economic and Social History Review*, 10.2.

Raychaudhuri, T. (ed.) (1963). *Contributions to Indian Economic History*, ii, Calcutta.

—— (1965). 'The Agrarian System of Moghul India', *Enquiry*, 2.

—— (1968). 'A Re-interpretation of 19th century Indian Economic History?', *Indian Economic and Social History Review*, 5.1.

—— (1969). 'Permanent Settlement in Operation: Bakargang District, East Bengal, in Frykenberg (1985).

—— and Habib, I. (eds.) (1982). *The Cambridge Economic History of India*, vol. i, *c. 1200–c. 1750*, Cambridge.

Reddy, A. M. (1979). 'Wages Data from the Private Agricultural Accounts, Nellore District 1893–1974', *Indian Economic and Social History Review*.

Rees, A. (1963). *The Economics of Work and Pay*, New York.

Reynolds, L. G. (ed.) (1975). *Agriculture in Development Theory*, New Haven, Conn.

—— (1983). 'The Spread of Economic Growth to the Third World, 1850–1980', *Journal of Economic Literature*, 21.

—— (1985). *Economic Growth in the Third World, 1850–1982*, New Haven, Conn.

Reynolds, N., and Sundar, P. (1977). 'Maharashtra's Employment Guarantee Scheme: A Program to Emulate', *Economic and Political Weekly*, 16 July.

Robinson, A., Brahmananda, P. R., and Deshpande, L. K. (1983). *Employment Policy in a Developing Country: A Case Study of India*, 2 vols., London.

Robinson, E. A. G., and Kidron, M. (eds.) (1970). *Economic Development in South Asia*, London.

Rodgers, G. B. (1975). 'Nutritionally Based Wage Determination in the Low-income Labour Market', *Oxford Economic Papers*, 27.

Rosenzweig, M. R. (1978). 'Rural Wages, Labour Supply and Land Reform: A Theoretical and Empirical Analysis', *American Economic Review*, 68.5.

—— (1980). 'Determinants of Wage Rates and Labour Supply Behaviour in the Rural Sector of a Developing Country', ADC–ICRISAT conference, Hyderabad.

Rudolph, L. J., and Rudolph, S. H. (1967). *The Modernity of Tradition: Political Development in India*, Chicago.

Rudra, A. (1973). 'Direct Estimation of Surplus Labour in Agriculture', *Economic and Political Weekly*, annual no.

—— (1975). *Indian Plan Models*, New Delhi.

—— (1978). 'Organisation of Agriculture for Rural Development in India', *Cambridge Journal of Economics*, 2.4.

—— (1981). 'Against Feudalism', *Economic and Political Weekly*, 16.52.

—— and Biswas, R. (1973). 'Seasonality of Employment in Agriculture', *Economic and Political Weekly*, 8.39.

—— and Sen, A. (1980). 'Farm Size and Labour Use: Analysis and Policy', *Economic and Political Weekly*, 15.5–7.

Russell, J. C. (1969). 'The Population of Hiuen Tsangs India (AD 629–645)', *Journal of Indian History*, Aug.

Ruttan, V. (1977). 'The Green Revolution: Seven Generalisations', *International Development Review*, 19.4.

Rybczynski, T. B. (1955). 'Factor Endowments and Relative Commodity Prices', *Economica*, Nov.

Saini, G. R. (1979). *Farm Size, Resource Use Efficiency and Income-Distribution*, New Delhi.

Samuelson, P. A. (1949). 'International Factor Price Equalisation Once Again', *Economic Journal*, June.

—— (1966). 'Economic Theory and Wages', in *Collected Scientific Papers of P. A. Samuelson*, vol. ii, Cambridge, Mass.

Sandesara, J. C. (ed.) (1974). *The Indian Economy: Performance and Prospects*, Bombay.

Sankalia, H. D. (1977). *Prehistory of India*, Delhi.

Sanyal, S. K. (1977a). 'Trends in Rural Unemployment: A Comment', *Economic and Political Weekly*, 12.5.

—— (1977b). 'Trends in Some Characteristics of Landholdings: An Analysis for a Few States I and II', *Sarvekshana*, 1.1–2.

Sastri, N. (1976). *A History of South India*, 4th edn., New Delhi.

Satyanarayana, Y. (1980a). *Trends in Employment and Unemployment in India: An Analysis, Discussion and Compilation of Data*, mimeo, Washington, DC.

—— (1980b). *Wage Trends in India–1830–1976: An Analysis, Discussion and Compilation of Data*, mimeo, Washington, DC.

Sau, R. (1981): *India's Economic Development: Aspects of Class Relations*, New Delhi.

Saxena, S. P. (1941). 'Cost of Living Indices and Wages', in R. K. Mukherjee and H. L. Deng (eds.), *Economic Problems of Modern India*, London.

Schelling, T. C. (1984). 'Self-command in Practice, in Policy and in a Theory of Rational Choice', *American Economic Review*, 74.2.

Schultz, T. W. (1964). *Transforming Traditional Agriculture*, New Haven, Conn.

—— (1967). 'Significance of India's 1918–19 Losses of Agricultural Labour: A Reply', *Economic Journal*, 77.

Schumpeter, J. A. (1959). *A History of Economic Analysis*, Oxford.

Scott, Fg. M., MacArthur, J. D., and Newberry, D. M. (1976). *Project Appraisal in Practice*, London.

Seal, A. (1968). *The Emergence of Indian Nationalism: Competition and Collaboration in the Later 19th Century*, Cambridge.

—— (1973). 'Imperialism and Nationalism in India', in Gallagher and Seal.

Sen, A. K. (1965). 'The Commodity Composition of British Enterprise in Early Indian Industrialization, 1954–1914', in *Deuxième Conférence International de l'Histoire Économique, Aix-en-Provence, 1962*, Paris.

—— (1966). 'Peasants and Dualism, with and without Surplus Labour', *Journal of Political Economy*, 74.5.

—— (1967). 'Isolation, Assuance and the Social Rate of Discount', *Quarterly Journal of Economics*, 81.1.

—— (1967). 'Surplus Labour in India: A Critique of Schultz's Statistical Test and Surplus Labour in India: A Rejoinder', *Economic Journal*, 77.

—— (1974). 'Dimensions of Unemployment in India', *Mainstream*, 12.

—— (1975). *Employment, Technology and Development*, Oxford.

—— (1976a). 'Famines as Failures of Exchange Entitlements', *Economic and Political Weekly*, special no. Aug.

—— (1976b). 'Poverty: An Ordinal Approach to Measurement', *Econometrica*.

—— (1977). 'Starvation and Exhange Entitlements: A General Approach and its Application to the Great Bengal Famine', *Cambridge Journal of Economics*, 1.1.

Sen Gupta, S. *et al.* (1969). 'Estimates of 19th Century Population of India', *Bulletin of the Socio-Economic Research Institute*, 13.1.

—— *et al.* (1970). 'Estimates of the 19th Century Population of Pakistan', *Bulletin of the Socio-Economic Resarch Institute*, 14.1–2.

Sen, S. R. (1965). Paper presented at the World Population Conference, cited in Clark and Haswell.

Shah, C. M. (1974). 'Growth of Indian Agriculture: Experience and Explanation', in Sandesara.

Sharma, A. (1972). 'British Raj and Indian Economic Development: The 19th Century as a case of Controversy and Methodology', *Indian Economic Journal*, Jan.–Mar.

Sharma, B. R. (1974). *The Indian Industrial Worker*, Bombay.

Sharma, R. S. (1954). *The Crescent in India*, Bombay.

Sharma, R. S. (1980a). *Sudras in Ancient India*, 2nd edn., Delhi.

—— (1980b). *Indian Feudalism*, 2nd edn., Delhi.

—— (1983). *Perspectives in Social and Economic History of Early India*, New Delhi.

Shukla, T. (1965). *Capital Formation in Indian Agriculture*, Bombay.

Simmons, C. P. (1976). 'Recruiting and Organizing an Industrial Labour Force in Colonial India: The Case of the Coal Mining Industry 1880–1939,'' *Indian Economic an Social History Review*, Oct.–Dec.

Simon, J. L. (1977). *The Economics of Population Growth*, Princeton, NJ.

Singh, B. (1979). 'Economics of Milk Production and Bovine Livestock Composition in a Growing Economy', *India Journal of Agricultural Economics*, 34.2.

Singh, I. J. (1978). 'Rural Works Programs in South Asia: A Note', mimeo, Washington, DC.

Singh, V. B. (ed.) (1965): *Economic History of India 1857–1956*, New Delhi.

—— (1973). *Wage Patterns, Mobility and Savings of Workers in India*, Bombay.

Sinha, J. N. (1972). *The Indian Working Force (Its Growth and Changing Composition)*, Census of India 1961, vol. i, monograph ii, New Delhi.

—— and Sawney, P. K. (1970). *Wages and Productivity in Selected India Industries*, Delhi.

Sinha, P. R. N. (1971). *Wage Determination*, Bombay.

Sivasubramonian, S. (1965). 'National Income of India 1900–1 to 1946–7, mimeo, Delhi.

—— (1970). 'Some Comments on the Source Material on Agricultural Output in India 1900–47', in Ganguli.

—— (1977). 'Income From the Secondary Sector in India 1900–47', *Indian Economic and Social History Review*, 14.4.

Smith, A. (1776). *The Wealth of Nations*, London.

Smith, V. A., ed. P. Spear (1981). *The Oxford History of India*, 4th edn., Delhi.

Spear, T. G. P. (1963). *The Nabobs*, Oxford.

—— (1965a). *A History of India*, vol. ii, London.

—— (1965b). *The Oxford History of Modern India 1740–1941*, Oxford.

Spence, A. M. (1974). *Market Signalling*, Cambridge, Mass.

—— (1975). 'The Economics of Internal Organisation: An Introduction', *Bell Journal of Economics*, spring.

Srinivas, M. N. (1965). 'Social Structure', in *The Gazetter of India*, vol. i, *Country and People*, New Delhi.

—— (1966). *Social Change in Modern India*, Berkeley, CA.

—— (1962). *Caste in Modern India*, Bombay.

Srinivasan, T. N. (1979a). 'Trends in Agriculture in India, 1949–50/1977–78', *Economic and Political Weekly*, 14.30–2.

—— (1979b). 'A Note on Bonded Labour', mimeo, Washington, DC.

—— (1979c). 'Agricultural Backwardness under Semi-feudalism: Comment', *Economic Journal*, 89.

Stein, B. (ed.) (1975). *Essays on South India*, Honolulu.

—— (1980). *Peasant State and Society in Medieval South India*, Delhi.

—— (1982). 'South India: Some General Considerations of the Region and its Early History', in Raychaudhuri and Habib.

Stiglitz, J. E. (1969). 'Rural–Urban Migration, Surplus Labour, and the Relationship between Urban and Rural Wages', *East Africa Economic Review*, 1.

—— (1974). 'Alternative Theories of Wage Determination and Unemployment in LDCs: The Labour Turnover Model', *Quarterly Journal of Economics*, 88.

—— (1975a). 'Information and Economic Analysis', in Parkin and Nobay.

—— (1975b). 'Incentives, Risk and Information: Notes Towards a Theory of Hierarchy', *Bell Journal of Economics*, autumn.

—— (1976). 'The Efficiency Wage Hypothesis, Surplus Labour and the Distribution of Incomes in LDCs', *Oxford Economic Papers*, 28.

Stokes, E. (1959). *The English Utilitarians and India*, Oxford.

—— (1975). 'The Structure of Landholding in Uttar Pradesh 1860–1948', *Indian Economic and Social History Review*, 12.2.

—— (1978). *The Peasants and the Raj: Studies in Agrarian Society and Peasant Rebellion in Colonial India*, Cambridge.

Stone, I. (1979). 'Canal Irrigation and Agrarian Change: The Experience of the Ganges Canal Tract, Muzzafarnagar District (UP), 1840–1900', in K. N. Chaudhri and C. J. Dewey (eds.), *Economy and Society*, Delhi.

Strotz, R. H. (1955–6). 'Myopia and Inconsistency in Dynamic Utility Maximisation', *Review of Economic Studies*, 23.

Sundaram, K. (1977). 'The Structure of the Work Force in Rural India: 1950/51–1971', *Indian Economic Review*, 12.1.

Symposium on *Cambridge Economic History of India* (1985), *Modern Asian Studies*, 19.3.

Thapar, R. (1966). *A History of India*, vol. i, London.

—— (1984). *From Lineage to State*, Delhi.

Thavaraj, M. K. (1955). 'Public Investment in India, 1898–1914, Some Features', *Indian Economic Review*, 2.

—— (1960). 'Capital Formation in the Public Sector, 1898–1938', in *Papers on National Income and Allied Topics*, vol. i.

—— (1963a). 'Pattern of Public Investment in India, 1901–1939', *Indian Economic and Social History Review*, 1.

—— (1963b). 'Rate of Public Investment in India 1898–1939', in Raychaudhuri (1963).

Thorner, A. (1982). 'Semi-feudalism or Capitalism', *Economic and Political Weekly*, 17.49–51.

Thorner, D. (1951). 'Capital Movement and Transportation: Great Britain and the Development of India's Railways', *Journal of Economic History*, 12.

—— (1980). *The Shaping of Modern India*, New Delhi.

—— and Thorner, A. (1962). *Land and Labour in India*, Bombay.

Timberg, T. (1978). *The Marwaris*, New Delhi.

Tinker, H. (1974). *A New System of Slavery*. London.

Tomlinson, B. R. (1975). 'India and the British Empire, 1880–1935', *Indian Economic and Social History Review*, 12.4.

—— (1979). *The Political Economy of the Raj 1914–1947: The Economics of Decolonization in India*, London.

Usher, D. (1983). Review of Brennan and Buchanan, *The Power to Tax, Journal of Economic Literature*, Sept.

Vaid, K. N. (1976): *The New Worker*, Bombay.

Vaidyanathan, A. (1977a). 'Constraints on Growth and Policy Options: Reply', *Economic and Political Weekly*, 14.

—— (1977b). 'Performance and Prospects of Crop Production in India', *Economic and Political Weekly*, 2.33–4.

—— (1977c). 'Constraints on Growth and Policy Options', *Economic and Political Weekly*, 12.38.

—— (1978). 'Aspects of India's Bovine Economy: Some Preliminary Results', *Indian Journal of Agricultural Economics*, 33.

Vicziany, M. (1979). 'The De-industrialisation of India in the 19th Century: A Methodological Critique of Amiya Kumar Bagchi', *Indian Economic and Social History Review*, 16.2.

Visaria, P. (1977). 'Trends in Rural Unemployment India: A Comment', *Economic and Political Weekly*, 12.5.

Voelcker, J. A. (1893). *Report on the Development of Indian Agriculture*, Bombay.

Wadhwa, C. D. (ed.) (1977). *Some Problems of Indian Economic Policy*, 2nd edn., New Delhi.

Weber, M. (1963). *The Sociology of Religion*, Boston, Mass.

von Weiszacker, C. C. (1971). 'Notes on Endogenous Changes of Tastes', *Journal of Economic Theory*.

Whitcombe, E. (1971). *Agrarian Conditions in Northern India*, vol. i, *The United Provinces Under British Rule 1860–1900*, Berkeley, C.A.

Wilson, E. O. (1975). *Sociobiology*, Cambridge, Mass.
Wolf, M. (1981). *Indian Exports*, Baltimore, Md.
Woodruff, P. (1953–4). *The Men Who Ruled India*, 2 vols., London.
Zarembaka, P. (1972). *Towards a Theory of Economic Development*, San Francisco, CA.

INDEX

Note: Sub-entries are in alphabetical order, except where chronological order is more significant.